# How the Chinese Economy Works
Second Edition

# How the Chinese Economy Works

**Second Edition**

By Rongxing Guo

First edition published 1999
Second edition published 2007 by
PALGRAVE MACMILLAN
Houndmills, Basingstoke, Hampshire RG21 6XS and
175 Fifth Avenue, New York, N.Y. 10010
Companies and representatives throughout the world

PALGRAVE MACMILLAN is the global academic imprint of the Palgrave Macmillan division of St. Martin's Press, LLC and of Palgrave Macmillan Ltd. Macmillan® is a registered trademark in the United States, United Kingdom and other countries. Palgrave is a registered trademark in the European Union and other countries.

ISBN 13: 978–0–230–54274–7   hardback
ISBN 10: 0–230–54274–3       hardback

This book is printed on paper suitable for recycling and made from fully managed and sustained forest sources. Logging, pulping and manufacturing processes are expected to conform to the environmental regulations of the country of origin.

A catalogue record for this book is available from the British Library.

Library of Congress Cataloging-in-Publication Data

Guo, Rongxing
    How the Chinese economy works / by Rongxing Guo. – 2nd ed.
        p. cm.
    Includes bibliographical references and index.
    ISBN-10: 0–230–54274–3      (cloth)
    ISBN-13: 978–0–230–54274–7  (cloth)
        1. China–Economic conditions. 2. China–Economic policy. I. Title.

    HC427.92.G86 2007
    330.951–dc22                                    2006052704

10   9   8   7   6   5   4   3
16   15   14   13   12   11   10   09   08

Printed and bound in Great Britain by
CPI Antony Rowe, Chippenham and Eastbourne

謹以此書紀念我的慈母赫玉花 (1927–2005)

# Contents

# List of Boxes

# List of Figures

# List of Tables

# Preface

## Features of this book

The book is intended to provide information and explanations of the operational mechanisms of the Chinese economy through both national and multiregional dimensions. This book was first published in the 'Studies on the Chinese Economy' series in 1999. In this enlarged edition, a more complete, up-to-date set of time-series data on the Chinese economy has been collected and, where appropriate, reconstructed. Specifically, in the second edition, Chapters 1, 5 and 9 are completely new, Chapters 3, 6, 7 and 10 are significantly revised and all the other chapters are updated with new data from 1995 onwards.

It should be noted that this book is not able to deal with all issues critical to the Chinese economy. Rather, the main objective of this book is to offer an analysis of the driving forces of the Chinese economy, providing insights into national and regional economic trends. Each chapter starts with an epigraph (or an ancient Chinese fable) that has an allegorical link with what will be discussed in the chapter. Besides, one or more boxes are inserted where necessary in each chapter. These are hoped to extend readers' knowledge of Chinese economics. The statistical information on the greater China area is also provided for those concerned with the comparative analysis of Taiwan, Hong Kong, Macau and mainland China. Except for a few of sections, this book is not technically complicated. Therefore, I hope that it will be read widely, as an introduction, by researchers as well as ordinary readers and students who want to acquire some general knowledge about the Chinese economy.

## Acknowledgements

The first edition of this book was the outcome of my previous teaching activities in Korea University (1994), Peking University (1996), University of Trier (1997–98) and Beijing Graduate School of CUMT (1998–2002). Many individuals have extended me with helps on the first edition of this book. During the first period of writing, many valuable comments and suggestions were received from Zhao Renwei (Chinese Academy of Social Sciences). During my visit to South Korea and Germany, I benefited from many discussions with Eui-Gak Hwang and Thomas Heberer who also kindly arranged my stay at their respective universities. The grants from the National Science Foundation of China (NSFC) and the East Asian Development Network (EADN) make it possible for me to conduct a series of field inspections in China and collect some specific regional data, both of which have contributed to the writing of this book. I am very grateful to T.M. Farmile (former Publishing Director of Macmillan) and to Mervyn Thomas (Linda Auld Associates) for helpful suggestions and corrections on the first edition of this book.

The finalization of the current edition of this book has been promoted by my various research activities conducted in China and abroad. Chapter 5 is based on the case study of the Global Research Project (GRP) 'Understanding Reform' sponsored by the Global Development Network (New Delhi, India). I have substantially benefited from the collaboration with Kaizhong Yang (BJDI/Peking University, China) and Renwei Zhao (Institute of Economics/CASS, China). José María Fanelli (University of Buenos Aires, Argentina and Coordinator of the GRP), Gary Mcmahon (Global Development Network, USA) and Leong Liew (Griffin University, Australia) provided insightful comments and suggestions at each stage of the research. I have also benefited from the comments provided by Isher Ahluwalia, Richard Cooper, Amara Pongsapich, and other participants at the 'Understanding Reform' workshops held in Cairo (16–17 January 2003) and New Delhi (28–30 January 2004). Some micro-level findings in this book are based on the field surveys that I conducted jointly with Zhao Renwei, Li Shi, Zhang Yong, Xing Youqiang, Xie Yanhong and Wang Xiaoping in March 2002. Research assistance received from Zhao Gongzheng is also appreciated.

The final appearance of this book has benefited from helpful discussions with Lyn Squire who also generously wrote a foreword for this edition. Among the Palgrave Macmillan staff contributing to the publication of this book, Amanda Hamilton (Economics Publisher) and Alec Dubber (Editorial Assistant for Economics) kept in regular communication with me when the draft was prepared. I am extremely grateful to Ann Marangos (Editorial Services Consultant) for editing the book. Nevertheless, the remaining errors in this book are my sole responsibilities.

R.X. Guo

# List of Abbreviations

| | |
|---|---|
| BECZ | trams-province border economic cooperative zone |
| CCP | Chinese Communist Party |
| CCPCC | Chinese Communist Party Central Committee |
| CEPA | closer economic partnership arrangement |
| COE | collectively-owned enterprise |
| CPE | centrally planned economy |
| CPPCC | Chinese People's Political Consultative Congress |
| FDI | foreign direct investment |
| FIE | foreign (Taiwan, Hong Kong and Macau) invested enterprise |
| FYP | five-year plan |
| GDP | gross domestic product |
| GNP | gross national product |
| GVAO | gross value of agricultural output |
| GVIAO | gross value of industrial and agricultural output |
| GVIO | gross value of industrial output |
| GVSP | gross value of social product |
| HRS | household responsibility system |
| MPS | material product system |
| NBS | National Bureau of Statistics of China |
| NIE | newly industrialized economy |
| NMP | net material product |
| NPC | National People's Congress |
| PCS | people's commune system |
| PPP | purchasing power parity |
| PRC | People's Republic of China |
| PSE | Private, share-holding or other enterprise |
| R&D | research and development |
| RMB | renminbi, Chinese currency |
| SAR | special administrative region |
| SARS | severe acute respiratory syndrome |
| SETC | State Economic and Trade Commission |
| SEZ | special economic zone |
| SNA | system of national accounts |
| SOE | state-owned enterprise |
| SPC | State Planning Commission |

| | |
|---|---|
| SSB | State Statistical Bureau |
| TVE | township and village enterprise |
| WHO | World Health Organization |
| WTO | World Trade Organization |

# Foreword

The world is watching the miraculous development of the Chinese economy with varied emotions: envy, hope, concern. Even a country like India that is experiencing its own miracle still casts a jealous eye at the success of the Chinese economy. Other less fortunate countries are looking to China for lessons to guide and accelerate their own development. And still others worry that China's emergence will squeeze them out of markets for their exports or their sources of energy.

The economics profession has devoted much time and effort to understanding what drives the growth of economies. Much of this research has employed cross-country regressions. Useful though such research may be, it can never provide a full understanding of the growth process in economies as *sui generis* and complex as that of China. Careful case studies employing appropriate empirical techniques offer the prospect of a much richer and deeper appreciation of the details of the growth process and of the interactions between key factors. The potential of such studies is increased several-fold when the research is undertaken by investigators with detailed local knowledge and personal understanding of the economy being investigated. For these reasons, the Global Development Network has promoted case studies undertaken by local authors as a vital means of providing a fuller understanding of the complex process of growth. I am therefore especially pleased to write a foreword for this volume, a volume that provides such an excellent example of this approach applied to perhaps the most important growth experience in recent history.

The volume's author, Guo Rongxing, has drawn on his extensive knowledge of the Chinese economy to update and expand the 1998 edition of his book *How the Chinese Economy Works*. The coverage and content illustrate the value of in-depth case studies. Guo Rongxing examines the functioning of the economy in both the pre-reform and the post-reform periods; he explores the operation of the economy at the national and the provincial level; he investigates the exploitation of and development of natural and human resources; he analyzes the institutional evolution of the economy; and he reports on the economic and social outcomes. The richness of the material and the clarity of the analysis will perhaps make the envious countries even more so; they will certainly provide valuable information for those hoping to learn from the Chinese experience; and they will provide a firmer basis for assessing the concerns of those competing in output and input markets.

On the evidence of this contribution, one can look forward to the third edition of this volume with great anticipation.

*Lyn Squire*
*Global Development Network*
*New Delhi*

# Notes to Readers

Unless stated otherwise, we have implied in this research that the geographical scope covers only mainland China (see Map in the separate page) and that the statistical data used in this book are from *China Statistical Yearbooks* (all issues) published annually.

The time domain of this research is mainly fixed for the years from 1949 to the early 21st century, with some exceptions when an analysis of the pre-1949 period is needed.

For the sake of convenience, specific autonomous regions and municipalities directly under the central government will be referred to alongside provinces by a single name.

The unit of the Chinese currency (RMB) is yuan (¥). The exchange and the PPP rates of the RMB (¥) are shown below:

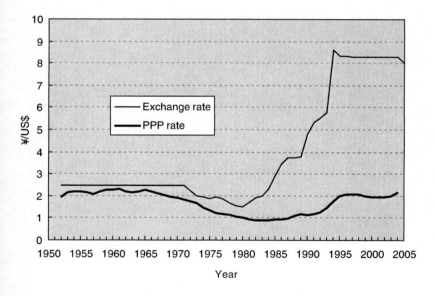

Chinese names are customarily written in the order of family name (which is in the single syllable in most cases) followed by given name, while the Western style is usually applied by the Taiwan, Hong Kong and other overseas Chinese.

Chinese names and geographical terms in mainland China are written in China's official (*pinyin*) form, while those outside mainland China are in the conventional form.

The regional percentages in the tables may not add up to 100 due to rounding errors.

*Map*  The spatial division of the Chinese economy

# Executive Summary

Chapter 1 starts with a brief history of China, focusing on the various factors that could have shaped China's existing political, economic and cultural characteristics. This chapter also investigates the causes and consequences of China's periodic changes of feudal dynasties as well as their political, economic and cultural implications to the PRC gigantism in the new millennium.

After having reviewed the historical evolution of China's administrative divisions and existing literature on Chinese economic regionalization, Chapter 2 presents a regional topology for the Chinese economy. Depending on different purposes and research preferences, five topological frameworks (provincial administrations, great regions, coastal and inland areas, eastern, central and western belts, and southern and northern parts) – through which the multiregional analysis and comparison of the Chinese economy will be conducted in other chapters – are provided in this chapter.

Chapter 3 analyzes the most important elements for economic development. Natural and human resources are unevenly distributed across China. In short, population and labour force densities are greater in the Eastern belt than in the Western belt. The northern part is much richer in deposits of mineral resources than the southern part, except for a few deposits of non-ferrous metals, while, in contrast, the southern part has an advantage for agricultural production and, in particular, dominates most of the nation's rice production. One of the most important implications of this chapter is that the unevenly distributed and coal-dominated energy structure is the major obstacle to Chinese industrialization and sustainable development. Besides, China's institutional and cultural issues are also addressed in this chapter.

According to the new institutional economics, system, like other production factors required in economic development, is a special kind of scarce resource and should thus be treated properly in economics. Chapter 4 sets out to examine the functional evolution of development planning, production ownership, public finance, banking and external economic relations. During the past decades, China has successfully transformed its centrally planned system to a decentralized and market-oriented one. In particular, it achieved a faster economic growth than any other socialist or former socialist countries in the world. However,

It is puzzling because it seems to defy the conventional wisdom. Although China has adopted many of the policies advocated by economists, such as being open to trade and foreign investment and sensitive to macroeconomic stability, violations of the standard prescriptions are striking. China's reform was implemented without complete liberalization and privatization. Besides, especially since the 1990s, China almost has not implemented any substantial political reforms.

Chapter 5 explores the elements underpinning the design and implementation of China's economic reform. It provides an explanation for the causes and timing of major reform programs, as well as for how the success and failure of reform efforts were associated with initial conditions and reform strategies. The analytic narrative of China's political economic events shows that a radical reform tends to be more efficient than a gradual/partial one at an early stage (from the late 1970s to the early 1980s), while a gradual/partial reform tends to be more efficient than a radical one at a late stage. During the past decades, China's reform has achieved two objectives at the same time: to improve economic efficiency by unleashing the standard forces of incentives and competition on the one hand; and to make the reform a win-win game and thus interest compatible for those in power on the other. And they take into consideration of China's specific political and cultural conditions. With its economic achievements, the rationale of the Chinese-style reform is rarely questioned today within China. However, China's economic growth has been obtained at the cost of a retardation of political reforms, not to mention worsening income inequalities as well as other social problems.

Since economic reform and open-door policies were implemented in the late 1970s, the Chinese economy has demonstrated an increasing asymmetry between different regions and resulted in a series of regional economic problems which need to be addressed properly by policymakers. In Chapter 6, the Chinese economy is analyzed generally and compared via multiregional dimensions. Due to the application of different statistical systems in the pre- and post-reform periods as well as the unavailability of statistical data in some provinces, a complete multiregional comparison of the Chinese economy is extremely difficult and, to some extent, meaningless. Using the best data and the regression approach, Section 2 tries to estimate a set of time-series data on GDP for all provinces, on which the multiregional comparison of the Chinese economy is based. In Section 3, efforts of consistent economic comparison will be attempted based on the indices of real living standards. Finally, in Section 4, inequality indexes are computed for the past decades. Not surprisingly, China's economic reform and open-door policies have for the past decades disproportionally aided the coastal provinces where per capita GDPs are several times higher than in the poor inland provinces.

Chapter 7 discusses China's industrialization and technological progress. Despite its long history of civilization, China has lagged far behind the advanced nations in industrial modernization. Generally, the poor industrial performances had to large extent been ascribed to the Chinese socialist construction of 'self-reliance and independence' and the irrational industrial structure in which heavy industry was given priority. The estimated production function based on the data of 500 enterprises suggests that resource-exploiting enterprises have the highest capital productivity in the Western belt and that high-technology enterprises have the highest labour productivity in the Eastern belt. Chinese rural industrialization in which the TVEs have played an important role is discussed. Finally, Chinese technological progress is reviewed briefly in this chapter.

Despite its mutually complementary conditions between different regions, the Chinese economy has been internally affected by various geographical, institutional and cultural barriers between provincial administrations. Following a theoretical analysis of the spatial efficiency of authoritarianism, Chapter 8 studies the possibilities and conditions under which the Chinese economy can (not) be optimized spatially. As a practical measure to overcome the interregional barriers and to provide a 'bridge' for spatial economic integration, China has established different forms and levels of multiregional economic cooperative zones since the early 1980s. The particular focus of the last part of this chapter will examine China's various efforts on the search for spatial economic integration as well as the 'West Region Development Strategy'.

Chapter 9 discusses the most critical problems that China is facing today: population, resource and environment. Basically, China's economic development has followed a traditional model that is characterized by high resource and energy (mainly coal) consumption and extensive management. This has not only led to a series of damages to the environment of today, but also affected its economic sustainability in the future. Therefore, shifting the development strategy and embarking on the path to sustainable development is the only correct choice for the Chinese economy. It should be noted that China, like many other developing countries, is facing many pressing problems related to the economic development which might, at least in the short-run, be contradicted with environmental protection. However, environmental policies and measures should never be treated independently from economic policies. Moreover, they can serve as a dynamic mechanism for the maximization of the real well-being of the entire people.

Chapter 10 deals with Chinese economic internationalization. The Chinese economy has been transforming from the autarkic to an outward-oriented pattern. The open-door policy was first implemented in the coastal area in the early 1980s, resulting in a rapid economic growth for China and the Eastern belt in particular. In the early 1990s, China embarked on another outward-looking policy to promote the cross-border trade and economic development of the inland frontier area. China's efforts on economic internationalization have greatly benefited every sphere of Chinese life. The Chinese government has attempted to adjust further its economic policies so as to meet gradually the needs of the multilateral trading system. Even though China has acceded to the WTO, it is hard to state all trading activities have done according to the provisions of the WTO. In essence it is still questionable whether China is in compliance with its obligations under the WTO. It is also questionable whether China can harmonize its rules with disciplines under the WTO since China has less experience with multilateral trade rules and an apparent poor understanding of WTO rule.

Finally, Chapter 11 performs extensive analysis of the Chinese economy through a larger geographical scope. Despite their common history and cultural and linguistic homogeneity, the greater China area (including Taiwan, Hong Kong, Macau and mainland China) has followed during the past decades divergent political and economic systems, from which different social and economic performances have resulted. Along with mainland China's economic reform and the return of Hong Kong and Macau, from the British and Portuguese governments, to China in 1997 and 1999, respectively, the economic ties between the three parts as a single sovereign nation have been accelerated under the principle of 'one country, two systems' in the 21st century. The two sides of the Taiwan strait, however, have been politically separated for over fifty years due to the mutual distrust and hostile strategies arising from the bloody conflict between the Nationalists and the Communists at the end of World War II. With the Cold War coming to an end and the surging tide of global participation in economic development, more and more Chinese believe that the cross-strait trade and economic cooperation must be *directly* conducted by the two sides, before the national reunification eventually becomes a possibility. Nevertheless, the creation of political harmony and reunification between Taiwan and the mainland may still require both more time and more patience from both parties.

吾十有五而志于學，三十而立，四十而不惑，五十而知天命，六十而耳順，七十而從心所欲，不逾矩。 　　　"論語·為政"

# 1
# A Brief History of China

It [Luoyi, a place in central China] is the center under heaven, from which all other states bear same distance when they come to pay tributes. (ci tianxia zhi zhong, sifang rugong daoli jun.)
King Wu of Zhou (c. 1066 BC)

## The origins of the nation

Geographically shaped as a rooster in East Asia, China has a 14,500 km coastline along the East China Sea, the Korean Bay, the Yellow Sea and the South China Sea. It has a total length of approximately 22,140 km land boundaries with North Korea, Russia and Mongolia in the northeast and north, Kazakhstan, Kyrgyzastan, Tajkistan, Afghanistan and Pakistan in the west, India and Nepal in the southwest, and Myanmar, Laos and Vietnam in the south.

The geography of China has shaped its special culture and philosophy. The Yellow river – which originates at the foot of the Kunlun mountains in the west and flows several thousand miles eastward to the Pacific ocean – has been generally known as the cradle of Chinese nation. It was along the banks of the river that Chinese civilization first flowered some 8000 years ago. The shift from Neolithic to Bronze Age culture marks the transition from prehistory to the beginning of recorded history in China. In the prehistoric period, the progenitors of the Han people (China's ethnic majority) were scattered in small tribes over the middle reaches of the Yellow river. Toward the end of the Neolithic period, these tribes were already using a primitive form of writing, and had developed a system to measure time and count numbers. They had also developed a variety of articles for daily use, including clothing, houses, weapons, pottery, money and so on.[1]

Chinese civilization, as described in mythology, begins with Pangu, the creator of the universe. Chinese today refer to themselves as *yanhuang zisun* (descendants of Emperors Yan and Huang – the legendary founders of the Chinese nation). But the traditional culture began to come into being with the emergence of Emperor Huang (huangdi). During the period of the reign of Emperor Huang and the following emperors, people were taught to observe 'five basic relationships' including 'good relations between sovereign and minister, father and son, husband and wife, brothers, and friends.' This code of conduct which was later developed systematically by Confucius (551–475 BC) and his disciples established an ethical philosophy which has influenced the Chinese society for more than 2000 years.

From the 22nd to the 2nd century BC, the three Chinese tribes – Xia, Shang, and Zhou – were established as the three ancient dynasties in the middle, eastern, and western sections of the Yellow river valley, respectively. In the Xia dynasty, which lasted from 2205 BC to 1766 BC, the territorial boundaries of China began to take shape. The country was divided into nine administrative prefectures and a system of land taxes was established. The Shang dynasty lasted more than six centuries from 1766 BC to 1122 BC. During this period, articles made of bronze were widely used.[2] In a war with the 28th ruler of the Shang dynasty, the allied forces under the commander of King Wu defeated the Shang's army. As a result a new dynasty named Zhou was founded. The power of the rulers in the Zhou dynasty was based on 'Zhongfa' – a system of inheritance and ancestral worship at a time when polygyny was the usual practice among the royalty and nobility.[3] In this way, a huge structure was built up, radiating from a central hub through endless infeudation and subinfeudation. Particularly noteworthy is that in the dynasty education was widespread with a national university in the capital and various grades of schools named. Scholars and intellectuals were held in high esteem. Art and learning flourished as never before.

The Chinese name *zhongguo* (central kingdom, or called 'China' in the Western Hemisphere) derives from the term 'center under heaven' which was first remarked by King Wu of the Zhou dynasty (see Box 1.1). The King's intention was to move the Zhou's capital from Haojing in western China to Luoyi (now known as Luoyang) in central China in order to keep more effective control over the whole nation. During the second half of the Zhou dynasty (also called 'Spring and Autumn and the Warring States'), a new group of regional rulers sought to obtain the services of talented individuals who could help enlarge their political influence. The result was an unprecedented development of

---

*Box 1.1*   He Zun

He Zun is a wine vessel made in the early period of the Zhou dynasty (1121–221 BC). With a height of 38.8 cm, top-opening diameter of 28.8 cm and a weight of 14.6 kg, He Zun is named after 'He', the owner of the vessel.

Unearthed in the fall of 1963 on the level of the Jiacun village, Baoji city, Shaanxi province. It is now a collection of the City Museum of Baoji. There is an inscription of 122 Chinese characters at the bottom inside. The main idea is: In 1059 BC King Cheng of the Zhou dynasty (reign 1063–1027 BC) was offering a sacrifice to his father (King Wu of the Zhou), saying: 'Once capturing Luoyi [today's Luoyang at central China's Henan province], the major city of the Shang dynasty, King Wu notified his liegemen that "it will, as the center under heaven, become a place in which I can govern the whole nation".' The remaining characters of the inscription tells that King Cheng taught a young man of the King's family named He a lesson on how the former Kings of the Zhou dynasty reigned the people.

The inscription in He Zun has been regarded as the earliest literal record for the name 'China' (central kingdom or *zhongguo*).

---

independent thinking and of original philosophies. The most celebrated philosophers were Laozi, Confucius, Zhuangzi, Mencius, Mozi, Hanfeizi, and Xunzi. These individuals were the leading sprits of the Taoist, Confucian, Mohist, Legalist schools of thought.

## Rise and fall of the empire

In 221 BC, China was unified by Qin shihuang, the first emperor of the Qin dynasty. The most important contribution of the Qin dynasty was the founding of a completely new social and political order under a strict system of rewards and punishment favoured by a group of scholars called Legalists. In place of feudalism, the country was reorganized into 36 prefectures and a number of counties. Under this prefecture-county administration, all authority was vested in the central government. For the first time in history, China's written language, currency, and weights and measures were all unified and standardized. In addition, Qin shi-huang undertook large-scale construction projects, including national roadways, waterways, and the Great Wall. After the conquest of the 'barbarians' in the south, the Chinese territory was extended to the shores of the South China sea. In spite of many political and military achievements, the multicultural development was monopolized in the Qin dynasty. Excessive trust was put on the efficacy of the Legalist method, while the books on Confucianism and other schools of thought were burned to keep the people ignorant. Even worse, the intellectuals and scholars criticizing the government were either executed or sent as slave labour to build the Great Wall.

The cruel and despotic rule, however, eventually resulted in the fall of the 15-year long dynasty. Five years later, Liu Bang reunited China and established a long-lived dynasty, called Han (206 BC–AD 220). Strong military forces made it possible for the Han dynasty to expand China's territories to the Western Dominion in today's Xinjiang and Central Asia and to Taiwan island in the East China sea. The Han dynasty was a glorious age in Chinese history. Political institutions of the Qin and the Han dynasties were typical of all the dynasties that were to follow. The nine-chapter legal code drawn up in the early days of the Han served as a model for all later versions of Chinese codes. The political and military might of the Han dynasty was so impressive that the Chinese since then have called themselves the 'Han' people. Confucianism was given special emphasis and those doing research on Confucian studies were given priority for public positions. Emperor Wudi (reign 140–87 BC) listed the Confucian classics as subjects of study for his ministers, and appointed well-read scholars to professorship called Boshi (doctor). Confucianism thus gained official sanction over competing philosophical schools and became the core of Chinese culture.

At the end of the Eastern Han period (AD 25–220)[4] political corruption and social chaos, together with widespread civil disturbances and royal throne usurpation, eventually gave birth to three independent kingdoms – the Wei (AD 220–265) in the north, the Shu (AD 221–263) in the southwest and the Wu (AD 222–280) in the southeast. China remained divided until AD 265 when the Jin dynasty was founded in Luoyang in central China. The Jin was not militarily strong compared with non-Han counterparts in the north, which encouraged the move of its capital southward to what is now Nanjing. Large-scale migration from the north to the south made the Yangtze river valley more prosperous than before, and the economic and cultural center shifted gradually to the southeast accordingly. In the Yellow river valley, the non-Han peoples lived with indigenous Han people, forming a more diverse and dynamic Chinese nation than ever before.[5]

China was reunified in the Sui dynasty (AD 581–618). The Sui is famous for its construction of the Grand Canal by which the Yellow river and the Huai and Yangtze rivers were linked for communication between the south and the north. Only the Great Wall – which was first built in the Qin dynasty – is comparable with the Canal in terms of human cost. Like the Qin, the Sui was also a short-lived dynasty, which was succeeded by a powerful dynasty, the Tang. At the height of its power, the Tang dynasty enlarged its territory to Mongolia in the north, Xinjiang in the west, the northern part of the Korean peninsula in the east and the northern part of Annam (today's Vietnam) in the south, which was larger than in any previous period. The Tang dynasty spanned the reigns of 21 sovereigns, totally for a period of 289 years, before five dynastic changes occurred along the Yellow river valley and ten regional powers controlled different sections of the Yangtze river.[6] In the Tang dynasty, the Chinese culture influenced as far away as India in the western side of the Himalayas and Japan in the east. For example, the traditional written language, architecture, and political institutions of Japan and Korea were to some extent imitations of the Tang model.

In 960, China was reunited. Unlike the Tang dynasty, the Song dynasty (AD 960–1279) was militarily confronted by powerful enemies from the north. The conflict between the Song and the Liao (a non-Han dynasty in the north) lasted for more than a century before another non-Han dynasty, the Jin, took the Song's capital, Kaifeng, and captured two Song emperors as hostages in 1127. With northern China falling into non-Han hands, the Song's capital moved from the Yellow river valley to Hangzhou. As a result, the economic and cultural center shifted from central to southeast China. Despite its military weakness, the Song dynasty contributed also a great deal to the world's civilization. Many Chinese inventions, such as the compass, gunpowder and movable-type printing were introduced to the western countries during this period.

In 1279 the Mongol cavalry, under Genghis Khan, controlled the entire Chinese territory. The 88-year long Yuan dynasty was an extraordinary one in Chinese history. Under the Mongol rule, China once again grew in size. During the strongest period of the Yuan dynasty, China's territory was even extended to the eastern part of Europe. In the internal affairs, however, the Mongolian caste system in which the Han people were ranked after all non-Han peoples, together with political corruption and misgovernment, eventually resulted in a successful anti-Mongol revolution let by Zhu Yuanzhang, who founded the Han-based dynasty, the Ming (1368–1644) in Nanjing. In 1421, the Ming dynasty moved its seat to Beijing, after defeating the nomadic tribes of the northern part of the Great Wall.

As the Ming dynasty was declining, China's last, also the last minority-based dynasty, the Qing (AD 1644–1911), was set up by the Manchus, who rose in Manchuria (today's northeast part of China). Compared with the Mongols, the Manchus' rule over China was successful. At the height of the Qing dynasty, the Manchus utilized the best minds and richest human resources of the nation, regardless of race. What is more important, the Han-based political ideologies and cultural traditions of the Chinese were adopted by the Manchus, resulting in virtually total cultural assimilation of the Manchus by the Han Chinese. Despite its early progress in political stability, China in the late Qing dynasty fell behind the west nations in science and technology, which eventually resulted in the disintegration of this nation. Entering the 19th century, the Chinese society became totally an autarkic one. Naturally, China found her place in the world's modern civilization but at the corner of it.

The 1840s decade marked a turning point in Chinese history. From early in the 19th century Britain was smuggling large quantities of opium into China, causing a great outflow of Chinese silver and grave economic disruption. In an effort to protect its opium trade, Britain initiated the First Opium War in 1840. The War was ended in 1842, after the corrupt Qing court signed the Treaty of Nanjing with Britain, bartering away China's national sovereignty. Subsequently, China declined into a semi-colonial and semi-feudal country. After the Opium War, Britain and other western powers such as Belgium, the Netherlands, Prussia, Spain, Portugal, the USA and France, seized 'concessions' and divided China into 'spheres of influence'. During the second half of the 19th century, many peasant leaders and national heroes rose time and again. The Revolution of 1911, led by Dr. Sun Yat-sen, is of great significance in modern Chinese history, since it discarded the feudal monarchial system that ruled China for more than 2,000 years with the founding of the Republic of China (ROC). In the following decades, however, the Chinese nation was on the edge of bankruptcy.[7]

## China in the new millennium

During the past century, China's economic development had been interrupted time and again. The Chinese economy was nearly bankrupted at the end of the Civil War in the late 1940s, and seriously

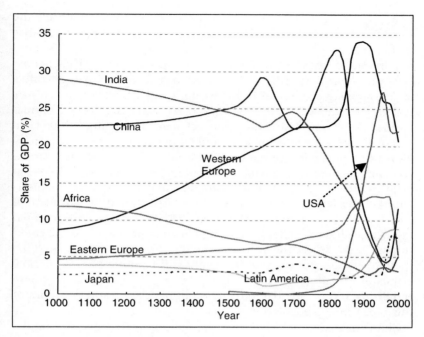

Source: Based on Maddison (2001), p. 261.

*Figure 1.1*   A horizontal view of the Chinese economy from AD 1000 to AD 2000

damaged in the Great Leap Forward (1958–60) and Cultural Revolution (1966–76) movements. However, since the late 1970s when the Chinese government began the gradual transformation of its Stalinesque centrally planned system, the Chinese economy has grown with exceptional rapidity. It has achieved an average gross national product (GNP) annual growth rate of near 10 per cent since the early 1980s (which is among the highest in the world during the same period).

There have been even many encouraging reports on the Chinese economy. For example, World Bank (1992) issues a range of evidence for why China looks set to become the world's largest economy by the year 2010 and that the Chinese economic area (including mainland China, Taiwan, Hong Kong, Macau, and other Chinese alien areas in Southeast Asia) has been one of the world's 'growth poles'.[8] Segal (1994, p. 44) notes that the current figures on Chinese GDP might have been misleading because they do not take into account real PPP rates. According to Noland (1994), the Chinese economy is already the second largest in the world if it is measured by purchasing power parity (PPP) rates instead of standard international prices.[9] What is more important, however, is the trend *per se*, rather than any specific figure.

In the reform era since 1978, China has been one of the world's fastest growing economies in the world. From 1978 to 2005, China's real gross domestic product (GDP) has grown at the average annual rate of 9.5 per cent. Using nominal exchange rates, China's 2005 GDP was about 30 per cent of Japan's and 12 per cent of the USA's. However, nominal exchange rates underestimate the size of the Chinese economy because Chinese prices are much lower than those in developed countries. Using the purchasing PPP measurements of the International Monetary Fund, China's 2005 GDP should be higher than Japan's, and 55 per cent of the size of the USA's. The International Monetary Fund estimates that, using PPP measurements, China could surpass the USA as the world's largest economy as early as 2007, though China's per capita GDP would still be quite low. While PPP estimates are subject to some margin of error, the Chinese economy certainly has the potential to rival that of the USA in size as a result of the huge Chinese population.

China has achieved vigorous economic growth since the implementation of market-oriented reform in the late 1970s. The remarkable performance has been accompanied and facilitated by, *inter alia*, historic, geographic, social, and cultural factors. Up to now, the Chinese model has been generally known as the most successful one among former Soviet-type economies according to the measure of economic performance. However, it should also be noted that China still lags far behind many marketized and industrialized economies. It is only the huge population that causes the Chinese economy to rank at the bottom of the world's economies by the per capita measure. The per capita income of China has still been much lower than that of USA, Japan and other Asian NIEs. While China's over-centralized planning system was mainly responsible for those poor socioeconomic performances, there were also historical, social, and cultural factors that hindered its socioeconomic development. Indeed, it is not easy to develop a market-system framework within a short period of time in China – a country utilizing the centrally planned system for nearly 30 years and that was, in particular, deeply influenced by long periods of feudalism but rarely by economic democracy.

The Chinese economy has experienced dramatic changes and a faster development than many other transitional centrally planned economies

(CPEs) during the past decades. This is certainly determined by both the internal and the external environments. At the same time, China's current situation poses many crucial challenges to the Chinese economy. Many inherent problems in relation to economic development persist. If the Chinese government does not address them properly, its efforts, based on the Chinese-style *laissez-faire* reform, inevitably would be jeopardized. Heading toward the 21st century, it can still be seen that China is scheduled to develop its economy according to its own characteristics. But the Chinese government should have a more cautious bearing on this matter. More than two thousand years ago, Confucius taught his pupils with the autobiographical story:

> Since the age of 15, I have devoted myself to learning; since 30, I have been well established; since 40, I have understood many things and have no longer been confused; since 50, I have known my heaven-sent duty; since 60, I have been able to distinguish right and wrong in other people's words; and 70, I have been able to do what I intended freely without breaking the rules.

Hopefully, with the approaching of the 60th year socialistic construction, the CCP and the People's Republic of China (PRC) leaders will perhaps have got out of the past confused age and know where to go and what to do next, both economically and politically.

# 2
# The Spatial Division of the Chinese Economy

Originally proliferated by Tao,
  (dao sheng yi)
One gives birth to Two in opposition.
  (yi sheng er)
The Two begets Three in triangle under which
  (er sheng san)
everything in the world is ready to be created.
  (san sheng wanwu)

Laozi (c. 600 BC)

When referring to the Chinese economy, at least two important points must be noted: first, China's vast territorial size and wide diversity in physical environments and natural resource endowments have inevitably resulted in great regional economic differences; second, China has a population of more than 1.3 billion, with 56 ethnic groups. It is geographically divided by 31 provincial administrations, each of which is equivalent to a medium-sized country in the rest of the world. In short, the Chinese economy is one of the most complicated and diversified spatial systems that can be found in the world. The only feasible approach one may apply is, therefore, to divide it into smaller geographical elements through which one can have a better insight into the spatial mechanisms and regional characteristics.

Usually, the method of regionalization of the Chinese economy may be different, depending upon the analytical purposes. In this chapter, we will divide the Chinese economy into (1) provincial administrations (2) great regions (3) coastal and inland areas (4) geographical belts, and (5) southern and northern parts.

10

## Provincial administrations

There had been 12 dependent states (*zhou*) in China during the Yao and Shun periods (about 4000 years ago).[1] Since then, China's provincial administrations have been named as, *inter alia*, *jun* in the Qin dynasty (221–206 BC), *junguo* in the Han dynasty (206 BC–AD 220), *zhou* in the Wei (AD 220–265), the Jin (AD 266–420), and North and South (AD 420–589) dynasties, *dao* in Tang dynasty (AD 618–907), *lu* in North and South Song (AD 960–1279) and the Jin (AD 1115–1235) dynasties, *zhongshu-xingsheng* in the Yuan dynasty (AD 1279–1368), *xingsheng*[2] in the Ming (AD 1368–1644) and the Qing (AD 1644–1911) dynasties, and so on.[3] While the formation of most provinces had taken place far before the PRC was founded, a few of others were either incorporated with their neighbouring provinces or divided into new provinces during the past decades. In addition, some sub-areas have been administratively transposed between the neighbouring provinces.

China has three kinds of provincial-level units in its territorial-administrative hierarchy: provinces, autonomous regions, and municipalities directly under the central government (see Table 2.1). In the Chinese state administration 'autonomous' refers to self-government by a large and single (but not necessarily majority) ethnic minority in any given unit within the territorial hierarchy. Autonomous regions are provincial-level units of state administration where the presence of an ethnic minority is officially recognized. They have the name of the specific ethnic minority incorporated in their title, as for example, in the Guangxi Zhuang autonomous region, where Guangxi is the geographic region and the Zhuang a nationality appellation. Municipalities are large cities, directly subordinate to the leadership of the central offices of the party-state.

It should be noted that, in China, the three kinds of provincial administrations (*sheng*, *zizhiqu*, and *zhixiashi*) have different functions from each other. For example, some top *zhixiashi* leaders have been appointed as members of the Political Bureau of the Chinese Communist Party Central Committee (CCPCC),[4] while very few *sheng* and *zizhiqu* leaders have. The autonomous regions (*zizhiqu*) are only established in areas where the ethnic minorities consist of the major portion of population. As a result of the cultural differences between the non-Han ethnic minorities and the Han majority, the *zizhiqu* is, at least in form, the most politically and socially autonomous among the three kinds of provinces. Furthermore, all provinces are independent from each other in designing local fiscal, tax, labour, and trade policies, and

*Table 2.1*　China's political and cultural conditions, by province

| Province | Population (m) | Land area (000 km²) | Political form | Main ethnic groups | Main languages |
|---|---|---|---|---|---|
| Anhui | 63.3 | 130.0 | S | Han, Hui, She | MD |
| Beijing | 13.8 | 16.8 | ZXS | Han, Hui, Man | MD |
| Chongqing | 31.0 | 82.4 | ZXS | Han, Yi | MD |
| Fujian | 34.4 | 120.0 | S | Han, She, Hui | MI |
| Gansu | 25.8 | 390.0 | S | Han, Hui, Tibetan | MD, MG |
| Guangdong | 77.8 | 180.0 | S | Han, Yao, Zhuang | CT, MY |
| Guangxi | 47.9 | 230.0 | ZZQ | Zhuang, Han, Yao | CD, TA |
| Guizhou | 38.0 | 170.0 | S | Han, Miao, Buyi | CD, TA |
| Hainan | 8.0 | 34.0 | S | Han, Li, Miao | CT, TA |
| Hebei | 67.0 | 190.0 | S | Han, Hui, Man | MD |
| Heilongjiang | 38.1 | 460.0 | S | Han, Man, Korean | MD |
| Henan | 95.6 | 160.0 | S | Han, Hui, Mongol | MD |
| Hubei | 59.8 | 180.0 | S | Han, Tujia, Hui | CD |
| Hunan | 66.0 | 210.0 | S | Han, Tujia, Miao | MY, CD |
| Inner Mongolia | 23.8 | 1100.0 | ZZQ | Mongol, Han | MG |
| Jiangsu | 73.6 | 100.0 | S | Han, Hui, Man | CD, MD |
| Jiangxi | 41.9 | 160.0 | S | Han, Hui, Miao | CD |
| Jilin | 26.9 | 180.0 | S | Han, Korean, Man | MD |
| Liaoning | 41.9 | 150.0 | S | Han, Man, Mongol | MD |
| Ningxia | 5.6 | 66.0 | ZZQ | Hui, Han, Man | MD |
| Qinghai | 5.2 | 720.0 | S | Han, Tibetan, Hui | TB, MG |
| Shaanxi | 36.6 | 190.0 | S | Han, Hui, Man | MD |
| Shandong | 90.4 | 150.0 | S | Han, Hui, Man | MD |
| Shanghai | 16.1 | 5.8 | ZXS | Han | WU |
| Shanxi | 32.7 | 150.0 | S | Han, Hui, Mongol | MD |
| Sichuan | 86.4 | 477.6 | S | Han, Yi, Tibetan | MD, TB |
| Tianjin | 10.0 | 11.0 | ZXS | Han, Hui, Korean | MD |
| Tibet | 2.6 | 1200.0 | ZZQ | Tibetan, Han, Menba | TB |
| Xinjiang | 18.8 | 1600.0 | ZZQ | Uighur, Han, Kazak | TK, MG |
| Yunnan | 42.9 | 380.0 | S | Han, Yi, Bai | MD, TB |
| Zhejiang | 46.1 | 100.0 | S | Han, She, Hui | CD |

*Notes*: S (sheng)=province; ZZQ (zizhiqu)=autonomous region; ZXS
(zhixiashi)=municipality directly under the central government; MD=Mandarin;
CD=Chinese dialects; TB=Tibetan; MY=Miao-Yao; MG=Mongolian; TK=Turkish dialects;
TG=Tungus; WU=Wu; TA=Tai (Dai); MI=Min.

*Box 2.1* How many provinces should be there in China?

Given China's huge land and population size in provincial adminis-trations, establishing new provinces (or other provincial level units) in the border areas of adjacent large-size provinces seem to have at least two positive functions. The first concerns the increase of the efficiency of spatial administration over the marginal, adjacent areas by transferring the multitude of administrative system into a unitary administrative structure; and the second relates to the real-ization of more economies of scale for provincial administration by separating the marginal areas out of the over-sized provinces.

Since the mid-1950s, the total number of China's provinces has increased from 29 up to 30 in 1988 and 31 in 1997. But economic geographers and regional scientists still believe that a smaller size of land area and population may be helpful in the improvement of efficiency for the spatial administration in China. For example, the optimum numbers of China's provinces have been suggested below:

| No. of provincial administrations | Author |
|---|---|
| 58 | Hong (1945a, b) |
| 40–3 | Hu (1991) |
| 43 | Guo (1993) |

*Source*: Liu (1996), pp. 153–6.

economic development plans which have, *ceteris paribus*, resulted in differing regional economic performances in China.|

Most of China's provinces, autonomous regions and municipalities directly under the central government (in what follows, unless stated oth-erwise, we will use the term 'province' as to denote all the three kinds of administrative divisions), which are the average size and scale of a European country in population and land area, are considerable political and economic systems in their own right. These large provincial adminis-trations have been known to lack of administrative efficiency. Various efforts have been made in order to find a solution (see Box 2.1).

## Great regions

When the PRC was founded on 1 October 1949, the Chinese economy was managed through six great administrative regions (i.e. North,

Northeast, East, Central South, Southwest, and Northwest regions). Except for the North region, which was under the administration of the central government, the other five great regions also had their own governmental bodies in charge of agriculture and forestry, industry, public finance, trade, and so on. In 1954, the six great administrative regions were abolished and, before they were re-organized in 1961, seven cooperative commissions were established in North, Northeast, East, Central, South, Southwest, and Northwest regions in 1958, respectively. The six great regional administrations were destroyed by the 'Red Guards' during the Cultural Revolution period (1966–76). In 1970 the Chinese economy was spatially organized *via* ten economic cooperative zones (i.e. Southwest, Northwest, Center, South, East, Northeast, North, Shandong, Fujian and Jiangxi, and Xinjiang zones). It is generally believed that this arrangement was based on the centrally planned system and reflected the state's efforts to meet the desperate need for regional self-sufficiency in the high tide of the Cold War era.[5]

From 1981 to 1985, and guided by the State Council (1980b), six economic zones were organized in Northeast, North, East, Central South, Southwest, and Northwest regions, respectively. Notice that Shandong was excluded from the six economic zones; Guangxi was included in both Central South and Southwest economic zones; and eastern Inner Mongolia was included in both North and Northeast economic zones. In 1992 when the Chinese government decided to build up a market-oriented economy, the State Planning Commission (SPC) was authorized to map out the development plans for the following economic regions (*People's Daily*, 1992, p. 1).

- Yangtze delta (Jiangsu, Zhejiang and Shanghai)
- Bohai Sea circle (Beijing, Tianjin, Hebei, Shandong, Shanxi, central Inner Mongolia and Liaoning)
- Southeast Coastal area (Guangdong, Fujian and Hainan)
- Northeast area (Liaoning, Jilin, Helongjiang and eastern Inner Mongolia)
- Southwest area (Sichuan, Guizhou, Yunnan, Tibet and Guangxi)
- Central area (Henan, Anhui, Hubei, Hunan and Jiangxi) and
- Northwest area (Shaanxi, Gansu, Ningxia, Qinghai, Xinjiang and western Inner Mongolia)

Besides the above definitions, regional scientists and economic geographers have also defined Chinese great regions, with differing numbers and geographical scope, for their own purposes. The following are some examples in which six, seven, and ten great regions have been used to divide the Chinese economy, respectively.

## Six great regions

Wright (1984, p. 78) roughly divides the Chinese economy into Northeast, North, Northwest, Central East, West and Southwest, and Southeast regions. As an economic geographer, Hu (1993, pp. 193–203) uses the following definitions

- Northeast region (Liaoning, Jilin and Heilongjiang)
- North region (Beijing, Tianjin, Hebei, Shanxi, Inner Mongolia, Shandong and Henan)
- Northwest region (Shaanxi, Gansu, Qinghai, Ningxia and Xinjiang)
- East Middle region (Shanghai, Jiangsu, Zhejiang, Anhui, Jiangxi, Hubei and Hunan)
- South region (Guangdong, Fujian, Guangxi and Hainan) and
- Southwest region (Sichuan, Guizhou, Yunnan and Tibet)

Based on the transprovincial commodity flows via the central rail network, Yang (1993, p. 270) groups the provinces into

- Northeast region (Liaoning, Jilin, Heilongjiang and eastern Inner Mongolia)
- North region (Beijing, Tianjin, Hebei, central Inner Mongolia, and northeastern, northern and eastern Shandong)
- Central East region (Shanghai, Jiangsu, Zhejiang, Anhui, Jiangxi (excluding southern area), Henan, northern Hubei, southern and southwestern Shandong and Hunan (excluding southwestern area))
- South region (Guangdong, Guangxi, Hainan, Fujian, southern Jiangxi and southern and central Hunan)
- West region (Shaanxi, Gansu, Qinghai, Ningxia, Xinjiang and Tibet) and
- Southwest region (Yunnan, Guizhou, Sichuan and southwestern Hubei)

In addition, based on the interregional division of labour, Liu (1994, pp. 36–7) frames

- Northeast region (Liaoning, Jilin, Heilongjiang and eastern Inner Mongolia)
- North region (Beijing, Tianjin, Hebei, Shanxi, and western Inner Mongolia, Shandong and Henan)

- Central region (Shanghai, Jiangsu, Zhejiang, Anhui, Jiangxi, Hubei and Hunan)
- Southeast region (Fujian, Guangdong, Guangxi and Hainan)
- Southwest region (Sichuan, Yunnan, Guizhou and Tibet) and
- Northwest region (Shaanxi, Gansu, Qinghai, Ningxia and Xinjiang)

## Seven great regions

Using the input-output table developed by the State Statistical Bureau (SSB), Li *et al.* (1994, pp. 139–65) analyze the mutually complementary conditions and industrial interdependence between the seven great regions:

- Northeast region (Liaoning, Jilin and Heilongjiang)
- North region (Beijing, Tianjin, Hebei, Shandong and Inner Mongolia)
- South region (Fujian, Guangdong and Hainan)
- Central region (Shanxi, Henan, Anhui, Hubei, Hunan and Jiangxi)
- Northwest region (Shaanxi, Qinghai, Gansu, Ningxia and Xinjiang)
- Southwest region (Sichuan, Guizhou, Yunnan, Guangxi and Tibet) and
- East region (Shanghai, Jiangsu and Zhejiang)

In addition, when estimating the Chinese economic disparities, Keidel (1995) uses

- Far Western region (Xinjiang, Tibet, Qinghai, Gansu and Ningxia)
- Northern Inland region (Heilongjiang, Jilin, Inner Mongolia, Shaanxi and Shanxi)
- Southern Inland region (Sichuan, Guizhou, Yunnan and Guangxi)
- Central region (Henan, Anhui, Jiangxi, Hubei and Hunan)
- Northern Coastal region (Liaoning, Hebei, Beijing, Tianjin and Shandong)
- Eastern Coastal region (Jiangsu, Shanghai and Zhejiang) and
- Southern Coastal region (Fujian, Guangdong and Hainan)

## Ten great regions

Taking into account the spatial characteristics in resource endowment, transport network, and central city, Yang (1989, pp. 238–40) divides the Chinese economy into Northeast, Beijing–Tianjin, Shanxi–Shaanxi, Shandong, Shanghai, Central South, Sichuan, Southeast, Southwest, and Great West zones. In this research, Inner Mongolia is divided into four sub-areas of Northeast, Beijing–Tianjin, Shanxi–Shaanxi, and

Great West zones, respectively. After clarifying the regional differences in physical environment and cultural identity, Yang (1990, pp. 38–40) groups China's provincial economies into the following regions:

- Northeast
- North
- East
- Central
- South
- Southwest
- Northwest
- Inner Mongolia
- Xinjiang and
- Tibet

It can be assumed that the vast land area and clear cultural identity are the main reasons for him to define each of the three autonomous regions (Inner Mongolia, Xinjiang, and Tibet) as a great region. In addition, Liu (1994, p. 36) demarcates the Chinese economy by 10 regions.

Since the early 1980s, China's official statistical authorities (such as the SSB (or the National Bureau of Statistics, NBS, as it is now called) and other statistical departments and divisions under ministries or administrations) have used six great regions as shown in Table 2.2. The six great regions have been also applied in many scholarly research works.[6]

*Table 2.2*   The six great regions

| Great region | Land area (%) | Geographical scope (provinces) |
| --- | --- | --- |
| North | 16.3 | Beijing, Tianjin, Hebei, Shanxi, and Inner Mongolia |
| Northeast | 8.2 | Liaoning, Jilin, and Heilongjiang |
| East | 8.3 | Shanghai, Jiangsu, Zhejiang, Anhui, Fujian, Jiangxi, and Shandong |
| Central South | 10.6 | Henan, Hubei, Hunan, Guangdong, Guangxi, and Hainan |
| Southwest | 24.6 | Sichuan, Chongqing, Guizhou, Yunnan, and Tibet |
| Northwest | 32.0 | Shaanxi, Gansu, Qinghai, Ningxia, and Xinjiang |

## Coastal and inland areas

The 12 provinces surrounded by the Yellow, East China, and South China seas are known as the coastal area, while the remaining 18 provinces comprise of the inland area (see Table 2.3). Generally, the coastal area is more developed than the inland area, as a result of its proximity to the market economies along the western shore of the Pacific ocean as well as the earlier introduction of economic reform and opening up to the outside world.

There have been different definitions of the coastal and inland areas from that in Table 2.3. For example, Mao (1956, p. 286) treats Anhui and eastern Henan provinces as a part of the coastal area according to the principle of geographical proximity to the coastal area, while the State Council (1993) classifies two coastal provinces of Guangxi and Hainan into the inland area according to the principle of economic similarity to the inland provinces.

## Eastern, central and western belts

Even though China's economic divergence has not been so large within the inland area as between the inland and coastal areas, there are still some plausible reasons for why the inland area needs to be further divided into smaller geographical units. As the western part of the inland area has less-developed social and economic infrastructures than the eastern part, China's inland area can be classified into two

*Table 2.3*   The coastal and inland areas and the Eastern, Central, and Western belts

| Area | Belt | Land area (%) | Geographical scope (provinces) |
| --- | --- | --- | --- |
| Coast | East | 13.5 | Liaoning, Hebei, Beijing, Tianjin, Shandong, Jiangsu, Shanghai, Zhejiang, Fujian, Guangdong, Hainan, and Guangxi |
| Inland | Center | 29.8 | Shanxi, Jilin, Heilongjiang, Anhui, Henan, Hubei, Hunan, Jiangxi, and Inner Mongolia |
| | West | 56.7 | Sichuan, Chongqing, Guizhou, Yunnan, Shaanxi, Gansu, Qinghai, Tibet, Ningxia, and Xinjiang |

parts – the Central belt which is next to the coastal area (here it is referred as the Eastern belt) and the Western belt.

The Eastern, Central, and Western belts first appeared in the proposal for national economic and social development in the Seventh five-year plan (FYP) (1986–90) which was adopted in April 1986 by the National People's Congress (NPC).[7] In this FYP, the government advocated that: 'The development of the eastern coastal belt shall be further accelerated and, at the same time, the construction of energy and raw material industries shall be focused on the Central belt, while the preparatory works for the further development of the Western belt shall be actively conducted.'[8] Generally, the Eastern, Central, and Western belts are geographically defined in Table 2.3.[9] Nevertheless, there have been different definitions on the tripartite division of the Chinese economy. For instance, Guangxi, a coastal province along the Gulf of Tonkin, is included in the Western belt by Yang (1989, pp. 90–6), Gu (1995, pp. 45–51) and Chen (1994, p. 57). In Gu's analysis, moreover, Jilin and Heilongjiang, two inland provinces in Northeast China, are included in the Eastern belt.

## Southern and Northern parts

The introduction of the 'North and South' concept in this book seems to be necessary for the bi-regional comparison of the Chinese economy. Besides the natural and climatic environments, social and cultural conditions also differ between northern and southern China. Without good reason, the Chinese are usually identified as Northerners and Southerners in terms of birthplaces and, occasionally, native places when they are introduced to each other. While it is not quite clear when the saying 'South China raises intelligent scholars while marshals mainly come from the North' was aired and whether or not it can be used to spatially characterize China's ethnic nature, many conflicts and wars in Chinese history did take place in the northern part.

The first major Han-Chinese migration from the northern to the southern part of Yangtze river took place during the Wei, the Jin, and the South and North dynasties (AD 220–589), and was accelerated during the Five Dynasties and Ten States period (AD 907–960) when China's northern part became the field of battle. Since then large-scale Han-Chinese migration was promoted by the frequent wars between the Chinese and Liao, Jin, Mongol, and other minorities in the North Song (AD 960–1126) and the South Song (AD 1127–1279) dynasties. In the wars with their far northern enemies, the Han–Chinese first lost their northern part after the late North Song dynasty. Naturally, the frequent wars greatly accelerated the emigration of the northern intellectuals to the southern part.

The geographical definition of the Southern and Northern parts may slightly differ in research circle. For example, Qinling range and Huaihe river are traditionally used to divide the South and North, while the Yangtze river is sometimes known as the boundary of northern and southern China. In most cases, nevertheless, there are 15 provinces in each of the Northern and Southern parts, as shown in Table 2.4. The only difference between the two definitions lies in the fact that the Qinling range and the Huaihe river are located in Shaanxi, Henan, Anhui, and Jiangsu provinces, while the Yangtze river runs through Sichuan, Hubei, Anhui, Jiangsu provinces and Shanghai municipality.

*Table 2.4*　The Northern and Southern parts

| Part | Land area (%) | Geographical scope (provinces) |
|------|---------------|-------------------------------|
| North | 59.8 | Beijing, Tianjin, Hebei, Shanxi, Inner Mongolia, Liaoning, Jilin, Heilongjiang, Shaanxi, Gansu, Qinghai, Ningxia, Xinjiang, Shandong, and Henan |
| South | 40.2 | Shanghai, Jiangsu, Zhejiang, Anhui, Fujian, Jiangxi, Sichuan, Chongqing, Guizhou, Yunnan, Tibet, Hubei, Hunan, Guangdong, Guangxi, and Hainan |

# 3
# China's Economic Foundations

When a seed is planted in spring
   (chun zhong yi li su)
There are thousands of grains harvested in the fall.
   (qiu shou wan ke li)
While all land across the country has been cultivated
   (si hai wu xian tian)
Why do farmers still die from starvation?
   (nong fu you e si)

                    'Linnong' by Li Shen (AD 772–846)

## Physical capital

Natural resources (such as land, climate, biology, water, minerals, energy, and so on) are the basic component among the factors that influence social and economic activities, especially for less-developed economies lacking capital and technology. Theoretically, in a nation whose manufacturing and other high-tech industries are not internationally competitive, one of the most feasible ways to eradicate its poverty and backwardness is to develop the natural resource-based sectors. During recent decades, Chinese economic development followed this path. Until recently, the natural resource-based sectors still played the most important role in the less-developed areas of China.

With its vast land area, comparable to the USA or Canada, China also possesses an abundance of other natural resources. According to a report published by the World Resources Institute, China's cropland (96,615,000 ha) accounts for 6.8 per cent of the world's, and is the fourth largest (after Russia, USA, and India); China has 9 per cent of the world's total permanent pasture (only after Australia and Russia),

21

3.4 per cent of the world's forestland and woodland (after Russia, Brazil, Canada, and USA), and 8.39 per cent of the world's reserves of 15 major metals (copper, lead, tin, zinc, iron ore, manganese, nickel, chromium, cobalt, molybdenum, tungsten, vanadium, bauxite, titanium, and lithium) (after Russia, South Africa, and USA) (WRI, 1992, pp. 322–3, 262–3).[1]

However, if population size is taken into account, China's natural resources are not richer than in the world as a whole. For instance, China's per capita cultivated land area is less than one-third the world's; its per capita forestland and woodland is approximately one-seventh the world's; and, except for tin and tungsten, China's per capita metal reserves are fewer than the world's, as shown in Table 3.1. In addition, natural resources are generally known to be low grade in China. For example, more than 95 per cent of the iron ore reserves are ferriferously poor, and the iron-rich ore that can be directly processed by refineries accounts for only 2.4 per cent of the proven reserves; about two-thirds of the proven copper ore reserves can be refined to only 1 per cent copper products. The phosphoric ore with the composition of phosphorous pentoxide ($P_2O_5$) at or higher than 30 per cent accounts for only 7.1 per cent – while, in contrast, that at or lower than 12 per cent accounts for 19 per cent – of the proven reserves.[2]

*Table 3.1*   Major metal reserves of China and the world

| Item | Million tons of contents[a] | | | Per capita kg[b] | | |
|---|---|---|---|---|---|---|
| | China (1) | World (2) | (1)/(2) (%) | China (3) | World (4) | (3)/(4) (%) |
| Bauxite | 150 | 21559 | 0.70 | 128.2 | 3934.1 | 3.26 |
| Copper | 3.00 | 321.00 | 0.93 | 2.56 | 58.58 | 4.37 |
| Iron ore | 3500 | 64648 | 5.41 | 2992 | 11797 | 25.36 |
| Lead | 6.00 | 70.44 | 8.52 | 5.13 | 12.85 | 39.92 |
| Manganese | 13.6 | 812.8 | 1.67 | 11.62 | 148.32 | 7.83 |
| Molybdenum | 0.55 | 6.10 | 9.02 | 0.47 | 1.11 | 42.34 |
| Nickel | 0.73 | 48.66 | 1.50 | 0.62 | 8.88 | 6.98 |
| Tin | 1.50 | 5.93 | 25.30 | 1.28 | 1.08 | 118.52 |
| Titanium | 30.0 | 288.6 | 10.40 | 25.64 | 52.66 | 48.68 |
| Tungsten | 1.05 | 2.35 | 44.68 | 0.90 | 0.43 | 209.30 |
| Vanadium | 0.61 | 4.27 | 14.29 | 0.52 | 0.78 | 66.67 |
| Zinc | 5.00 | 143.90 | 3.47 | 4.27 | 36.26 | 16.26 |

*Notes:* [a] WRI (1992, pp. 322–3); [b] figures of population are 1.17 billion for China and 5.48 billion for the world in 1992.

⸻The Chinese economy is characterized by heterogeneous and diversified natural conditions: the climate ranges from the tropical zone in the south to the frigid zone in the north and from the arid and semiarid zones in the northwest to the humid and semi-humid zones in the southeast. As a result, in China the regional distribution of natural resources is extremely unequal. In general, the agricultural and biological resources diminish from the south to the north and from the

*Table 3.2* Regional distribution of major mineral resources

| Mineral resource | Major provinces (in order of reserves) |
|---|---|
| Argentum (Ag) | Jiangxi, Guangdong, Guangxi, Yunnan, Hunnan |
| Bauxite | Shanxi, Guizhou, Guangxi, Sichuan |
| Bismuthum (Bi) | Hunan, Guangdong, Jiangxi, Yunnan, Inner Mongolia |
| Chromium (Cr) | Tibet, Inner Mongolia, Gansu |
| Coal | Shanxi, Inner Mongolia, Shaanxi, Guizhou, Ningxia |
| Collat. (Co) | Gansu, Yunnan, Shandong, Hebei, Shanxi |
| Copper (Cu) | Jiangxi, Tibet, Yunnan, Gansu, Anhui |
| Gold (Au) | Shandong, Jiangxi, Heilongjiang, Jilin, Hubei |
| Hydragyrum (Hg) | Guizhou, Shaanxi, Hunan, Sichuan, Yunnan |
| Iron (Fe) ore | Liaoning, Sichuan, Hebei, Shanxi, Anhui |
| Kaolin (Ka) | Hunan, Jiangsu, Fujian, Guangdong, Liaoning |
| Lead (Pb) | Yunnan, Guangdong, Hunan, Inner Mongolia, Jiangxi |
| Manganese (Mn) | Guangxi, Hunan, Guizhou, Liaoning, Sichuan |
| Molybdenum (Mo) | Henan, Jilin, Shaanxi, Shandong, Jiangxi |
| Natural gas | Sichuan, Liaoning, Henan, Xinjiang, Hebei, Tianjin |
| Nickel (Ni) | Gansu, Yunnan, Jilin, Sichuan, Hubei |
| Petroleum | Heilongjiang, Shandong, Liaoning, Hebei, Xinjiang |
| Platinum (Pt) | Gansu, Yunnan, Sichuan |
| Silica stone (SiO$_2$) | Qinghai, Beijing, Liaoning, Gansu, Sichuan |
| Stibium (Sb) | Hunan, Guangxi, Guizhou, Yunnan |
| Tantalum (Ta) | Jiangxi, Inner Mongolia, Guangdong, Hunan, Sichuan |
| Tin (Sn) | Guangxi, Yunnan, Hunan, Guangdong, Jiangxi |
| Titanium (Ti) | Sichuan, Hebei, Shaanxi, Shanxi |
| Tungsten (WO$_3$) | Hunan, Jiangxi, Henan, Fujian, Guangxi |
| Vanadium (V) | Sichuan, Hunan, Gansu, Hubei, Anhui |
| Zinc (Zn) | Yunnan, Inner Mongolia, Guangdong, Hunan, Gansu |

*Source*: CISNR (1990, p. 644).

east to the west. Except for hydropower resource which concentrates in Southwest and Central South regions, energy resources are richer in the north than in the south; while metals are mainly distributed in the transitional area (such as Sichuan, Gansu, Hunan, and so on) between the plateau in the west and the mountain and hilly areas in the east. Table 3.2 lists the major mineral resources by province.

*Table 3.3*  Monetary values of minerals, by provinces

| Province | Monetary value (billion yuan)[a] | Share to China (%)[b] | Million yuan per km$^2$ of land[c] | Thousand yuan per capita[d] |
|---|---|---|---|---|
| Anhui | 1988.45 | 3.49 | 15.30 | 36.98 |
| Beijing | 160.07 | 0.28 | 9.53 | 2.98 |
| Fujian | 116.09 | 0.20 | 0.97 | 2.16 |
| Gansu | 1048.13 | 1.83 | 2.69 | 19.49 |
| Guangdong[e] | 546.42 | 0.95 | 3.04 | 10.16 |
| Guangxi | 488.35 | 0.85 | 2.12 | 9.08 |
| Guizhou | 1736.85 | 3.03 | 10.22 | 32.30 |
| Hebei | 2198.26 | 3.84 | 11.57 | 40.88 |
| Heilongjiang | 2194.40 | 3.83 | 4.77 | 40.81 |
| Henan | 2179.13 | 3.80 | 13.62 | 40.53 |
| Hubei | 388.70 | 0.68 | 2.16 | 7.23 |
| Hunan | 1249.79 | 2.18 | 5.95 | 23.24 |
| Inner Mongolia | 5035.61 | 8.79 | 33.57 | 93.65 |
| Jiangsu | 401.77 | 0.70 | 0.37 | 7.47 |
| Jiangxi | 595.58 | 1.04 | 5.96 | 11.08 |
| Jilin | 492.13 | 0.86 | 3.08 | 9.15 |
| Liaoning | 2436.64 | 4.25 | 13.54 | 45.32 |
| Ningxia | 802.29 | 1.40 | 12.16 | 14.92 |
| Qinghai | 748.18 | 1.13 | 1.039 | 13.91 |
| Shaanxi | 144.49 | 2.52 | 0.76 | 2.69 |
| Shandong | 2374.53 | 4.14 | 15.83 | 44.16 |
| Shanghai | 3.46 | 0.01 | 0.60 | 0.06 |
| Shanxi | 11529.22 | 20.1 | 76.86 | 214.42 |
| Sichuan[f] | 13239.37 | 23.1 | 23.64 | 246.22 |
| Tianjin | 121.59 | 0.21 | 11.05 | 2.26 |
| Tibet | 43.57 | 0.07 | 0.03 | 0.81 |
| Xinjiang | 1012.33 | 1.77 | 0.84 | 18.83 |
| Yunnan | 2648.74 | 4.62 | 6.97 | 49.26 |
| Zhejiang | 55.73 | 0.09 | 0.56 | 1.04 |

*Notes:* [a] based on Sun (1987, pp. 4–8); [b] the first column divided by the total amount of the first column; [c] the first column divided by the land area of each province; [d] the first column divided by the population of each province; [e] includes Hainan; [f] Includes Chongqing.

Using the total monetary value of 45 major minerals, land area and population of each province (shown in Table 3.3),[3] we may estimate that the five richest provinces are Sichuan, Shanxi, Inner Mongolia, Yunnan and Liaoning, and the five poorest provinces are Shanghai, Tibet, Zhejiang, Fujian and Tianjin according to the absolute and per-capita values (shown in the second and fifth columns, respectively); while the five richest provinces are Shanxi, Inner Mongolia, Sichuan, Shandong and Anhui, and the five poorest provinces are Tibet, Jiangsu, Zhejiang, Shanghai and Shaanxi according to the per-square-kilometer value (shown in the fourth column).

Energy resource is disproportionally distributed in China, as shown in Table 3.4. For example, about 70 per cent hydropower reserves are concentrated in Southwest region, while the North, Northeast, and East regions as a whole shares only less than 10 per cent; more than 60 per cent of coal reserves are distributed in the North region, with only a small portion, sparsely distributed, in the Northeast, East, and Central South regions; Northeast region accounts for nearly a half of the nation's petroleum and natural gas reserves, while Central South and Southwest regions as a whole only shares a meager 5 per cent. Nevertheless, Northwest is the only region which is modestly rich in coal, hydropower, petroleum, and natural gas. In addition, the energy structure is disproportional among regions. For example, coal nearly monopolizes the North region, while the Southwest and Central South regions are mostly dominated by hydropower. Nevertheless, the East,

*Table 3.4* Energy resources by great region (%)

| Great region | Coal | Hydropower[a] | Petroleum[b] | All energy |
|---|---|---|---|---|
| North | 64.0 (98.2) | 1.8 (1.3) | 14.4 (0.5) | 43.9 (100.0) |
| Northeast | 3.1 (54.6) | 1.8 (14.2) | 48.3 (31.2) | 3.8 (100.0) |
| East | 6.5 (72.9) | 4.4 (22.5) | 18.2 (4.6) | 6.0 (100.0) |
| Central South | 3.7 (44.5) | 9.5 (51.8) | 2.5 (3.7) | 5.6 (100.0) |
| Southwest | 10.7 (25.2) | 70.0 (74.7) | 2.5 (0.1) | 28.6 (100.0) |
| Northwest | 12.0 (66.7) | 12.5 (31.3) | 14.0 (2.0) | 12.1 (100.0) |
| China | 100.0 (85.9) | 100.0 (13.1) | 100.0 (1.0) | 100.0 (100.0) |

*Notes*: (1) figures in parentheses are energy structures. (2) the geographical scopes of the great regions are defined in Table 2.2. (3) standard coal equivalent conversion rates are as 0.714 t/t for coal, 1.43 t/t for petroleum, 1.33 t/1000 m³ for natural gas, 0.143 t/t for oil shale, and 350 g/kWh for hydropower;
[a] the theoretical reserves multiplied by 100 years;
[b] includes natural gas and oil shale.
*Source*: MOE (1991, p. 101).

*Table 3.5*   Regional distribution of agricultural products

| Product | Major provinces (in order of output) |
| --- | --- |
| Rice | Hunan, Sichuan, Jiangsu, Hubei, Guangdong |
| Wheat | Henan, Shandong, Jiangsu, Hebei, Sichuan |
| Maize | Shandong, Jilin, Hebei, Sichuan, Henan |
| Soybean | Heilongjiang, Henan, Jilin, Shandong, Anhui |
| Cotton | Shandong, Hebei, Henan, Hubei, Jiangsu |
| Rapeseeds | Shandong, Sichuan, Anhui, Jiangsu, Henan |
| Tobacco | Henan, Yunnan, Shandong, Guizhou, Hunan |
| Tea | Zhejiang, Hunan, Sichuan, Anhui, Fujian |
| Fruits | Shandong, Hebei, Guangdong, Sichuan, Liaoning |

Northwest and Northeast regions are mainly served by coal rather than by petroleum, hydropower and natural gas.

The distribution of water is extremely irregular in China. In general, the northern part is poor in surface water, but modestly rich in groundwater in a few provinces such as Qinghai, Xinjiang, Inner Mongolia and Heilongjiang. The precipitation is more than 1000 mm/year in the southern part and more than 1600 mm/year in the southern coastal area; while it ranges from 100 to 800 mm/year in the northern part. In particular, the Talimu, Tulufan and Chaidamu basins in Northwest region have less than 25 mm of precipitation per annum. As a result of the suitable climate and adequate rainfall, the southern part is the dominant rice producer; wheat is the main foodstuff in the lower Yellow river (such as Henan, Shandong, Hebei, northern Jiangsu and Anhui provinces) and southern Great Wall areas. Table 3.5 lists the major agricultural provinces in order of output for the selected products.

## Human capital

> If you plan for a year, sow a seed; if for ten years, plant a tree; if for a hundred years, teach the people. You will reap a single harvest by sowing a seed once and ten harvests by planting a tree; while you will reap a hundred of harvests by teaching the people.
>
> Guanzhong (551–479 BC)

Since Confucianism began to influence Chinese society, people have placed a high value on education in China. However, education has not been successfully achieved in China particularly for the past century. In 1964, when the second national population census was conducted, as high as 56.76 per cent of the total population aged 16 and over were illiterate or semi-literate. Thereafter, the illiterate and semi-literate rate decreased considerably but was still estimated at 31.88 per cent and 20.61 per cent in the third and fourth national population census in 1982 and 1990, respectively.[4] According to the UNESCO (1995, table 1.3), the literacy rates for China were 87 per cent for males and 68 per cent for females in 1990, which are higher than that of India (62 per cent and 34 per cent), Pakistan (47 per cent and 21 per cent), and many other low-income countries, while still lower than that of Indonesia (88 per cent and 75 per cent), the Philippines (90 per cent and 89 per cent), Thailand (95 per cent and 91 per cent), Malaysia (86 per cent and 70 per cent), and many other low- and upper-middle income countries, and much lower than that of Japan, the USA, Germany, and other high income countries.

⊫ China's modestly high illiteracy has been decided by both historic and institutional factors. Before 1949, China's education was very backward and had been seriously damaged by the long-lasting wars. For instance, more than 60 per cent of people born in the 1930s and more than 70 per cent of people born in the 1920s were illiterate or semi-literate. During the two peaks of population growth in the 1950s and the 1960s, neither the government nor their homes were able to provide an equal education opportunity for each child.[5] ⊣

During the Cultural Revolution period (1966–76), China's education system which, to a large extent, had represented Confucianism was effectively reformed. Primary school education was reduced from six years to five years and junior and senior middle school education were each cut by one year. In those cases the textbooks were highly revised and simplified. Even worse, the school teachers who had been highly ranked in traditional Chinese society were the subjects of political discrimination. During this period, the destruction of the higher education system was even more serious because universities were closed during 1966–70 and operated on political merit rather than academic performance during 1971–76. The Cultural Revolution resulted in a 'break-point' of ages for scientists and engineers, which has already affected China's socioeconomic development negatively.

Education in China has experienced dramatic changes during the post-Mao era. In 1977 the national entrance examinations for higher learning institutes were resumed. One year later, the Chinese government first recognized during the First National Conference on Science and Technology (NCST) that 'science and technology is a productive force' and began to treat intellectuals as 'a branch of the working class'.[6] Since then education has been the scene of much action. Particularly praiseworthy is the fact that China's primary education has achieved much progress with the percentage of school-age children enrolled increased from only 49.2 per cent in 1952 to near 100 per cent in 2000. However, problems still remain in middle school education. For instance, almost a half of the graduates from junior middle schools had not been able to enter senior middle schools in 2000 (see Figure 3.1).

A regression based on the data on China's educational expenditure and national income from the 1980s and the early 1990s reveals that when the per capita national income grew from 250 yuan to 1000 yuan, the ratio of educational expenditure to national income decreased from 6.3 per cent to 2.8 per cent accordingly (Hsueh, 1994b, pp. 80–1). Obviously, the empirical estimate is inconsistent with the hypothesis that there exists a positive correlation between the income level and

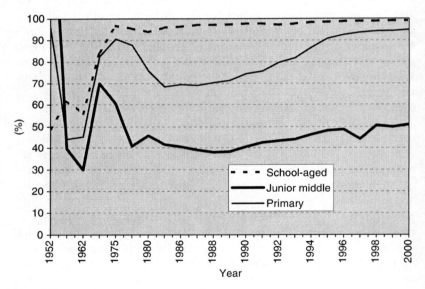

*Notes*
(1) the proportion of graduates of junior middle schools entering senior middle schools was higher than 100 per cent in the early 1950s as the students graduated from junior middle schools were less than the students enrolled in senior middle schools; (2) graduates of junior middle school include vocational schools.

*Figure 3.1*   School-aged children enrolled and graduates of primary and junior middle schools entering higher level schools (1952–2000)

the ratio of educational expenditure to GNP, as estimated by Chenery and Syrquin (1975, p. 20).[7] Even though the two estimates are based on different statistical definitions, it can still be seen that China's education lagged behind its economic growth. In 1978, China's expenditure on public education as a percentage of GNP was 2.07 per cent. Thereafter, this ratio increased gradually up to 2.69 per cent in 1986 but then dropped back to 2.08 per cent in 1995. But since 1995 it has increased considerably (see Figure 3.2).

Expenditure on public education as a percentage of GNP of China only leads that of a few of poor nations such as Nigeria (0.5 per cent, 1992) but still lags far behind that of the world as a whole (5.1 per cent, 1993) and many other nations such as Canada (7.6 per cent, 1992), Hungary (7.0 per cent, 1992), Bulgaria (5.9 per cent, 1992), Portugal (6.1 per cent, 1990), USA (5.3 per cent, 1990), and Japan (4.7 per cent, 1991).[8] Besides, China's education is unevenly provided among the provinces. According to Knight and Li (1993, pp. 292–3), the mean value of education is 9.19 years in Beijing, almost three times that in Qinghai. However, the mean values of education in years are more even in urban area, the reasons for which may be twofold. First, the central government attempts to equalize educational opportunities among provinces: the richer provinces tend to receive less and the poor provinces more central government funding for education. Second, the

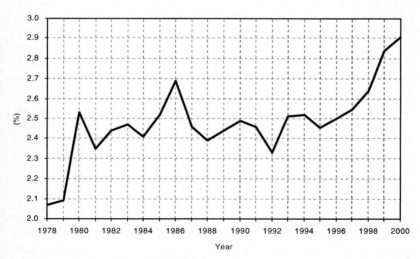

*Figure 3.2*  Government expenditure on education as a % of GNP (1978–2000)

assignment of college graduates to employment is done on a national basis. Government gives preferential treatment to the poor provinces by assigning graduates from colleges in rich provinces to work in poor provinces (Knight and Li, 1993, p. 300).

## Political and institutional bases

According to the new institutional economics, system, like other production factors required in economic development, is a special kind of scarce resource and should thus be treated properly in economics. Economic system of any nation is the mechanism that brings together natural resources, labour, technology, and the necessary managerial talents. Anticipating and then meeting human needs through production and distribution of goods and services is the end purpose of every economic system. While the type of economic system applied by a nation is usually artificially decided, it is also to a large extent the result of historical experience, which becomes over time a part of political culture.

Historical evidence suggests that the Western countries gradually pulled ahead of the rest of the world from the 16th century.[9] Northern Italy and Flanders played the leading role from the 16th to 17th century, the Netherlands from then until the end of the 18th century, the UK and Germany in the 19th, and the USA since then. The main institutional characteristics of the Western society that have favoured its development can be broadly summarized as follows: (1) the recognition of human capacity to transform the forces of nature through rational investigation and experiment and (2) the ending of feudal constraints on the free purchase and sale of property, followed by a whole series of developments which gave scope for successful entrepreneurship (Maddison, 1996, p. 50).

After the fall of the socialist system in 1990, old institutions that provided certain economical and social stability in the society have been rapidly destroyed and new market-oriented fundamentals have been hardly spreading in the economic environment of the former Soviet Union. Whereas by the late 1990s many elements of a market-based formal framework had been established, its implementation was often weak. The enforcement of new laws and regulations has been constrained by the presence of old informal institutions – the strong bureaucracy, the weak respect for law, informal networking, and other social factors, which were historically rooted in the behavior of the Soviet society. As a result the speed and sequencing of the economic reforms, which were important at the beginning of the transition, seems not to be so important nowadays comparing with the necessity of institutional transformation.

During the 20th century the failure of the CPEs to keep pace with their market-oriented counterparts demonstrated clearly enough that planning entire economies at the central government level is not a productive path to long-term development. Since 1978, economic reforms in China have sought to improve, among others, enterprise incentive systems with greater relative decision-making autonomy. The dynamism of the Chinese economy may be attributed to a variety of reform measures. One such measure was the lifting of previous restrictions on the development of non-state sectors and the policy of promoting a diversified ownership structure. This has led to the explosive growth of the non-state sectors that are increasingly acting as the engine of economic development particularly since the early 1990s when China formally tried to transform its economy to a socialist market system.

## Cultural issues

If you understand others you are smart.
If you understand yourself you are illuminated.
If you overcome others you are powerful.
If you overcome yourself you have strength.

Laozi (c. 600 BC)

As well as describing the content of libraries, museums, moral and religious codes of conduct the world 'culture' is commonly used to describe social life. As such, 'culture' is the living sum of symbols, meanings, habits, values, institutions, behaviors, and social artifacts which characterize a distinctive and identified human population group. It confers upon individuals identity as members of some visible community; standards for relating to the environment, for identifying fellow members and strangers; and for deciding what is important and what is not important to them (Goulet, 1980, p. 2). The differences between intra- and inter-cultural behaviors can be summarized as four aspects: (1) feelings of superiority (and occasionally inferiority) toward people who are perceived as being very different; (2) fear of and lack of trust in such people; (3) difficulty of communication with them as a result of differences in language and what is considered civil behavior; (4) lack of familiarity with the assumptions, motivations, such as relationships, and social practices of other people (Huntington, 1996, p. 129).

To a certain extent, cultural differences have decisively influenced economic and marketing decisions. Although it is not the only tool in building trusting relationships, doors usually open more quickly when knocked on by someone who shares a familiar culture. While others usually suggested more complicated compositions for a culture, we will only discuss three elements – ethnicity, language and religion – in this research. Of course, our discussion of these cultural elements is not definitive and perhaps would not satisfy anthropologists. Nevertheless, our consideration is due to the concerns that (a) 'ethnicity' provides a genetic basis in which socioeconomic behaviors between same and different groups of people can be easily differentiated; (b) 'language' is an effective tool of communication; and (c) 'religion' can provide the insights into the characteristics of culture.

### Ethnicity

Members of the ethnic majority in China have for most of the Christian era traditionally referred to themselves as the Han race. This may well be because of the relatively long period of social, political, economic and military consolidation and stability enjoyed by the Chinese nation during the Han (206 BC–AD 220) dynasty. The Han people consisting of more than 90 per cent of the population in China display the physical characteristics of Continental Asian Mongoloids. They are, in general, of medium stature, with slightly rounded heads, less prominent foreheads, low nose bridges, straight black hair and yellow-brown to white pigmentation.

The term 'Han', however, does not fully account for the cultural and ethnic origins of the Chinese people. It is, instead, an inclusive name for the various tribes that lived together on the Central China Plains much prior to the time of Christ. The trend over the ages was for many ethnic groups living adjacent to the Hua-Xia people to be assimilated at different times and to different degrees into what ultimately the Chinese have termed the Han culture.[10] The original ethnic stock for this amalgam seems to have primarily included the Hua-Xia, Eastern Yi, Chu-Wu, and Baiyue groups. Other non-Han peoples were assimilated into the evolving culture of the Han group at different points in China's history: for example, the Xiongnu and Xianpi between the third and fifth century AD, the Eastern Hu and the Jurchens (ancestors of the Manchus) from the tenth through the early 13th century, later the Mongols toward the end of the 13th century, and the Manchus through their conquest of Central China in the 17th century. All have fused with and become key elements of Han culture, which most

Chinese regard as the cultural mainstream of the Chinese nation, although the last two groups retain a separate ethnic identity to a greater or lesser extent today within the Chinese culture.

Besides the Han majority which can be found throughout the country, though mainly in the lower reaches of the Yellow and the Yangtze rivers, the Pearl river valleys and the Northeast China plain, there exist 55 ethnic minorities that are scattered over a vast area of China (see Appendix I for details). As a matter of fact, the total number of ethnic groups has never been fixed in China. For example, in 1953, only 42 ethnic peoples were identified, while the number increased to 54 in 1964 and 56 in 1982, respectively. According to the 1990 National Census, there had 752,347 and 3,498 persons with unknown ethnic identity and foreigners with Chinese citizenships, respectively, in mainland China.[11] From a geographical perspective, most of the ethnic minorities are concentrated on the western inland areas, such as Hui in Ningxia, Ugyur in Xinjiang, Mongol in Inner Mongolia and Qinghai and Tibetan in Tibet and the surrounding areas. The only exception is the ethnic Zhuang which concentrates in Guangxi in southern China.

Each of the ethnic minorities has one or more names in China. In most cases, the names used by minorities for themselves tell the legend of their origin. For example, the name Kirgiz means '40 girls'. A legend says that the ancestors of the Kirgiz people were 40 sisters. Kazak means 'swan'. The first Kazak was said to be the child of a swan who turned into a beautiful girl. Some other ethnic groups are named after their customs or costumes. For example, as the Xibe people liked to wear a hooked leather belt, they used 'Xibe' (leather belt or hooked belt) to name their ethnic group. The Yi people who live in Southwest China like to wear black clothes, so they call themselves Nisu, meaning the 'black people'. But the Bai people have a preference for white, so they call themselves Baini, or the 'white people'. Ethnic names in many cases relate to the values and activities of the ethnicity. Sometimes, the names also indicate the natural and geographical conditions under which the ethnic peoples lived. For example, Ewenki means 'people living in the mountain forests'. Another example is the Maonan people whom were given the name because they resided in an area called Maonan. The names of ethnic people in China have also been subject to the process of formation, development and confirmation. The Yi people, for instance, were called Yi, Yizou or Loulou, depending on where they lived, in addition to dozens of other names they called themselves.

The names of ethnic groups can lead to information about their economic and cultural conditions. Quite a few reveal the major occupation of these peoples. For example, in the language of Lahu people, it means 'roasting tiger-meat on fire', which can be gathered that the Lahu people used to live by hunting. This can also be witnessed by their neighbours in Southwest China, the Dai and Hani, who called themselves Mushe ('the hunters'). There is a small ethnic group entitled 'Oroqen' (which has two meanings: 'people who herd tamed deer' and 'people who live on the mountains') living in the Greater and Lesser Xing'an Mountains in Northeast China. Another ethnic group also living in Northeast China call themselves the Daur (meaning 'cultivator'), indicating that the Daur people engaged in agriculture during the ancient times.

Since the dawning of China's Neolithic period, agriculture has been the economic mainstay of the Han people. In the embryonic stages of its ethnic development, the Han group lived primarily along the banks of China's major rivers. The area along the Yellow river, characterized by a semi-arid climate, with loose, fertile soil, was suitable for growing millet; while the tropical and semi-tropical climate of the areas along the Pearl and Yangtze rivers was good for rice production. Thus millet and rice could be said to be the staple crops that delineated early Han culture. While the Han culture continued to develop, commerce, industry, education, and government service were also viable livelihoods, as for example in the case of the transportation of food, clothing, and jewelry between the large walled cities and smaller, more remote towns. The non-Han minorities, such as the Tibetans, in western China, on the other hand, have traditionally had a mixed economy of nomadism. The minority peoples in northeast China rely on either fishing and hunting or nomadism, while the Mongols have been mainly nomadic. The other minorities, such as the Uygurs in Xinjiang, have historically engaged in either agriculture or nomadism, but supplemented by commerce.

During their histories, many ethnic groups have also established a series of festivals, reflecting the diversified cultural backgrounds of their own. Spring Festival (i.e., the new year by the lunar calendar) has served as the most important festival of the Han people and has become now the nation-wide holiday in China. Traditional festivals of non-Han ethnic people include, for example, the Dai people's Water-Splashing Festival (the middle of April), the Mongol's Nadam (Recreation) Fair (April or May), the Yi people's Torch Festival (24 June), the Yao people's Danu Festival (or Woman Ancestor's Day), the Bai people's

Third Month Fair, the Uygur Bairam Fair, the Uygur and Hui's Corban Fair (the 10th day of the 12th month in the Muslim calendar), Li people's 3 March Festival (the third day of the third month in the lunar calendar), the Zhuang people's Gexu (Singing) Fair (the third day of the third month in the lunar calendar), and the Tibetan's New Year and Onghor (Expecting a Good Harvest) Festival), and so on.

## Language

China's linguistic system is comprehended in terms of lexicon, grammar, syntax, phonetics, and so on. Chinese, the language of the Han people, is the most commonly used language in China and one of the most common languages in the world. Written Chinese emerged in its embryonic form of carved symbols approximately 6000 years ago. The Chinese characters used today evolved from those used in bone and tortoise shell inscriptions more than 3000 years ago and the bronze inscriptions produced soon after. Drawn figures were gradually reduced to patterned strokes, pictographs were reduced to symbols, the complicated became more simple. Earlier pictographs and ideographs were joined by pictophonetic characters. Chinese is monosyllable. The vast majority of Chinese characters used today are composed of an ideogramatic portion on the left and the phonetic on the right. For example, the Chinese character for the tree that produces tung oil, is composed of an ideogram on the left representing a tree, phonogram on the right indicating that the word should be pronounced *tong* (as would this phonetic element if it were an independent character).[12]

China's linguistic system is diversified (see Table 3.6). Besides Chinese – China's official language that belongs to the Han-Tibetan language family – many other languages are also used regionally and locally by most of the 55 minorities that have their own languages except Hui and Manchu who employ Chinese as their native language in China. 23 of these languages have taken written forms. Five linguistic systems are represented: 29 languages, including Zhuang, Dai, Tibetan, Yi, Miao and Yao, are within the Han-Tibetan language family; 17 languages, including Uygur, Kazak, Mongolian and Korean, are within the Altaian language family; three languages, the Va, Deang and Blang, are within the South Asian language family; and Gaoshan is an Austronesian language. The Jing language has yet to be classified typologically. The main non-Han Chinese languages used in China are: Zhuang (spoken) in most parts of Guangxi and some parts of Guangdong, Yunnan, and Guizhou; Ugyur (spoken and written) in Xinjiang and some parts of Qinghai; Tibetan (spoken and written) in Tibet and the surrounding

---

*Box 3.1*   The evolution of Chinese characters

The diverse Chinese characters which were individually developed with different styles by various kingdoms in ancient China were first unified in the Qin dynasty 2000 years ago. Since then, the written Chinese has been standardized as different forms. For example, the standard script of the Qin dynasty is referred to as the larger seal script (*dazhuan*), which was later developed into the smaller seal style (*xiaozhuan*). Compared with the larger seal script, the latter is characterized by thin, meticulously rendered lines. Although the clerical script (*Lishu*) which was also developed in the Qin dynasty was easier and faster to write, and sped up the processing of official documents, the cursive script (*chaoshu*) emerged as a faster alternative one later on. The regular script (*kaishu*) was developed in the second century AD based on the official script style. The regular script shed the wavy, thickened stroke of the earlier style, and established a standard in the face of increasingly fanciful cursive scripts as used as the standard script today. The running script (*xingshu*) which was invented in the second century AD is a flowing style that falls somewhere between the regular and cursive scripts.

Since the 1950s different versions of Chinese characters have been applied. While the traditional (complex) form continues to be used in Hong Kong, Macau and Taiwan, a new form of Chinese characters, based on a list of 515 and 2236 new simplified characters, was adopted in mainland China in 1956 and 1964, respectively. The traditional form of Chinese characters never disappeared in mainland China, due to the fact that they were used to record all of China's traditional cultural heritages on the one hand and the increasing links between mainland Chinese and the traditional Chinese characters' users in Hong Kong, Macau and Taiwan on the other hand.

---

areas; Mongolian (spoken and written) in Inner Mongolia, Qinghai, and the surrounding areas; Yi (spoken) in some parts of Sichuan, Yunnan, Guizhou and Guangxi provinces; and English (spoken and written) in Hong Kong, and so on.

While Chinese has been the mainstream of China's multi-linguistic system, some Chinese dialects are so far removed from each other that

*Table 3.6*   Changes of population shares of the major linguistic groups (1985 and 1995)

|  | 1985 (%) | 1995 (%) | % change 1985–95 |
|---|---|---|---|
| Chinese (Han) | 88.654 | 91.956 | 3.302 |
| Zhuang | 1.266 | 1.366 | 0.100 |
| Manchu | 0.407 | 0.867 | 0.460 |
| Hui | 0.683 | 0.759 | 0.076 |
| Miao | 0.476 | 0.652 | 0.176 |
| Uighur | 3.214 | 0.636 | –2.578 |
| Yi | 0.516 | 0.580 | 0.064 |
| Tujia | 0.268 | 0.503 | 0.235 |
| Mongol | 0.323 | 0.424 | 0.102 |
| Tibetan | 0.366 | 0.405 | 0.039 |
| Bouyei | 0.201 | 0.225 | 0.024 |
| Dong (Tung) | 0.135 | 0.222 | 0.087 |
| Yao | 0.133 | 0.188 | 0.055 |
| Korean | 0.167 | 0.169 | 0.002 |
| Bai (Pai) | 0.107 | 0.141 | 0.034 |
| Hani | 0.100 | 0.111 | 0.011 |
| Kazakh | 0.086 | 0.098 | 0.012 |
| Li | 0.077 | 0.098 | 0.020 |
| Dai (Tai) | 0.080 | 0.090 | 0.011 |
| She | 0.035 | 0.055 | 0.020 |
| Lisu | 0.046 | 0.050 | 0.005 |
| Gelo | 0.005 | 0.038 | 0.033 |
| Lahu | 0.029 | 0.037 | 0.008 |
| Dongxiang | 0.026 | 0.033 | 0.007 |
| Va (Wa) | 0.028 | 0.031 | 0.003 |
| Shui | 0.027 | 0.030 | 0.003 |
| Naxi | 0.023 | 0.024 | 0.001 |
| Qiang | 0.010 | 0.017 | 0.007 |
| Tu | 0.015 | 0.017 | 0.002 |
| Xibe | 0.008 | 0.015 | 0.008 |
| Mulam | 0.009 | 0.014 | 0.005 |
| Kirgiz | 0.011 | 0.012 | 0.001 |
| Daur | 0.009 | 0.011 | 0.002 |
| Jingpo | 0.009 | 0.011 | 0.002 |
| Blang (Bulang) | 0.006 | 0.007 | 0.002 |
| Salar | 0.007 | 0.007 | 0.001 |
| Maonan | 0.004 | 0.007 | 0.003 |
| Tadzhik (Tajik) | 0.003 | 0.003 | 0.001 |
| Achang | 0.002 | 0.002 | 0.001 |
| Ewenki (Evenk) | 0.002 | 0.002 | 0.001 |

*Source*: Based on *Britannica Book of the Year* (1986 and 1996).

they could be considered different languages of the same family. In fact, the line between language and dialect is often drawn by factors having little to do with linguistics such as geographical boundaries. Though the Mandarin is standardized nationwide as *putonghua*, each region speaks its own local version of it, usually reflecting influence from the native dialect of the area. These regional variations of Mandarin are perhaps as great as, or even greater than, those of other languages in the rest of the world. Roughly speaking, the Mandarin group is subdivided into Northern, Northwestern, Eastern, and Southwestern Mandarin. Dialects of the Mandarin group which are characterized by relatively simple phonological and tone systems are spoken in three-quarters of the country by two-thirds of the population throughout China, which is the main reason why Mandarin has been chosen for the national language.

The Chinese dialects can be generally classified into six groups of Xiang (in Hunan area), Gan (in Jiangxi area), Kejia (in Guangdong, Taiwan and other scattered areas), Wu (in Shanghai and the adjacent areas), Min (in Fujian and Taiwan areas), and Cantonese, or Yue (in Guangdong and the adjacent areas). The Xiang dialect as spoken in Changsha and the Gan dialect as spoken in Nanchang each has six tones, including the entering tone. The Changsha and Nanchang dialects do not distinguish between the constants *l*- and *n*-. The Kejia dialect, whose speakers are mostly found in Guangdong, Taiwan, and Southeast Asia, also has six tones. There is a great deal of variation among the Wu dialects, mostly spoken in Jiangsu and Zhejiang provinces. The Suzhou dialect of Jiangsu province, representing the northern Wu, has seven tones; the Wenzhou dialect of Zhejiang province, treated as the southern Wu, has eight tones; and Shanghai dialect has five tones. The Min dialects are spoken widely in Fujian, Taiwan, Hainan and many areas of Southeast Asia, including Singapore and the Philippines. The Min group includes Northern and Southern Min. While the Northern Min is represented by Fuzhou, the Southern Min dialect, which has seven tones, is mostly spoken in eastern Fujian and most parts of the Taiwan area. Southern and Northern Min dialects are for the most part mutually unintelligible. Cantonese (Yue), with a total of nine tones which is more than any other dialect, is the main dialect of Guangdong, Hong Kong, Macau and many overseas Chinese communities.[13]

The main unifying force of China's many diverse dialects is the shared written system. While the exact number for the Chinese characters has not been clear, the Qing Dynasty *Kangxi Dictionary*, completed in 1716, contains 47,035 characters. The recently published *Hanyu Da Cidian* (Chinese Lexicon) contains over 56,000 characters. However, many of these characters are not in common use. About 3000 characters account for 99 per cent of those used in modern books and newspapers. While it still remains unclear whether or not the economic behavior differs between the Chinese language and other languages users. It is generally believed that the unified Chinese characters used by people speaking different dialects makes it possible for the central government to maintain control effectively over a vast size of territory. However, it is really a very long and time-consuming process to grasp the dozens of thousands of Chinese characters, which, as argued by Maddison (1996, p. 54), strengthened the Chinese ethnocentrism, encouraged self-satisfaction, and inhibited the intellectuals' deviance or curiosities. On the other hand, Fairbank (1980, p. 41) notes that the written Chinese is not a widely open door through which the mass peasants gain the truth and knowledge; rather it is the stumbling block for their progresses.

## Religion

According to the *Oxford Advanced Learner's Dictionary* (1974, 3rd edn, p. 712), religion is 'belief in the existence of a supernatural ruling power, the creator and controller of the universe, who has given to man a spiritual nature which continues to exist after the death of the body'. In general, the main religions in China are Confucianism, Buddhism, Taoism, Islam, Catholicism, Protestantism, along with shamanism, Eastern Orthodox Christianity and the Naxi people's Dongba religion. The native religions are Confucianism, Buddhism, Taoism, shamanism and animism, while Buddhism was imported from India and evolved later into a Chinese-style religion. Features of some of these religions are as follows.

Founded by Kongzi or Confucius (551–479 BC), Confucianism was reputed to have served as the basis of the traditional Chinese culture. *Lunyu* (Analects of Confucius) records the saying and deeds of Confucius and his disciples. It covers a wide scope of subjects, ranging from politics, philosophy, literature and art to education and moral cultivation. With only 12,000 characters, it is terse but comprehensive, rich yet profound; as the major classic of Confucianism as well as the most authoritative, it has influenced Chinese society for over two thousand years. Its ideas have taken such firm root in China that all Chinese – both Han and non-Han ethnicities – have been more or less influenced by it. Since the Han dynasty, every ruler has had to pay at least some heed to this, and people also expected their ruler to act accordingly in China.[14] Confucian philosophy concerning the relationship between politics and morality serves as the basis of the Confucian school's emphasis on moral education, becoming one of the major characteristics of Confucianism. This idea also represented the distinguishing feature of the Oriental culture realm under the influence of Confucianism.

Taoism probably took form as a religion during the second century AD. It originated from sorcery, pursuit of immortality and other supernatural beliefs found in ancient China. Taoists look to the philosopher Laozi (born in about 604 BC) as their great leader, and take his work *The Classic of the Way and Its Power* ('Daode Jing') as their canon. Mystifying the philosophic concept of 'Dao' or 'Tao' (the way, or path), they posit that man could become one with the 'Dao' through self-cultivation and achieve immortality. As an escape from Confucianism, Taoism has been promoted by each revulsion of scholars against the overnice ritualism and detailed prescriptions of the classics. It has also denoted the common people's belief in certain traditional super-institutions. Applying the idea of balance in all things, Taoism argues that human moral ideas are the reflection of human depravity, that the idea of filial piety springs from the fact of impiety, that the Confucian statement of the rules of propriety is really a reflection of the world's moral disorder.

Throughout the whole process of Chinese history, Chinese culture has been reconstructed under external religions. Among the first, and the most important, is the importation of Buddhism from India in the first century BC. Springing from Hinduism in about 600 BC, Buddhism is one of the most influential religions in Asia. As a reformation of Hinduism, it did not abolish caste but declared that Buddhists were released from caste restrictions. At the heart of Buddhism there are the Four Noble Truths: (1) existence is suffering; (2) suffering has a cause, namely craving and attachment; (3) there is a cessation of suffering, which is Nirvana; and (4) there is a path to the cessation of suffering, which includes the 'eight-fold path' of the right views (that is, right desires, right speech, right action, right occupation, right effort, right awareness and right contemplation). Nirvana is the ultimate goal of the Buddhism. It represents the extinction of all cravings and the final release from suffering. To the extent that such ideal reflects the thinking of the mass of people, a Buddhist society's values would be considered antithetical to such goals as acquisitions, achievement, or affluence. From another early school of Buddhism there developed the lines of thought that led toward the positions advocated by Mahayana

Buddhism. The Mahayana (greater vehicle) gave itself this name in polemical writings to distinguish itself from what it called the Hinnayana (lesser vehicle), Theravada, and related schools. The main philosophical tenet of the Mahayana is that all things are empty, or devoid of self-nature. Buddhism became increasingly popular after the fourth century AD and has now been a Chinese religion and an important part of Chinese culture. Tibetan Buddhism, or Lamaism as it is sometimes called, is founded primarily in Tibet and Mongolia. One of the tenets of Buddhism is that life is painful and that it is not limited to the mortal span with which we are familiar.

Islamic adherents probably first reached China in the mid-seventh century. During the Tang (AD 618–907) and the Song (AD 960–1279) dynasties, Muslim Arab and Persian merchants of the Islamic faith came overland through Central Asia to northwest China and by sea to Guangdong and other southeastern ports, bringing with them the Islamic faith. Christian belief was first introduced to China during the Tang dynasty. The name Islam is the infinitive of the Arabic verb 'to submit'. Muslim is the present participle of the same verb, thus, a Muslim is one submitting to the will of Allah – the only God of the universe – of which Mohammed is the Prophet. Muslim theology, *Tawhid*, defines the Islamic creed, whereas the law, *Shariah*, prescribes the actions of adherents. The Koran (*Qur'an*) is accepted as the ultimate guide and anything not mentioned in the Koran is quite likely to be rejected. The Five Pillars of Islam, or the duties of a Muslim, are (1) the recital of the creed (2) prayer (3) fasting (4) almsgiving and (5) the pilgrimage. A Muslim must pray five times a day at definite hours. During the month of Ramadan, in the midsummer in the lunar year, Muslims are required to fast from sunrise to sunset with no food, no drink and no smoking. The fast is meant to develop both self-control and sympathy for the poor. By almsgiving the Muslim shares with the poor. The pilgrimage to Mecca is a well-known aspect of Islam. There have been two major groups in Islam – namely, *Sunni* and *Shia*. While they are similar in many ways, Sunni Muslims adhere to both the Koran and *Sharia*, while Shia Muslims only believe in the Koran.

Shamanism originated from the Evinki people of Siberia, and literally means 'the one who knows'. Today, in the Western world, 'shaman' is often taken to mean any kind of native medicine man or woman or anyone with a strong personality and an intense stare (Horwitz, 1998). Shamanism goes hand in hand with the animist's experience of the world: first, all that is alive, and being alive embodies a spirit; second, all that is alive is connected by these spirits. Therefore, we all – humans, trees, dogs, cats, bees, stones, mountains, seas, Earth and Sky – are connected. Shamans believe that there exists a medium, or 'witch' between the God and themselves. The witch, according to the shamanism, can convey the God's decrees.

As a primeval religion, followers of animism tend to be found in remote and mountain areas. Animists believe that the hills, valleys, waterways and rocks are spiritual beings, as are the plants and animals. Furthermore, they believe that there are other, less obvious spiritual beings not commonly associated with the phenomena of everyday experience. Animists worship the natural bodies (most of which are animals) with which they have special causal relations. Magic, a key element of animism, is the attempt to achieve results through the manipulation of the spiritual world. It represents an unscientific approach to the physical world.

During the Qing (1644–1911) dynasty, a large number of Christian missionaries began arriving in China. They brought not only their religion but also new concepts of science and technology. Catholicism and Protestantism came to China much later than Buddhism and Islam, and their influence on Chinese society has been much less, being mainly restricted to large cities such as Shanghai, Beijing, Guangdong and Wuhan and certain rural areas.[15]

In brief, China is a country with great diversity in religion (see Table 3.7). Except for the Protestants and Roman Catholics across China as a result of the western missionary efforts, most of the other religious followers have either a geographical or ethnic orientation in China. Most Han people engage in folk religious practices, usually mixed with elements of Confucianism, Taoism and Buddhism. The remaining minority peoples in China adhere to different religious cultures. The Hui, Uygur, Kazak, Kirgiz, Tatar, Ozbek, Tajik, Dongxiang, Salar, and Bonan peoples, mostly in Northwest China, adhere to Islamic culture. The Tibetan people in Southwest China, Mongol people in North and West China, Lhoba, Moinba, Tu and Yugur believe in Tibetan Buddhism known as Lamaism; the Blang and Deang in Southwest China to Theravada Buddhism. Quite a few of the Miao, Yao, and Yi peoples in South and Southwest China follow Catholicism or Protestantism. Moslems constitute a significant minority that is scattered across the whole country. The minority peoples of southwestern China such as the Dai tend to be adherents of the Hinayana school of Buddhism prevalent in Thailand and Myanmar. Some minority peoples of Jilin and Heilongjinag provinces in northeast China subscribe to shamanism and other ethnic groups living in the valleys of the southwestern mountain ranges embrace animist beliefs.

*Table 3.7*   Changes of population shares of the major religious groups (1985 and 1995)

| Item | 1985 (%) | 1995 (%) | % change 1985–95 |
| --- | --- | --- | --- |
| Non-religion | 59.200 | 51.915 | –7.285 |
| Chinese folk-religion | 20.100 | 20.130 | 0.030 |
| Atheism | 12.000 | 11.980 | –0.020 |
| Buddhism | 6.000 | 8.476 | 2.476 |
| Western Christianity | – | 5.949 | na |
| Islam | 2.400 | 1.467 | –0.933 |
| New-Religion | – | 0.252 | na |
| Traditional beliefs | – | 0.081 | na |
| Sikh | – | 0.080 | na |

*Notes*: (1) '–' denotes that figures are too small or that data are not available; (2) 'na' denotes not available.

*Source*: Based on *Britannica Book of the Year* (1986 and 1996).

## Policy implications

The ultimate goal of any economic system is the allocation of scarce resources among competing factions. To accomplish this goal, the economic system must explicitly deal with the supply and demand of goods and services as well as the interaction between the two. There is no exception for the Chinese economy.

The uneven distribution of natural resources in China has heavily influenced the disequilibrated regional structures of exploitation and supply of those resources used as inputs of production to produce desired final goods and services for the society. China's mineral and energy resources are mainly distributed in the northern and western inland areas, while the largest industrial consumers are located in the eastern and southern coastal areas. Therefore, the long-distance transfers of raw materials and semi-finished products from the northern and western inland areas to the eastern and southern coastal areas should be the only feasible approach by which to efficiently create an equilibrium between supply and demand in the Chinese economy. The Chinese government should recognize this fact and try to deal carefully with the national economic cooperation.

The Chinese economy has been mainly fuelled by coal rather than by petroleum and natural gas as in most industrialized economies. Given its abundance in reserves compared with other energy resources such as hydropower, petroleum and natural gas, coal which accounts for more than 80 per cent of China's total energy resources has supplied near 70 per cent of the nation's total energy supply until recently. Without stressing the low heating conversion rate of coal consumption, the serious environmental damage resulting from the exploitation, transportation, and consumption of coal resources has already posed challenges to the sustainable development of the Chinese economy (this will be discussed in details in Chapter 9).

A huge population does not represent an advantage in human resources for economic development, particularly when a country is transformed from an agricultural society that uses mainly traditional methods of production to an industrial society that requires not only advanced sciences and technologies but also qualified workers. A well-educated and law-abiding population that possesses a strong work ethic is the *sine qua non* of modern economic growth. At present, the development of education is particularly urgent for China – a country with a high proportion of illiteracy and whose educational system had been seriously destroyed in the Cultural Revolution period (1966–76). At the same time, ways must be found to raise the technical and professional level of the workers already in employment.

For most of its past thousands of years, China's political culture was based on Confucius theory. Ethical beliefs have consistently remained within the bounds of a set of orthodox principles governing interpersonal relationships that have officially applied to all strata of society: loyalty, filial piety, benevolence, righteousness, love, faith, harmony, and peace. As a result, China has developed a different culture regarding economic development from the rest of the world, in response to its own particular environment and social conditions (see Box 3.2). For instance, unlike other peoples, the Chinese would care about their spiritual interests (including the richness of spiritual life and harmonization of feeling) more than the material ones. This characteristic results largely from the Confucian philosophy which emphasizes 'faithfulness', 'kindheartedness', 'trustworthiness', 'ritualism', 'peace' and so on. All of these have patterned Chinese economic life and structure, which eventually results in China's economic culture.

China's religious package aiming at a harmonious balance between Confucianism, Buddhism, and Taoism worked quite well for a long period. Probably due to this fact, the Chinese were too intoxicated with its past prosperity and still had proudly treated itself as the 'central kingdom' (*zhongguo*) of the world even since it lagged economically far behind Western nations. This kind of ethnocentrism and self-satisfaction eventually made China a typical autarkic society for a long time. With

*Box 3.2*   Chinese characteristics

More than one hundred years ago, Arthur H. Smith, who had served as the Missionary of the American Board for 22 years in China, wrote a book entitled *Chinese Characteristics*. The book was first published in Shanghai by an English newspaper in 1890. The second edition of the book was published in London in 1892. The third, fourth, and fifth revised editions were published in New York, London, Edinburg and London in 1894, 1895 and 1900, respectively. Based on the rural Chinese life during the late nineteenth century, Smith presented an interesting description of Chinese characteristics. To make comparison easier, we classify them (each appears as a chapter in Smith's book) into three types, as the following:

| Positive | Negative | Neutral |
|---|---|---|
| • Economy | • Disregard of time | • Face |
| • Industry | • Disregard of accuracy | • Flexible inflexibility |
| • Politeness | • Talent for | • Absence of nerves |
| • Physical vitality | misunderstanding | • Indifference to |
| • Patience and | • Talent for indirection | comfort and |
| perseverance | • Intellectual turbidity | convenience |
| • Contempt for | • Benevolence | • Content and |
| foreigners | • Absence of public | cheerfulness |
| • Mutual responsibility | spirits | • Filial piety |
| and respect for law | • Conservation | |
| • Polytheism, pantheism | • Absence of sympathy | |
| and atheism | • Social typhoons | |
| | • Mutual suspicion | |
| | • Absence of sincerity | |

*Source*: Smith (1972).

regards to the cultural differences between the Chinese and Japanese economies, Maddison (1996, p. 53) argues that:

> In China, the foreigners appeared on the fringes of a huge country. The ruling elite regarded it as the locus of civilization, and considered the 'barbarian' intruders as an irritating nuisance. In Japan, they struck in the biggest city, humiliated the Shogun and destroyed his legitimacy as a ruler. The Japanese had already borrowed important elements of Chinese civilization and saw no shame in copying in a Western model which had demonstrated its superior technology so dramatically.

# 4
# China's Economic Systems in Transition

Doctor Bianque went to see King Wu of the state of Qin. The King told the doctor about his health condition and Bianque was ready to give him a treatment. The ministers at the King's sides said to him: 'Your Majesty, the malady is in front of your ears and below your eyes. Even with treatment it might not be cured and very likely you will lose your hearing and sight.' The King passed these messages to Bianque. Bianque was enraged and threw down the stone needle which he used for giving treatment, saying: 'Sire, you discuss your illness with one who knows how to effect a cure but you allow those who know nothing about medicine to spoil the whole thing. If the Qin is governed in this way, then a single such mistake on your part is enough to bring down the state.'

Zhanguoce (475–221 BC)

## General review

In 1978, Deng Xiaoping and his senior supporters took decisive control of the CCPCC. This ended what has been described as two years of uncertainty and indecisive strategy and policy after the death of Mao Zedong. The Third Plenum of the Eleventh CCPCC, which was held in December 1978, marked a major turning point in China's reform and development. After a decade of turmoil brought about by the Cultural Revolution (1966–76), the new direction set at this meeting was toward economic development and away from class struggle. The course was laid for the Chinese Communist Party (CCP) to move the world's most populous nation toward the ambitious targets of the Four Modernizations in sectors of industry, agriculture, science and technology and national defence.

46

In brief, the institutional evolution in the Chinese economy since 1978 has demonstrated a gradual process and may be outlined by six phrases as the following:

1. centrally planned economy (before 1978);
2. economy regulated mainly by planning and supplementally by market 1978–84.;
3. commodity economy with a plan (1985–87);
4. combination of planned and market economy (1988–91);
5. socialist market economy with *state* ownership as main form (1992–97);
6. socialist market economy with *public* ownership as main form (from 1998 onwards).

Before the third Plenum of the 11th CCPCC was held on 18 December 1978, China had been a CPE.[1] Generally, this kind system has at least three problems. First of all, it makes almost all productive enterprises subordinate to administrative organs. To large extent, this neglects the economic independence of the enterprises and thereby leads to the neglect of their material interests and responsibilities, blunting their initiative and enthusiasm. Second, the system involves excessive command planning from above and is too rigid. So long as the enterprises meet their stipulated targets, they are considered to have performed satisfactorily regardless of whether or not its products satisfy the needs of society. Third, the system of unified income and expenditure means that everyone has an 'iron rice bowl' (*tie fanwan*) and 'eats from the same pot' (*daguo fan*), that is, people have guaranteed employment regardless of whether that are productive or not and they can rely on the work of others from their income. Egalitarianism, lack of interest in economic results and a low sense of economic and legal responsibility are all expressions of this mentality.

Guided by the CCPCC (1984), the roles of central planning and market regulation were reversed in the modified system 'commodity economy with a plan'.[2] Generally, Phase 3 was known to be loosely based on the Hungarian model of market socialism. Nevertheless, the state continued to own the bulk of large- and medium-sized enterprises and to regulate production and pricing of a number of strategic commodities, but the market mechanism was permitted to play an increasing role in the pricing and allocation of goods and services and in the allocation and remuneration of labour in some non-strategic sectors. In the ideological struggles between the radical reformers and the conservatives in China's reform circle, there was a new term 'social-ist commodity economy'[3] from 1988 to 1989, but which was replaced by Phase 4 ('combination of planned and market economy') immediately after the Tian'anmen Square incident during May–June 1989. Nevertheless, Phase 4 was extremely important in terminology insofar as it legitimates the abolition of traditional mechanisms of central planning system in favour of an introduction of market regulation.

During the 1980s, China's reform and open-door policy had also resulted in, besides economic prosperities, political and social instabilities. This can be witnessed by the CCP's 'anti-spiritual pollution' and 'anti-bourgeois liberalization' campaigns in 1983 and 1987, respectively. This kind of political disequilibria between the CCP conservatives and intellectuals reached the highest tide in 1989, which, together with other factors such as high inflation and official corruption, eventually became a leading cause of students' protests against the CCP and central government during May-June 1989. As soon as the Tian'anmen incident was calmed down, there was a shift of power in economic decision-makings from reformers to conservatives. China's economic reform slowed down thereafter, so did China's economic growth temporarily.

The socialist camp in Eastern Europe and the former Soviet Union fell suddenly in the beginning of the 1990s. China's immediate reaction to the collapse of these communist regimes was re-centralization, but the CCP soon realized that its legitimacy could only be sustained by economic growth through further reforms. Amid the political dead-lock between the reformers and conservatives concerning how to combine the planned and market economic systems, Deng Xiaoping made his now famous southern tour to the province of Guangdong in early 1992. Using the regional support for continued reforms, Deng's visit tipped the political balance at the CCPCC and the central government. This resulted in China's official declaration in October 1992 to build a 'socialist market economy', as well as a calling for faster reforms and economic development.

In the early 1990s, some treatments of the coastal specific economic zones (SEZs) were extended to a list of inland regions and cities along the Yangtze River and, as a result of China's diplomatic normalization with the former USSR, to the border cities and towns adjacent to Russia and other neighbouring countries. Furthermore, many inland cities, which did not qualify for these special treatments, established numerous economic and technological development zones (ETDZs) inside their regions. It is worth noting that the wide-ranging pro-development reforms during the above years brought about not only high economic growth but also the two-digital inflationary pressures that were built in 1993. Facing the overheating of the economy, the Chinese government announced a series of banking and financial reforms in 1994, aiming at eliminating some of the structural inefficiencies in the financial sector.

Even though China's ambitious agenda geared towards transforming the Chinese economy into a market-oriented one was unveiled as early as 1992, when Deng Xiaoping's Southern Speech[4] eventually influenced China's decision-makers, the formal document entitled 'Decision of the CCPCC on Several Issues Concerning the Establishment of a Socialist Market Economic Structure' was finally approved by the Third Plenum of the 14th CCPCC on 14 November 1993. According to the decision, the government should withdraw from direct involvement in enterprise management. Instead, 'Government functions in economic management consist mainly of devising and implementing macro-economic control policies, appropriate construction of infrastructure facilities and creation of a favourable environment for economic development' (Article 16). The Plenum also declared that 'the government shall take significant steps in the reform of the system of taxation, financing, investment and planning, and establish a mechanism in which planning, banking and public finance are coordinate and mutually check each other while strengthening the overall coordination of economic operations' (Article 17).

China's commitment to the creation of a market-oriented economy has been the central plank of its program of economic reform, and considerable progress towards this end has been achieved since 1978, through the gradual withdrawal of the government from the allocation, pricing, and distribution of goods.[5] Reforms introduced have so far exhibited remarkable results. Particularly praiseworthy are the facts that the Chinese-type reforms have avoided the output collapse characteristic of transitions in other former CPEs and generated unprecedented increases in the level of living standards across the country. For the last decades, China has successfully implemented a stable economic reform and opening up to the outside world and, in particular, achieved a faster economic growth than any other socialist or former socialist countries in the world.

## Development and planning

The economic development in a traditional socialist economy is realized mainly through a plan worked out by the central planning authorities.

The plan, however, is a mental construct which may or may not correctly reflect the objective requirements of economic development. If the plan is correct, economic development is smooth; if it is incorrect, not only is it of no help but it may even cause stagnation and decline. This has been obviously proven in China's economic circle.

When the PRC was founded in 1949, the transformation of private ownership of the means of production into public ownership and the establishment of a powerful socialist sector paved an effective way for planned development of the national economy. During the First FYP period (1953–57), much attention was paid to industrial construction, especially in heavy industry. At the same time, the socialist transformation of agriculture, handicrafts, and capitalist industry and commerce was effectively carried out. In line with these goals, 156 key projects and other items were arranged with the guidance of the Soviet Union. The First FYP was generally known by the PRC's central planners and economists to be very successful because all scheduled targets were fully met during this period: the GVIO grew at 18 per cent annually, higher than the planned rate (14.7 per cent); the annual GVAO growth rate (4.5 per cent) exceeded the planned rate (4.3 per cent).[6] Facing the economic difficulties during the late 1950s and the early 1960s, the CCPCC and the State Council put forward the policy entitled 'readjustment, consolidation, filling-out, and raising standards' (*taiozheng, gonggu, chongshi, tigao*). The production targets for heavy industry were reduced and investment in capital construction was cut back. The accumulation rate which had stood at as high as 39.9 per cent in 1960 was adjusted sharply down to only 10.4 per cent by 1962. The enterprises with high production costs and large losses were closed or switched to other products. With the adjustments, the economy rapidly returned to normal. From 1962 to 1965, the gross value of industrial output (GVIO) was growing at an annual rate of 17.9 per cent, gross value of agricultural output (GVAO) at 11.1 per cent, and national income at 14.5 per cent.[7]

In contrast to the First FYP and the readjustment period (1963–65), the years 1958–60 provided a typical case of errors in planning, resulting in serious economic imbalances. During this period, the Great Leap Forward movement was effectively launched by setting up a series of high targets within a given period, while most of which, however, were impossible to be fulfilled due to the limitation of resources and production capacities.[8] To accomplish its ambitious target for an overnight entrance to the 'communist heaven', large quantities of raw materials and labour force were diverted toward heavy industry while, in contrast, the development of agriculture and light industry received less attention. This situation lasted until 1960 when the serious imbalances between accumulation and consumption and between heavy industry on one hand and agriculture and light industry on the other hand occurred suddenly. Despite this profound lesson, similar problems arose again thereafter.[9]

Since a socialist economy is rigorously directed by state planning, as soon as errors occur in the plan, all economic activities are affected. China bore witness this point by its experience and lessons. Theoretically, it is essential to make a 'perfect' plan for the healthy operation of the economy. However, it is almost impossible for the state planners to accurately manage a balance between social production and social needs and efficiently distribute the scarce resources even with the use of the sophisticated computers. In fact, the central planners could never obtain complete and accurate information on economic activities from which to formulate plans due to information constraints and asymmetries. Furthermore, the centrally planned system also generated many other problems. For example, as wages were fixed workers had no incentive to work after the output quota of the factory had been reached. Any extra production might have led to the increase of the following year's quota while salaries remained unchanged. Factory managers and government planners frequently bargained over work targets, funds, and material supplies allocated to the factory. Usually, government agencies allocated less than managers requested so managers requested more than they needed; when bargaining over the production, the managers, however, asked a smaller quota than they were able to finish, so they were usually ordered by a larger quota than requested.[10]

China's decentralization of its mandatory planning system and introduction of market mechanisms which began at 1978 first focused on a gradual transition from the PCS to the HRS under which farmers were free to decide what and how to produce in their contracted farmlands and, having fulfilled the state's production quotas, could sell their excess products on the free market and be able to purse some non-agricultural activities. In 1984 when urban reform was implemented, China aimed at regulating industrial production by market forces, in the same way, after fulfilling their output quotas, enterprises could make profits by selling their excess products at free or floating prices. It is worthy noting that the above efforts resulted inevitably in dual prices for commodities during the transition period and had both positive and negative effects (this will be discussed in detail in next chapter).

No matter how difficult the transformation of the CPE to a market economy was, mandatory planning in the Chinese economy has been reduced many times, following a double-track system (see Box 4.1). By the end of 1986, the number of key industrial products under direct control of the State Planning Commission (SPC) has decreased from 120 to 60; accordingly, the share of industrial production fell from 40 per cent to 20 per cent; the number of commodities and materials

---

*Box 4.1*  Double-track economics

China's economic reform began in the late 1970s, carrying out a double-track system in which the share of production subject to both central and local governments declined continuously. The reform was first implemented in agricultural products and spread slowly to consumer goods and intermediate goods. In each case, a free market in which the price was subject to the market regulations developed in parallel with a controlled market in which the price was kept almost unchanged at an officially fixed level. Because the price was higher in the market-regulated track than in the state-controlled track, supply in the free market grew rapidly, so its share in total output rose steadily. Meanwhile, the planned price was able to raise incrementally until it approached the market price when the gap between supply and demand narrowed. The dual pricing system provided opportunities for people who had access to state-controlled goods and materials to make large profits by buying them at an officially fixed low price and reselling them at a market-based price, which often led to unequal competition as well as official corruption. Nevertheless, this dual market created various distortions and speculative transactions. But it was at least better than taking no action at all during the process of rationalizing prices.

During the 1980s and the early 1990s the double-track system extended through almost every sphere of the Chinese economy, from agriculture, industry, commerce, transportation, post and tele-communications to health care, education, and so on. By the late 1990s, the dual pricing system had decontrolled more than 90 per cent of retail prices and agricultural and intermediate product prices and removed the mandatory plans of a large number of products including fuel and raw materials.

distributed by the state (i.e., *tongpei wuzhi*) dropped from 250 to 20 and the goods controlled by the Ministry of Commerce (MOC) decreased from 188 to 25; the share of prices which were 'free' or 'floating' increased to about 65 per cent in agriculture and supplementary products, 55 per cent of consumer goods and 40 per cent of production materials.[11] Between 1979 and 1992, the proportion of industrial goods and materials distributed under the central plan system declined from 95 per cent to less than 10 per cent. There was a parallel reduction in the planned allocation of consumer goods: the number of the first class goods distributed by the state dropped from 65 to 20 and that of the production materials distributed by the state was reduced from 256 to 19 during those period.[12]

Between regions there are some slight differences in the process towards the decentralization of mandatory planning. Roughly speaking, the Eastern belt is more marketized than the Central belt, while the Western belt is the least marketized. With in China, according to Table 4.1, the share of the marketized agricultural products ranged between 20.3 per cent (Qinghai) and 43.3 per cent (Jilin) in 1988 and 60.0 per cent (Henan) and 98.8 per cent (Guangdong) in 1994. It is more interesting to note that some developed provinces (such as Shanghai, Beijing, Jiangsu, and so on) were not so highly marketized as the poor provinces (such as Anhui, Guangxi, Hainan, and so on) in 1988. The probable cause of this is the fact that China's agricultural reform was first carried out in Anhui and other poor and agriculture-based provinces, whereas Shanghai and Beijing – the centrally administered municipalities with strong industrial bases – lagged behind those agriculture-based provinces. Using the data given in Table 4.1, we can make further analysis for the correlation between the share of marketized agricultural products and the ratio of market-regulated price to state-controlled price:

$$\ln(SMAP94/SMAP88)= 0.9960+1.4664\ln RMP \qquad (4.1)$$
$$(33.51) \ (4.21)$$
$$(N=23, \ R^2=0.46, \ F=17.73)$$

where, *SMAP*=share of marketized agricultural products, and *RMP*=ratio of market-regulated price to state-controlled price. From the estimated coefficients shown in Equation (4.1), we may find that *SMAP*88 is negatively related to *RMP*, implying that the higher the market-regulated price to the state-controlled price, the lower of the share of the marketized agricultural products. This was reasonable and reflected to some

*Table 4.1* Share of marketized agricultural products by province, (1988 and 1994)

| Province | SMAP (%) 1988 | SMAP (%) 1994 | RMP 1988 |
|---|---|---|---|
| Anhui | 40.1 | 81.7 | 0.822 |
| Beijing | 29.6 | 94.2 | 1.116 |
| Fujian | 32.5 | 91.0 | 0.984 |
| Gansu | 20.8 | 85.0 | 1.119 |
| Guangdong | 36.0 | 98.8 | 0.887 |
| Guangxi | 35.9 | 81.2 | 0.940 |
| Guizhou | 24.8 | | 1.690 |
| Hainan | 34.1 | | 0.887 |
| Hebei | 29.3 | 88.8 | 0.993 |
| Heilongjiang | 29.3 | 81.2 | 0.996 |
| Henan | 26.4 | 60.0 | 1.049 |
| Hubei | 27.3 | 72.7 | 1.030 |
| Hunan | 35.1 | 79.3 | 0.970 |
| Inner Mongolia | 26.9 | | 0.837 |
| Jiangsu | 29.5 | 77.4 | 1.015 |
| Jiangxi | 31.6 | 74.7 | 0.897 |
| Jilin | 43.3 | 85.9 | 0.957 |
| Liaoning | 33.1 | 90.4 | 1.042 |
| Ningxia | 28.5 | 81.5 | 0.961 |
| Qinghai | 20.3 | 77.5 | 1.215 |
| Shaanxi | 31.0 | 77.2 | 1.026 |
| Shandong | 28.9 | 73.5 | 0.953 |
| Shanghai | 27.8 | 91.7 | 1.024 |
| Shanxi | 23.3 | 80.9 | 1.005 |
| Tianjin | 38.4 | | 1.020 |
| Tibet | 23.0 | | 1.008 |
| Yunnan | 21.5 | 67.3 | 1.164 |
| Zhejiang | 33.5 | 76.5 | 1.004 |

*Notes*: (1) SMAP=share of marketized agricultural products; (2) RMP=ratio of market price to state-controlled price.

*Sources*: (1) SSB (1989b, p. 130); (2) Riskin (1994, p. 350, table 10.11); and (3) PYC (1995, p. 19, table 2).

extent the government's efforts to stabilize the market, i.e., letting the provinces with market-regulated price close to or lower than the state-controlled one share a higher proportion of the market-oriented reform in agricultural sector during the early period of economic reform (1978–88). In 1994, the agricultural marketization was positively related to *RMP*.

## Labour and employment

After the establishment of the new China, the labour market was officially eliminated because according to Marxist theory labour is not a commodity to be bought and sold. From the late 1950s, the system of the state allocation for all urban employment was gradually introduced. After 1966, the state became responsible for job allocation for the entire urban labour force. All labour was allocated either to units owned by the states or to large collectives which were essentially as same as the state-owned units. In the centrally planned system, labour force was allocated to enterprises by the state and lifetime employment was guaranteed. Wages were also determined by the state in the principle of 'distribution according to working performance' (*anlao fenpei*). There is no doubt that this kind of system eliminated the widespread occurrence of unemployment that had usually existed in the old China and has universally existed in all capitalist countries. It also effectively equalized wages and considerably reduced gaps between the haves and the have-nots.

This rigid system of job allocation, however, has resulted in some disadvantages. Once people were employed in state sector, their jobs were secure, regardless of the quality of their work. The system thus became known as the 'iron rice bowl' (*tie fanwan*) because of the employment security it implied. Employing units could not freely employ whom they needed and had to provide almost equal pay to those who performed differently. This hindered the improvement of labour productivity. Furthermore, the system did not encourage people to develop their talents and enthusiasm fully since they could not choose the work which best suited them, thus reducing considerably the incentive for them to work harder. Under the equal wage system (namely, 'eating from the same pot', or *daguo fan*) human resources were not allocated in the efficient way and labour productivity growth was not as fast as it might have been.

Realizing the negative effects of this labour system, the government began to carry out a series of reforms in the early 1980s. The earliest effort included the introduction of a contract system – setting up a production quota for each employee. Nevertheless, this system was not so successful in the industrial (mainly state-owned) sector as in the agricultural sector due to the complicated production processes of the former. In July 1986, the NPC announced four laws concerning employment. According to the laws the governmental allocation of workers and lifetime employment were abolished and, at the meantime, a

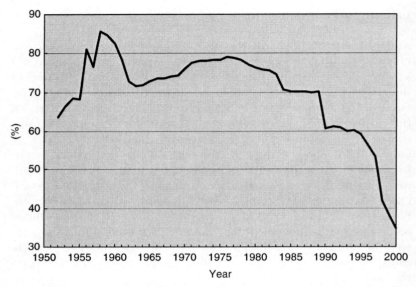

*Figure 4.1*   Shares of employment of the state sector in urban area (1950–2000)

contract system (*hetong zhi*) was introduced. In the contract system, all employees were hired as contractual workers (*hetong gong*) and the employed terms varied from less than one year to more than five years. Naturally, when the contract expired, either the worker was laid-off or the contract was renewed. Unfortunately, in practice the contract system has not worked so well in the state sector as in the non-state sector.

Since reform and opening up to the outside world, Chinese employment pattern has been experiencing structural changes, along with the declining of the state sector and the growing of the non-state sector (see Figure 4.1).

## Production and ownership

### Agriculture

After the founding of the PRC, the Chinese government reformed the ownership of land (*tugai*) and proportionally distributed the cultivated land among farmers. As a result, the farmers' incentive to work increased significantly. However, the new leadership only took this land reform as a provisional measure and did not consider it to be proper for a socialist economy. In the second half of the 1950s, China began to transform its private ownership of land. By 1958, the PCS had been adopted as a universal form of agricultural production throughout mainland China. About 150 million rural households were grouped into five million production teams which in turn were organized nationwide into 50,000 people's communes (Minami, 1994, p. 77). Under the people's commune system (PCS), land was owned collectively and the output was distributed to each household according to the work points (*gongfen*). The state purchased a major share of the grain output and distributed it to the non-agricultural population through government agencies. For much of the pre-reform period, the independent accounting unit was the production team. In the Great Leap Forward and the high tide of the Cultural Revolution, the production brigade (usually including several production teams) and even the people's commune (usually including several production brigades) were selected as independent accounting units in some 'advanced' areas where peasants were persuaded to have meals with 'big-pot'. Naturally, the PCS generally has been known to provide disincentives for the farmers to work harder.

The PCS lasted for more than 20 years in China before the government began to introduce a household-based and production-related responsibility system (i.e., household responsible system, HRS) in the early 1980s. Under the HRS each household may be able to sign a contract with the local government to obtain a certain amount of arable land and production equipment depending on the number of rural population in this family and have a production quota. As long as the household completes its quota of products to the state, it can decide freely what to produce and how to sell. Although land is still owned by the state, the HRS and the PCS are definitely different from each other.

In rural sector, collective ownership of land has been retained but farmers' right and responsibilities are now clearer since the leasing period is long (15 years for the initial stage with an extension of a further 30 years). Figure 4.2 provides a broad picture of the benefits to farmers through price and ownership reform. Before the reform, farmers had to sell to the government all the remaining gains (which was treated as of vital to the huge Chinese population at that time) and other important agricultural products at a very low price. The benefit is the area ACDF. After reform, the additional benefit to farmers is the area HJAC. This area can be decomposed into two parts: one that arises from 'price adjustment' within the planned price framework, i.e., area HIAB; the other that from 'price release',[13] i.e., area IJBC. 'Price

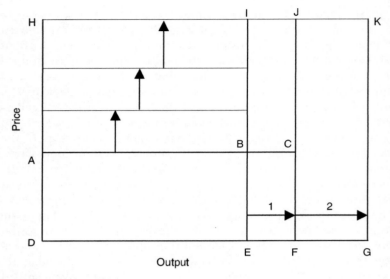

*Source*: Zhao, 1999, p. 194.

*Figure 4.2*   Price and ownership reform in rural sector

adjustment' entailed the government gradually increasing the planned purchased price and changing the relative price of agricultural goods to manufactured goods (depicted by the three little arrows in Figure 4.2); while 'price release' involved the gradual reduction of the quota that farmers were required to sell to the government. The reduction of the quota enabled farmers to sell part of their products in the market at market prices (as shown by arrow 1 in Figure 4.2). The policies behind rural price reform were thereafter introduced as part of many urban sector reforms.

## Industry

Generally, China's industrial organization experienced a period of concentralization and then a period of decentralization. In much of the pre-reform period, China's industrial organization was implemented via a centrally planned system which offered the advantages of rapid structural transformation through direct and strong government participation and large-scale mobilization of resources and their selective disposition to priority sectors. Such a system enabled the industrial sector to grow at highly creditable rates between 1953 and 1978. The advantages of rapid structural change under a centrally planned system, however, were soon outweighed by the problems of low efficiency, slow technological progress, sectoral disproportion, and sharp annual fluctuations in growth rates.

In general, the state-owned enterprises (SOEs) were established to serve as five important roles in the Chinese economy: (1) they had in many cases led to improved efficiency and increased technological competitiveness; (2) they had generally taken a more socially responsible attitude than the purely private enterprises; (3) they had helped to prevent oligopolistic collusion by refusing to collude; (4) they had helped the government to pursue its regional policy by shifting the investment to the poor west of the country; and (5) they had been used by the government as a means of managing aggregate demand to enable it to operate its counter-cyclical policy. Closely copying the Soviet prototype, the SOEs followed a 'unified supply and unified collection' system in which the state supplied all inputs (such as labour, funds, raw material, power supply, an so on) necessary to execute production targets and claimed all output and financial revenues.[14]

The main substantive difference between the collectively-owned enterprises (COEs) and SOEs lies in the extent of government control. The SOEs serve to some extent as the concrete manifestation of the socialist principle of public ownership of the means of production by the whole people. Local governments are responsible for the provision of inputs to the COEs within their jurisdiction and conversely have first if not sole claim their output and revenues. Usually, the COEs are classified into two parts: urban COEs are directly controlled by local governments and subjected to state plans; rural COEs are fully under the jurisdiction of the township and village government units (this will be discussed in detail in Chapter 8).

Obviously, the PSEs were the freest to decide on investment, labour, output, and pricing and, above all, the most market-oriented. China's PSEs practically ceased to exist from 1958 when the socialist transformation of national capitalist industry was completed to 1979 when the Chinese government began to reform its CPE (see Figure 4.3). During the reform era, the PSEs have experienced a recovery during 1978–88, a short hover during 1989–91, and a mushrooming since 1992. According to the Chinese definition, an individually owned enterprise employing up to eight people is defined as *getihu* (individual household), but one with eight or more employee is defined as *shiyingqiye* (privately-owned enterprise).[15]

The foreign invested enterprises (FIEs) mainly comprise joint-ventures and wholly foreign-owned enterprises. Like the PSEs, the FIEs also have grown rapidly since the early 1980s, as a result of dramatic inflows of foreign capitals into China. We will discuss this issue in detail in Chapter 10.

Since 1978, industrial reforms in China have sought to improve enterprise incentive systems, utilize indirect economic levers (price, tax, interest rate, credit, banking, and the rest) to regulate industrial production, endow enterprises with greater relative decision-making autonomy and above all, to compel enterprises to operate according to market regulations. The positive effects of reform on industrial performance are evident from the dramatic industrial growth during the reform period (see Chapter 8 for more details). The dynamism of the industrialization may be attributed to a variety of reform measures. One such measure was the shift in sectoral priorities within industry which allowed a greater share of resources to be diverted away from the input- and capital-intensive producer goods industries towards the more efficient and profitable consumer goods industries. Another measure was the lifting of previous restrictions on the development of the non-state sectors and the policy of promoting a diversified ownership structure. This has led to the explosive growth of the non-state sectors which are increasingly acting as the engine of industrial development

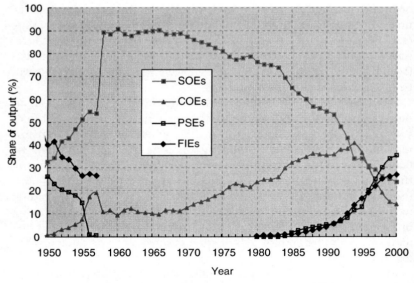

*Figure 4.3*   Shares of industrial output by ownership (1950–2000)

particularly since the early 1990s when China formally tried to transform its economy to a socialist market system. From 1978 to 2000, the shares of industrial output produced by the SOEs, COEs, PSEs, and FIEs changed greatly, with the GVIO growing much slower in the SOEs than in the COEs, PSEs, and FIEs. It is particularly noteworthy that the SOEs' share in GVIO firstly began to rank after the PESs and FIEs in 1997 and 1998, respectively (see Figure 4.3).

The substantial reform of the state industrial organization started in 1984 with the CCP and government's decision to shift the emphasis of reforms from the agricultural sector to the non-agricultural sectors. On 10 May 1984, the State Council issued the 'Provisional Regulations on the Enlargement of Autonomy of State-owned Industrial Enterprises' which outlines ten specific decision-making powers to be enjoyed by enterprises. The 'invigoration' of large- and medium-sized SOEs and the application of indirect means to regulate SOEs were adopted as policy in the State Council's governmental report to the Fourth Session of the Sixth NPC on 25 March 1986. In December, the 'Bankruptcy Law Concerning the State Enterprises' was adopted by the NPC. However, the Bankruptcy Law was not effectively applied until the early 1990s due to fears of unemployment and social instability as China has not a relatively complete social security system.[16]

Following the call for faster economic growth and reform by Deng Xiaoping, the government began to accelerate and intensify market-oriented reforms after 1992. Industrial reform was focused on the issue of property right reform by granting more autonomies for the SOEs. In June 1992, State Commission for Restructuring the Economic Systems (SCRES), State Planning Commission (SPC), Ministry of Finance (MOF), the People's Bank of China (PBC), and the Production Office of State Council (the former name of SETC) jointly issued the 'Provisional Regulations on Joint-Stock Companies' to govern the formation of shareholding companies. The regulations cover the standardization of joint stock companies, their accounting system, financial management, taxation and auditing, labour and wage system. This was followed by the State Council's 'Regulations on the Transformation of the Operating Mechanisms of State-owned Industrial Enterprises' on 22 July 1992, which codified the independent decision-making powers of the SOEs in 14 key areas (including production, investment, labour, marketing, independent profit and loss accounting, assets, mergers, closures, bankruptcy, and so on).

Since Deng Xiaoping's theory on the construction of a socialist market economy with Chinese characteristics was formally adopted in

1993, there has been rapid and substantial changes in the industrial management. One important policy is the importation of 'modern enterprise system' which in practice follows the modern western-type and market-based corporate system. Besides its critical role in the sustainable improvement of productivity in industrial sector, industrial reform is also the institutional *sine qua non* of establishing an effectively functioning competitive market system.

The reform on non-performing SOEs was debated once again in the Fifth Plenum of the Fourteenth CCPCC held during September 1995. The outcome was the policy of 'grasping the large and releasing the small' (*zhua da fang xiao*). To 'grasp the large' (*zhua da*) is to turn a select group of 300 out of a list of 1000 already successful large enterprises and enterprise groups into world-class businesses. To 'release the small' (*fang xiao*) is to privatize or to contract out small SOEs or to let them go bankrupt. This policy allows most small SOEs to be sold off to private individuals and the management of those not sold is contracted out (see Box 4.2). The majority of the remaining large and medium SOEs are to be turned into corporations with various forms of ownership, ranging from corporations with 100 per cent private ownership to those with a mixture of private and state capital and others with 100 per cent state capital. The central government, however, will continue to be the only shareholder in companies that produce 'special-category' and defence related products.

The state ownership, which had been defined as the classic feature of socialism, was discussed in the 15th CCP National Congress during October 1997. The CCP's final conclusion was that public (*gongyou*), instead of state (*guoyou*), ownership is to be the dominant form of ownership.[17] Besides, the development of all other forms of ownership, including private ownership, is encouraged. Furthermore, private and individual businesses are not only tolerated but are now considered as making valuable contributions to the economy. The shift in the CCP's view on ownership is now enshrined in the Chinese constitution with two amendments to the constitution at the Ninth National NPC held in March 1998. The first amendment was to Article 6 of the constitution, with the addition of a clause stating that China is now at its preliminary stage of socialism. This amendment is used to justify having public, instead of state, ownership as the main form of ownership of the means of production. The clause further states that public ownership will develop together with other forms of ownership. The second constitutional amendment was to Article 21, with the addition of a

*Box 4.2* After ownership reform: a tale of two companies

Zibo Mining Bureau (ZMB) is a large state-owned mining enterprise located in Shandong province. By the end of June 2001, the ZMB has a total number of 36,447 staff, and 25,922 retired personnel and 10,198 other dependent personnel. It has ¥4.249 billion gross assets and ¥3.325 billion debt (with a debt/asset ratio of 78.25 per cent). The ZMB decided to introduce ownership reform in its two subsidiary companies (Guangzheng and Chuangda) in 1997 and 1999, respectively. The following table reveals that, since ownership reform, there has an increasing tendency for income inequalities; 'position' variable has played a more important role in the distribution of earnings.

| | *Guangzheng* | | *Chuangda* | |
|---|---|---|---|---|
| | Dec.1997 | Dec.2001 | Dec.1997 | Dec.2001 |
| *1. Earnings per worker (yuan)* | | | | |
| Total earnings | 490.64 | 735.54 | 493.97 | 660.63 |
| Wage | 490.64 | 563.63 | 493.97 | 566.38 |
| Share bonus | na | 171.91 | na | 94.25 |
| *2. Gini coefficients* | | | | |
| Total earnings | 0.265 | 0.326 | 0.186 | 0.276 |
| Wage | 0.265 | 0.320 | 0.186 | 0.247 |
| Share bonus | na | 0.601 | na | 0.590 |
| Samples | 229 | 382 | 36 | 345 |

*3. Determinants of wage level\**

| Explanatory variable | Coefficient | Coefficient | Coefficient | Coefficient |
|---|---|---|---|---|
| Constant | 6.820 (13.93) | 5.503 (24.95) | | 5.898 (18.99) |
| Experience | −0.116 (−2.52) | 0.015 (1.08) | | 0.030 (1.81) |
| Experience$^2$ | 0.0037(2.39) | 0.00001 (0.03) | | −0.0009 (−2.19) |
| Male | 0.138 (1.00) | 0.303 (5.27) | | 0.177 (2.71) |
| Education | −0.022 (−0.47) | 0.0536 (3.06) | na | −0.0075 (−0.30) |
| Top managers | 1.051 (1.59) | 1.151 (5.44) | | 1.195 (5.25) |
| Middle-class managers | | 1.091 (7.75) | | |
| | 0.747 (2.34) | −0.015 (−0.12) | | 0.449 (3.64) |
| Clerks | −1.184 (−2.82) | −0.013 (−0.19) | | 0.396 (3.04) |

*Box 4.2*    continued

| Technical workers | –0.135 (–0.87) | | –0.229 (–1.79) |
|---|---|---|---|
| $R^2$ | 0.186 | 0.389 | 0.223 |
| F | 3.335 | 26.55 | 11.67 |
| Samples | 125 | 322 | 334 |

*Notes*: *: Results are estimated based on ordinary least squares (OLS). Figures within parentheses are T-statistic values.

*Source*: Guo *et al.* (2003).

clause stating that individual, private and other forms of non-public ownership are 'important components of a socialist economy' and they 'supplement the system of socialist public ownership'.

An example of the 'grasping the large' policy is the restructuring of China's oil industry and the four state-owned oil companies – China National Offshore Oil Corporation (CNOOC), China National Petroleum Corporation (CNPC), China Petrochemical Corporation (Sinopec) and China National Star Petroleum Corporation (CNSPC).[18] In August 1999 CNOOC grouped all the shares of all its subsidiaries into the newly formed, China Offshore Oil Corporation (COOC). Three months later in November 1999, CNPC did likewise and formed China Oil & Gas Stock Co. Ltd. (Petrochina). Sinopec is expected to follow suit. Meanwhile, China National Star Petroleum Corporation (CNSPC), the smallest state-owned oil company, was merged with Sinopec in late November 1999. The aim behind the formation of the new companies and the merger was to reduce the four state oil companies to three state holding companies and to consolidate the shares of their subsidiaries into three companies for overseas listing. As part of the restructuring, core and non-core businesses of the state oil companies are to be separated, some debt converted to equity and their workforce reduced with state financial help. Adverse stock market reactions towards the end of 1999 led to the postponement of the initial public offering (IPO) of CNOOC in Hong Kong and New York. But despite continuing uncertainties over the potential success of their IPOs, CNOOC, CNPC and Sinopec were pushed ahead with their restructuring plans in 2000 because of China's expected entry into the WTO after its successful negotiation with the US.

## Public finance and banking

Public finance decides to a large extent the use of a nation's aggregate resources and, together with monetary and exchange rate policies, influences the macro balance of payments, the accumulation of foreign debt, and the rates of inflation, interest, and so on. However, the degree of impact may differ significantly and depend upon whether the economy is managed under the market-oriented system or centrally planned system. Public finance usually plays an important role in promoting balanced development and equilibrium in both wealth accumulation and distribution for a planned economy in which central government collects and directly dispenses much of its budget for society, while the local budget is collected from and used for local administrative organs, factories, enterprises, and welfare facilities. As the market economy is a private-ownership system, the channels of policy influences are much more indirect and mainly through the *laissez-faire* approach.

Since the late 1970s, public finance, as an important component of the Chinese economic system, has undergone a series of reforms on the central–local relations.[19] The goals of these reforms were to decentralize the fiscal structure and strengthen the incentive for local government to collect more revenue for themselves and for the central government to maintain an egalitarian fiscal redistribution among the provinces. Briefly, China's efforts towards this end have experienced four different stages, all of which sought to find a rational revenue-raising formula between the central and local governments:

### The first stage (1980–84)

The Chinese government began to implement the fiscal system entitled *'huafen shouzhi, fenji baogan'* (divide revenue and expenditure, set up diversified contract system) in 1980. The main contents of the fiscal reform included (1) the transformation from the traditional system of 'having meals in one pot' (*yizhao chifan*) to that of 'having meals in different pots' (*fenzhao chifan*); (2) the transformation of financial redistribution from mainly through sectors directly under the central government to mainly through regions; and (3) the transformation of the divisions of revenue and expenditure and the proportion of revenue sharing between the central and local governments from being fixed annually to being fixed for every five years.

During this period, the basic structure of the central-local fiscal relations was framed and amended frequently. In 1980, there were ten provinces (Inner Mongolia, Fujian, Guangdong, Guangxi, Guizhou, Yunnan, Tibet, Qinghai, Ningxia and Xinjiang) on which the central government taxed a zero marginal rate. Specifically, Guangdong – a coastal province with close proximity to Hong Kong and Macau – was required to pay a lump-sum (LT) tax to the central government; Fujian – another coastal province with close proximity to Taiwan – was able to retain all the revenue it collected plus a lump-sum subsidy (LS) from the central government; the rest eight poor provinces and ethnic minority-based autonomous regions could retain all the revenue they collected and additionally receive a lump-sum but growing subsidy (GS) from the central government. In five provinces (Beijing, Tianjin, Liaoning, Shanghai and Jiangsu), the total revenue collected was to be shared with the central government in fixed proportions (SOR), varying from 12 per cent to 90 per cent.[20] In the remaining provinces, revenue was shared between the central and local governments in more complicated ways and, as a result of considerable and frequent politicing, negotiating and bargaining with central government, the fiscal arrangements were amended and the shares of these provinces were generally raised in 1982 and lowered in 1983 in accordance with central government's revenue requirement (see Table 4.2).

### The second stage (1985–87)

The fiscal system entitled *'huafen shuizhong, heding shouzhi, fenji baogan'* (divide the categories of tax, verify revenue and expenditure, and set up diversified contract system) was introduced from 1985. This system, which was to strengthen the method of 'having meals in different pots', divided revenue into three parts: the centrally fixed revenue, the locally fixed revenue, and the revenue shared by the central and local governments. Among other changes of the central–local fiscal relations, Jilin, Jiangxi and Gansu provinces moved from DRS to LS, Shaanxi province from SOR to LS, Heilongjiang province from DRS to SOR in 1985 and LT in 1986, respectively. Simultaneously the favourable fiscal policies were still applied in Guangdong and Fujian provinces and other minority-based autonomous regions, as demonstrated in Table 4.2.

### The third stage (1988–93)

A fiscal responsibility system entitled *'chaizheng baogan'* was introduced through two sub-stages below.

(a) *1988–90*: Seven methods were introduced during this period: (1) STR (*shouru dizheng baogan*); (2) SOR (*zhong'e fencheng*); (3) GT

*Table 4.2* Changes of the central–local fiscal relations (1980–93)

| Province | 1980–81 | 1982 | 1983–84 | 1985 | 1986–87 | 1988–90 | 1991–93 |
|---|---|---|---|---|---|---|---|
| Anhui | DR | SOR | SOR | SOR | SOR | SOR | SOR |
| Beijing | SOR | SOR | SOR | SOR | SOR | STR | STR |
| Fujian | LS | LS | LS | LS | LS | LS | LS |
| Gansu | DR | SOR | DRS | LS | LS | LS | LS |
| Guangdong | LT | LT | LT | LT | LT | GT | GT |
| Guangxi | GS | GS | GS | GS | GS | GS | LS |
| Guizhou | GS | GS | GS | GS | GS | GS | LS |
| Hainan | | | | | | GT | LS |
| Hebei | DR | SOR | SOR | SOR | SOR | STR | STR |
| Heilongjiang | DRS | DRS | DRS | SOR | LT | LT | LT/STR |
| Henan | DR | SOR | SOR | SOR | SOR | STR | STR |
| Hubei | DR | SOR | SOR | SOR | ROR | ROR | LT/SGT |
| Hunan | DR | SOR | SOR | SOR | SOR | GT | GT |
| Inner Mongolia | GS | GS | GS | GS | GS | GS | LS |
| Jiangsu | SOR | SOR | SOR | SOR | SOR | STR | STR |
| Jiangxi | DRS | DRS | DRS | LS | LS | LS | LS |
| Jilin | DRS | DRS | DRS | LS | LS | LS | LS |
| Liaoning | SOR | SOR | SOR | SOR | SOR | STR | STR/SGT |
| Ningxia | GS | GS | GS | GS | GS | GS | LS |
| Qinghai | GS | GS | GS | GS | GS | GS | LS |
| Shaanxi | DR | SOR | SOR | LS | LS | LS | LS |
| Shandong | DR | SOR | SOR | SOR | SOR | LT | LT/SGT |
| Shanghai | SOR | SOR | SOR | SOR | SOR | LT | LT |
| Shanxi | DR | DR | SOR | SOR | SOR | SOR | SOR |
| Sichuan | DR | SOR | SOR | SOR | ROR | ROR | LS/STR |
| Tianjin | SOR | SOR | SOR | SOR | SOR | SOR | SOR |
| Tibet | GS | GS | GS | GS | GS | GS | LS |
| Xinjiang | GS | GS | GS | GS | GS | GS | LS |
| Yunnan | GS | GS | GS | GS | GS | GS | LS |
| Zhejiang | DR | SOR | SOR | SOR | SOR | STR | STR |

*Note*: The definition and formulation of the contents are given in Table 4.3.

*Sources*: World Bank (1990, p. 89), Oksenberg and Tong (1991, pp. 24–5), Argarwala (1992, p. 68), Wei (1994, p. 298), and Knight and Li (1995).

(*shangjie'e dizheng baogan*); (4) LT (*ding'e shangjie*); (5) LS (*ding'e buzhu*); (6) GS (*ding'e buzhu, meinian dizheng*); and (7) ROR (*zhong'e baogan*).

(b) *1991–93*: Six methods were introduced during this period:[21] (1) STR: Beijing (*a*=50 per cent, *r*=4 per cent), Hebei (*a*=70 per cent, *r*=4.5 per cent), Liaoning (*a*=58.25 per cent, *r*=3.5 per cent), Jiangsu (*a*=41 per cent, *r*=5 per cent), Zhejiang (*a*=61.47 per cent, *r*=6.5 per cent), and Henan (*a*=80 per cent, *r*=5 per cent)) and Shenyang of

*Table 4.3* Definition and formulation of the fiscal policies

| Fiscal policy | Definition | Revenue goes to provincial govt. | Revenue goes to the central govt. | Marginal tax rate |
|---|---|---|---|---|
| DR | dividing revenue | $\sum\alpha_i C_i$ | $\sum(1-\alpha_i)C_i$ | $\sum(1-\alpha_i)C_i/\sum C_i$ |
| DRS | dividing revenue and receiving growing subsidy | $\sum\alpha_i C_i + S_0(1+r)^t$ | $\sum(1-\alpha_i)C_i - S_0(1+r)^t$ | $\sum(1-\alpha_i)C_i/\sum C_i$ |
| GS | receiving lump-sum but growing subsidy | $C + S_0(1+r)^t$ | $-S_0(1+r)^t$ | 0 |
| GT | paying lump-sum but growing tax | $C - T_0(1+r)^t$ | $T_0(1+r)^t$ | 0 |
| LS | receiving lump-sum subsidy | $C+S$ | $-S$ | 0 |
| LT | paying lump-sum tax | $C-T$ | $T$ | 0 |
| ROR | retaining overall revenue | $C$ | $0$ | 0 |
| SGT | sharing overall revenue and paying growing tax | $(1+\alpha)C - T_0(1+r)^t$ | $-\alpha C + T_0(1+r)^t$ | $-\alpha$ |
| SOR | sharing overall revenue | $\alpha C$ | $(1-\alpha)C$ | $1-\alpha$ |
| STR | sharing target revenue but retaining residual revenue | $C-(1-\alpha)C_0(1+r)^t$ | $(1-\alpha)C_0(1+r)^t$ | 0 |

*Notes:* $C$=revenue collected by province ($C_0$ denotes $C$ at time zero); $C_i$=revenue collected by province from source $i$ ($i$= 1, 2, 3 denote revenue from source $i$ goes to central government, to provincial government, and is shared between them respectively) $S$=lump-sum subsidy from central government ($S_0$ denotes $S$ at time zero); $T$=lump-sum tax to central government ($T_0$ denotes $T$ at time zero); $r$=annual growth rate; $\alpha$=fixed share of revenue accruing to province ($0<\alpha<1$); $\alpha_i =\alpha_1, \alpha_2, \alpha_3$ (where $\alpha_1 =0$, $\alpha_2=1$, $0<\alpha_3<1$).

Liaoning ($a$=30.29 per cent, $r$=4 per cent), Harbin of Heilongjiang ($a$=45 per cent, $r$=5 per cent), Ningbo of Zhejiang ($a$=27.93 per cent, $r$=5.3 per cent), and Chongqing of Sichuan ($a$=33.5 per cent, $r$=4 per cent); (2) SOR: Tianjin ($a$=46.5 per cent), Shanxi ($a$=87.55 per cent), and Anhui ($a$=77.5 per cent); (3) GT: Guangdong ($T_0$=¥1.413 billion, $r$=9 per cent) and Hunan ($T_0$=¥0.8 billion, $r$=7 per cent); (4) LT: Shanghai ($T_0$=¥10.5 billion), Shandong ($T$=¥289 million), and Heilongjiang ($T$=¥299 million); (5) LS: Jilin ($S$=¥107 million), Fujian ($S$=¥50 million), Jiangxi ($S$=¥45 million), Shaanxi ($S$=¥120 million), Gansu ($S$=¥125 million), Inner Mongolia ($S$=¥1.852 billion), Guangxi ($S$=¥608 million), Yunnan ($S$=¥673 million), Guizhou ($S$=¥742 million), Qinghai ($S$=¥656 million), Hainan ($S$=¥138 million), Hubei ($S$=4.78 per cent of Wuhan's revenue), and Sichuan ($S$=10.7 per cent of Chongqing's revenue); and (6) SGT (*zhong'e fencheng jia zhengzhang fencheng*): Dalian of Liaoning ($a$=27.74 per cent, $a'$=27.26 per cent), Qingdao of Shandong ($a$=16 per cent, $a'$=34 per cent), and Wuhan of Hubei ($a$=17 per cent, $a'$=25 per cent).[22]

Coming to an end, the economic incentives facing the provinces appeared to improve over time for the post-reform period. In 1980, for example, no fewer than 19 provinces were on some form of revenue sharing or division, whereas in 1985 revenue division had ceased and 15 provinces shared their respective revenues. In 1988's reform, most of these provinces were switched to lump sum taxation or the sharing of target revenues, while only three provinces remained on a revenue sharing formula. In sum, this account of the fiscal relationship between the central and local governments highlights four problems: first, the non-uniform treatment of provinces appeared neither efficient nor equitable; second, the uncertainty associated with changing rules and bargaining had disincentive effects on the revenue collection of the province governments; thirdly, the high marginal tax rates faced by some provinces could be expected to deter revenue collection; lastly, the various efforts to reform the centralized fiscal system was to reduce the share that central government received of the revenue collected by the provinces.[23]

### The fourth stage (1994– )

Since 1994, China has implemented the 'tax-sharing system' (*fenshui zhi*) under which central government collects all shared as central taxes, and local government collects only those designated as local

(a) Total revenue/expenditure

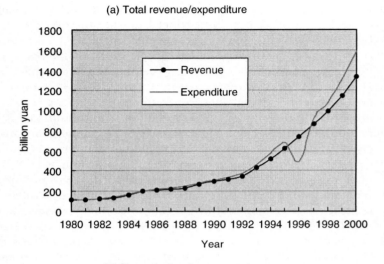

(b) Shares by local government

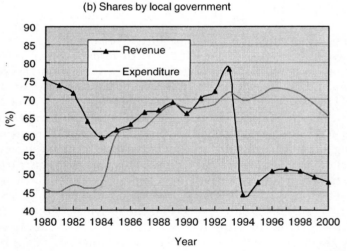

*Notes*: (1) 'revenue' excludes borrowing from domestic and abroad, 'expenditure' excludes repayment of the principal and payment of interest, borrowing from domestic and abroad.

*Figure 4.4*   China's revenue and expenditure (1980–2000)

taxes. The fourth stage fiscal reform, by transferring much of the revenue collection function to central government, attempted to tackle the principal-agent problem of the revenue contracting period. The solution was essentially to transpose the principal and agent. It can be seen from Figure 4.4 that China's diversified fiscal systems have resulted in differing central-local relations since the early 1980s. During 1980–84 when the first stage fiscal reform was implemented, China's share of central revenue to total revenue increased from 24.5 per cent to 40.5 per cent; while its share of central expenditure to total expenditure decreased from 54.3 per cent to 52.5 per cent accordingly. In the following years, both the share of central to total revenue and the share of central to total expenditure had decreased considerably before the 'tax-sharing system' was implemented in 1994.[24]

Banking reforms have played an important role in China's overall effort to transform a centrally planned economy into a market-based economy since 1978. Although the banking sector has undergone remarkable changes over the period, deep-seated structural problems of asset quality, capital adequacy and profitability continue to pose a challenge to the sector. Arguably, the major problem in the Chinese banking sector is the high level of non-performing loans (NPLs) – and continued lending to loss-making SOEs. Until recently, banking reforms were mainly focused on introducing competition, broadening the channels of financial intermediation and providing a legal framework for bank supervision. In 1995, notable developments in this respect were introduced: the promulgation of the Central Bank Law that firmly established the PBC as the sole government agent to supervise and regulate the banking sector, and the enactment of the Commercial Banking Law that clearly defined the scope of business for commercial Banks.

The 1997 Asian financial crisis speeded up the reform pace of China's banking system. China quickened the pace of reform in 1998 and seems to be aware of two lessons that can be drawn from the Asian financial crisis. The first lesson is that a sound banking system is crucial for an economy to withstand external shocks. The second lesson from the Japanese banking saga is that delay only allows NPLs to grow and erode bank capital. Under the reforms starting in December 1998, the directors of the regional branches of the PBC would be appointed directly by its headquarters in Beijing without consultations with the provincial governments. Instead of a PBC branch previously being established in each province and SEZ, the regional PBC branches were only located in nine cities.[25] Furthermore, previous powers delegated to PBC branches to control the volume of credit were decentralized back at the PBC headquarters. Moreover, projects above a certain scale would now have to be approved by central bank headquarters. However, only the above reform effort was enough for the construction of a healthy banking and financing system, since there had been too much amount of bad loans to the SOEs (we will discuss this in greater detail in next section).

The reform of the SOEs was delayed due to the 1997 Asian financial crisis.[26] Two years later in 1999, China introduced a debt-equity swap scheme (*zhai zhuan gu*) to convert a portion of SOEs' bank debt into equity. China's four largest state-owned commercial banks set up their own state asset management companies – 'Cinda' (of China Construction Bank), 'Huarong' (of Industrial and Commercial Bank of China), 'Great Wall' (of Agricultural Bank of China) and 'Oriental' (of Bank of China – to deal respectively with their bad loans to selected SOEs that have potential as going business concerns but are burdened by heavy debts. The bad loans are converted into equity and then sold at a discount to investors. The immediate objectives of debt–equity swaps are to improve the balance sheet of the commercial banks and reduce the debt service of the SOEs. In the longer term, it is hoped that investors in these debt-equity swaps would have the managerial and technical expertise to turn the SOEs permanently around. There are strict guidelines specifying conditions that the first enterprises have to fulfill before they are allowed to have their debts converted into equity.

Conditions under which enterprises were chosen include: (1) they must have good marketing records and competitiveness; (2) their technical equipments must be line with environmental protection; (3) they must have high quality of management level and good accounting system; (4) their leaderships must be specialized in business and administration; and (5) they must take 'effective reform measures', including plans to 'cut the number of employees to increase efficiency'. By the end of 1999, 601 non-performing SOEs had been approved by the State Economic and Trade Commission (SETC) to transform their debts (459.6 billion yuan) into equity.

On 1 April 2000, China introduced 'real name' banking system under which all the household bank deposits require a depositor's ID. This is an important step in moving from anonymous banking to real-name banking, an international practice. Frankly speaking, this change was not so much about increasing tax revenue, but to reduce political corruption by making the flow of money transparent. What is interesting is the particular way China introduced the real name banking: It followed a dual-track approach. The real name policy only applies to the new deposits made after 1 April 2000. Withdrawing from the existing deposits, which amounted to more than 6 trillion yuan (or about three-fourth of China's GDP in 1999), continued to be anonymous. As

a result, the existing bank deposits were 'grand fathered' and thus protected, and only the new deposits are required to follow the new rule.
Nevertheless, the dual track approach reduced the opposition to this
reform drastically.

Several measures have been taken since the late 1990s to establish a
strong prudential framework that encompasses all types of banking
and nonblank financial institutions. However, the pressing issues after
China's WTO accession still need to be addressed (Chi, 2000). They are:

1 Governance, transparency, and the private sector
   - Moving ahead with public administration reform
   - Increasing transparency to enhance public understanding of land
     support for reform
   - Improving the efficiency and transparency of the public adminis-
     tration will also strengthen law enforcement
   - Strengthening corporate governance by accelerating the trans-
     formation of SOEs to join stock companies
   - Supporting the development of non-state enterprises
2 Infrastructure and Public Utilities
   - Separating the government from enterprises is the key reform for
     infrastructure and public utilities
3 Commercial banks, bad debts, and the financial sector
   - Transforming state-owned commercial banks to joint stock own-
     ership
   - Accelerating the development of non-state financial institution
   - Strengthening the management supervision of banks, investment
     companies, and securities markets
4 Agriculture and rural development
   - Liberating trade of farm products
   - Introducing rural land reform and a market for land use rights
5 Human resources
   - Reforming the mechanism for human resources selection
   - Reforming the residential registration

## External economic relations

Another key element of China's reforms was its open-door policy.
In order to attract foreign investment, the NPC enacted the 'Law
of the People's Republic of China Concerning the Joint Ventures
with Chinese and Foreign Investment' in 1979. Also in this year, the
CCPCC and the State Council decided to grant Guangdong and Fujian

provinces 'special policies and flexible measures' in foreign economic affairs. On 26 December 1979, the People's Congress of Guangdong province approved the Guangdong provincial government's proposal that a part of Shenzhen (next to Hong Kong), Zhuhai (next to Macau) and Santou be designed as SEZs in which the market-oriented system with Chinese characteristics can be experimented. At the same time, Xiamen in Southeast Fujian province (near Taiwan) also became a SEZ with the approval of the NPC. Subsequently, Guangdong and Fujian gained substantial autonomy in developing their regions as the central government granted them authority to pursue reform 'one step ahead' (*xian zhou yibu*). Not only did these areas enjoy lower tax rates, but also they gained more authority over economic development. The four cities are below the provincial level but have independent budget agreements with the center.[27]

Prior to the early 1980s, the management of foreign economic affairs rested in the hand of one government ministry that controlled things too finely and rigidly. In the first years when China implemented the outward-oriented development strategy, reform of the foreign economic system was conducted via three aspects. First, under the unified control of the state, a closer relationship between production and marketing and between industry and trade was arranged, which enabled production units to participate directly in foreign trade. Second, the special policies and measures relating to foreign trade were handed to the local governments. A third type of reform was to expand the autonomy of the SOEs to act on their own initiatives and have direct links with foreign traders at meetings arranged by specialized export SOEs. In 1982, the Ministry of Foreign Trade (MFT) was renamed the Ministry of Foreign Economic Relations and Trade (MFERT). At the same time, trade bureaux at provincial and local levels were established to manage both foreign trade and foreign direct investment (FDI).

In 1984, the trade management system was further reformed. Foreign trade enterprises were given autonomy to deal with international trade. The MFERT and local trade bureaux were, in principle, not allowed to interfere in the management of foreign trade enterprises. Many large SOEs received permission to engage in foreign trade. Local enterprises were also able to establish their own foreign trade companies. In 1988, foreign trade was reformed by a system of contracts under which the separation between ownership (state) and management (enterprise) was maintained and thus the foreign trade enterprises were able to operate independently. Despite these reforms, the fundamental structure of central planning and state ownership has not been changed fundamentally, particularly in large- and medium-sized SOEs.

In parallel with the gradual intensification of its economic reforms, China has increasingly amplified its foreign-related legal system, steadily improved its trade and investment environment and enforced the intellectual property rights protection system. On the issue of trade system transparency, China has sorted out and publicized all management documents that used to be deemed confidential. In 1993, the Ministry of Foreign Trade and Economic Cooperation (MFTEC) was established to reform laws and regulations on the management of foreign trade and economic cooperation. Import restrictions were further eased. By the end of 2000, China had rescinded import licensing and quota control on over 1000 tariff lines (see Chapter 10 for details).

## Summary

The advocates of new institutional economists recognize that a good market economy requires 'getting institutions right' (Coase, 1992; North, 1997; and Williamson, 1994). This is because institutions in general set the rules to affect the behavior of economic agents in a fundamental way. The institutional economists thus regard the conventional wisdom of transition focusing on stabilization, liberalization, and privatization as inadequate, missing the important institutional dimension. To them, a set of institutions are critical for sustained growth, including secure private property rights protected by the rule of law, impartial enforcement of contracts through an independent judiciary, appropriate government regulations to foster market competition, effective corporate governance, transparent financial systems, and so on (Qian, 2002). Standing in marked contrast with the failures of Russia, which was to some extent based on a 'blueprint' or 'recipe' from western advisors, has been the enormous success of China, which created its own path of transition (Stigliz, 1999, p. 3).

Many efforts have attempted to probe into the characteristics of the Chinese reform that has been successfully introduced since the late 1970s. For example, Montinola *et al.* (1995) suggest that the system of federalism[28] and the inherent jurisdictional competition places striking limits on this system of patronage and political spoils. In an extensive discussion about the topics central to the success of China's economic reforms, Shirk (1994) included the importance of gradualism, the initial role of agrarian reform, and the political mechanisms underpinning reform within the central government. In comparison with other researchers, Shirk placed greater weight on the political organization of local governments and their control over the economy, arguing that local political officials should be viewed as creating systems of patronage and loyalty.

Obviously, the Chinese reform experience defies conventional explanations. In the late 1950s, the same authoritarian regime was waging a massive campaign under the name of the 'Great Leap Forward,' resulting in a loss of huge lives. From 1966 to 1976, the same regime was launching a so-called 'Great Cultural Revolution,' causing serious cultural and economic damages to this nation. Meanwhile, influential theories of the political economy of the former socialist systems emphasizes that unless the one-party (Communist Party) monopoly is abolished, reforms are doomed to fail (Kornai, 1992). Consequently there will be questions such as: Why has Chinese-style reform worked during the past decades? Can China's market-oriented reform be sustained in the long run? If China's reform had adopted a big bang *vis-à-vis* the gradual approach that it has utilized, how would the Chinese economy have performed in the past decades?

China's reform experience has provided ample and valuable narrative for this regard. But narrative alone cannot answer the above questions sufficiently since they relate to events that did not occur and the motivation for not behaving in a particular way. Addressing these questions requires an appropriate model for linking what we observe with what we do not observe. Understanding China's economic reform cannot be based on theories alone. The narrative matters because from the historical point of view some specific events can yield a multiplicity of equilibria. To be sure, the Chinese reform has been demonstrated a complicated process in which a series of endogenous and exogenous factors are linked with each other and play differing roles in the institutional changes. Thus, in order to evaluate such issues as what have determined or influenced the Chinese reform process and how well the Chinese reform has performed, we require resorting to theory able to guide an empirical analysis.

In the next chapter, on the basis of an analytic narrative approach, we will compare the outcomes of the major reforms that have been implemented during the past decades.

# 5

# How Well the Chinese-style Reform Performs

Bianque was granted an audience by Duke Huang of Cai. He stood looking at the ruler for a while and spoke, 'Your Majesty is suffering from an ailment, which now remains in between the skin and the muscles. But it may get worse without treatment.' 'I am not at all indisposed,' replied the Duke complacently. When Bianque left, the Duke remarked, 'It is the medical man's usual practice to pass a healthy person as a sick man in order to show his brilliance.' Ten days later, Bianque had another chance to see the Duke. This time, he pointed out to him: 'The ailment has developed into the muscles. It will go from bad to worse if no treatment is conducted.' To this the ruler said nothing but showed a greater displeasure than before. Another ten days went by. On seeing the Duke again, Bianque warned him that the illness had gone into the stomach and the intestines and that unless an immediate treatment be given, it would go on worsening. Again the Duke said not a word but looked angrier. After a third ten days, when Bianque saw the Duke, he simply turned round and went away. Feeling it strange, the Duke sent a man to ask Bianque for the reason.

'Well, an ailment lying in between the skin and the muscles remains on the surface, and so external application with warm water and ointment can cure it,' said Bianque, 'If it sinks into muscles, acupuncture will do good; if it resides in the stomach and the intestines, a decoction of herbs will take effect. But when the sickness penetrates into the bone marrow, it becomes fatal and nothing can be done about it. Now, as the Duke has come to that last stage, I have nothing to recommend.' Five days after that, the Duke felt pains and ordered his men to look for Bianque, but to find that he had fled to the state of Qin. Soon afterwards, the Duke died.

Hanfei (280–233 BC)

# Chinese-style reform, the (un)successful cases[1]

### Radical reform, the successful cases

China's agricultural reform started at September 1980 and had been successfully completed before the end of 1982. The CCP and Chinese government used only about two years to de-collectivize about 700 million farmers throughout the huge nation, via a method known as HRS. Under the HRS, each household may be able to sign a contract with the local government and then obtain a certain amount of arable land and production equipment depending on the number of rural population in this family and have a production quota. As long as the household completes its quota of products to the state, it can decide freely what to produce and how to sell. Although land is still owned by the state, the incentive for agricultural production has increased significantly. The decollectivization of agriculture, which has been recognized as a radical reform (Sachs and Woo, 1994; and Zhao, 1999, p. 192), has universally been recognized as a success. For example, from 1978 to 1984, grain output increased by 56 per cent (Lin, 1992). Even more rapid was the growth in the output of other agricultural commodities (during the pre-reform period, the growth in grain output had been at the expense of these commodities). Over the longer period of reform from 1978 to 2002, gross agricultural output had grown in real terms at more than 5 per cent annually (NBS, 2003).

The special political and economic features of China determine the driving forces and the outcomes of the reform in agricultural ownership. First, more than 80 per cent of China's population still lived in 1978 in rural area – a backward and autarky society.[2] Second, China's agricultural sector had been dominated by the collectivist ownership before the reform – which did not fit for a standard socialism. As a result, reforming the collective sector (while keeping the state-owned sector unchanged) would have not been regarded by the conservatives as of fundamentally affecting China's socialist orthodox. Third and most importantly, the Chinese policymakers – from both reformist and conservative cliques – still had remembered the three-year famine (1959–61) during which millions of farmers died from starvation. They should have recognized that the horrible famine had (at least partially) attributed to China's highly centralized agricultural system, and that if it would occur again, the CCP would lose its power base in China.

Since the initial and external conditions of the agricultural sector were similar to those of the industrial sector (especially those of the small state-owned and collectively-owned industrial enterprises), we argue that at least some industrial reforms – which had followed a too gradual/partial pace (as will be discussed below) – were misguided during the early 1980s. Had the industrial reform followed a more radical approach in speed and scope at the early stage of reform, there would have been more positive economic performances in the industrial sector.

Another successful case is the reform of Chinese bureaucracy. The first thing done by Deng Xiaoping after he resumed his job was to reform bureaucratic institution. Manned by millions of cadres, the system was acknowledged officially to be overstaffed and sluggish. The drive to weed out tens of thousands of aged, inactive, and incompetent cadres was intensified. Even more revolutionary, the life tenure system for state and party cadres was abolished, and age limits for various

*Table 5.1*  Reforming the Chinese bureaucracy (February 1982–September 1984)

| Statistic | Provincial governors | Ministers | City mayors or department chiefs | County sheriffs or division chiefs |
|---|---|---|---|---|
| Mandatory retirement age (years) | 65 | 65 | 60 | 55 |
| Average retirement age (years) | | | | |
|     Before reform | 62 | 64 | 58 | – |
|     After reform | 55 | 58 | 50 | <45 |
| Percentage with college degree (%) | | | | |
|     Before reform | 20 | 37 | 14 | 11 |
|     After reform | 43 | 52 | 44 | 45 |
| Average tenure (years) | | | | |
|     Pre-1982 | 6.43/6.23[a] | 6.56 | – | – |
|     Post-1982 | 3.84/4.05[a] | 4.44 | – | – |

*Notes:* [a] Governor/party secretary.

*Source:* Li (1998, p. 394).

offices were established and, on a less restrictive basis, an education requirement for each level of government positions (see Table 5.1 for a summary of the reform). While removing superfluous personnel, the reform leaders stressed the importance of creating a 'third echelon' of younger leadership to enter responsible positions and be trained for future authority.

The major and direct consequence of the bureaucratic reform is that many younger and educated bureaucrats have replaced the older revolutionary veterans. The new and young officials were generally more supportive of reforms, more adaptable, and more pragmatic. Being better educated in almost all cases, they were also generally more competent than their predecessors (Li, 1998, p. 394). Clearly, the Chinese-style reform of bureaucracy served as a stable political foundation for the implementation of the economic reform during the past decades. Without that reform, in which more younger cadres were able to play an important role, the afterwards reforms would have been impossible.

Although the above two reforms have been regarded as successful cases, they had some negative effects. For example, the cooperative medical care system that had worked quite well before the reform in rural areas was abandoned as a result of the HRS. The implementation of the buying-out plan of the old-aged cadres also had negative effects. An implicit and informal arrangement for most senior officials was that their children were allowed to enter politics in senior positions, which resulted in the birth of the infamous taizhidang (party of crown prince) in China. It is worth noting that the rise of the taizidang was always paralleled with political and economic corruptions. However, the above problems were not because the reforms were too radical but that they were too mild (especially in the case of bureaucratic reform) and limited in scope (especially in the case of agricultural reform).

### Gradual/partial reform, the successful cases

The key component of China's gradual/partial reform was the introduction of a dual-track system. This system was first implemented in agricultural products and spread slowly to consumer goods and intermediate goods. In each case, a free market in which the price was subject to the market regulations developed in parallel with a controlled market in which the price was kept almost unchanged at an officially fixed level. Because the price was higher in the market-regulated track than in the state-controlled track, supply in the free market grew rapidly, so its share in total output rose steadily. Meanwhile, the planned price was able to rise incrementally until it approached to the market price when the gap between supply and demand narrowed. The dual-track system extended through almost every sphere of the Chinese economy, from agriculture, industry, commerce, transportation, post and telecommunications to health care, education, and so on during the transition. For example, between 1979 and 1992, the proportion of industrial goods and materials distributed under the central plan system declined from 95 per cent to less than 10 per cent. There was a parallel reduction in the planned allocation of consumer goods: the number of the first class goods distributed by the state dropped from 65 to 20 and that of the production of materials distributed by the state was reduced from 256 to 19 during those period (Liu, 1995, p. 53).

The smooth implementation of the dual-track system depended on the compensation of losers. For example, although consumers can buy foodstuffs in the market since 1980, urban food coupons (for purchasing grain, meat, oil, and so on) were finally removed only in the early 1990s. Guangzhou completed the removal of the above coupons in 1992 and spent on average 103 yuan in 1988, 113 yuan in 1990, and 43 yuan in 1992 per urban resident for compensation. Beijing also spent 182 yuan in 1990, 185 yuan in 1991, and 123 yuan in 1994 per head before its removal of the coupons (Qian, 2002). In general, the dual-track reform has been recognized as of success, since it not only avoided output declining but also improved efficiency (Wu and Zhao, 1987; and Li, 1997). It must be noted that the dual-track system did not always work well, especially when there existed large gap between market-regulated and officially fixed prices (we will discuss this point later).

In short, a brief review of the gradually declining trend of the plan track throughout the 1980s provides evidence that, ex post, there is no 'ratcheting up' of the plan. Moreover, recent data reveal that the plan track in product market has been largely 'phased out' in the 1990s, and this phasing out of the plan track was generally accompanied by explicit compensation. With rapid growth, the plan track becomes, in no time, a matter of little consequence to most potential losers, which in turn reduces the cost required for compensating them (Lau *et al.*, 2000, p. 142).

Another key initiative of China's gradual reform was the decentralization of authority, i.e., transferring economic management and decision-making from central government to provincial and local governments (see Chapter 4 for details). How did the reform work in practice and to what extent had the provincial governments' fiscal incentives been strengthened as a result of this reform? Jin *et al.* (2001), based on the panel data of 28 provinces between 1982 and 1992, find that the marginal fiscal incentives of provincial governments increased during the reform period between 1982 and 1992, compared with those during the pre-reform 1970–79 period. A comparison of these findings with parallel investigations in Russia is also revealing. Zhuravskaya (2000) examined the fiscal incentives of city governments in the region-city fiscal relationship in post-reform Russia (city is one level below region, which in turn is one level below the federal government). Using the data of 35 cities for the period 1992–97, she found that increases in a city's own revenue were almost entirely offset by decreases in shared revenues from the region to the city.[3]

Economic reforms of many former CPEs followed their domestic political crises (such as the collapse of the Soviet Union in Russian, and the death of Mao Zedong and the fall of the leftist 'Gang of Four' in China). But successful reforms are also promoted by favourable international environment. It has now generally believed that the Chinese outward-oriented development policy has borrowed in part from the NIEs in East Asia. On the one hand, the reformist leaders were deeply aware as well that their rivals from the Chinese Civil War across the Taiwan strait, their compatriots in colonial Hong Kong, and their cold war enemies in southern Korea were enjoying sustained economic success that raised deeply challenging questions about China's own continuing backwardness (Garnaut, 1999, pp. 2–3). On the other hand, China and the US saw the Soviet Union as their common enemy and this led Mao and Nixon to normalize the Sino–US relations in 1971, which paved the way for China's reengagement with the non-communist world. Later the defeat of the US in Vietnam made the West seemed a less threatening place to China's leaders, facilitating China's reentry into the global economy (Liew *et al.*, 2003). Consequently, it is not difficult to understand why China's open-door policy was first introduced and successfully implemented in the eastern/coastal vis-à-vis the western/inland areas.

China's foreign exchange system used to be severely controlled by the central government. Since China started its economic reform in the late 1970s, the foreign trade system has been liberalized in gradualism. In the early 1980s, Chinese currency RMB was non-convertible and the foreign exchanges were strictly supervised by the state. There existed two exchange rates at that period: an official rate published by the government and another one special for foreign trade. Such a system was aimed to enhance the country's export and to restrict its import, for

China suffered from a lack of foreign exchanges seriously at that time. In 1984, as a result of the improving performances in the foreign trade and the economy as a whole, the government adopted a new exchange retaining policy. This policy allowed domestic enterprises and institutions to retain a part of their foreign currency earnings, compared with the previous one in which these units turned in all their foreign currency earnings to the state. Although a larger part of foreign exchanges was still in the control of the government, the new retaining policy stimulated domestic enterprises to increase their exports, and hence the foreign trade performance of China improved significantly. However, this kind of gradual/partial reform, together with other gradual and partial reforms on the external economic sectors, also has faced difficulties, as will be discussed in detail on p. 85.

## Radical reform, the unsuccessful cases

After nearly ten years of reforms and debates over plan and market, a radical price reform was introduced suddenly in June 1998. This was based on the idea that 'long pain is not better than short pain', and that market prices should be put in place at once. The macroeconomic environment was not favourable for such an implementation: inflation was very high (18.5 per cent in 1988) and friction from dual pricing was at its worst (for example, the planned price for steel was 700 yuan per ton while the market price was 1800 yuan per ton) (Zhao, 1999, p. 195).

If price subsidies are a significant cause for deficits and if supply is highly elastic then fiscal stabilization calls for early and speedy price liberalization (Liew *et al.*, 2003). According to their argument, the greater are fiscal deficits (if they are not due to price subsidies) and value of forced savings and smaller are supply elasticities, the longer should be the lag between fiscal and monetary stabilization and price liberalization. From 1985 to 1988, price subsides increased (Jin *et al.*, 2001), as did the fiscal deficit stemming from it. The supply was constrained as a result of the decreasing marginal return from the early reform in agricultural sector on the one hand, and the unsuccessful reform in state-owned industrial sector (as will be discussed on p. 85) on the other. Implementing the price reform under these circumstances was both politically and socially impractical.[4] This dual market provided opportunities for people who had access to state-controlled goods and materials to make large profits by buying them at an officially fixed low price and reselling them at a market-based price. Consequently, it created various distortions and speculative transactions, which have often led to unequal competition as well as official corruption.

Another noticeable case was China's various attempts at the radical SOE reform during the late 1980s and the 1990s. It had been delayed for several times, due to the serious concerns about the social instability that could result from the reform. The SOE reform is sufficiently extensive to cause large increases in unemployment. In December 1986, the 'Bankruptcy Law Concerning the SOEs' was adopted by the NPC. However, the Law was not effectively applied until 1994 due to fears of unemployment and social instability, as China did not have a relatively complete social security system.

The reform on non-performing SOEs was debated once again in the Fifth Plenum of the Fourteenth CCPCC held during September 1995. The outcome was the policy of 'grasping the large and releasing the small'. To 'grasp the large' (*zhuada*) is to turn a select group of 300 out of a list of 1000 already successful large enterprises and enterprise groups into world-class businesses. To 'release the small' (*fangxiao*) is to privatize or to contract out small SOEs or to let them go bankrupt. This policy allows most small SOEs to be sold off to private individuals and the management of those not sold is contracted out (Liew, 1999, p. 93). During the first two years when the government began to release small and non-performing SOEs and to lay off superfluous workers, the major protests organized by workers are reported in the following: (i) more than 10,000 retrenched and retired SOE workers held sit-down protests and demonstrations in April 1997 (Panzhihua city, Sichuan province); (ii) about 100,000 retrenched workers and their relatives protested on the streets against the withdrawal of housing benefits and misappropriation of their retirement funds in June 1997 (Mianyang city, Sichuan province); (iii) 30,000 textile workers protested against non-payment of wages. They interrupted local traffic and surrounded the airport on December 3, 1997 (Jiamusi city, Heilongjiang province); and (iv) 100,000 workers in 4 cities rioted during protests against retrenchments, non-payment of wages, official corruption and other grievances during November–December 1997 (Heilongjiang province).[5]

Notice that since the mid-1990s the CCP and the central government have particularly worried about the increasing number of illegal organizations established to organize protests against the SOE reform.[6] Unlike in the western democratic countries in which protests against government can be regularly found, the abovementioned protests were unusual in the PRC's history. They could easily remind the CCP and central government of the Tian'anmen incident in June 1989. Consequently, they could retard any further efforts on the radical reforms of the SOEs.

We are not able to verify if or to what extent the SOE reform, when implemented earlier, could have been more successful than it has been now. But, arguably, if the substantial ownership reform of the small and rural-based SOEs were introduced in parallel with or immediately following the radial agricultural ownership reform during the early stage (that is, in the late 1970s or the early 1980s), there would have been similar, positive economic performances. The primary reason lies in the fact that the market culture based on private ownership – the main form of ownership before the 1950s – still remained in the memory of most middle-aged SOE workers in China in the early 1980s. The critical role that the retired SOE workers played in the dramatic growth of the township and village-based enterprises (McMillan and Naughton, 1992; and World Bank, 1996, p. 51) indicates that the SOEs and the SOE workers could become more productive if the property right and incentive system went away from those of state-ownership.

## Gradual/partial reform, the unsuccessful cases

Not all gradual/partial reforms performed well in China. The typical unsuccessful examples were the introduction of the responsibility system and the contract system in the SOEs in 1983 and 1986, respectively. These reforms had some positive impacts on SOEs' performance, but overall they still did not achieve the objective of turning SOEs into efficient enterprises. In brief, there are at least the following problems for this system. First, the operating mechanism of the contract system strengthened the vertical one-to-one bargaining relationship between government and firm. It did not strengthen the competitive horizontal relationship between firms, and therefore was not consistent with market-oriented reform (Zhao, 1999, p. 196). Second, it did not guarantee that the SOEs became independent economic identities. Last but not least, the contract did not solve the long-term behavioral problems of the managers and employees. Their behavior was still driven by short-term motivations, impinging on the interests of the owner, the state, and damaging firms' long-term development (Huang, 1999, p. 103).

To understand the characteristics of the Chinese-style reform, one must keep in mind two important facts: first, China's vast territorial size and wide diversity in physical environments have inevitably resulted in great differences in regional economic conditions; second, with China's 1.3 billion population and 56 ethnic groups, most provinces, which are equivalent to a medium-sized country in the rest of the world, are considerable political and economic systems in their own right. The differences between these provinces have long been a defining characteristic of China's politics since in most cases their boundaries have been created over some two thousand years ago (Gottmann, 1973; and Goodman, 1997). Besides, Chinese culture is not homogeneous across provinces, in terms of ethnic and linguistic groups as well as provincial politics. As a result, the chances of the adoption of a common standard and interprovincial coordination between different groups of people are not likely to be enhanced if there are markedly differing religious beliefs and cultural values.

The Chinese-style decentralization of economic authority (as discussed in Chapter 5, p. 1) did not always work well, especially during the early stage of reform. Precisely, it provided less incentives and opportunities for provincial and local governments to make use of the comparative advantages for interregional cooperation in the 1980s than in the 1990s.[7] Since the advent of administrative decentralization, China's national economy had become effectively 'cellularized' into a plethora of semi-autarkic regional enclaves during the 1980s. In order to protect local market and revenue sources, it became common in China that provinces restrict import (export) from (to) other provinces by levying high, if informal, taxes on commodities and by creating non-tariff barriers. Xinjiang autonomous region, for example, effectively banned the import of forty-eight commodities on the grounds that they would harm its domestic economy. Jilin refused to market beer produced in its neighbouring provinces of Heilongjiang and Liaoning. Hunan province prohibited exporting grain to its neighbour, Guangdong province. In some provinces, local authorities established, and provided finance for, a variety of schemes so as to promote the sales of local products. Enterprises from other provinces, however, often had difficulties in finding office spaces, accommodation, or land for their business activities.[8]

Another case is the reform of China's banking system, which is generally recognized to lag far behind China's dramatic moves toward a market economy evident in other sectors. Prior to the beginning of reforms in 1983, the People's Bank of China (PBC), China's central bank, dominated the country's highly centralized financial scene. It not only controlled the money supply, but it also managed all banking and savings activities. In effect, before the reforms the PBC was only an accounting department of the Chinese central government. At the end of 1993, the State Council issued a new plan to spur changes in the monetary and financial system that would strengthen the PBC's grip on the macroeconomic environment, create specialized banks to serve priority sectors, and push the other banks toward becoming true commercial banks. The overall objective was to separate monetary policy from normal banking functions and to convert most banks into truly independent financial entities. However, the PBC remains subservient to the finance ministry and thus cannot refuse to finance government expenditures. Branches of the PBC in the provinces and districts are also subject to the dictates of both PBC and local government officials. As a result, it is very difficult for them to refuse loans to local government entities that demand more and more credit (Xu, 1995).

The 1997 Asian financial crisis, in an instructive way, alerted Chinese leaders to dangers of a weak financial system. Aware of lessons drawn from the Asian financial crisis, China wanted to quicken the pace of banking reform in 1998. The major measure was that ¥270 billion (US$33 billion) in special bonds was issued in 1998 so as to recapitalize the state banks. Then in 1999, it created an asset-management company (AMC) for each of the big four state banks. The AMCs received ¥400 billion (US$48 billion) in seed capital from the Ministry of Finance (MOF) and issued ¥1 trillion (US$121 billion) worth of MOF-guaranteed bonds. They then used these funds to buy ¥1.4 trillion (US$170 billion) of bad loans from the state banks at face value. But the program has failed to cure the banks' woes, since other relevant financial and economic reforms had not been implemented. Since 1998, the percentage of bad loans on the banks' books has not fallen much, and the AMCs have had limited success in recovering or selling off the bad assets. Meanwhile, corporate governance, transparency, and risk management at the state banks have only shown slight improvement (Lo, 2004).

China's gradual/partial open-door policy has serious implications for its legal system and its lack of transparency, and problems of assimilating a non-market economy.[9] For example, about 220 Chinese laws that are incompatible with WTO rules have to be changed (Reti, 2001). Besides, by the WTO requirements, banks, insurance companies, telecommunications and other service industries of the rest of the world will be allowed to operate in China according to the negotiated timetable. The impact may eventually break up the status of monopoly and state control that have existed in China for about a half-century. The new bank reforms starting on December 1, 2003, opening the sector further to foreign competition, have been still too mild and limited in

*Table 5.2*    Pressing banking and financial reforms after access to WTO

| Item | Short-term (2002–05) measures | Long-term (2005–11) measures |
|---|---|---|
| Monetary policy | Liberalizing interest rates for bank deposits and bank loans. Improving indirect policy tools. Abolishing directed (political) lending. | Adopting a fully market-based strategy of demand management. Exploiting new channels of monetary transmission. Adopting policies of greater independent and accountability. |
| Banking | Continuing the commercialization process by allowing more competing and accepting diversified ownership structure. Improving the quality of banks' assets through debt destructing and debt transfer. Increasing operational efficiency while reducing overstaffing and over branching. | Finishing the process of cleaning up banks' balance sheets and introducing uniform capital adequacy ratios based on internationally accepted standards. Giving up majority state ownership. |
| Financial service | Screening and rectifying the numbers and business scope of local trust and investment corporations. Modernizing the payment system. Supporting new financial products while dealing carefully with associated risks. | Streamlining the structure of the financial service industry. Expanding the supply and improving the quality of products. |
| Direct finance | Continuing to develop securities markets by simplifying trading procedures, improving information disclosure procedures, and upgrading the legal framework. | Liberalizing asset prices and allowing the stock market to reflect borrowers' financial conditions and to execute corporate control. |
| Regulation/ supervision | Strengthening prudential supervision. Clarifying and harmonizing operational standards, provision requirements, and accounting rules. Developing a new law for closure and bankruptcy of financial institutions. | Finishing the process of replacing direct state intervention and state protection with a market-oriented regulatory framework. Reconsidering the segmentation of banking, investment, and insurance. |
| External liberalization | Further simplifying the foreign exchange administration. Allowing more exchange rate flexibility. Starting a gradual removal of capital controls. Permitting foreign banks and other financial institutions to enter China, in accordance with the WTO agreement. | Adopting a fully flexible exchange rate regime. Continuing the gradual and cautious removal of capital control and ultimately, if preconditions are met, adopting full capital account convertibility. Allowing foreign banks and other financial institutions to compete on a level playing field with domestic banks. |

*Source*: von Gemert (2001, p. 11).

scope. Pressing banking and financial reforms are needed in both short- and long-terms (see Table 5.2).

Indeed, China is now facing with a dilemma in whether to follow the past tune (that is, the gradual and partial strategy) so as to minimize the risk of macroeconomic transition or to go faster so as to satisfy the WTO requirements with the fixed timetable. According to its WTO accession proposal, China must have put all the above reforms altogether within 3–5 years after 2002. However, it seems that the Chinese government is not prepared; neither is it willing to bear the potential risk of any substantial or radical reforms. One example is the reform of foreign exchange system. As stated earlier on p. 83, China's gradual/partial reform on foreign exchange system has contributed significantly to its robust foreign trade performance on the one hand and the domestic economic stability on the other. But since 1994 when a unitary and floating exchange-rate system was established, there has not had any substantial reform. Obviously, this system is to a large extent determined by the government and that the foreign exchange rate is controlled officially and the central bank is one of the biggest participants in the market.

## Simulating the reform process: a model

> A cat, no matter whether its color is black or white, would be a good one if it catches rats.
>
> Deng Xiaoping (1903–97).

In this section, we try to present a theoretical framework to examine the dynamic behaviors of market reform under different initial and exogenous (domestic and external) conditions. Frankly speaking, there is no single, well-defined political and institutional framework for carrying out market-oriented reforms. For example, in most cases, a market-oriented reform implies a reduction in depth and scope of government participation and interference in an economic activity; in other cases, however, government intervention is necessary (see, for example, Williamson, 1995; Rodrik, 1996). To avoid the ambiguity, we would temporarily put aside the Chinese economy. Instead, we consider a highly simplified CPE which is transformed toward to a market-oriented economic system within a given time period. Specifically, the CPE is characterized by the following assumptions:

I.  The reform scheme may either be accelerated or be reversed, depending on the improvement or deterioration of political stability, respectively.

II.  Political stability is associated with three factors – public satisfaction (as will be defined in Assumption III), social shock resulting
from the reform, and external irritation (which is positively related
to the extent to which the CPE opens its economy to the outside
world).

III.  Population is treated as constant. Public satisfaction is positively
related to the increment of income level.

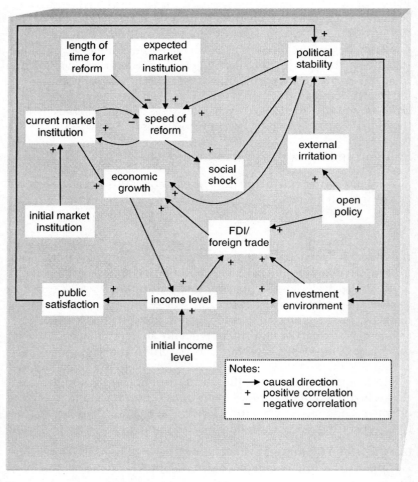

*Figure 5.1*   A simplified model of economic reform

IV. External environment refers to economically marketized and politically democratized economies. The CPE's open-door policy has two effects: economically, it will promote economic growth through foreign trade and FDI inflows; politically, it will affect political stability through external irritation (as defined in Assumption II).

In order to simulate the CPE's reform process and its outcomes under different initial and exogenous conditions, we must identify the correlations between the important factors that can influence the dynamic behaviors of the CPE endogenously. Figure 5.1 shows a simplified model in which the feedback mechanisms are based on the assumptions made above. The model can further be roughly quantified by various linear equations, as shown in Appendix III. The exogenous (policy) variables and the initial conditions of the CPE are set as the following:

(i)   The length of time for reform ($T$) is fixed at two values: $T=2$ (it denotes 'big bang reform'); $T=10$ (it denotes 'gradual reform').

(ii)  The stock of initial market institution ($I_0$) ranges from 0.0 (that is, there is no market institution at the start of reform) to 1.0 (that is, there is a 100 per cent share of market institution at the start of reform).

(iii) The initial income (per capita and total) is set as $Y_0=\$100$.

(iv)  External policy ($O$) has two values: $O=1$ (it denotes 'open-door policy'); and $O=0$ (it denotes 'closed-door policy').[10]

To evaluate how institutional evolutions are influenced by reform strategies and initial conditions and external policies, we run our model under different values of $I_0$, $O$ and $T$. The simulated results (shown in Figure 5.2) may help us to derive the following corollaries.

*Corollary 1.* Initial institutional conditions decide the extent to which a reform is successfully implemented. Specifically, the initial stock of market-oriented institutions encourages the smooth implementation of the reform; while the initial stock of centrally planning institutions retards the smooth implementation of the reform.

When looking at the remarkable differences between the Chinese and Russian reforms, one must not ignore the different initial institutional conditions of these two countries. Prior to reform, the centrally planning system lasted relatively a short period of time in China (that is, from the late 1950s to the late 1970s) compared to that in the former Soviet Union (FSU) (that is, from the early 20th century to the

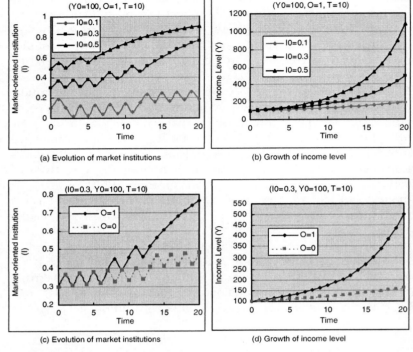

*Figure 5.2*   The simulated results of the CPE's dynamic behaviors

late 1980s). As a result, the capitalist ideology and market culture still had a strong base in China *vis-à-vis* the FSU.[11]

*Corollary 2.* External environment plays an important role in a market-oriented reform. Specifically, an open-door policy encourages implementation of a reform; while a closed-door policy retards the implementation.

Haggard and Webb (1994) have found that international factors influence reform through a number of channels, such as the prospect of trade concessions and agreements, conditionality and ideas brought by external advisers and technocrats trained abroad. The significant role of the open-door policy in market-oriented reform can be witnessed by the Chinese experience. China's application to get access to the GATT/WTO lasted for 16 years from 1986 to 2002. After each of the long-running negotiations, China's centrally planned system on foreign trade had a gradual reform toward the market-oriented economic system. During the 1990s, almost all major Chinese reforms on foreign trade system were marked by the WTO accession negotiations (Chi, 2000).

*Corollary 3.* Reform strategy matters in the whole reform process.

Consider now a reform program consisting of two reform measures that can be carried out simultaneously or sequentially. Suppose that the economic outcome of the full reform is in most circumstances better than that of each partial reform measure. Without considering the cost of implementation, a big bang reform may have an advantage over a gradual one.[12] However, once reforms are turned back sometimes due to the political and economic uncertainties (as defined in Assumption I), the reversal is more costly for the full reform than the partial one, which means reversing the full reform costs more than reversing a single partial reform measure.[13] With regard to the case of the simplified CPE, we can investigate how the economic differences between the gradualism and the big bang are related to the initial market institutions. In Figure 5.3, the vertical axis is represented by ratio of the income level of the gradualism (T=10) to the big bang (T=2), that is, $Y_{T=10}/Y_{T=2}$.[14] Obviously, gradualism is better than big bang if $Y_{T=10}/Y_{T=2}>1$, while big bang is better than gradualism other-

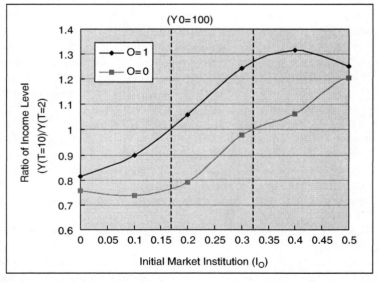

*Figure 5.3* How reform strategy matters under different conditions

*Table 5.3*    The CPE's optimal reform strategies: simulated results

| External policy (O) | Open-door policy (O=1) | Closed-door policy (O=0) |
|---|---|---|
| *Initial market institutions ($I_0$)* | | |
| $I_0 < 1/6$ | Big Bang | Big Bang |
| $1/6 < I_0 < 1/3$ | Gradualism | Big Bang |
| $I_0 > 1/3$ | Gradualism | Gradualism |

*Source*: Derived from Figure 5.3.

wise. Since $Y_{T=10}/Y_{T=2}$ equals to 1 when $I_0$ is around 1/6 for open-door policy (O=1) and when $I_0$ is around $1/3$ for closed-door policy (O=0) in Figure 5.3, we can derive a set of optimal strategies for reform under different initial and external conditions (see Table 5.3). Consequently, Corollary 3 includes the following:

*Corollary 3.1*. When there is only a very small stock of initial market-oriented institutions, big bang is better than gradualism.

*Corollary 3.2*. When there is a large stock of initial market-oriented institutions, gradualism is better than big bang.

*Corollary 3.3*. When there is a moderate stock of initial market-oriented institutions, external environment matters in the optimization of reform strategies. Specifically, gradualism is better than big bang under open-door policy, while big bang is better than gradualism under closed-door policy.

It is reasonable to assume that the CPE has relatively weak market institutions at the beginning of the market-oriented reform, while at the late stage its market institutions will be improved as a result of the reform implemented during the early stage. Consequently, Corollary 3 can be roughly translated into the following:

*Corollary 4.1*. During the early stage of reform, big bang is better than gradualism.

*Corollary 4.2*. During the late stage of reform, gradualism is better than big bang.

*Corollary 4.3*. During the middle stage of reform, big bang is better than gradualism under closed-door policy, while gradualism is better than big bang under open-door policy.

## Interest groups, stakeholders and reform

In this section, reform is allowed to be determined endogenously. Our task is to find how the players and stakeholders interact with each other during the whole reform process and how they have decisively influenced the reform outcomes. For simplicity of our analysis, we assume that the CCP is the only player (policymaker), which can be further divided into different cliques (such as radicals and conservatives) in different reform period. Interest groups can be defined as collections of individuals who share a specific common interest. Various interest groups can overlap. For instance, the same individual can be an entrepreneur and a university professor. Stakeholders then are members of an interest group whose interests are affected by a particular decision.

The evidence described below will demonstrate how the Chinese-style reform has been evolved from the collusion of the CCP radicals and conservatives (during the early stage of reform) to the collusion of the political, economic and cultural elites (during the late stage of reform) as well as how this evolution has influenced the outcomes of the Chinese reform *per se*.

### Radicals and conservatives in the early reforms

To understand the implications of the incentives for the implementation of a reform in China, we must make a point of the relation between the CCP radicals and conservatives.[15] Both Deng Xiaoping and his senior supporters in power had been victims in the Cultural Revolution (1966–76) during which Mao criticized them for economic liberalism. The special event of Cultural Revolution made them – regardless of their liberal or conservative ideology – must unite, or at least must not challenge each other in mutually tolerable matters during the early period of reform.[16]

An initial challenge facing the Chinese leadership was to provide for a rational and efficient governing system to support economic development. In pursuit of that goal, the cult of personality surrounding Mao Zedong was unequivocally condemned and replaced by a strong emphasis on collective leadership. An example of this new emphasis was the CCP's restoration in February 1980 of its Secretariat, which had been suspended since 1966. The new CCP constitution, adopted in 1982, abolished the post of CCPCC chairman – a powerful post held by Mao Zedong for more than four decades, thereby providing a degree of balance between the CCP radicals and conservatives.

The striking feature of the Chinese reform during the 1980s was the collusive game between the radicals and conservatives. In considering a reform strategy, the radicals must take into account not only the benefit from the reform but also the political cost stemming from the possibility of losing the coalition with the conservatives. Since deterrence implies cost, the reform strategy that both players (radicals and conservatives) would find optimal to cooperate does not equate the marginal economic benefit with the marginal economic cost. Instead, a player's optimal strategy of reform equates the marginal economic cost with the marginal economic and political costs. In other words, it is political cost that creates a wedge between the efficient and optimal strategies of reform. Although the strategy with a faster reform maximizes the radicals' gross payoff, it does not maximize its net payoff. The radicals would find it optimal to have a strategy with a slower reform in which the marginal economic gains from cooperation equal the marginal political and economic costs.[17] For example, Li Peng's long-lasting political career as premiership is one of the outcomes resulting from the collusion of the radicals and conservatives. In 1987, Li became a member of the Politburo's powerful Standing Committee, and a year later Deng Xiaoping picked Li to succeed Zhao Ziyang as premier after Zhao became the CCPCC general secretary. The choice was unusual because Li Peng did not appear to share Deng's advocacy of economic reform. But Deng must compromise with the conservatives.[18] However, this might be an early case of the CCPCC's *Baiping* game (see Box 5.1).

As a matter of fact, during the massive mandatory retirement program which was facilitated by a one-time buyout strategy (as stated on pp. 78–80), the outgoing CCP officials were partially compensated both economically and politically. For example, a special name was coined for this kind of retirement, *lixiu* – which means literally 'to leave the post and rest'. After *lixiu*, retired officials continued to enjoyed all their former political privileges, such as reading government circulars of the same confidentiality level. Some served as special counselors for their successors. As economic compensations, they could keep using their official cars with chauffeurs and security guards. In addition, officials under *lixiu* received an extra month of wages each year and extra housing that their children and grandchildren were entitled to enjoy after their death (Li, 1998, p. 394). As discussed in Chapter 5, p. 79, without that reform, in which many younger cadres were able to play an important role, the reforms that followed afterwards would have been impossible.

---

*Box 5.1*    Playing with *Baiping*

Since the late 1990s, a new Chinese terminology – Baiping – has been popularized in mainland China. The Chinese term 'Baiping' is composed of two Chinese characters – 'bai' (place, put, arrange, etc.) and 'ping' (flat, uniform, fair, etc.). The original meaning of Baiping is 'to put flat; or to arrange uniform.' The term had been so informal before the 21st century that even the 1999 edition of *Cihai* – the largest and the most influential Chinese dictionary published by Shanghai Cishu Publishing House – didn't collect it. Notice that the frequently used Baiping has extended from its original meaning to that of 'to treat fairly; to compromise; to tradeoff; to punish.' It has been so popular that even elementary students have been using it in their oral communications.

After the death of Deng Xiaoping in 1997, Jiang Zemin exerted a powerful hold on the CCPCC, deftly playing its various wings against each other. In this scenario, Li Peng, the eighth NPC Chairman, held the CCPCC's No. 2 post, higher than that of Zhu Rongji – the State Council Premier – during the 1998–2003 term. It was the first in the PRC's history that NPC Chairman held a political rank higher than the Premiership. Moreover, the heads of major non-Communist parties and other non-party prominent personages were selected as state leaders with the titles of vice Chairpersons of the NPC and Chinese People's Political Consultative Congress (CPPCC) in exchange of their support of the CCP as the permanent ruler of the state. For example, as for the 2003–08 term, China's state-level leaders include nine standing members of the CCPCC Politburo (some of whom also held the posts of President, Premier, the NPC and CPPCC Chairmen), and dozens of vice Chairpersons of the NPC and of the CPPCC (too many to account!).

---

Past reform events shows that the institutional improvement towards a market-oriented system followed a non-linear pattern in China. From the late 1970s to the early 1990s, China's reform indicated a recurring pattern of reform and retrenchment identified by a four stage: 'decentralization immediately followed by disorder, disorder immediately followed by concentralization, concentralization followed by rigidity, and rigidity followed by decentralization,' a cycle of 'decentralization (*fang*) – disorder – concentralization (*shou*) – rigidity.'[19] As a matter of fact, the shou-fang circle represents the dynamic process of the political games between radicals and conservatives. Specifically, the fang (decentralization) was initiated by the radicals, while the shou (concentralization) was insisted by the conservatives. As a result of their very nature (as stated at the beginning of this section), both radicals and conservatives have compromised with each other's initiatives during most of the reform era.

When dealing with the early reforms, it is necessary to mention other stakeholders as well as their attitudes towards reforms. Farmers and urban workers – both benefited from the reform-driven economic growth – did not oppose the CCP and the reform in particular. Intellectuals, most of whom had received westernized training and been seriously mistreated during the Cultural Revolution. They had a strong desire for western democracy *vis-à-vis* China's old political system. On the other hand, however, the CCP elites, especially the CCP conservatives, could not at all accept a totally western-oriented reform (Kang, 2002). Since the radical reformers had been much less powerful than the CCP conservatives at the period when most CCP seniors were still alive, their attempt at uniting with intellectual elite failed during Tian'anmen incident in June 1989.

It seems likely that, as a result of the disappearance of the CCP seniors and the conservatives on the one hand and the emergence of more young and western-learning officials on the other, the Chinese reform should have become more and more radical since the mid-1990s. What have happened since then?

### Political, economic and cultural elites in the late reforms

As the initiation and sustainability of a reform requires political, economic and cultural supports, identifying interest groups and stakeholders of the reform in general but especially those who are politically (and otherwise) active as allies and opponents of reform is an important step toward successful completion of the reform. An important distinction is whether interest groups and stakeholders are organized – in other words, whether they pursue their common interest jointly in a coordinated fashion. It is nature to believe that stakeholders will exert pressure on policymakers. This, however, needs not to be always the case, as not all stakeholders are organized (Fidrmuc and Noury, 2003). Because organized interest groups are better informed than the citizenry at large, they can provide key personalities (the government officials, legislators) with intelligence of various kinds.

Starting in the mid-1980s, the bureaucratic reform generated a large surplus of government officials. At the same time, many government agencies began establishing business entities, and bureaucrats became managers of these businesses. As a result, a phenomenon that later came to be known as *xiahai* ('jumping into the ocean'). Since the early 1990s, *xiahai* has been an immensely popular phenomenon among Chinese government officials.[20] By joining the business world, the former bureaucrats obtain much higher economic payoffs as well as personal freedom, despite being exposed to more economic uncertainty. On the other hand, there is high demand for those bureaucrats, since in the half-reformed economy many nonstate enterprises need their knowledge and skills to deal with the remaining government regulations.

Since the 16th National Congress of the CCP, which was held in Beijing in November 2002, the CCP membership has been formally open to China's business elite. The removal of the clause in the CCP's constitution that officially prohibits private businessmen from becoming party members and serving in the government is intended to bring the CCP constitution into line with the reality of the party's character and social composition as it prepares to accelerate market reforms. In a rambling opening address to the Congress, Jiang Zemin articulated the class interests of the new Chinese elite. He called for the Beijing regime to persevere in opening up to the capitalist market and declared that the CCP should protect the 'legitimate rights and interests' of businessmen and property owners (Jiang, 2002). The formal opening of the CCP to business layers in 2002 represented a turning point. The fact that Jiang's 'Three Represents' theory formalizes what has already emerged was highlighted by the year 2002 *Forbes* magazine list of China's 100 richest multi-millionaires. A quarter declared they were CCP members (Chan, 2002). In addition, many Chinese CEOs of private companies or transnational corporations also have connections with the CCP.

Since the mid-1990s, cultural elites (including noted intellectuals, popular entertainers and ethnic minority-based social elites) have been getting close to political and economic elites in China.[21] The factors resulting in the collusion of the political and cultural elites might include the following. First, the disappearance of the CCP elders has weakened the power of the conservatives since the early 1990s, while the younger political leaders are usually with higher educations than their predecessors. Second, after Tian'anmen incident, radical intellectuals were seriously retaliated, most of them either fleeing the country or disappearing from academic field. Third, the changing external environment (such as the collapse of the former Soviet Union followed by the unsuccessful big-bang reform of Russia and the U.S. transferring from standing against the CCP to against China) helped most if not all intellectuals to cooperate with the CCP and the government.

Several books have portrayed the post-Tian'anmen period as one of intense political disagreement (Fewsmith, 1999; and Lam, 1999). Certainly, this was true until the mid-1990s. Yet, disagreements since then have been expressed more and more through non-sanctioned means by non-sanctioned actors. The elite battles evident today are based on illegitimate end-running, not legitimate contestation. Thus the politics of contestation – legitimate competition within the structures of the polity properly used by a range of agreed actors – remains absent. The earnestness of contestation in the early reform era has been replaced by the anomie of compliance or the intrigue of crypto-politics in the post-reform era (Gilley, 2004, p. 121).

Among China's rural peasantry and the industrial working class, a seething hostility is building up over official corruption, poverty, the loss of services, unemployment and the widening income gap between rich and poor. After several years of factional debate within the CCP, a consensus has emerged that the lesson to be drawn from the Tian'anmen events is that the regime must build a solid base among the urban upper and middle-classes, while making no democratic concessions to the masses (Chan, 2002). The government believed it could weather the opposition of workers and peasants by keeping them like 'scattered sand', lacking any national organization or coherent political program (Kang, 2002). Commenting on the sentiment of the political establishment, Kang (2002) points out: 'There is a stable alliance between the political, economic and intellectual elite of China. The main consequence is that the elite won't challenge the CCP and the government. The economic elite love money, not democracy. Their vanity will also be satisfied as the CCP has promised them party membership and government positions.'

How has the Chinese reform been linked with the collusion of the political, economic, and cultural elites? First of all, faced with the failure of the radical reforms in the former USSR, the political elite – no matter how radical they had been during the past period of reform – has become rational over time. Precisely, they would rather choose more gradual/partial (or alternatively, less radical) reform strategy than they did in the 1980s. Second, the political, economic and cultural elites have increasingly become beneficiaries of the existing system

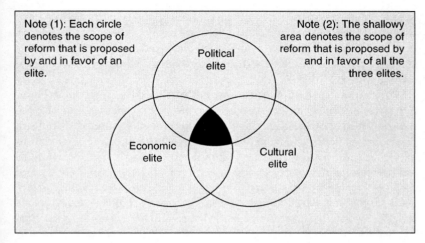

Note (1): Each circle denotes the scope of reform that is proposed by and in favor of an elite.

Note (2): The shallowy area denotes the scope of reform that is proposed by and in favor of all the three elites.

Political elite

Economic elite

Cultural elite

*Figure 5.4*    Collective actions of the Chinese elites on reforms

that was based on the past gradual and partial reforms. As a result, there will be less and less incentive for them to see any (radical and thorough) political and economic reforms that could affect their existing benefits.[22] Last but not least, in contrast to the reforms that had been merely decided by the political elite (including both CCP radicals and conservatives) before the mid-1990s (as discussed in Chapter 5, p. 95), the reforms that have been decided by the political elite in cooperation with the economic and cultural elites since then have been far more limited in scope (as shown in Figure 5.4).

## Can the Chinese-style reforms be sustained?

It is almost certain that the Chinese-style reform would not be reversed in the foreseen future. This is not only because the Chinese-style reform has become a win-win game for all who are in power, but also it has made the Chinese economy more and more dependent on the outside world. Since China's entrance into the WTO in November 2002, external stakeholders (such as international financial organizations, foreign owned enterprises) have been increasingly influencing the Chinese economic reform. However, the collective actions of these stakeholders on the Chinese reforms are much more complicated than those of the Chinese domestic stakeholders. For example, with regard to the reform on the current exchange-rate system under which the Chinese currency has been, as generally recognized, devaluated, there are two different voices from the outside world. While countries having large trade deficits with China have requested the Chinese currency to be more freely decided by the market, their overseas enterprises in China have benefited significantly from this currency devaluation by exporting their made-in-China products to the outside world.

While China's reform has been strongly driving its economic growth, it has also derived a series of socioeconomic problems. Prior to the reform, China was an egalitarian society in terms of income distribution. The policy of 'letting some people get rich first' (rang yibufen reb xian fu qilai) was adopted to overcome egalitarianism in income distribution, to promote efficiency with strong incentives and to ultimately realize common prosperity based on an enlarged pie. But this policy has quickly enlarged income gaps between different groups of people (see Chapter 6, p. 128). By openly proclaiming itself a party of the 'economic elite' that has benefited from its free market agenda, the CCP has been hoping to consolidate a reliable base of support for its continued rule. With its pro-growth polices, ban on independent trade unions and low environmental standards, the CCP has created an advantageous atmosphere for the economic elite to make money. Policies so favour the rich and business that China's economic program, in the words of one western ambassador, resembles 'the dream of the American Republican Party'[23]

China's big surge in economic inequalities is not the only unwanted result of the Chinese-style reform. The one-party political system lacks the informational and incentive roles of democracy that, working mainly through open public discussion, can be pivotally important for the reach of social and public policies. The worsening of social and human progress from 1996 to 2002 is a typical example (see Figure 5.5). Sen (2004), for example, presents an interesting comparison between China and an Indian state, Kerala:

> At the time of economic reforms, when China had a life expectancy of about 67 years or so, the Indian state of Kerala had a similar figure. By now, however, Kerala's life expectancy of 74 years is very considerably above China's 70. Going further, if we look at specific points of vulnerability, the infant mortality rate in China has declined very slowly since the economic reforms, whereas it has continued to fall very sharply in Kerala. While Kerala had roughly the same infant mortality rate as China – 37 per thousand – at the time of the Chinese reforms in 1979, Kerala's present rate, below 14 per thousand, is less than half of China's 30 per thousand (where it has stagnated over the last decade).

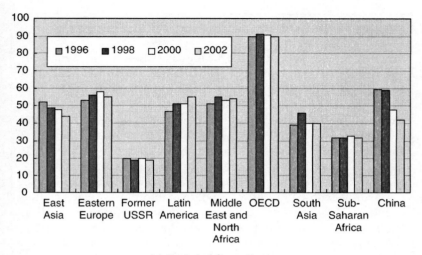

(a) Control of Corruption

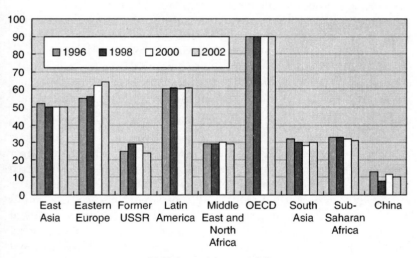

(b) Voice and Accountability

*Source*: www.worldbank.org/wdi/governance/govdata2002/index.html

*Figure 5.5*  Social and political capacities, China and the world (1996–2002)

---

*Box 5.2*　What does the SARS crisis mean?

From November 2002 to 2003, Severe Acute Respiratory Syndrome (SARS) infected over 8000 people in 30 countries and killed more than 500. Beyond the human toll, it was wreaking significant economic damage across Asia. Besides Hong Kong, which was among the worst hit, GDP growth rates in Taiwan, Singapore and Thailand were also lowered in 2003. Nowhere was SARS having more impact than on mainland China, where the disease started.

Yet the greatest impact of the SARS crisis may be on China's antiquated political system. Chinese mismanagement of the outbreak has plainly exposed just how far political reform has lagged behind economic development. Beijing's long concealment of the truth is exposing political fault lines by simultaneously weakening the economy, damaging the government's credibility. The crisis has undermined traditional supporters, aggravating old demographic strains, and emboldening detractors to more assertively protest government policy. While growing pressure from a more demanding public and an increasingly interdependent world has forced China to reevaluate its political and socioeconomic policies, the extent of any resulting political reform depend on whether the enhanced incentives for accountability and transparency among public officials override the traditional incentives for party and factional loyalty.

---

Since the beginning of its economic reforms, China has increasingly benefited from global interdependence and the modern world's free flow of goods, capital, and people. However, with those benefits the responsibilities of accountability and transparency also come. China's 'two-in-one' party-state system has exposed the dearth of political dynamics. The severe acute respiratory syndrome (SARS) epidemic spread throughout China in April 2003 exposed some of China's institutional weakness (see Box 5.2). As China continues to integrate with the world economy and accepts other global values, pressures for political reform mount.

## Concluding remarks

This chapter explores the elements underpinning the design and implementation of the Chinese economic reform from 1978 to 2003.

It provides an explanation for the causes and timing of the major reform programs, as well as for how the success and failure of the reform efforts were associated with the initial conditions and the reform strategies.

The importance of initial conditions and strategies for economic reforms has been noted (Fischer and Gelb, 1991; and De Melo *et al.* 1997). Problems on such issues as how they affect the final results of economic reforms however still remain unresolved (Campos and Coricelli, 2002, p. 828). The analytic narrative of the political economic events shows that the efficiency of China's reform depended on: (i) the initial institutional conditions (ii) the external environment, and (iii) the reform strategy. We argue that a radical reform tends to be more efficient than a gradual/partial one at the early stage (the late 1970s and the early 1980s), while a gradual/partial reform tends to be more efficient than a radical one at the late stage. Finally, we find that from 1978 to 2003 the Chinese-style reform has been evolved from the collusion of the CCP radicals and conservatives to that of the political, economic and cultural elites, at the cost of sacrificing the benefit of the rest of the people.

In comparison to those of Eastern Europe and the former Soviet Union, reforms in China have some distinct characteristics. First, the degree to which the economic system derived form the former Soviet Union exerted influence on the Chinese economy varied from sector to sector. The sector that was most influenced was the industrialized sector of the national economy, while the influence on the disaggregated agricultural sector and small industries was less. Second, the economic reforms in China started when China was regarded as a quasi-militaristic model of communism (Zhao, 1999, p. 186), which was different from the reforms in Eastern Europe. Third, the economic reform in China preceded political reform.

Except for a few cases in which reform followed an approach similar to that of big bang, most Chinese economic reforms can be identified as of gradualism. The Chinese-type reform introduced since 1978 has so far exhibited remarkable results. Particularly praiseworthy are the facts that the Chinese-type reform has avoided the output collapse characteristic of transitions in other former centrally planned economies and generated unprecedented increases in the level of living standards across the country. For the last two decades, China has successfully transformed its centrally planned system and, in particular, achieved a faster economic growth than any other socialist or former socialist countries in the world. However, China's unusual reform experience might not be generalizable to other transition economies, since it has been shaped by a set of unique initial conditions. A particularly intriguing and understudied initial condition is the legacy of the Great Famine (1959–61) and the Cultural Revolution (1966–76), which not only boosted Deng Xiaoping's credibility and authority as a reformer, but it also set up a foundation for the smooth of implementation of agricultural and bureaucratic reforms. Our narrative is developed in the specific context of the Chinese economy in the reform era. It does not afford general tests on a series of other cases.

In short, during most of the past two decades, China's reform has achieved two objectives at the same time: to improve economic efficiency by unleashing the standard forces of incentives and competition on the one hand; and to make the reform a win-win game and thus interest compatible for those in power on the other (Qian, 2002). And they take into consideration of China's specific political and cultural conditions. With its economic achievements, the Chinese reform is rarely questioned today. However it still remained problematic in social and political perspectives throughout the reform era. Ironically, China's economic growth was obtained at the cost of a retardation of political reforms, not to mention worsening income inequalities as well as other social problems.

Nevertheless, we believe that the Chinese government would have been quite familiar with Hanfei's (280–233 BC) story as stated at the beginning of this chapter, and that they do already learn something useful from the death of Duke Cai!

# 6
# A Multiregional Economic Comparison

A man from the state of Zheng wanted to buy a pair of shoes. He measured his foot and put the measurement on a chair. When he set out for the market he forgot to bring it along. It was after he had found the pair he wanted that this occurred to him. 'I forgot the measurement,' said he. He went home to get it but when he returned the market had broken up and he did not get his shoes after all. 'Why didn't you try on the shoes with your feet?' someone asked. 'I would rather trust the measurement than trust myself,' he replied.

Hanfei (280–233 BC)

## About statistical data

The lack of high-quality and comparable cross-section data is always the major hurdle in the study of multiregional economic issues, particularly in the CPEs. During the pre-reform period, China only published a fragmentary set of data on such indicators as national income, GVSP, GVAO and GVIO, the reliability of which, however, is not certain. The recent research environment has been increasingly improved, along with the transformation of the Chinese economy from the centrally planned system to a market-oriented system. Since the early 1980s, an increasingly complete set of data on regional economic performances have been released, as shown in Table 6.1. Regardless of this progress, many problems, however, still exist when one tries to apply the officially published data to compare the Chinese economy multiregionally.

Since the mid-1980s, China has started compiling national income statistics according to the United Nations' SNA.[1] Many theoretical and

*Table 6.1*   Main sources for China's statistical data

| Title | Years | Editor(s) | Publisher |
|---|---|---|---|
| China Statistical Yearbook | 1981–99 | SSB | CSP |
| | 2000– | NBS | CSP |
| A Compilation of Historical Statistical Materials of China's Provinces, Autonomous Regions and Municipalities (1949–89) | 1949–89 | SSB (1990) Hsueh et al. (1993) | CSP WVP |
| Almanac of China's Economy | 1981– | EMP | |
| China Economic Science Yearbook | 1986–89 | Xiao et al. | ESP |
| | 1990– | Li et al. | CSP |
| China Industrial Economic Statistical Yearbook | 1988– | SSB | CSP |
| China Yearbook for Energy Statistics | 1986–92 | SSB | CSP |
| | 1993– | SETC | CSP |
| Price Yearbook of China | 1990– | ECPYC | CPP |

*Notes*: NBS=National Bureau of Statistics of China; SSB=State Statistical Bureau; CSP=China Statistics Press; EMP=Economics and Management Press; ESP=Economic Science Press; SETC=State Economic and Trade Commission; ECPYC=editing committee of *Price Yearbook of China*; CPP=China Price Press; WVP=Westview Press.

practical problems on how to adopt the SNA to Chinese economic accounting, however, still remain unsolved. For instance, the sum of the regional GDPs may not equal the national GDP published by the SSB, the reason for which is that the statistical data compiled by the SSB are derived from the records of the various ministries in charge of their related sectors whereas the regional statistical data are compiled by the regional statistical bureaux.[2]

The compilation of the GDP data left many unpersuaded in China, especially under the dual pricing system. With the exception of the data on the tertiary sector, the transformation of net material product (NMP) data to the corresponding GDP data were simply devised by the SSB and, therefore, some question whether the GDP data may be arrived at by multiplying the NMP by some conversion factors. In fact, since socialist accounting system does not take into account output value of service sector, historical records of this sector were very fragmentary. China has published the GDP indices at constant prices with 1978 being the base year. The GDP data at constant prices are inextricably linked to the real NMP data collected by the old system. Unlike

Western countries that derive real GDP using a system of price indices, the basic production units at the lowest level of the statistical reporting system are responsible for computing the real output value based on a catalogue of fixed prices (*bubian jia*) handed down from above. The raw data are then reported to the higher level of the system to be further aggregated. Many analysts argue that problems may arise in this reporting process of the compilation of GDP data.[3]

There is another question: should real or nominal GDP/NMP data be used for a multiregional comparison of the Chinese economy? Ideally, the adjusted GDP/NMP based on the PPP method in the sprit of Wolf (1985) and Summers and Heston (1991, pp. 327–68) should be used in China because of the vast range of natural and social environments and varying price levels and inflation rates across the country. Unfortunately, few such efforts have been made on the measurement of China's regional GDPs using the PPP methodology due to the lack of sufficient and up-to-date information and data. Hsueh (1994a, pp. 22–56) modifies the nominal NMP data of 29 provinces using the 1980's fixed prices of industrial and agricultural products of which Beijing's relative price index is assumed to be 100 in 1981, while the data on national income (NI) of the remaining provinces are converted by their Beijing-based price levels respectively. Hsueh's attempt to estimate China's NMP, although heroic, is surely controversial and will leave many unpersuaded, particularly when the provinces' industrial structures differ greatly from one another.

Difficulties may arise from the multiregional economic comparison between the pre-reform period during which China was virtually a CPE and the post-reform period during which China has been gradually approaching to a market economy. In market economies, GNP is the total value of all final products and services generated and national income is the total of all incomes received by all factors in production during a defined period of time. In the CPEs, however, the national income accounts record only productive activities carried out in their territories, rather than incomes received by their residents. China's national income accounts during the pre-reform period were virtually based on the MPS, whose most important aggregate is NMP. The NMP comprehensively covers value added in the 'material' sectors of production. The sum of the outputs of all separately enumerated production units multiplied by relevant prices of outputs is called gross value of social product (GVSP). As GVSP includes also the values of intermediate products which are simply the material costs for consecutive production units, values of products were counted more than once. Obviously, the use of the GVSP concept might result in a series of negative effects particularly when using it as an indicator to evaluate multiregionally the sizes of the economies, as a part of the GVSP is contributed by intermediate products that are never meaningful to the social welfare no matter how large it is. The national income represents the sum of net product (value added) of all separately enumerated branches of the economy during a given period. In terms of value, it is equivalent to the value of the total social product within the time period minus the value of the means of production consumed during that period; in terms of materials, it is equivalent to the total social product (including means of production and means of consumption) within the given period minus the means of production consumed during that period.[4] The national income was only created in China by material production sectors, such as industry, mining, agriculture, forestry, animal husbandry, building construction, and service trades that were of a productive nature and carried out such activities as assembly, processing and repairs. However, it ignored the contributions from non-productive labours, particularly in such non-material spheres as banking, insurance, science, education, culture, health, administration, military, and so on.

With regard to most official publications that can be taken as they exist, economic data with political implications such as income distribution, inflation, credit rationing, shadow interest rates, use of foreign capital, and military expenditure, and so on are, at least partially, under government control, they had been so particularly before the early 1990s. Furthermore, the decline of professional ability and job ethics of some local officials in charge of the collection and processing of economic data could largely devalue the quality of data. For instance, it is not uncommon for rural industrial enterprises to report nominal output under the rubric of output at constant prices; government cadres and business officers in rural areas whose promotion is partly based on agricultural and industrial growth may falsify the statistical data by enlarging the output valuation.[5] Therefore, some care should be taken in the use of these published time series data.

In addition, some cares should be taken when one uses the official data to estimate and compare China's economic performances for the pre- and post-reform periods during which different statistical systems were employed.

## Macroeconomic indicators

### General situation

Briefly, China's macroeconomy has experienced dramatic changes during the past decades (see Figure 6.1), which includes a steady

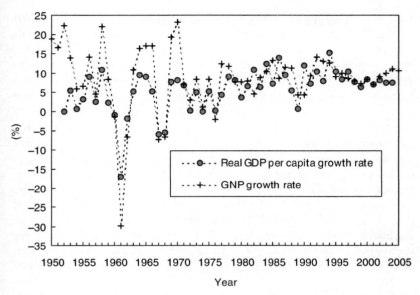

*Notes*: GNP growth rates from 1952 to 1977 are represented by national income growth rates (SSB, 1996); the real GDP per capita growth rates are based on Heston *et al.* (2006).

*Figure 6.1*　China's economic growth (1950–2005)

growth in the First FYP (1953–57), a short leap forward followed by a sudden economic disaster between 1958–62, a rapid growth period (1963–65), a chaotic period stemming from the Cultural Revolution movement (1966–76), a fast growth period (1977– ) during the post-reform era with a few exceptions in 1981 and 1989–90. Particularly praiseworthy is that economic growth in China has sustained at an average rate of about 10 per cent annually since 1978 and has been among the highest of the dynamic nations during the same period. It is approximately three times that of the developed nations, more than double that of India, whose conditions are similar to those of China, and even larger than that of the NIEs such as South Korea, Taiwan, Hong Kong, Singapore, and so on.

China's GNP has already been one of the largest in the world, behind the US, Japan, Germany, and France. Although China's total GNP is large, its per capita GNP is lower than that of South Korea, Malaysia, and Thailand, but higher than that of other neighbouring nations such as India, Mongolia, North Korea and Vietnam.[6] Besides, according to the World Bank standard, China has just move from the least developed economy to a lower-middle-income economy by per capita GNP.[7] It should be noted that, however, if it is calculated by the PPP rates, China's economic size would be much larger than that is measured by the current exchange rate. Table 6.2 gives some different estimates on the per capita GNP/GDP in accordance to the PPP and exchange rate conversion methods. Generally, even though they differ greatly, the per capita GDPs adjusted by PPP rates are approximately two to four times that measured by the exchange rate. Of course, the optimistic estimations of Chinese GDP have not been widely accepted, due to incomplete price statistics.[8] Nevertheless, it is unbelievable that the gaps of real living standards between China and the advanced nations are as large as that of the per capita GNPs in US dollars between them.

Arguably, the Chinese economy could have been underestimated if the international statistical standards are applied. For example, according to the evidence released by the SSB, China's actual GDP could have been over 30 per cent larger than the current figure, which is contributed by (1) real estate sector (10 per cent) (2) government, science

---

*Box 6.1*   Underground economics

The size of underground economic activities varies enormously from country to country. Obviously, it is impossible to get precise estimates because, by their very nature, the details have been largely hidden from the authorities. Nevertheless, the following factors determine the size of the underground economy (Sloman, 1991, p. 574):

1. The level of taxes and regulations. The greater their level, the greater the incentive for people to evade the system and 'go underground'.
2. The determination of the authorities to catch up with evaders, and the severity of the punishments for those found out.
3. The size of the service sector relative to the manufacturing sector. It is harder for the authorities to detect the illicit activities of motor mechanics, gardeners and window cleaners than the output of cars, bricks and soap.
4. The proportion of the population that is self-employed. It is much easier for the self-employed to evade taxes than it is for people receiving a wage where taxes are deducted at source.

and technology, education, culture, and health care sectors (4 per cent) (3) self-service within enterprises (3 per cent) (4) rural construction (2.2 per cent) and other rural economic activities (2 per cent), and (5) national defense and underground economic activities (10 per cent).[9]

## Estimation of GNP for the pre-reform period

Since the founding the PRC, China has adopted two different concepts (NI/GVSP and GNP/GDP) to measure its national and regional economic performances. As explained earlier, the concept of NI (national income) deviates from that of GNP *ex facto*, because the former is based on the traditional MPS used by most CPEs, while the latter is based on the SNA used by the market economies. The PWT v6.2 provides a consistently estimated time-series data for China's per capita GDP under constant prices (Heston *et al.*, 2006), but it does not include provincial and regional data. Therefore, it is useful for us to estimate China's GNP/GDP for the pre-reform period during which the MPS was introduced.

Different approaches have been suggested to estimate the GNP for the CPEs. Marea (1985, pp. 15–6 and 27–119), for example, presents five alternative approaches. The first approach entails building a more or less complete set of national accounts from disaggregated data, and then computing GNP as the sum of value added in the production sectors. This approach needs production data aggregated according to some sort of labour cost valuation. The second approach is scaling up from NMP to GNP on the basis of an average relationship found to hold for either other CPEs or market economies. Differences in economic systems as well as in qualities and levels of development must be taken into consideration. The third approach relates to scaling up from NMP by adding net value added in the non-material sectors plus depreciation, and otherwise adjusting as necessary to make the GNP estimates for CPEs comparable with those for market economies. The method is subject to estimation errors, and is also time-consuming because of the need for data reconstruction and adjustments. The fourth method is to derive GNP as the sum of the end-use values of all economic units (consumption, investment, government expenditure, and net export). This is an expenditure approach which is widely used in estimating income in market economies. The fifth method is called 'physical indicators approach', which involves GNP directly in dollars by currency exchanges rate conversion or some type of PPP. The essence of this approach is the determination of a regression relationship between a set of physical indicators (such as consumption and the stock of certain assets) of development and the per capita dollar GDP of arbitrarily chosen sample countries. This approach sounds well grounded and practical, but it too encounters the problems of structural and development-level differences between the target country and the reference country.

None of the above methods, as argued by Hwang (1993, p. 108), could be applied to the CPEs with no comprehensive, consistent, and up-to-date statistical information on the NMP or physical aggregation data for direct use. Before the reform, China had been an autarkic CPE, therefore, Marea's approaches could not be applied to estimate the GNP for that period. As China has adopted the SNA since the mid-1980s while at the same time did abandoning the MPS until 1994, it is possible for us to quantitatively estimate the correlation between the MPS and the SNA. Based on the data from 1985 to 1993, we may estimate three linear equations between GNP and GVSP, NI (national income) and GVIO:[10]

$$GNP = 0.4837GVSP \qquad (1985–93, R^2=0.991) \qquad (6.1)$$
$$(78.456)$$
$$GNP = 1.3259NI \qquad (1985–93, R^2=0.993) \qquad (6.2)$$
$$(84.587)$$
$$GNP = 0.5799GVIAO \qquad (1985–93, R^2=0.967) \qquad (6.3)$$
$$(39.210)$$

Using Equation 6.2 (as it is the most significantly estimated among the three equations), we can approximately derive China's GNP series from 1952 to 1978. By replacing the NI series into Equation 6.2, the GNP derivation is shown in the second column of Table 6.2. It is worth noting that China's NI/GNP ratio ($1/1.3259{\approx}0.7542$) estimated in Equation 6.2 is less than North Korea's (0.8) estimated by Hwang (1993, p. 118). The causes of the difference between China and North Korea need to be explored in detail.

The differences between the estimated GNP per capita (the fourth column of Table 6.2) and the SSB's GNP (the second column of Table 6.2) may be possibly explained by (1) the estimation errors produced in Equation 6.2 and (2) the official miscalculation arising from the incomplete application of the system of national accounts (SNA).

If national income had been more accurately stated by SSB than GNP from 1986 to 1993, we may conclude that China's actual GNP had been understated before 1992 and overstated after 1992 by the SSB.[11]

*Table 6.2*    Various estimates of China's GDP per capita (1952–2004)

| Year | NBS (2005) | | Equation (6.2) | WPT v6.2 | Other sources |
|------|-----------|---------------------------|----------------|----------|---------------|
|      | RMB (Y)[a] | Exchanges rate (US$)[a] | RMB (Y)[a] | PPP ($)[b] | PPP ($) |
| 1952 | 119 | 48  | 136  | 334  | |
| 1953 | 142 | 58  | 160  | 351  | |
| 1954 | 144 | 58  | 165  | 349  | |
| 1955 | 150 | 61  | 170  | 363  | |
| 1956 | 165 | 67  | 186  | 394  | |
| 1957 | 168 | 68  | 186  | 402  | |
| 1958 | 200 | 81  | 225  | 438  | |
| 1959 | 216 | 88  | 241  | 441  | |
| 1960 | 218 | 89  | 244  | 445  | |
| 1961 | 185 | 75  | 201  | 378  | |
| 1962 | 173 | 70  | 182  | 372  | |
| 1963 | 181 | 74  | 192  | 390  | |
| 1964 | 208 | 84  | 219  | 426  | |
| 1965 | 240 | 97  | 254  | 462  | |
| 1966 | 254 | 103 | 282  | 485  | |
| 1967 | 235 | 95  | 258  | 458  | |
| 1968 | 222 | 90  | 239  | 432  | |
| 1969 | 243 | 99  | 266  | 467  | |
| 1970 | 275 | 112 | 276  | 500  | |
| 1971 | 288 | 117 | 323  | 534  | |
| 1972 | 292 | 130 | 325  | 536  | |
| 1973 | 309 | 155 | 345  | 562  | |
| 1974 | 310 | 158 | 343  | 561  | |
| 1975 | 327 | 176 | 359  | 589  | |
| 1976 | 316 | 163 | 343  | 592  | |
| 1977 | 339 | 182 | 369  | 616  | |
| 1978 | 379 | 225 | 415  | 668  | |
| 1979 | 417 | 268 | 455  | 724  | 1000 (WB) |
| 1980 | 460 | 307 | 495  | 751  | |
| 1981 | 489 | 287 | 522  | 803  | |
| 1982 | 526 | 278 | 556  | 889  | |
| 1983 | 582 | 295 | 613  | 944  | |
| 1984 | 695 | 300 | 724  | 1061 | |
| 1985 | 855 | 291 | 882  | 1135 | |
| 1986 | 956 | 277 | 974  | 1293 | 2440 (HS) |
| 1987 | 1103 | 296 | 1136 | 1414 | |
| 1988 | 1355 | 364 | 1406 | 1489 | 2472 (K) |
| 1989 | 1512 | 402 | 1550 | 1497 | |
| 1990 | 1634 | 342 | 1668 | 1678 | 1031 (RC); 2140 (LS) |

Table 6.2   Various estimates of China's GDP per capita (1952–2004) – contd.

| Year | NBS (2005) | | Equation (6.2) | WPT v6.2 | Other sources |
|------|------------|---------------------------|----------------|------------|---------------|
| | RMB (Y)[a] | Exchanges rate (US$)[a] | RMB (Y)[a] | PPP ($)[b] | PPP ($) |
| 1991 | 1879 | 353 | 1895 | 1798 | 1680 (BUAA) |
| 1992 | 2287 | 415 | 2288 | 1983 | 1600 (IMF) |
| 1993 | 2939 | 510 | 2753 | 2131 | 2120 (WB) |
| 1994 | 3923 | 455 | | 2453 | 2510 (WB) |
| 1995 | 4854 | 581 | | 2702 | |
| 1996 | 5576 | 671 | | 2925 | |
| 1997 | 6054 | 730 | | 3229 | |
| 1998 | 6307 | 762 | | 3475 | |
| 1999 | 6547 | 791 | | 3691 | |
| 2000 | 7084 | 856 | | 4002 | |
| 2001 | 7543 | 911 | | 4281 | |
| 2002 | 9047 | 985 | | 4630 | |
| 2003 | 10500 | 1262 | | 4970 | |
| 2004 | 12300 | 1485 | | 5333 | |

Notes: [a] at current prices. [b] at constant prices. HS=Hesiods and Samorse; K=Kravis; RC=Rand Mc. Nolly & Company; LS=Lorentz Samoese; BUAA=Beijing University of Aero. & Astro.; IMF= International Monetary Fund; WB=World Bank staff estimates.

Sources: (1) World Bank (1996, p. 21), (2) Zheng (1996, p. 1) and (3) Penn World Table (PWT) v6.2 (Heston et al., 2006).

## A multiregional comparison

The provinces' national income statistical data were only reported from 1952 to 1993, while their GDP statistical data have been available since 1978. In order to conduct a consistent multiregional comparison of the Chinese economy across the pre- and post-reform periods, we have to apply the national income data and Equation 6.2 to estimate the GDP indicators for the pre-reform period. As the GDP data were not statistically reported by a few provinces (such as Liaoning in 1978 and 1979, Qinghai in 1979 and 1981–84, Guangxi in 1979, 1981–85 and 1987, and Tibet in 1978–84) during the early period when the MPS was transferred to the SNA, we have to make some approximations of per capita GDP for these provinces according to their national income data and Equation 6.2. Finally, there still exists an obstacle in the multiregional comparison of the Chinese economy: Tibet had not officially reported any statistical data before 1980. The only possible method we can use is to estimate Tibet's per capita GDP using other provinces to which Tibet is the most similar in economic conditions as reference. In 1980, the per capita national income of Tibet was 266 yuan, approximately 1.127 times that of Yunnan. Based on Yunnan's GDP data and a conversion factor of 1.127, we may obtain Tibet's per capita GDP data for the period from 1952 to 1979.[12] The estimated per capita GDP data for the selected years (1952, 1979, 1990, and 1995) are shown in Table 6.3, from which the provinces that prospered and those that stagnated can be derived:

Table 6.3   Per capita GDPs by province (1952, 1980, 1990 and 2000)

| Province | 1952[a] | 1980 | 1990 | 2000 |
|---|---|---|---|---|
| Anhui | 102(22) | 170(27) | 1090(24) | 4806(24) |
| Beijing | 330(3) | 2234(2) | 4881(2) | 22946(2) |
| Chongqing | NA | NA | NA | 5187(19) |
| Fujian | 126(14) | 265(20) | 1551(12) | 11341(7) |
| Gansu | 124(16) | 299(16) | 1059(27) | 3807(30) |
| Guangdong | 117(18) | 274(18) | 2395(5) | 12527(5) |
| Guangxi | 81(27) | 169(28) | 933(29) | 4313(29) |
| Guizhou | 73(29) | 136(29) | 794(30) | 2660(31) |
| Hainan | NA | NA | 1473(15) | 6553(15) |
| Hebei | 145(9) | 383(7) | 1367(17) | 7693(11) |
| Heilongjiang | 276(4) | 485(5) | 1901(8) | 8553(10) |
| Henan | 101(23) | 262(21) | 1045(28) | 5432(18) |
| Hubei | 110(20) | 277(17) | 1493(13) | 7161(13) |
| Hunan | 102(21) | 261(22) | 1159(20) | 5554(17) |
| Inner Mongolia | 198(7) | 338(14) | 1328(18) | 5899(16) |
| Jiangsu | 126(13) | 375(10) | 1953(7) | 11726(6) |
| Jiangxi | 137(11) | 254(24) | 1118(23) | 4799(25) |
| Jilin | 189(8) | 389(6) | 1617(10) | 6987(14) |
| Liaoning | 257(5) | 870[a](4) | 2452(4) | 11048(8) |
| Ningxia | 138(10) | 266(19) | 1320(19) | 4850(22) |
| Qinghai | 125(15) | 378(9) | 1478(14) | 5119(20) |
| Shaanxi | 100(24) | 343(12) | 1148(21) | 4605(27) |
| Shandong | 112(19) | 340(13) | 1599(11) | 9509(9) |
| Shanghai | 774(1) | 3792(1) | 5818(1) | 33922(1) |
| Shanxi | 124(17) | 303(15) | 1423(16) | 5037(21) |
| Sichuan | 76(28) | 198(26) | 1064(26) | 4808(23) |
| Tianjin | 347(2) | 1447(3) | 3620(3) | 17989(3) |
| Tibet | 94[b](25) | 255[b](23) | 1127(22) | 4705(26) |
| Xinjiang | 208(6) | 371(11) | 1688(9) | 7320(12) |
| Yunnan | 83(26) | 206(25) | 1074(25) | 4569(28) |
| Zhejiang | 135(12) | 382(8) | 1978(6) | 13262(4) |

Note: [a] estimated based on the data of national income (NI) (SSB, 1990b) and Equation 6.2; [b] estimated by the author. Figures in parentheses are ranks; per capita GDP, which are measured at current prices are based on SSB (1986, 1991) and NBS (2001) except for (a) and (b).

1. *1952–80* (29 provinces are included): 15 provinces (Beijing, Hebei, Shanxi, Liaoning, Jilin, Jiangsu, Zhejiang, Shandong, Henan, Hubei, Sichuan, Yunnan, Tibet, Shaanxi and Qinghai) ranked higher than before, ten provinces (Tianjin, Inner Mongolia, Heilongjiang, Anhui, Fujian, Jiangxi, Hunan, Guangxi, Ningxia and Xinjiang) ranked lower than before, and four provinces (Shanghai, Guangdong, Guizhou and Gansu) remained unchanged.
2. *1980–90* (29 provinces are included): ten provinces (Jiangsu, Zhejiang, Anhui, Fujian, Shandong, Hubei, Guangdong, Yunnan, Tibet and Xinjiang) ranked higher than before, 11 provinces (Hebei, Shanxi, Inner Mongolia, Jilin, Heilongjiang, Guangxi, Sichuan, Guizhou, Shaanxi, Gansu and Qinghai) ranked lower than before and eight provinces (Beijing, Tianjin, Liaoning, Shanghai, Jiangxi, Henan, Yunnan and Ningxia) remained unchanged.
3. *1990–2000* (30 provinces are included): nine provinces (Fujian, Hebei, Henan, Hunan, Inner Mongolia, Jiangsu, Shandong, Sichuan and Zhejiang) ranked higher than before, 13 provinces (Gansu, Guizhou, Heilongjiang, Jiangxi, Jilin, Liaoning, Ningxia, Qinghai, Shanxi, Shaanxi, Tibet, Yunnan and Xinjiang) ranked lower than before and eight provinces (Anhui, Beijing, Guangdong, Guangxi, Hianan, Hubei, Shanghai and Tianjin) remained unchanged.

## Real living standards

What a man of virtus Yan Hui was! Living in a mean alley on homely fare was a hardship others would find intoterable, but Yan was still no less cheerful and would never change his aspirations. Only Yan was able to cultivate a virtue!

Confucius (551–479 BC)

## General situation

The standard of living improved significantly in China during the First FYP (1953–57) but suffered a sudden decline thereafter due to the failure of the Great Leap Forward (1958–60). It did not start to improve significantly until the end of the Cultural Revolution (1966–76) during which people were largely encouraged to be rich in 'sprit' but *not* 'material'. Since the early 1980s, the Chinese living standard has improved steadily. Among China's eight FYPs the Eighth FYP (1991–95) is the best one in which the per capita personal consumption growth rate is the highest for China as a whole, while the Sixth FYP (1981–85) is the best one in which the per capita personal consumption growth rate is the highest for the agricultural households. This was not only because of economic growth but also because of continuous reduction in population growth.

If China's per capita personal consumption is measured in US dollars, the figure is still quite small. However, China's commodity prices are very low. If the Chinese standard of living were measured by purchasing power, it would definitely increase. For instance, after having calculated personal consumption in China and Japan using exchange rate, Mizoguchi *et al.* (1989, p. 28) find that China's per capita personal consumption expenditure is only 3.1 per cent of Japan's. However, when per capita personal consumption expenditure is recomputed using purchasing power, China's figure is 21.5 per cent of Japan's when Japan's consumption structure is used for weighting and 15.7 per cent when China's consumption structure is used for weighting.

China's data on people's livelihood (such as employment, disposable income and expenditure of residents, level of consumption, housing condition, quantity of consumer goods owned, and so on) have been compiled annually by the SSB (which has been renamed NBS) based on surveys of different samples. Some questions and ambiguities remain when different samples and measurements are chosen. For instance, the SSB makes no allowance for the rental value of housing. Furthermore, the SSB coverage of income in kind and subsidies also appears to be much less comprehensive than it is. Moreover, Khan *et al.* (1993, pp. 34–7) explain in detail why their estimates are different from the SSB's: the difference in the case of the rural sample is almost certainly due to differences in the definition of income and the method of estimation rather than difference in sampling method or in measurement errors; for the urban area, as the sample is much more weakly related to the SSB sample, the difference between the two estimates could therefore be due in part to differences in sampling and to measurement errors. If we can assume that their calculations are more accurate than the SSB's, we may thus conclude that the national income under China's macroeconomic accounting was underestimated during the 1980s, which is consistent with our hypothesis in the Section on 'Macroeconomic indicators' on p. 112.

When comparing China's living standards with other countries, one should remember that China has had a very comprehensive social welfare system (even if it is not available to all Chinese citizens), especially during the pre-form period. Ma and Sun (1981, p. 568), for example, estimate that the total work-related insurance and other types of social welfare expenditure might have been as high as 526.7 yuan per year for each worker, or 81.7 per cent of the average wage before 1980. In addition, urban residents have also access to low-cost housing. According to the urban surveys conducted by the SSB, the per capita expenditure for residence in most urban area is only 32.23 yuan in 1985 and 250.18 yuan in 1995, which accounts for approximately only 4.3 per cent and 5.8 per cent of the total per capita incomes, respectively, far lower than that of the market economies.[13]

One important indicator reflecting real living standards is 'life expectancy at birth'. In demography, the term 'life expectancy at birth' is expressed by number of years newborn children would live if subject to the mortality risks prevailing for the cross-section of population at the time of their birth. During the 1980s and 1990s, China's economic growth was faster than the rest of the world. However, its life expectancy was not improved proportionally. Table 6.4 shows that in 1980 five economies in the Asia-Pacific region have a higher level of life expectancy than China. From 1980 to 1998 China's level of life expectancy rose by two years, while Australia, Hong Kong, Japan, New Zealand and Singapore, all having a higher base level of life expectancy than China, achieved 4–6 years of increase in life expectancy. Sri Lanka, with the same level of life expectancy as China's in 1980, had increased its

*Table 6.4*   Life expectancy and infant mortality rates, selected economies

| Country | Life expectancy (years) | | Infant mortality rate (per thousand) | |
|---|---|---|---|---|
| | *1980* | *1998* | *1980* | *1998* |
| China | 68 | 70 | 42 | 31 |
| Australia | 74 | 79 | 11 | 5 |
| Hong Kong | 74 | 79 | 11 | 3 |
| Japan | 76 | 81 | 8 | 4 |
| South Korea | 67 | 73 | 26 | 9 |
| Malaysia | 67 | 72 | 30 | 8 |
| New Zealand | 73 | 77 | 13 | 5 |
| Singapore | 71 | 77 | 12 | 4 |
| Sri Lanka | 68 | 73 | 34 | 16 |
| Low-income economies | 51 | 55 | 108 | 79 |
| Middle-income economies | 64 | 69 | 53 | 30 |
| High-income economies | 73 | 77 | 15 | 6 |
| World average | 61 | 65 | 67 | 44 |

*Source*: Wang (2003, p. 55).

life expectancy by five years in 1998. Infant mortality rate of China was also higher than that of the Asia-Pacific economies.

### Rural–urban disparity

Since the reform, income differentials between urban and rural China have experienced different patterns. In the early period of the economic reform which was concentrated on the introduction of HRS to the agricultural sector, rural income increased very rapidly and the gap between the rural and urban areas narrowed until 1985. Since then, the rural-urban gap began to increase again as a result of the diminishing marginal returns of the agricultural sector in one hand and the urban industrial reform in the other hand. As demonstrated in Figure 6.2, the ratio of urban to rural per capita income fell from 2.36 in 1978 to 1.70 in 1983; it then exceeded 3.0 in 2000.[14] Before starting our in-depth analysis for the causes, some issues relating to the definition of the rural and urban income should be clarified. The estimates of China's rural and urban incomes conducted by the SSB and World Bank as well are based on the conventional definition of income which excludes several items such as subsidies and payments in kind and undervalues others (production for self-consumption). The understatement of

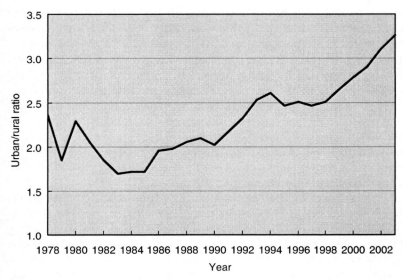

*Figure 6.2* China's rural–urban income gaps (1978–2003)

income sources will of course artificially decrease both rural and urban true incomes and may miscalculate the income gap between the two.

Before the reform, the distribution of income between rural and urban areas was rather uneven. In 1957 when the Chinese economy was the most prosperous, per capita personal income in urban area was 3.48 times that in rural area (SSB, 1986, pp. 667 and 673). As shown in Figure 6.2, the income gap between the rural and urban areas continued to decrease until 1983, but after 1985 the gap began to widen again and by 1994 the rural-urban inequalities were even greater than in the mid-1960s and 1970s. How can one explain these changes in the relative incomes of the rural and urban populations in China? Zhao (1993, pp. 82–3) argues that China's income differentials between rural and urban areas have resulted largely from government policy. For example, in the pre-reform era, it was the policy to keep agricultural prices low in order to accumulate funds for industrialization. Migration of labour from the low-income countryside to the high-income cities was strictly controlled by the government through a system of registration of urban residents. The consequence of these policies, however, was to aggravate rural-urban inequalities.

## A multiregional comparison

As we have seen in Chapter 3, natural and human resources are irregularly distributed in China. Specifically, the Eastern belt is blessed with mild climate and rich soil, while the Western belt has a vast territory and sparse population. The northern part is much richer in mineral resources than the southern part, except for a few non-ferrous metals. In contrast, most of the southern part, given its favourable climate and terrain, has an agricultural advantage over most, if not all, of the northern part, the desert North and Northwest regions and, in particular, dominates most of the nation's rice production. All the above regional characteristics in the distribution of resources, together with the spatially diversified economic systems and policies and other historical and cultural factors, have unevenly decided the spatial structure of the Chinese economy.

The vast size of, and diversified natural conditions, in China generate many regional differences in terms of climate, geography, soil fertility and other resource endowments, which in turn make the living standard vary from region to region. In particular, South and East regions have natural advantages for agriculture over the Northwest region. Mineral and energy resources are much richer in the North than in the South. In other aspects, the eastern coastal area, due to its geographical proximity to the market economies, may introduce more easily the *laissez-faire* approach than the central and the western inland areas. All these factors have inevitably resulted in great economic disparities among regions.

A brief look at the Chinese composition of personal consumption shows that the proportion of total expenditure going on food and beverages has dropped in both rural and urban areas since the reform, reflecting Engel's Law (SSB, 1996); while demand for housing, furniture and utensils, clothing, health care, education and others is seen to be more income-elastic, as the Law suggests. However, economic transformation in China has raised some problems in relation to the application of the Law. For instance, when estimating the Engel coefficients with respect to the per capita net incomes, we obtain a significant regression for the rural area and an insignificant regression for the urban area:

$$REC=69.47-5.87\times10^{-5}RNI \qquad (N=30,\ R^2=0.48,\ F=25.64) \qquad (6.4)$$
$$(-5.06)$$
$$UEC=50.20+9.75\times10^{-5}UNI \qquad (N=29,\ R^2=0.001,\ F=0.02) \qquad (6.5)$$
$$(0.15)$$

where, *RNI* and *UNI* are the per capita rural and urban net incomes; *REC* and *UEC* are the rural and urban Engel coefficients, the data of which are calculated based on SSB (1996, pp. 288–9, 303 and 305). Equation 6.4 demonstrates a negative correlation between the rural Engel coefficient (*REC*) and per capita net income (*RNI*), which is consistent with the Engel's Law. It should be noted that the insignificant and positive correlation between *UEC* and *UNI*, with far smaller t-statistical values in parentheses, $R^2$ and F-values in Equation 6.5, does not mean that Engel's Law has been overthrown by the Chinese urban data, rather, it implies that the Chinese data need to be further clarified in detail. Briefly, two major factors may have miscalculated and perhaps enlarged the Engel coefficients for the Chinese urban areas: first, subsidies coming from the government usually ascribe to the personal consumption in housing and health care; second, the Chinese meals are more complex and therefore more costly to prepare than Western style food.

The vast territory size, together with a less-developed transport system and rigid spatial economic barriers (as will be discussed in Chapter 7, p. 140) differentiates regional purchasing powers, that is, the same monetary income level may result in different real living standards in different regions. Theoretically, if the price indices and consumption structures are known, the personal consumption expenditure can be recomputed for different regions of China based on the purchasing power. Due to the difficulties in collecting the comparable regional data, we have to leave this ambitious task. Nevertheless, one is still able to witness the regional differences of purchasing power based on the retail prices of consumers goods at free markets. On 25 December 1995, for instance, the price tags of some foodstuff demonstrate that 1 kg of rice costs only ¥2.8 in Xi'an and Chengdu but ¥4.2 in Guangzhou; 1 kg of oil costs ¥7.8 in Zhengzhou and Shanghai but ¥12.2 in Guangzhou; 1 kg of chicken costs ¥8.8 in Yinchuan but ¥20.0 in Chengdu; 1 kg of fish costs ¥4.4 in Hefei but ¥11.0 in Chengdu, Guiyang, Tianjin and Beijing; 1 kg of eggs costs ¥6.2 in Harbin but ¥9.4 in Guiyang; 1 kg of apples costs only ¥3.0 in Taiyuan, Kunming and Lhasa but ¥7.0 in Beijing, Tianjin and Hohhot.[15]

## Inequality index

With the use of different data and measurements, it seems that there is never a consensus on this issue. For example, Zhang (1994, p. 300) uses 27 provinces (excluding Qinghai and Tibet) for 1980, 28 provinces (excluding Tibet) for 1981–88 and 28 provinces (excluding Tibet and Hainan, a new province established in 1988) for 1989–90 and obtains an increasing regional inequality in terms of per capita income in rural China. Based on the multiregional data in which three municipalities directly under the central government are incorporated into their neighbouring provinces (Beijing and Tianjin into Hebei, Shanghai into Jiangsu) and Tibet and Hainan are excluded from the analysis, Tsui (1993) shows inter-provincial inequality declined from the late 1970s to the mid-1980s and a reversal tend preceding the reform era. Jian et al. (1996, pp. 1–22) use the data of 28 provinces (Tibet and Hainan are excluded) and obtain a V-shaped pattern for China's multiregional inequalities from 1978 to 1993. Obviously, the regional inequalities will demonstrate differing patterns if different measurements and regionalizations are employed. In addition, sore care should be taken when one uses the official data to estimate China's regional inequalty index for the pre- and post-reform periods during which different statistical systems were employed.

The simplest measurement for regional inequalities is standard error (SR).[16] SR is a statistical approach by which regional disparities are measured in absolute terms, while other approaches, such as Gini coefficient, coefficient of variation (CV), weighed mean error ($M_W$) and so on, may be used to derive the regional disparities in relative terms.[17] It must be noted that SR, CV, Gini and $M_W$ approaches can only deal with the measurement of regional inequalities in terms of a single index. However, it is necessary sometimes for one to jointly analyze the regional disparities according to different indices, particularly when these indices are contradictory with each other. For instance, Nolan and Sender (1992, pp. 1279–303) and Sen (1992, pp. 1305–12 and 2004) argue that China has paid more attention to the economic growth rather than education, health care and other service sectors since the early 1980s. Thus, when evaluating the income inequalities in China, one should take different indices into account.[18]

Due to the diversified natural and social conditions among different regions, China's regional inequalities have had a long history. It is generally admitted that the Eastern belt has a relatively higher per capita GNP and, of course, higher living standard than the Western belt. It is noticeable that different results have emerged in the estimates of the regional economic inequalities in China. Some researchers believe that China's regional inequalities have definitely increased, reflecting the first stage of the inverted U process in Williamson (1965, pp. 165–204) as well as China's uneven regional development strategy.[19] In contrast, others argue that only the gaps between the Eastern, Central, and Western belts have been widened for the past years while the interprovincial gaps have been substantially narrowed since the economic reform was introduced in 1978.[20]

Let us first look at the poorest and richest provinces in China. In 1952, the per capita national income of Shanghai was estimated at 584.15 yuan which is 10.67 times that of Guizhou (54.77 yuan). In 1979, Shanghai's per capita national income rose to 2860.92 yuan, 27.85 times of Guizhou's (102.72 yuan).[21] Obviously, during the prereform period, the economic gap between the richest and poorest provinces widened rapidly. How large is this gap during the postreform period? Briefly, the economic gap has experienced two different patterns if we take into account the per capita GDP (see Table 6.3). Shanghai's per capita GDP was 27.88 times of Guizhou's in 1979 and 7.34 times of Guizhou's in 1990, which implies that the per capita GDP ratio of Shanghai to Guizhou decreased greatly during the above period. From 1990 to 2000, however, the per capita GDP ratio of Shanghai to Guizhou increased once again to 12.6. Until now, we may

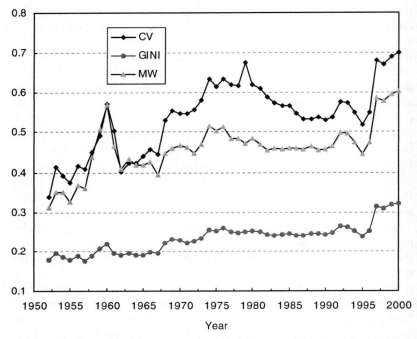

*Sources*: (1) estimation by the author for 1952–78 and (2) SSB (various issues) for 1979–2000 with some exceptions of the provinces whose GDPs are estimated by the author (more details may be found in Section 6.2).
*Note*: 29 provinces are considered from 1952 to 1988 (during which Hainan is included in Guangdong province) while 30 provinces are considered from 1989 to 1997 and 31 provinces from 1998 onwards (since then Chongqing has been separated from Sichuan province).

*Figure 6.3*   Changes of regional inequalities (1952–2000)

conclude that the economic gap between the richest and the poorest regions has been very high in China.

How about China's regional inequalities when all provinces are taken into account? Using the provinces' per capita GDP data which have been officially reported by the NBS (SSB) for the years from 1978 to 2000[22] and estimated in Section 6.2.2 for the years from 1952 to 1977, we may calculate the Gini, CV and $M_W$ coefficients for the years from 1952 to 2000 (see Figure 6.3).

Regional inequalities (measured by Gini, CV, and $M_W$) fluctuated frequently during the above period (see Figure 6.3). Except for a few years (such as 1954–55, 1957, 1961–62, and 1967), China's regional inequalities increased from the early 1950s to the late 1970s. For instance, the Gini, CV and $M_W$ were 0.178, 0.339 and 0.312 in 1952; in 1980, however, they increased significantly to 0.253, 0.621 and 0.483, respectively. Obviously, China's egalitarian did not bring about any economic equalities among the provinces during this period. From the early 1980s to the mid-1990s, except for a few years in the early 1990s, regional inequalities have decreased among the provinces, however, they have increased steadily since then.

A glance at the year-to-year per capita GDPs of the Eastern, Central and Western belts simply reveals that the regional inequalities have increased significantly, as demonstrated in Figure 6.4. For instance, the per capita GDP in the Eastern belt was 87 per cent higher than that in the Western belt in 1978; in 2000, however, it was almost 150 per cent higher than that in the Western belt.

While China's reform has been strongly driving its economic growth, it has also derived a series of socioeconomic problems. Prior to the reform, China was an egalitarian society in terms of income distribution. In the initial stage of the reform, the policy of 'letting some

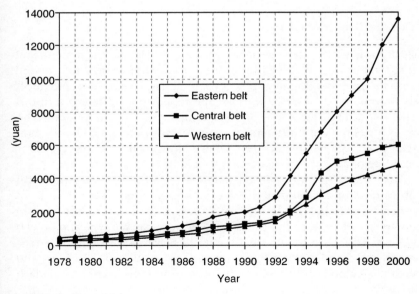

*Source*: As for Figure 6.3.

*Figure 6.4* Per capita GDP gaps of the Eastern, Central and Western belts (1978–2000)

*Table 6.5*   China's income Gini coefficients (1978, 1988, 1995 and 2002)

| Year | Rural area | Urban area | China as a whole |
|---|---|---|---|
| 1979/80 | 0.310 | 0.160 | 0.330 |
| 1988 | 0.338 | 0.233 | 0.382 |
| 1995 | 0.381 | 0.280 | 0.437 |
| 2002 | 0.366 | 0.319 | 0.454 |

*Sources*: (1) World Bank (1983, pp. 83, 92) for 1979/80; (2) Zhao (2001) for 1988 and 1995; and (3) Li (2004) for 2002.

people get rich first' was adopted to overcome egalitarianism in income distribution, to promote efficiency with strong incentives and to ultimately realize common prosperity based on an enlarged pie. But this policy has quickly enlarged income gaps between different groups of people (see Table 6.5).

An empirical framework for analyzing the positive and negative effects of various factors (economic growth and various institutional and policy reforms) on China's income inequality is shown in Table 6.6.

## Concluding remarks

Beginning with a common background of ideological system and history, but proceeding with differing paces of economic reform and with different development policies, China has developed its provinces and promoted the welfare of urban and rural people differently. In this chapter, a multiregional economic comparison has been conducted, with the emphases on the macroeconomic indicators, real living standards, and regional inequalities. When addressing the Chinese economy multiregionally, at least two issues should be noted.

First, China's rural-urban inequalities are very high compared with other developing countries. For example, in Indonesia the ratio of urban to rural income was 1.66 in 1987. In Bangladesh the highest observed ratio during the 1980s was 1.85 whereas the typical ratio was close to 1.5.[23] Admittedly the household surveys on which these estimates are based make a less than full accounting of subsidies and incomes in kind. But these components in Indonesia and Bangladesh are tiny compared to that in China.

Second, even though not taking into account its two SARs (Hong Kong and Macau) and Taiwan (an economic comparison of Taiwan, Hong Kong, Macau and mainland China will be conducted in Chapter

*Table 6.6* Determinants of income inequality in China

| Item | Within urban or rural areas | Between urban and rural areas |
|---|---|---|
| **1. Economic growth or development** | | |
| Faster growth of urban nonstate-owned economy | + | + |
| Faster growth of rural nonagricultural economy | + | – |
| Development of agriculture | + | – |
| **2. Economic reform or institutional changes** | | |
| *Order changes* | | |
| Price reform in rural areas | – | – |
| Household responsibility system in rural areas | – | – |
| Internal migration of rural laborers | ? | – |
| Commercialization of urban housing | + | + |
| *Disorder changes* | | |
| Rent-seeking activities | + | ? |
| Insider control[a] | + | + |
| Monopoly | + | + |
| Corruption | + | + |
| **3. Economic policy and its changes** | | |
| Low purchasing price for agricultural products | ? | + |
| Taxation on agricultural products | ? | ? |
| Extrataxational burden peasants | ? | + |
| Personal income tax | – | – |
| Reduction of urban subsidies | | |
| a. Per head | + | – |
| b. By position | – | – |
| Transfer of urban residents' benefits to private property | + | + |
| Access to the WTO | ? | + |

*Notes*: [a]: 'Insider control' is described here as a mechanism through which public assets can be appropriated to serve the interests of a particular government organ or individuals. '+' denotes increase of inequality; '–' denotes decrease of inequality; '?' denotes difficulty to judge.

*Source*: Zhao (2001, p. 36; 2003, p. 284).

11), China still had a per capita GDP ratio of more than 12 for the richest (Shanghai) to the poorest (Guizhou) at the end of 1990s, which is only lower than Indonesia (20.8, 1983), but much higher than many other countries, such as former Yugoslavia (7.8, 1988), India (3.26, 1980), the Netherlands (2.69, 1988), Italy (2.34, 1988), Canada (2.30,

1988), Spain (2.23, 1988), France (2.15, 1988), West Germany (1.93, 1988), Greece (1.63, 1988), UK (1.63), South Korea (1.53, 1985), Japan (1.47, 1981), USA (1.43, 1983), and Australia (1.13, 1978).[24]

How large will China's regional inequalities be and how will they eventually affect the Chinese economy and society? We are watchimg with open eyes.

# 7
# Can the Chinese Economy Be Spatially Optimized?

> Zigong asked what was needed for government. Confucius said, 'Sufficient food, excellent armaments, and people's trust in the government.' Zigong asked, 'Suppose you were forced to get rid of one of the three, which one would you get rid of first?' 'Armaments,' said Confucius. Zigong went on asking, 'Which one would you get rid of if you were to get rid of one of the remaining two?' Confucius answered, 'The food. Although man will die of hunger without food, man has been destined to die since time immemorial. But if people lose their trust in the government then the state has lost its basis.'
>
> *Analects of Confucius*

## Spatial efficiency of authoritarianism: a theory

There have been two potentially contradictory metaphors pervading contemporary commentary on the nature and trajectory of the Chinese political economy. First of all, there is the more benign metaphor of the 'nationalization' of economic activities, which presents a picture of an environment in which economic agents, especially multiregional firms, are increasingly indifferent to political boundaries, competing in the 'national market' and satisfying the demands of consumers whose tastes are increasingly homogeneous across borders. Second, there is the view of the national economy as increasingly defined by different 'regional blocs' which are marked by high levels of intra-regional interdependence but which compete nationally.

The term 'authoritarian' refers to an organization or an independent state which enforces strong and sometimes oppressive measures against the population, generally without attempting to gain the consent of

131

the population. In an authoritarian state, citizens are subject to state authority in many aspects of their lives, including many that other political philosophies would see as matters of personal choice. Authoritarianism often arises from the presumption that governing bodies know what is right or wrong for the country and from intolerance of dissent. The government then enforces what it thinks is right, often with use of considerable force. Dissenting voices are ignored, or, more strikingly, are considered to be plotting against the best interests of the country. Such was, for instance, the case during the Reign of Terror in France or in Spain under Franco. In most cases, the leadership (government) of an authoritarian regime comprises an elite group that uses repressive means to stay in power. However, unlike totalitarian regimes, there is no desire or ideological justification for the state to control all aspects of a person's life, and the state will generally ignore the actions of an individual unless it is perceived to constitute a direct challenge to the state. Totalitarian governments tend to be revolutionary, intent on changing the basic structure of society, while authoritarian ones tend to be conservative.[1]

There is a series of challenges to the study of the economic mechanisms within as well as between authoritarian states differing in size. Why have some small economies that are culturally different from each other voluntarily formed a large economic zone, while large economies that are culturally similar to each other have not? Why are the political and economic agreements of the culturally heterogeneous economies less stable than those of the culturally homogeneous economies that are politically different? In order to explore the above dilemmas, we will define below our ways of creating a new authoritarian regime or eliminating an existing one.

> *Rule A*. If the net benefit of governing a defined state is larger than zero, then the existing authoritarian regime will survive or a new authoritarian regime will be born.
> *Rule B*. If the net benefit of governing a defined state is less than zero, then the existing authoritarian regime will disappear or a new authoritarian regime will not be born.

Furthermore, in order to model state formulation as a result of specific trade-off between the benefits of large jurisdictions and the costs and risks of diversity resulting from large populations, let us first consider an isolated authoritarian state and make the following assumptions:

1. There is mobility of socioeconomic factors within the authoritarian state, but not with the outside world.
2. All these socioeconomic factors are uniformly distributed throughout the authoritarian state.
3. There exists an isotropic communication and transport network in the authoritarian state.
4. The size of the authoritarian state can change freely, which means that it can be as small as zero, or as large as is necessary in the analysis.
5. The aim of the authoritarian state is to be seeking to maximize its well-being through the behavior of its economic agents.

Obviously, assumption (1) is characteristic of all kinds of isolated authoritarian states. Assumptions (2) and (3) are very common in most spatial economic analyses. In assumption (4), there are different ways to measure the size of authoritarian states: (i) land area reflects the size of natural resources on which a culture is necessarily based; (ii) population size usually reflects the size of social resources on which a culture is necessarily based; and (iii) economic output reflects all the final products and services generated within the authoritarian state or all the income items produced by and distributed to the population of the authoritarian state. But since the authoritarian state defined here is spatially uniform, the use of all these approaches will not affect the consistency of our analysis. Finally, assumption (5) simplifies our topic to a pure economic issue, in which consumers seek to maximize satisfaction and firms seek to maximize their return from productive activity.

For a given set of sizes for the authoritarian state (as defined in assumption (4), above), there is an expansion that defines the least-cost combinations of culture size inputs and thus specifies the lowest total variable cost attainable at each rate of administered size. Generally, the sources of benefit from economies of scale for the authoritarian state may be grouped into three categories:

- Technical economies. The large authoritarian states can make relatively efficient uses of their fixed cost and hence gain considerable advantages over small authoritarian states.
- Marketing economies. Marketing in a larger economy has many benefits, but the main economies of scale from marketing include the bulk purchases and distribution potentialities.
- Risk-bearing economies. A number of advantages can lead to larger authoritarian states experiencing risk-bearing economies. The underlying factor is that large authoritarian states frequently engage in a

range of diverse activities, so that a fall in the return from any one unit of economy does not threaten the stability of the whole economy.

While increases in size frequently confer advantages on an authoritarian state, there is a limit to the gains from growth in many cases. In other words, there is an optimal level of spatial capacity, and increases in size beyond this level will lead to a loss of economies of size and manifest themselves in rising average cost. Without doubt, the increasing complexity of managing a large authoritarian state is the major source of administrative inefficiencies when the state grows beyond a certain size, and control and management of diverse socioeconomic affairs and risks become increasingly difficult. Diseconomies of scale mainly result from managerial difficulties, which are, under certain circumstances, positively related to cultural diversity. Since a large population is likely to be less homogeneous, the average cultural distance between individuals is likely to be positively correlated with the size of the authoritarian state.[2]

On the basis of the above assumptions and rules, we can derive the following results:[3]

*Proposition 1.* Given the homogeneous natural and social conditions, the transaction cost (benefit) of an isolated authoritarian state can be minimized (maximized) at the geographical center of, and be maximized (minimized) at the geographical periphery of the state.

*Proposition 2.* Given the homogeneous natural and social conditions, the optimal size of an open authoritarian state is larger than that of an isolated one; and that the optimal size of a developed authoritarian state is larger than that of a less developed one.

*Proposition 3.* In a world of two or more authoritarian states, economic centers will move close to each other, if the inter-political and intercultural barriers are removed or reduced.

*Proposition 4.* Different authoritarian states that are open to each other may be integrated, under conditions that the actual size of each authoritarian state is smaller than its optimal size and that the actual size of the integrated authoritarian state is not larger than its optimal size.

## Spatial separation in China

In principle, spatial economic separation may effectively be reduced to a minimum level within a sovereign country by the central government. Due to the diversified natural, geographical environments and the heterogeneous social and cultural conditions in China, however, the Chinese economy has been spatially separated by a series of natural and artificial barriers. This kind of spatial separation became particularly serious during the period when the centrally planned system was transformed into a decentralized administrative system. Let us look briefly at this spatial separation and its negative effects on the Chinese economy through three aspects – geography, institution and culture.

## Geographical barriers

China is one of the countries with the most complicated topography and diversified physical environment in the world. Glancing at the map of China, one may find that many administrative regions, especially provinces, have been naturally bordered by geographical barriers such as mountains, rivers, lakes, and so on. This kind of geographical separation between adjacent provinces could seriously affect the regional economic developments if the inter-provincial transport and communication linkages are established inefficiently. After checking the highway networks of ten provinces (Beijing, Shanghai, Tianjin, Hebei, Shanxi, Liaoning, Gansu, Qinghai, Inner Mongolia and Ningxia) in *China Atlas* published in 1983, for example, Guo (1993, p. 119) estimates that, of the 453 highways in the peripheral areas, about 60 per cent were trans-provincially connected, whereas about 40 per cent reached the ends near the province's border. Obviously, fragmentary highway networks have exacerbated the inconveniences for every sphere of the local inhabitant's lives and adversely affected the Chinese economy in particular.[4]

Many provinces, autonomous regions, and municipalities directly under the central government have been informally demarcated in China. As a result, cross-border relations between the relevant provinces have never been easily coordinated and, sometimes, could become a destabilizing source for social stability and economic development, even though the regulations concerning the resolution of the border disputes have been issued and revised by the State Council (1981, 1988a). After 1986, the Ministry of Civil Affairs (MCA) conducted a series of field surveys on the provinces of Xinjiang, Inner Mongolia, Ningxia, Gansu, Shaanxi, Qinghai, Jilin, Hebei and Shandong in order to provide legal, formal, geographical boundaries for those provinces. Many problems, however, still remained unsolved. For example, after having compared the locally mapped borders, Zhang (1990, p. 8) points out that among China's 66 cross-province border lines (about 52,000 km), 59 cross-province borders have been discordantly portrayed and 54 cross-province borders have been disputed by the relavent local governments along a section of about 9500 km long borders.

Moreover, there is another geographical characteristic in the Chinese economy: many provinces' borders are naturally marked by mountains, rivers, and lakes which bless the border-regions with abundant natural and environmental resources. Given the cross-border *imbroglios* between the provinces, the sustainable exploitation and utilization of natural resources (such as energy, metals, forests, fishery, and so on) as well as environmental protection in the border regions will undoubtedly pose problems and disputes for both central and local governments in China (see Box 7.1).

---

**Box 7.1   Who owns Lake Weishan?**

The Lake Weishan area has experienced drastic changes in provincial administration during the 20th century. This has placed the Shandong-Jiangsu interprovincial relation on an unstable foundation. The 1953 border re-adjustment scheme created many problems. The fact that changes in natural conditions could result in either a rise (during rainy season) or a fall (during dry season) of water level in Lake Weishan, which would in turn either reduce or increase the size of lake and lakeshore land, was not taken into consideration. Naturally, this would cause frequent changes in the location of the interprovincial borderline which followed the decision that: 'Wherever water reaches is under Shandong's jurisdiction; but the land is regarded as Jiangsu's territory.' The argument about ownership of Lake Weishan continued, so did the border conflict between the provinces. From the founding of the People's Republic in 1949 to the year 2000 there have been nearly 400 cases of cross-border conflicts in the region with nearly 400 people killed or seriously wounded (Guo, 2005, pp. 197–226).

Given the difficulties in the current administrative arrangements, is the establishment of a new province (or provincial unit) in the lake area a practical solution? Although the establishment of the new province will not guarantee that all the border-related problems will be solved. Nevertheless, it would transform the interprovincial border disputes into a set of issues that could reasonably be solved by a single province administration. In such a case, the question 'Who owns Lake Weishan?' will no longer be part of an unsolved interprovincial equation!

Non-cooperative cross-border relations between provinces eventually could become a source of disturbance to economic development. Even worse, some inter-provincial disputes led to armed conflicts and seriously affect the social security and economic sustainability in border regions regardless of the regulations concerning the resolution of border disputes between administrative regions issued by the State Council (1981, 1988b). For example, there have been over 800 cross-province border disputes in 333 counties (or about 39 per cent of the total border counties in all provinces except for Hainan province) in mainland China. The total disputed areas (about 140,000 km$^2$) include grassland (about 96,000 km$^2$), mining areas (about 5000 km$^2$), water (about 1000 km$^2$), and mixed grass-mining-forestland (about 30,000 km$^2$) and are distributed unevenly in the Western belt (about 130,000 km$^2$), the Central belt (about 17,000 km$^2$), and the Eastern belt (about 700 km$^2$).[5]

## Administrative barriers

One of the key initiatives of China's economic reform that started in the late 1970s was the promotion of decentralization in economic operations, i.e. transferring economic management and decision-making from central government to provincial and local governments. For example, retail trade which used to be under the control of local government is now determined by collectively and individually owned enterprises. Decentralization and the introduction of market forces together imply that the centers of economic power are moving away from central government to the localities. Since the advent of administrative decentralization, China's national economy had become effectively 'cellularized' into a plethora of semi-autarkic regional enclaves. Let us analyze it below in detail.

There exist many multiregional differences in terms of natural and social resources, industrial structure, and economic development in China. For example, Shanxi (west Mt. Taihang) province has abundant coal resources but poor mineral, petroleum, and agricultural resources; except for petroleum, non-metal, and agricultural resources, metals and coal resources are relatively not rich in the province of Shandong (east Mt. Taihang); Hebei (north R. Yellow) province has a surplus supply of metals and coal resources but lacks petroleum and non-metals; Henan (south R. Yellow) province has rich coal, metal and agricultural resources but low non-metals. To facilitate understanding of the multiregionally complementary conditions in China, let us introduce a quantitative index ($Q_{ij}$) as formulated below:

$$Q_{ij}=\frac{x_{ij}\big/\sum_{i=1}^{6}x_{ij}}{\sum_{j=1}^{30}x_{ij}\big/\sum_{i=1}^{6}\sum_{j=1}^{30}x_{ij}} \tag{7.1}$$

where $x_{ij}$ is the output value of the $j$th sector ($j$=1, 2, ..., and 6, representing 'coal', 'petroleum', 'metal', 'non-metal', 'timber', and 'food') in

*Table 7.1*  Interprovincial comparative advantages ($Q_{ij}$), by industrial sector

| Province | Coal | Petroleum | Metal | Non-metal | Timber | Food |
|---|---|---|---|---|---|---|
| Anhui | 1.42 | 0.00 | 0.93 | 1.61 | 0.18 | 1.34 |
| Beijing | 0.63 | 0.00 | 0.44 | 0.62 | 0.00 | 1.90 |
| Fujian | 0.43 | 0.00 | 0.33 | 1.55 | 6.23 | 1.45 |
| Gansu | 0.75 | 2.22 | 1.01 | 0.92 | 0.83 | 0.46 |
| Guangdong | 0.21 | 0.16 | 0.82 | 1.58 | 0.14 | 1.78 |
| Guangxi | 0.32 | 0.00 | 2.58 | 1.16 | 0.34 | 1.59 |
| Guizhou | 2.63 | 0.00 | 1.30 | 0.97 | 1.94 | 0.76 |
| Hainan | 0.04 | 0.00 | 3.58 | 0.83 | 0.54 | 1.59 |
| Hebei | 1.51 | 1.30 | 2.05 | 0.75 | 0.00 | 0.57 |
| Heilongjiang | 0.58 | 2.79 | 0.12 | 0.16 | 3.12 | 0.32 |
| Henan | 1.57 | 0.94 | 1.24 | 0.37 | 0.00 | 0.91 |
| Hubei | 0.23 | 0.71 | 0.66 | 2.45 | 0.17 | 1.37 |
| Hunan | 1.21 | 0.00 | 2.53 | 1.44 | 0.43 | 1.19 |
| Inner Mongolia | 1.48 | 0.38 | 1.33 | 0.95 | 5.60 | 0.78 |
| Jiangsu | 0.79 | 0.14 | 0.16 | 1.62 | 0.00 | 1.66 |
| Jiangxi | 1.08 | 0.00 | 3.43 | 1.36 | 1.38 | 1.05 |
| Jilin | 0.79 | 0.95 | 0.56 | 0.54 | 6.50 | 0.88 |
| Liaoning | 1.03 | 1.51 | 1.18 | 0.99 | 0.00 | 0.75 |
| Ningxia | 3.70 | 0.42 | 0.05 | 0.25 | 0.00 | 0.52 |
| Qinghai | 0.26 | 2.70 | 1.13 | 1.37 | 0.09 | 0.37 |
| Shaanxi | 1.22 | 0.58 | 3.47 | 0.64 | 0.67 | 0.82 |
| Shandong | 0.90 | 1.13 | 0.97 | 1.22 | 0.00 | 1.01 |
| Shanghai | 0.00 | 0.00 | 0.01 | 0.07 | 0.04 | 2.31 |
| Shanxi | 4.70 | 0.00 | 0.89 | 0.25 | 0.03 | 0.20 |
| Sichuan | 1.10 | 0.61 | 0.43 | 1.35 | 1.74 | 1.16 |
| Tianjin | 0.01 | 2.05 | 0.02 | 0.56 | 0.00 | 1.12 |
| Tibet | 0.03 | 0.00 | 5.05 | 1.88 | 10.7 | 0.53 |
| Xinjiang | 0.35 | 3.11 | 0.44 | 0.26 | 0.21 | 0.37 |
| Yunnan | 0.71 | 0.40 | 3.24 | 0.66 | 1.83 | 1.09 |
| Zhejiang | 0.21 | 0.00 | 0.62 | 2.21 | 0.01 | 1.82 |

*Source*: Based on Equation (7.1) and SSB (1996b, pp. 118–36).

the $j$th province ($j$=1, 2, ..., and 30, representing China's provinces listed in the first column of Table 7.1). Specifically, China's provinces can be classified into three groups according to the values of $Q_{ij}$ (shown in Table 7.1):

1. when $Q_{ij}$>1, it means that supply exceeds demand in the $i$th sector of the $j$th province;
2. when $Q_{ij}$<1, it means that supply is less than demand in the $i$th sector of the $j$th province; and
3. when $Q_{ij}$=1, it means that supply and demand are in equilibrium in the $i$th sector of the $j$th province.

Generally, China's resource demand and supply may be geographically identified through four different zones which are labeled as (1) $S_LD_L$ (low supply, low demand) (2) $S_HD_L$ (high supply, low demand) (3) $S_HD_H$ (high supply, high demand), and (4) $S_LD_H$ (low supply, high demand). Obviously, Zones $S_LD_L$ and $S_HD_H$ can reach their respective optimum equilibrium point of social welfare even under the condition that inter-zone trade is not available, as their resource supplies can meet their resource demands. However, under the disequilibrated supply–demand conditions, neither Zone $S_LD_H$ nor Zone $S_HD_L$ can optimize its social welfare. As a matter of fact, as these two Zones' resource supply–demand structures are complementary with each other, the optimization of their social welfare can benefit greatly from their inter-zone trade, more specifically, from the import from Zone $S_HD_L$ to Zone $S_LD_H$, or the export to Zone $S_LD_H$ from Zone $S_HD_L$.

The trade-off between Zones $S_HD_L$ and $S_LD_H$ can be further explained by Figure 7.1 in which $S_0S$ illustrates a society's resource supply possibility curve of Zone $S_LD_H$, $W_0W_0'$ denotes the Zone's social preference curve and $OS_0$ and $OS$ denote the maximum possibilities of resource supplies of Zones $S_HD_L$ and $S_LD_H$, respectively. Consider the availability of the inter-zone trade and the absence of the resource supplies from other external sources, the optimum allocation of resource between Zones $S_HD_L$ and $S_LD_H$ will be at point $E_0$ where $S_0S$ and $W_0W_0'$ meet. When a trade embargo rises from Zone $S_HD_L$, the $S_0S$ curve shifts to the left to, say, $S_1S$. As a result, Zone $S_LD_H$ will have to end up with more supply of local resources and less social welfare consumption. In this case, the optimum equilibrium will occur at point $E_1$, which is lower than $E_0$, indicating a lower social welfare level upon the introduction of trade barriers between Zones $S_HD_L$ and $S_LD_H$. It must be noted that, the more Zone $S_LD_H$ is committed to the importing of resources in a

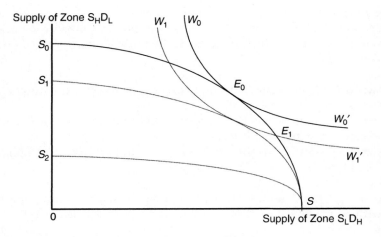

*Figure 7.1*   Regional optimum with resource allocation

world of resource constraints, the less is its social welfare consumption, since higher risks and more extra costs will result from the resource imports.[6]

According to the principle of comparative advantage, the uneven distribution of natural resources and industrial structure among different provinces enhances the mutual complementarities for the Chinese economy. However, administrative separation had formed, to some extent, a rigid self-reliant agricultural and industrial system for each province and seriously affected cross-border economic relations, particularly during the high tide of administrative decentralization stemming from economic reform. In order to protect local market and revenue sources, it became very common in China for some provinces to restrict import (export) from (to) other provinces by levying high, if informal, taxes and by creating non-tariff barriers on commodities ranging from tobacco to clothing, alcohol, washing machines, TV sets, refrigerators and even automobiles whose production is seen as important to their provincially 'domestic' economies. Xinjiang autonomous region, for example, effectively banned the import of 48 commodities on the grounds that they would harm its local economy. Jilin refused to market beer produced in its neighbouring provinces of Heilongjiang and Liaoning. Hunan province prohibited the export of grain to the neighbour, Guangdong province.... In some provinces, local authorities established, and provided finance for, a variety of schemes that promoted the sale of local products. Enterprises from other provinces, however, often have difficulties in finding office spaces, accommodation or land for their business activities. These protectionist measures, which were often in violation of central directives, were enforced through a patchwork system of roadblocks, cargo seizures, *ad hoc* taxes, commercial surcharges, and licensing fees, and in a number of well-publicized cases, highway robbery across the inter-provincial borders.[7] Moreover, this unfair competition between provinces could be fierce in the 'battlegrounds' of their border regions and there were numerous tales of 'trade embargoes' or 'commodity wars' between provinces over, among other items, rice, wool, tobacco, soy beans and mineral products.[8]

Experience and lessons from advanced countries have shown that the success of a nation in promoting its economic development depends to a large extent on a complete legislative structure and effective instrumental incentives of its own. China's efforts to this end have achieved much progress, but some still remain to be done in depth. In fact, China's 'commodity wars' between provinces stemmed from the fact that China does not have any constitutional clauses to specifically prohibit barriers against inter-provincial commerce, even though the relevant regulations and laws have been issued time and again by the State Council (1980a, 1982, 1986, 1990) and NPC (1993). More often than not, the state's orders were not accorded the priority status of a self-contained law, but took the form of less formal circulars, or were included as minor elements of larger pieces of portmanteau legislation.[9]

Difficulties in coordinating cross-border weather modification activities are another example. The following gives more details in this regard.

Largely due to the complicated pattern of clouds' mobility and the frequently changing distribution of moisture in the skies, many issues related to rainmaking have apparently been ignored by rainmakers and policymakers. The first neglected issue is how to answer the question of who owns the right to use the extra water to be produced by cloud seeding. The answer to that question might depend on who owns the right to use the cloud resource. In contrast to Brooks (1949, p. 119), who analogized clouds to be like wild ducks flowing over the land, Davis (1968, p. 104) suggested that 'clouds are rivers flowing through our skies.'[10] Even more complicated is that of the deprivation of rainfall downwind from where cloud seeding has enhanced rainfall. Obviously, the downwind atmosphere (clear air and clouds together) has less water content as a result of the greater rainfall upwind, hours, or a day, earlier. If the upwind landowners have the legal right to use an artificial manner to receive a larger amount of rainfall than the naturally occurring rainfall, then downwind landowners have been deprived of rainfall.

The controversy over who gets access to which clouds demonstrates the need for regulations and agreements on the exploitation and utilization of scarce natural resources. However, as the rain cloud case study (shown below) emphasizes, conditions for scientific regulation have not been mature, since many inherent features of meteorology are still not known. For example, it has been difficult for meteorologists to test the effects of weather modification, such as determining precisely how much rainfall has been caused by rainmaking activities. The natural changes in the atmosphere are very fast and complex. Since it is not able to observe the atmosphere everywhere at all times, so the data collected are not complete. The most effective way to manage rainfall is for government entities to coordinate efforts. The following cases can provide evidence in support of the above point of view.

On 25 July 2004, the Meteorological Bureau of Jiangsu province in Southeast China conducted some unsuccessful precipitation enhancement activities in its five cities with close proximity to Shanghai municipality and Zhejiang province at the Yangtze River delta. It has been suggested that if the rainmaking activities had been coordinated and jointly conducted by the whole cities of the delta area, there would have had better effects. The reason was that since each of the three provincial meteorological bureaux of Jiangsu, Zhejiang and Shanghai can only monitor the cloud movement for an area of up to 500 km in length. If the three provincial bureaux could share the monitored information and data that they collected on the cloud resources, the rainmakers can find more suitable time and locations to conduct more fruitful precipitation enhancement activities for their own.[11]

Similar stories can be found in Jilin province in Northeast China. In areas around Mt Changbai bordering with North Korea, the clouds' complicated mobility and the frequently changing distribution of water vapor make the enterprise unpredictable. Jilin's joint actions with its neighbouring provinces (and perhaps with North Korea, if the latter also needs rainmaking for its own) on cloud-monitoring and cloud-seeding will have better results than the separate ones. But there existed little cooperation and combined action in that area, as an official of the Weather Modification Bureau of Jilin province said: 'Although the effect would be great if several provinces work together when there is a huge cloud system in the sky, in reality, we seldom do that.'[12]

In China, when rare rain clouds appear over some often-parched regions, it has been a routine practice for workers at the local weather bureaux to roll out anti-aircraft guns and blast away at the sky. The shells that explode contain fine particles of silver iodide which scatter through the moisture-laden clouds. Provincial, county and municipal governments in almost all of Mainland China's 31 provinces, autonomous regions and municipalities have set up weather modification bureaux assigned to regularly bombard the heavens with chemicals in the hope of extracting more rainfall for farmers and city dwellers among China's 1.3 billion residents. In contrast to the possible problems resulting from the wide use of the precipitation enhancement technology, China is facing severe shortage in water supplies. Consequently, the use of this rainmaking technology will continue.

Indeed, the irrational utilization of cloud resources among the neighbouring administrative areas is increasingly becoming a legal and institutional problem in China. Till now, China, like most of other countries, has not had any laws and administrative regulations dealing with the cloud resources as well as the rational application of man-made precipitation enhancement. If the disordered competition mentioned above in rainmaking continues to exist among the neighbouring administrative areas, further conflicts will inevitably occur in cross-border areas. However, utilization of this largely ineffective man-made precipitation enhancement technology will become an issue to be faced by all stakeholders concerned. With persistent drought still plaguing China, some neighbouring regions have begun squabbling over the rights to clouds. The most hotly debated topic is that upwind neighbours will unfairly intercept clouds, thereby depriving downwind areas of rainfall (see Box 7.2 for a typical case of the accusation of 'rain theft'). Given the severity of water scarcity, such sensitivity is not surprising.

## Cultural barriers

Many sociologists and historians believe that the Chinese culture has not been homogeneous from its beginning. Besides the Han-Chinese who account for more than 90 per cent of the nation's total population, 55 minority groups which include Zhuang (15.6 million persons), Manchu (9.8 million persons), Hui (8.6 million persons), Miao (7.4 million persons), Uygur (7.2 million persons), Yi (6.6 million persons) and so on also exist in mainland China (SSB, 1996, p. 56). From a geographical perspective, the Han majority are dominant in the

*Box 7.2* Fighting for rainfalls

On an overcast day in the western vicinity of Beijing, you will hear the booming sound of anti-aircraft guns from the mountainside of Xiangshan Hills Park. Please don't be startled. That was neither an air raid drill, nor in preparation for a coming war. Rather, it was the sound of Beijing meteorologists shooting canisters of silver iodine into the gathering clouds. In addition to Beijing, other major cities and provinces also have ordered their respective meteorological workers to shoot at any clouds that could enhance rainfall over the drought city. The following is a case in point, as reported by Liu (2004):

In order to obtain a larger share of rainfall for their own, the five administrative areas (Pingdingshan, Zhumadian, Luohe and, Xuchang cities and Zhoukou prefecture) competed with each other, with thousands of rocket shells and old anti-aircraft guns shooting canisters of chemicals into the cloud. The final result of the rainmaking was significantly uneven: the largest rainfall occurred in Pingdingshan and Xuchang cities (with a rainfall of 100 mm or more); while Zhoukou prefecture, with the same input as the other four cities, had only a 27 mm rainfall in urban area and a meager 7 mm in the rural area where the need of rainfall was the most crying. Zhoukou officials complained that the neighboring cities had repeatedly seeded clouds that, if nature had been allowed to follow its course, would have scudded along to other places – such as Zhoukou – before delivering their rainfall.

Indeed, the rational and optimal utilization of cloud resources among the neighboring administrative areas is increasingly becoming a legal and institutional problem that must be solved appropriately by the Chinese authorities at both central and local levels. Till now, China, like most of other countries, has not had any laws and administrative regulations dealing with the cloud resources as well as the rational application of man-made precipitation enhancement. However, if this disordered competition in rainmaking continues to exist among the neighboring administrative areas in China, maybe some day in the future, the anti-aircraft guns and missiles that were used to shoot clouds would shoot each other.

Eastern and Central belts with the only exception of Guangxi which is a Zhuang autonomous region. The other minority-dominative autonomous regions include Ningxia (Hui minority-based) and Xinjiang (Ugyur minority-based) in Northwest region, Inner Mongolia (Mongolian minority-based) in North region, Tibet (Tibetan minority-based) in Southwest region, and so on. In addition, there are also 78 minority-based autonomous prefectures and prefecture-level municipalities and further 641 minority-based autonomous counties and county-level municipalities under the administrations of the above autonomous regions and other provinces in China.

Most of China's provinces, autonomous regions and municipalities directly under the central government, which are the average size and scale of a European country in population and land area, are considerable political and economic systems in their own right. The differences between these provinces have long been a defining characteristic of China's politics since in most cases their boundaries have been created over some two thousand years ago. Besides, Chinese culture is not homogeneous across provinces, in terms of ethnic and linguistic groups as well as religious adherents (Gottmann, 1973; and Goodman 1997). What is more important, there are heterogeneous religious believes in China. For example, people in Tibet and its adjacent autonomous areas in Southwest China usually believe in Tibetan Buddhism, while most minorities in Northwest China are closely related to Islam. The Han-Chinese representing the majority of Chinese population in the Central and Eastern belts are traditionally in favour of a mix of Buddhism, Confucianism and Taoism, with the exception of a few of others. Naturally, it is unlikely that people with markedly differing attitudes as well as different cultural values could emphasize the adoption of a common standard and the socioeconomic coordination. Apart from abstract questions of justice, this circumstance would not lead itself to an agreement between the cultural regimes concerned.

## China's search for spatial integration

Rooted in a single culture, the Chinese economic area is politically separated. Hong Kong and Macau had been for a long period two colonial territories ruled by the UK and Portugal for centuries before 1997 and 1999, respectively. Far before their returns to China under the principle of 'one country, two systems', the two capitalist economies had already set up close and efficient economic links with their communist rival in the mainland throughout the postwar history. Mainland China traditionally supplied most of Hong Kong's food and fresh water, and Hong Kong traditionally served as China's main port. Since 1978 the links between the two economies have been extended to production, investment, provision of services, and financial relations (Dodsworth and Mihaljek, 1997). Particularly, regardless of the political and military tensions between Taiwan and the mainland of China, bilateral trade and economic exchanges cross the Taiwan strait have grown dramatically, so have been tourism, technological and labour cooperation. It is unbelievable that this kind of economic ties could have been sustained between the two politically distrustful and hostile economies.

However the large size of the Chinese nation does insert some negative influences on the Chinese economy, especially in its huge and backward inland areas. Since the advent of the administrative decentralization in the early 1980s, China's national economy had become effectively 'cellularized' into a plethora of semi-autarkic regional enclaves. Public finance, as an important component of the Chinese economic system, has undergone a series of reforms on the central-local relations. The main goals of these reforms were to decentralize the fiscal structure and to strengthen the incentive for local governments to collect more revenue for themselves. Obviously, the economic decentralization has been a major factor in China's current economic success.[13] However these reforms have also had negative impacts on interprovincial relations. For example, in order to protect local market and revenue sources, it became common in China for some provinces to restrict import (export) from (to) other provinces by levying high, if informal, taxes and by creating non-tariff barriers on commodities whose production is seen as important to their provincially 'domestic' economies.[14] Moreover, this unfair competition between provinces has created fierce economic 'battlegrounds' in border-areas and there have been numerous examples of 'trade embargoes' or 'commodity wars' between provinces over, amongst other items, rice, wool, tobacco, soy beans, and mineral products.[15]

Most of China's provinces, autonomous regions and municipalities directly under the central government are on a size and scale equivalent to a European country in population and land area. They are considerable political and economic systems in their own right. The differences between these provinces have long been a defining characteristic of China's politics. In most cases their boundaries were created over two thousand years ago (Gottmann, 1973). In addition, Chinese culture is not homogeneous across provinces. There is a broad range of ethnic and linguistic groups as well as religious adherents in the nation.

This to a large extent implies that the chances of the adoption of a common standard between different groups of people are not likely to be enhanced if they have markedly differing religious beliefs and values. Consequently, China's great diversity in physical geography, resource endowment, political economy and ethnical identity has given rise to many difficulties in interprovincial administration.

For example, of China's 66 interprovincial borderlines, 65 are disputed and have even been published, according to their own preferences, by the provincial level authorities in their official maps and documents (Zhang, 1990, p. 8). According to the statistics released by the Ministry of Civil Affairs, of the 52,000 km of interprovincial borders in the Peoples Republic of China, only 5 per cent are legally fixed; 77 per cent are regarded as informal (or customary borderlines); and about 18 per cent (about 9,500 km) remain the subject of active dispute.[16] According to the various sources, there were more than 800 cases of cross-border disputes in 333 of the 849 interprovincial border counties of almost all provinces. In defiance of the State Council (1981, 1988b) regulations concerning the resolution of interprovincial border disputes, many disputes were the subject of armed fights between different groups of people. This has seriously affected the social security and sustainability of economic development in those cross-border areas.

Along with the increasing global participation of economic activity, the concept 'economic integration' has become a hot point in the political agenda of both developed and developing nations since the end of World War II, particularly in the late 1980s when the Cold War came to an end. During the last decades, international economic integration has achieved substantial progress, including the establishment of the European Union (EU) and its transformation into European Union (EU), the North America Free Trade Agreement (NAFTA), Asia-Pacific Economic Cooperation (APEC), Association of Southeast Asian Nations (ASEAN), and so on.

Beside its active participation in APEC and other international economic organizations, the Chinese government has also recognized the importance of tearing down the internal barriers disrupting transprovincial trade and economic cooperation. In 1979 the CCPCC and State Council implemented a new spatial development strategy entitled 'evading weakness, exerting advantages, protecting competitiveness, and promoting unification'. This strategy first attempted to replace the traditional economic method by which the Chinese economy was constructed into several self-supported regional systems. On 20 October

1984, the Third Plenum of the 12th CCPCC claimed that 'All administrative divisions should open up to each other, the barriers between economically developed and lagging regions, between coastal, inland and frontier regions, between urban and rural areas, and between different sectors and enterprises should be removed for economic unification according to the principle of evading weakness, mutual complementarity and joint development'.[17] Generally, it has been believed that multiregional economic cooperation was greatly promoted during the above period. From 1981 to 1985, more than 30 regional economic and technological cooperative organizations were established in China.

China's spatial economic integration drive was further promoted by the 'Regulations on Some Issues Concerning the Further Promotion of Horizontal Economic Unification' promulgated by the State Council in 1986. According to CASS (1992, pp. 561–7), more than 100 multiregional economic cooperative zones have been established by central and local governments. Generally, China's multiregional economic cooperative zones are usually voluntarily established and jointly administered by adjacent local government. Many of them also have liaison officers and convene regular (annual) meetings co-chaired by the participating sides. The main tasks of the meetings are to, *inter alia* (1) discuss the key issues related to all sides concerned, such as the regional economic development strategy, regional economic structure, and so on; (2) coordinate the policies and measures concerning the promotion of regional economic development; (3) develop bilateral and multilateral economic cooperation; (4) study reconstruction and unification in the fields of production, circulation, science and technology, and (5) implement the specific coordination between all sides concerned.

According to their objectives and functions, the multiregional economic cooperative zones can be classified into seven categories: (1) synthesized economic cooperative zones (2) resource-exploiting cooperative zones (3) open economic zones (4) municipal economic cooperative zones (5) municipal economic cooperative networks (6) cooperative zones for economically lagging areas, and (7) sectoral economic cooperative zones. In addition, these economic cooperative zones can generally be classified into three categories in terms of administrative level: first-class economic cooperative zones, each of which is usually composed of two or more adjacent provinces; second-class economic cooperative zones (trans-province border economic cooperative zones, or BECZs), each of which is composed of two or more adjacent prefectures, municipalities, or counties under different provinces; and third-class economic cooperative zones, each of which is composed of

*Table 7.2* Average per capita national income by type of border-region

| Type | 2-provincial border county | | 3-provincial border county | |
|------|---------|------|---------|------|
| | *non-BECZ* | *BECZ* | *non-BECZ* | *BECZ* |
| Plain | 489.79 | 942.40 | 391.61 | 467.69 |
| Mountain | 460.07 | 566.96 | NA | 623.01 |
| All | 473.79 | 686.42 | 391.61 | 584.18 |

*Notes*: 'BECZ' denotes that the trans-provincial border economic cooperation is available.
*Source*: Guo (1991, table 15).

two or more adjacent prefectures, municipalities, or counties within a single province.

Among the above economic cooperative zones, the BECZs are worthy of further note, due to their special geographical locations and multi-dimensional administrative structures. The BECZs were new entries to regional economic sphere in 1983. By the end of 1989, the total number of the BECZs had increased dramatically to 41.[18] The proliferation of BECZs has provided an efficient channel for provincially peripheral areas to develop cross-border economic ties and cooperation. From Table 7.2, we see that the average per capita national income is always higher in BECZs than in other border areas. Specifically, the per capita national income was only 473.79 yuan and 391.61 yuan in 2- and 3-province border counties (an *i*-province border county is one which is bordered by *i* provinces), respectively, given the unavailability of trans-province border economic cooperation; after trans-province border economic cooperation, however, the per capita national income in the 2- and 3-province border counties increased by 44.88 per cent and 49.17 per cent, to 686.42 yuan and 584.18 yuan, respectively.

## West China development strategy

In the middle of 1999 members of the CCPCC, headed by Jiang Zemin, started talking publicly about a change to China's regional development policy. For just over twenty years, ever since Mao's principles of equal development and regional self-sufficiency – encapsulated in the description of 'The whole country a chessboard' – had been set aside, a more differentiated approach to regional development policy had privileged the eastern and coastal economies of the People's Republic of China. Without abandoning the regional development policy of the previous twenty years, the new policy initiative has placed greater emphasis on the development of the interior.

One challenge facing China in this era of globalization is to prevent its uneven growth pattern. In order to narrow the gap with the prosperous coastal area, Jiang Zemin propagated a campaign called 'Open Up the West' during the second half of 1999. In January 2000 followed the Western Region Development Strategy (*xibu da kaifa*), which constitutes a cornerstone of the 10th Five-Year Plan (2001–2005) intended to foster future development of the inland regions. The stated goals were to bring about social and economic development of the interior and western regions of China. In November 1999, the State Council appointed the newly formed 'State Council Leading Group for Western Region Development' to define a new policy. The 'Office' was established in January 2003 to deal with day-to-day business. The main goals of the Western Region Development Strategy set by the central government are as follows:

- Promote the development of the Western and Central regions
- Eliminate regional disparities gradually
- Consolidate the unity of ethnic groups
- Ensure border security and social stability
- Promote social progress

It is expected that the strategy will initiate a number of programs and projects to stimulate domestic demand, expand the market, and to maintain sustained, rapid and healthy development of the national economy. The main tasks are as follows: (1) to construct the infrastructure: water conservancy, communications, energy, telecommunication, and urban infrastructure; (2) to improve the environment: to convert cultivated land back into forestry and pasture, to protect natural forests, recover and increase the vegetation of forestry and pasture, to reduce water loss and soil erosion, and to develop agriculture with local characteristics: processing industry and by-products. Rural poverty alleviation is also on the agenda. Enterprises are called to be active players in restructuring and upgrading traditional industries, to take advantage of military industries concentrated in the Western Region, and to develop high-tech industries in filed such as biology, engineering, aerospace, renewable energy, new materials, electronic information processing, and advanced manufacturing.[19] At the 10th NPC held in March 2003, the State Council raised the issue of uneven development between urban and rural areas and between the regions of the country, stressing that the Western Development Strategy and east-west interaction must be pushed ahead and that it must be ensured that these objectives are fulfilled.[20]

To these ends the detailed planning concentrates on improving infrastructure. Ten large scale infrastructural projects were originally identified and approved by the State Council as part of the proposal to develop China's West. These were:

- The construction of the Xi'an-Hefei section of the Xi'an-Nanjing Railway;
- The construction of the Chongqing-Huaihua (Hunan) Railway;
- Highway construction – five north-south, and seven east-west highways of 35,000 km; with work to start on the Liangping-Changshou section of the Shanghai-Chengdu Highway, and the Kuitan-Sailimuhu section of the Lianhu-Huocheng Highway;
- Airport construction – in particular the development of Xianyang International Airport, Xi'an and a feeder aviation network;
- The development of an overhead light railway in Chongqing;
- The construction of a natural gas pipeline from Sebei in Qinghai to Xining, and then to Lanzhou;
- The development of irrigation projects at Zipingpu in Sichuan, and at Shapotou, Ningxia;
- The restoration of farmland to forests and pastures, ecological construction, afforestation and the development of programs of sapling breeding;
- The development of a potassic fertilizer project in the Qaidam Basin, Qinghai; and
- The construction of infrastructure facilities for colleges and universities, funded by the issue of state bonds.[21]

To these have subsequently been added other specific projects, such as the spectacular proposal to extend the railway line from Golmud (in western Qinghai) that links into the national system, in the other direction to Lhasa, across some of the most inhospitable country for railway development in the world. Indeed, later formulations of proposals to develop China's West have placed even greater emphasis on transport and communications, and particularly the linkages with external economies. In December 2000 the State Council talked about the success of the entire project resting on the development of three 'economic belts' and their links with the main lines of communication.

The three were the new Tibet-Qinghai-Gansu Railway, and its links with the Eurasian continental bridge; the upper reaches of the Yangtze River (Chongqing and Sichuan) and its links to the coastal areas; and the Nanning-Guiyang-Kunming region, and its links with Southeast Asia. This interpretation of the project to 'Open Up the West' provides another point of contrast with the Third Front strategy. Inevitably because the Third Front strategy was less openly-announced and more tightly focused with a highly-specific policy goal (defence in the event of invasion) the project to 'Open Up the West' has been considerably more contested in its formulation and may also be in its implementation.[22]

While the policy to develop 'West China' has clearly been introduced from the top-down, and under the leadership of a dedicated office of the State Council, the wider political environment is very different from that of the 'Third Front Strategy' (see Chapter 8, p. 158). Not only has the project been more openly discussed, but there has been greater lower level involvement in its development. Even at the planning stage, provinces such as Shaanxi, Sichuan and Chongqing were centrally involved. A West China Development Research Institute was established in Xi'an as a cooperative project of the central government's Ministry of Science and Technology, the Shaanxi Province Committee of the CCP, the Science Commission of the Shaanxi Provincial People's Government, and Northwest University in order to provide advice on strategy and policy.

## Concluding remarks

In theory, multiregional economic cooperation and trade must be mutually beneficial to all provinces concerned, given the complementarity in natural resource endowments as well as other economic attributes. However, in China the costs arising from trans-province transactions cannot be underestimated. Discoordinating factors are the differing sub-administrative systems of the provinces and their specific internal social and cultural conditions. Thus, the extent of progress in economic cooperation between the provinces must depend upon the extent to which the related sides pragmatically reorganize and respond to the economic and non-economic benefits and costs involved. In this section, we have analyzed the economic impacts of China's sub-political borders. The result shows that the multiregional complementarities have not been fully utilized and that the Chinese economy cannot be spatially optimized due to the existing cross-border separation. If the Chinese economy falls under the jurisdiction of a single political authority, the economic relationship between its internal locations and sectors may be easily regulated by means of unified economic policies, and the inefficiencies of allocation of production factors can, therefore, be eliminated. But as the Chinese economy is administered by different regional authorities, the problem cannot easily be solved.

The experiences and lessons from both developed and developing countries during the postwar period have demonstrated that the success of a nation in promoting its economic development depends to a large extent on a complete legal system and effective management and supervision mechanisms of its own. China's efforts to this end have achieved some progress, but some large-scale changes are still needed. In fact, the 'commodity wars' between provinces and autonomous regions derived from the fact that China does not have any constitutional clauses which specifically prohibit constrains against interprovincial commerce, even though the central government has been increasingly concerned and many regulations and laws relating to the protection of multiregional cooperation and the removal of local economic blockades have been issued by the State Council (1980a, 1982, 1986, 1990) and the NPC (1993).

# 8
# Industrialization and Technological Progress

A man of the state of Song was worried about his seedlings growing too slowly. He pulled up the seedlings one by one and came home exhausted, saying to his family 'I am tired out today because I have helped the seedlings to grow'. Hearing this, his son hurried to the fields and found that all the seedlings had shrivelled up.

There are very few in the world who will refrain from helping the seedlings grow. But there are some who think it useless to give any help and give up. They are those who do not weed the fields. Whereas there are others who want the shoots to grow quickly by pulling them upward. In their case, not only is it of no help, it actually does harm.

Mencius (372–289 BC)

## China's efforts on industrialization

China had been a typical agrarian society with more than 90 per cent of its population living in rural areas before the PRC was founded in 1949. Thereafter, the Chinese government abandoned the old political and economic systems through socialist transformation of the capitalist industry and commerce. Between 1949 and 1956, some 123,000 capitalist enterprises were transformed into 87,900 industrial units under joint state-private ownership and, at the same time, many small workshops run by individual labourers were reorganized as collectives.[1]

During the early period of the PRC, the development of modern and comprehensive industry had always been given priority. With the direct involvement of central and local government, the targets of the First FYP (1953–57) were fully completed. Among the pre-reform FYPs, the First FYP (1953–57) has been generally known to be most success-ful, because many key macroeconomic issues, such as the relationship between industry and agriculture and the setting of an appropriate rate of accumulation, were properly handled in this FYP. However, some economic problems in relation to over-centralized administration and non-economic methods of management that have been reformed since the late 1970s had their origins in that period.

During this period, the national income increased annually by 8.9 per cent and the annual GVIO growth rate was 18.0 per cent (see Table 8.1). As the First FYP was nearing completion, Mao Zedong pointed out at an enlarged meeting of the Political Bureau of the CCPCC held on 25 April 1956: 'The emphasis in our country's con-struction is on heavy industry. The production of the means of pro-duction must be given priority, that's settled. But it definitely does not follow that the production of the means of subsistence, especially grain, can be neglected.'[2] In the subsequent years, however, the construction of heavy industry was overheated.

Guided by Mao's general line of building socialism with 'greater, faster, better and more economical results' (*duo kuai hao sheng*), the Great Leap Forward movement was launched by the Chinese govern-ment, calling for a doubling of output within one year.[3] In 1958, the target for steel production was raised from the planned output of 6.3 million ton to 10.7 million ton, amounting to a doubling of the real output of the previous year.[4] Obviously, achievement of this target was impossible due to the limitations of production capacity and resource bases. Nevertheless, the fulfilment was stubbornly insisted upon and consequently tens of millions of people had to be mobilized for steel production. The scale of capital construction grew dramati-cally so that the rate of accumulation suddenly rose from 24.9 per cent in 1957 to 33.9 per cent in 1958.[5]

Stimulated by the arbitrary directions given by the central authori-ties, many heavy industrial enterprises were set up blindly during the Great Leap Forward period (1958–60), without any consideration given to their sources of raw materials and their technological requirements. Quality was low and many unwanted and unusable goods were produced, resulting in great losses. Even worse, as large quantities of materials and labour were diverted towards heavy industry, the development of agricul-ture and light industry received accordingly less attention.[6] This situ-ation lasted until 1960, resulting in serious imbalances between accumulation and consumption and between heavy industry and agriculture and light industry. Consequently, from 1959 onwards,

*Table 8.1* Major economic indicators (1950–78)

| Item | 50-52 | 53-57 | 58-62 | 63-65 | 66-70 | 71-75 | 76 | 77 | 78 |
|---|---|---|---|---|---|---|---|---|---|
| *1 Annual growth rate* | | | | | | | | | |
| 1.1 National income (%) | 19.3 | 8.9 | -3.1 | 14.5 | 8.4 | 5.6 | -2.7 | 7.8 | 12.3 |
| 1.2 GVAO (%) | 14.1 | 4.5 | -4.3 | 11.1 | 3.9 | 4.0 | 2.5 | 1.7 | 9.0 |
| 1.3 GVIO (%) | 34.8 | 18.0 | 3.8 | 17.9 | 11.7 | 9.1 | 1.3 | 14.3 | 13.5 |
| (1) heavy industry | 48.8 | 25.4 | 6.6 | 14.9 | 14.7 | 10.2 | 0.5 | 14.3 | 15.6 |
| (2) light industry | 29.0 | 12.9 | 1.1 | 21.2 | 8.4 | 7.7 | 2.4 | 14.3 | 10.8 |
| 2 Accumulation/national income (%) | | 24.2 | 30.8 | 22.7 | 26.3 | 33.0 | 30.9 | 32.3 | 36.5 |
| 3 National income/100 yuan investment | | 35 | 1 | 57 | 26 | 16 | -10 | 26 | 34 |
| *4 Distribution of capital construction* | | | | | | | | | |
| 4.1 Agriculture (%) | | 7.8 | 12.3 | 18.8 | 11.8 | 11.3 | | | |
| 4.2 Light industry (%) | | 5.9 | 5.2 | 3.9 | 4.0 | 5.4 | | | |
| 4.3 Heavy industry (%) | | 46.5 | 56.1 | 49.8 | 57.4 | 54.8 | | | |

*Sources:* Liang (1982, p. 63, table 4); Dong (1982, pp. 88–9, table 9).

agricultural production dropped spectacularly. The GVAO in 1961 was 26.3 per cent below that in 1958; compared with the preceding year, industrial production dropped by an incredible 38.2 per cent in 1961 and 16.6 per cent in 1962. The productivity of industrial labor was 5.4 per cent lower in 1962 than in 1957, while national income declined by 14.4 per cent over the same period.[7] Although natural disasters and the deterioration of the Sino-Soviet ties played some role in these setbacks, the major cause should ascribe to China's overheated industrial policy.

In the following period, economic readjustment was attempted so as to correct some of the previous errors. Factories were either closed, suspended, merged or switched to other lines of production. The construction of some large-sized plants was cancelled or delayed. Many industrial workers were redeployed to the countryside (*xiafang*). During the readjustment period (1963–65), some sound progress towards industrial construction was made. The launching of the Cultural Revolution in 1966 and the ten years of social chaos that followed, however, disrupted this process. Similar errors of blind and subjective

---

*Box 8.1*   World dynamics: a pessimist viewpoint

Based on systems dynamics – a technique based on conceptions in control theory, organization theory, and on the available techniques of computer simulation – developed by Jay W. Forrester at MIT, a large-scale computer model was constructed to simulate likely future outcomes of the world economy. The most prominent feature of systems dynamics is the use of feedback loops to explain behavior. It is a unique tool for dealing with questions about the way complex systems behave through time.

The standard model run assumes no major change in the physical, economic, or social relationships that have historically governed the development of the world system. All variables included in the model follow historical values from 1900 to 1970 (Meadows, 1972).

One of main conclusions reached by this study suggests that within a time span of less than 100 years, society will run out of the nonrenewable resources on which the world's industrial base depends. When the resources have been depleted, a precipitous collapse of the economic system will result, manifested in massive unemployment, decreased food production, and a decline in population. The characteristic behavior of the system is collapse.

leadership of industrialization were committed. Many large-scale industrial enterprises were built without adequate sources of raw materials
and with no consideration of transport availability and social needs.[8]

From the early 1960s to the late 1970s, China spatially divided its
economy into three fronts according to the principle of 'preparing for
wars': (1) the eastern (coastal) provinces were defined as the first line
due to their proximity to the capitalist world; (2) a number of inland
provinces (such as Sichuan, Guizhou, Shaanxi, Gansu, Qinghai, Ningxia,
Yunnan, the western parts of Hubei, Hunan, Henan, Shanxi and Hebei,
the northern part of Guangdong, and the northwest part of Guangxi) –
most of which are covered by mountains – were treated as the third-
front; (3) the remaining provinces were treated as the second-front.
During the Cultural Revolution period (1966–76), the development of
the third-front area was given priority in the Chinese industrialization
as it was believed that World War III would occur very soon and that
the first-front area could inevitably become the battlefield. As a result
of governmental involvement, the third-line area's share of China's
capital investment sharply increased from 30.60 per cent in the First
FYP (1953–57) up to 52.70 per cent in the Third FYP (1966–70) and the
per capita GVIO increased from 22.04 yuan in 1952 to 373.97 yuan in
1983, while the coastal area increased from 93.77 yuan to 871.3 yuan
during the same period.[9] Promoted by the third-front development
strategy, many large and key enterprises (mainly in military, aeronautic
and astronautic, electronic, and other high-tech industries), universities, and research institutions were transferred from the coastal (urban)
area (the first-line) to the mountainous, remote, and, usually, rural
inland area (the third-front).[10]

The third-front area development policy quickly industrialized some
areas of China's inland provinces (see Table 8.2) and provided a pecu-
liar pattern for developing countries to avoid the 'polarization' between
rich and poor areas. During 1953 and 1978, the annual GVIO growth
rates of Shaanxi, Qinghai, Shanxi, Guizhou and Sichuan provinces
reached 20.1 per cent, 16.3 per cent, 12.0 per cent, 11.2 per cent and
11.8 per cent, respectively, which were much higher than that of the
coastal provinces.[11] However, it has not been known as a successful
approach to modernize the Chinese economy as a whole. This can be
demonstrated by the fact that the average annual capital output coefficient (that is, output/investment ratio) of the third-front area was only
0.256, far less than that of the coastal area (0.973) during 1953–79.[12] In
addition, Yang (1989, p. 76) estimates that there would have been a
net increase of 1434 billion yuan GVIO (in other words, approximately

*Table 8.2*  Industrial outputs of the third-front area as % of China (1952, 1965, and 1978)

| Item | 1952 | 1965 | 1978 |
|------|------|------|------|
| GVIO | 17.9 | 22.3 | 25.7 |
| Steel | 13.9 | 19.4 | 27.9 |
| Coal | 33.0 | 40.9 | 47.6 |
| Electricity | 10.5 | 25.2 | 33.5 |
| Machine tools | 2.2 | 15.7 | 27.3 |
| Car | – | – | 12.1 |
| Tractor | – | 77.4 | 30.6 |
| Cement | 14.1 | 13.6 | 37.0 |
| Clothing | 15.9 | 27.9 | 30.7 |
| Paper | 7.1 | 14.5 | 23.0 |
| Cigarette | 28.6 | 34.5 | 42.0 |

*Source*: Liu (1983).

45 per cent of China's total GVIO in 1975), had the investment been distributed in the coastal area rather than the third-front area during that period.

After the death of Mao Zedong in September 1976, the Chinese government once again tried to speed up economic development by setting up targets that were much higher than maximum capabilities. These impetuous and unrealistic plans started in 1978 and resembled, in many ways, those of the Great Leap Forward started in 1958. Proposals were made enthusiastically by the post-Mao leadership to produce 400 million ton of grain, 60 million ton of steel, 250 million ton of oil, and to develop 120 large- and medium-sized projects, including ten major oil fields, ten major steel plants and ten major coal mines, and to import large amounts of modern equipment and technology by the end of the Sixth FYP (1981–85).[13] It was not until the Third Plenum of the 11th CCPCC in December 1978 that the Chinese government began to shift its main focus of national task from the 'class struggle' to the realization of socialist economic construction, calling on the entire people to strive to achieve the four modernizations of industry, agriculture, national defense and science and technology at the end of the 20th century. However, many economic problems had been cyclically generated by the previous political struggles and could not be solved immediately. In late 1979, China decided to temporarily halt industrial expansion and carried out a policy entitled 'readjustment, reform, consolidation and improvement' (*tiaozheng, gaige, gonggu, tigao*) in order to tackle properly the existing structural imbalances of the Chinese economy. This policy lasted for three years and many industrialization programs did not start to work until 1984.

During the pre-reform period, China's industrialization was mainly implemented via a centrally planned system. Direct and strong government participation and large-scale mobilization of resources and their selective disposition to priority sectors enabled the industrial sector to grow at an average rate of over 10 per cent annually (with a few exceptions in 1961–62, 1967–68 and 1974), resulting in a dramatic increase of its share in national income from 19.5 per cent in 1953 to 49.4 per cent in 1978 (see Table 8.1 and Figure 8.1). The shares of agricultural, light and heavy industrial outputs in GVIAO structurally changed from 56.9 per cent, 27.8 per cent and 15.3 per cent in 1952 to 24.6 per cent, 35.4 per cent and 40.0 per cent, respectively, in 1980.[14] The advantages of rapid industrial expansion from a centrally planned mechanism, however, were soon outweighed by problems of low efficiency, disequilibriated industrial structure dominated by heavy industry, slow technological progress, sectoral disproportions, and sharp annual fluctuations in growth rates. In addition, the self-reliant and inward-looking policies that had been implemented by the Chinese government for most of the pre-reform period were bore responsibility for these poor industrial performances.

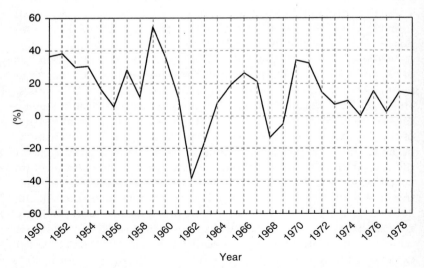

*Figure 8.1*   Industrial growth during the pre-reform period (1949–78)

## Post-reform industrialization

Industrialization contributes directly to economic development through an increase in income levels, job opportunities, exports and the availability of foreign capital and technology, and so on. In the NIEs, industrialization served as the key engine in the early period of economic takeoff. Therefore, most developing nations (especially poor and agrarian nations) have placed great emphasis upon it. China's industrialization had been affected to a large extent by political movements during the pre-reform period. Since the end of the Cultural Revolution, industrial fluctuations have been significantly reduced. At the beginning of economic reform, the industrial output increased annually by over 10 per cent, but declined to a meager 5 per cent in 1981. The industrial growth rate rose by over 20 per cent in 1985, followed again by less than 10 per cent during 1989–90 as a result of the conservative and tight monetary policy employed by the government. Since the early 1990s, China's industrial output has achieved the longest and fastest growth in the post-reform period (see Figure 8.2).

Economic development, on the other hand, decides the industrial structure of a country. Increases in per capita income usually lead to increased consumption, which in turn shifts the industrial structure away from agriculture towards manufacturing and service sectors. This also determines the distribution of labour force among industries.

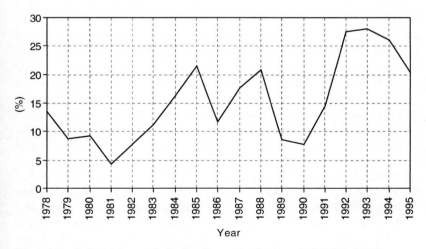

*Figure 8.2* Industrial growth during the post-reform period (1978–1995)

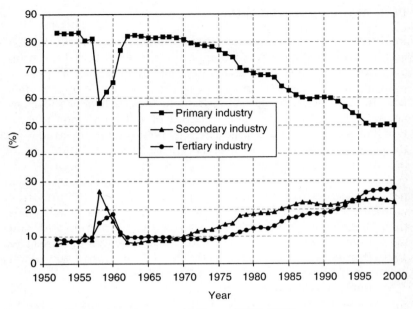

*Figure 8.3*   Employment by type of industry (1952–2000)

From 1952 to 2000, China's sectoral employment shares had changed from more than 80 per cent to about 50 per cent for primary industry, and less than 10 per cent to more than 20 per cent for both secondary tertiary industries (shown in Figure 8.3). Regardless of the increasing transference towards secondary and tertiary industries, Chinese employment has still been dominated by primary industry, especially in the western provinces (such as Tibet, Yunnan, Guizhou, Guangxi), with the exception of a few of provinces whose employment is dominated by secondary industry (such as Shanghai, Tianjin and Liaoning) and by tertiary industry (such as Beijing) in the coastal area.

'Industry' refers to the material production sector engaging in extraction of natural resources and processing of natural resources and agricultural products and reprocessing. With regard to light and heavy industry, there exist differing definitions in different countries. In China, 'light' refers to an industry that produces consumer goods and tools. It comprises two categories: (1) using farm products as raw materials, and (2) using non-farm products as raw materials. Heavy industry refers to general products used by other manufacturers. According to the purpose of production or use of products, heavy industry consists of three branches: (1) extraction of petroleum, coal, metal, and non-metal ores and timber felling (2) smelting and processing of metals, coke making and coke chemistry, chemical materials and building materials such as cement, plywood, and power, petroleum and coal processing, and (3) machine-building industry which equips sectors of the national economy, metal structure industry and cement works, industry producing the means of agricultural production, and the chemical fertilizers and pesticides industry.[15]

Between the early 1950s and the end of the Cultural Revolution, China devoted much of its energy to heavy industrialization at the expense of agriculture and light and service sectors (see the last rows of Table 8.1). Since the early 1980s, the Chinese government has effectively shifted the emphasis away from heavy industry to industries more directly connected with people's lives. This is a correct approach for China to undertake not only because those industries can meet people's demands but also because they are *labour-intensive* and therefore more appropriate for China – a country with the advantage of a cheap and surplus labour supply.

After three years (1950–52) of recovery, the PRC government began to construct its economy through a centrally planned approach. To overcome effectively the disequilibrated industrial distribution between the coastal and inland areas, the government shifted the investment to the inland area from the coastal area. During 1953–78, the basic construction funded by the state was split by 35.7 per cent in the coastal area and 55.2 per cent in the inland area (see Table 8.3). As a result industrial production grew unevenly between the coastal and inland areas. From 1952 to 1978, the inland area's share of GVIO increased from 31.8 per cent to 40.2 per cent, while the coastal area's share of GVIO decreased from 68.2 per cent to 59.8 per cent accordingly (Liu, 1994, p. 3). After 1978 when the Chinese government began to realize the importance of reforming its CPE and paying more attention to efficiency rather than regional equality, the capital investment had inclined on the coastal area. Between 1979 and 1990, the coastal area accounted for 49.9 per cent of the nation's capital investment, while the inland area's share decreased accordingly to 43.2 per cent, as demonstrated in Table 8.3.

Since the early 1980s, there has been a fundamental change in the investment system, mainly characterized by decentralization and regional autonomy. Concerning decentralization, the responsibilities are proportionally shared between central and local governments: (1) projects which are closely related to the overall structure of the

*Table 8.3*   Spatial distribution of investment between coastal and inland areas, (1953–90)

| Period | Coastal (%) | Inland (%) | Coastal/inland |
|---|---|---|---|
| 1953–57 (1st FYP) | 36.9 | 46.8 | 0.788 |
| 1958–62 (2nd FYP) | 38.4 | 56.0 | 0.686 |
| 1963–65 | 34.9 | 58.3 | 0.599 |
| 1966–70 (3rd FYP) | 26.9 | 64.7 | 0.416 |
| 1971–75 (4th FYP) | 35.5 | 54.4 | 0.653 |
| 1976–80 (5th FYP) | 42.2 | 50.0 | 0.844 |
| 1981–85 (6th FYP) | 47.7 | 46.5 | 1.026 |
| 1986–90 (7th FYP) | 51.7 | 39.9 | 1.296 |
| 1953–78 (pre-reform) | 35.7 | 55.2 | 0.647 |
| 1979–90 (post-reform) | 49.9 | 43.2 | 1.155 |
| 1953–90 | 45.0 | 46.8 | 0.962 |

*Note*: total investment of coastal and inland areas are less than 100.00% due to the exclusion of the spatially 'unidentified' investment which includes (1) the trans-provincial investment in railway, post and telecommunication, electric power, etc.; (2) the unified purchase of airplanes, ships, vehicles, etc.; (3) the investment in national defense.

*Sources*: (1) SSB (1991, 1992) and (2) Li and Fan (1994, p. 65).

national economy, such as key energy, raw material industry bases, trans-provincial communication and transportation networks, key mechanical, electronic and other high-tech development projects, key agricultural bases as well as the national defense industry, are still financially con-trolled by the state; (2) the primary industrial and local projects, such as agriculture, forestry and wood, local energy, raw material industries, regional communication and transportation networks, mechanical and light industries, science and technology, education, culture, public health, urban public infrastructure and services and so on, are mainly invested and managed by local government. In the case of regional autonomy, the quotas of industrial construction and technological remoulding items needed to be approved by the State Planning Com-mission (SPC) increased from 30 million yuan or over to 50 million yuan or over for energy, communication and raw material industries and from 10 million yuan or over to 30 million yuan or over for light and other industries. Production construction items beyond the above limits and non-productive construction items are decided by the provinces themselves.[16]

In order to compare China's industrial performances during the post-reform period internationally, one may simply employ the results by Hsueh (1994b, pp. 74–99) for China and the results by Chenery and

Syrquin (1975, pp. 20–1) for the international case. Both results are estimated using the same specification below:

$$X = \alpha + \beta_1 \ln Y + \beta_2 (\ln Y)^2 + \gamma_1 \ln N + \gamma_2 (\ln N)^2 + \Sigma(\delta_i T_i) \qquad (8.1)$$

where, $X$ denotes each of the variables shown in the first column of Table 8.4; $Y$ is the per capita national income (RMB yuan) at the constant price of 1980 for the Chinese case and per capita GNP (US dollar) for the international case; $N$ is population size (million persons); and $T_i$ denotes the time period. In Hsueh's analysis, two periods (i.e. 1980–84 and 1985–89) were selected. Arguably this is reasonable, because the year 1985 was generally known as the watershed for China's HRS-based agricultural reform and urban industrial reform, while it was the latter that significantly influenced industrialization. For most provinces, per capita national income ranged between ¥250 to 1000 yuan during the 1980s, which can be approximately converted to the per capita GNP of US$100 to 400 for the international case during the 1950 to 1970 period in Chenery and Syrquin (1975).

From Table 8.4, we find that the Chinese industrial structure was similar to the international version. For both versions, the ratios of value-added agricultural output were declining, while that of industrial output were increasing. However, the only difference is that China had

*Table 8.4* China's industrialization at different stage of economic development, with an international comparison

| Variable | International case[a] | | | Chinese case[b] | | |
|---|---|---|---|---|---|---|
| | US$100 (1) | US$400 (2) | (2)–(1) (3) | ¥250 (4) | ¥1000 (5) | (5)–(4) (6) |
| Va | 0.452 | 0.228 | –0.224 | 0.513 | 0.196 | –0.317 |
| Vm | 0.149 | 0.276 | 0.127 | 0.276 | 0.584 | 0.308 |
| Vl | | | | 0.118 | 0.282 | 0.164 |
| Vh | | | | 0.164 | 0.303 | 0.139 |
| Lp | 0.658 | 0.438 | –0.220 | 0.892 | 0.462 | –0.431 |
| Lm | 0.091 | 0.135 | 0.144 | 0.041 | 0.323 | 0.282 |
| Ls | 0.251 | 0.327 | 0.076 | 0.067 | 0.215 | 0.149 |

*Notes:* [a] Chenery and Syrquin (1975, pp. 20–1); [b] Hsueh (1994b, p. 80).

*Variables:* Va=ratio of value-added agricultural output in NI (national income); Vm=ratio of value-added industrial output in NI; Vl= ratio of value-added light industrial output in NI; Vh=ratio of value-added heavy industrial output in NI; Lp=ratio of labor of primary sector in total social labor; Lm=ratio of labor of manufacturing sector in total social labor; and Ls=ratio of labor of service sector in total social labor.

larger marginal changes in industrial structure with respect to economic growth than the international version. For example, when the per capita GNP ranged from US$100 to US$400, the changes of the ratio of value-added agricultural output and the ratio of value-added industrial output in GNP were −0.224 and 0.127, respectively, for the international case; while the changes of the ratio of value-added agricultural output and the ratio of value-added industrial output in national income for the Chinese case were −0.317 and 0.308, respectively, during the approximately same development stage. Furthermore, when the per capita national income increased from 250 yuan to 1000 yuan, the ratio of value-added light industrial output and the ratio of value-added heavy industrial output in national income increased by 0.164 and 0.139, respectively, implying that light industry served as a stronger engine on the Chinese economy than heavy industry. In Table 8.4, when the per capita national income increased from 250 yuan to 1000 yuan, the ratio of value-added agricultural output in national income decreased from 0.513 to 0.196, and the ratio of labour of primary sector in total social labour decreased from 0.892 to 0.462 accordingly; in contrast, when the per capita national income increased from 250 yuan to 1000 yuan, the ratio of value-added industrial output in national income increased from 0.276 to 0.584, while the ratio of labour of industrial sector in total social labour increased from 0.041 to 0.323 accordingly.

Chinese industrialization differs greatly from region to region, as demonstrated in Table 8.5. For instance, the Eastern belt, with only 12 provinces and 13.5 per cent of the land area, has 244,183 industrial enterprises under independent accounting system, 10.5 per cent more than that of the Central and Western belts as a whole (18 provinces) which account for 86.5 per cent of the land area. The regional industrial differences can be further explored in detail. In 1994, the number of employees and fixed assets in the Eastern belt were 62.6 per cent and 105.9 per cent higher than that in the Central belt, and 249.2 per cent and 292.6 per cent higher than that in the Western belt, respectively; while the GVIO, newly-added output and pre-tax profit in the Eastern belt were 185.7 per cent, 136.4 per cent and 134.0 per cent higher than that in the Central belt, and 536.5 per cent, 397.6 per cent and 325.9 per cent higher than that in the Western belt, respectively. From Table 8.5, we find that the relative industrial indicators of the Eastern belt were the best among the three belts. A glance at the Central and Western belts reveals that, except for the output/capital ratio (O/K), all other relative industrial indicators were better in the Western belt

*Table 8.5* Major industrial indicators[a] by the Eastern, Central, and Western belt

| Item | Eastern | Central | Western |
|---|---|---|---|
| Number of enterprises (N) | 244183 | 156075 | 64981 |
| Employees (thousand persons) (L) | 44770 | 27527 | 12822 |
| Fixed assets (billion yuan) (K) | 1921.51 | 933.25 | 489.39 |
| GVIO (billion yuan) | 3407.3 | 1192.7 | 535.3 |
| Newly-added output (billion yuan) (O) | 905.15 | 382.93 | 181.92 |
| Pre-tax profits (billion yuan) (P) | 296.93 | 126.88 | 69.72 |
| Average (million yuan) (K/N) | 7.87 | 5.98 | 7.53 |
| Size (persons) (L/N) | 183.3 | 176.4 | 197.3 |
| Capital/labor (yuan/person) (K/L) | 429196 | 339031 | 381680 |
| Output/capital ratio (O/K) | 0.47 | 0.41 | 0.37 |
| Labor productivity (yuan/person) (O/L) | 202178 | 139111 | 141881 |
| Income/output share (%) (P/O) | 32.80 | 33.13 | 38.32 |
| Profit/capital share (%) (P/K) | 15.45 | 13.60 | 14.25 |

*Note*: a: for industrial enterprises under independent accounting system only.

*Source*: calculated by the author based on SSB (1996b, pp. 79–81).

than in the Central belt, which is inconsistent with the results in Figure 6.4.

In order to conduct an in-depth comparison of industrial performances between different regions, we may build a multiregional production function. The general form of a Cobb–Douglas function can be written as $Y=e^\lambda K^\alpha L^\beta e^\mu$, where, $Y$=output, $K$=capital, $L$=labour, $\alpha$=elastic coefficient of capita, $\beta$=elastic coefficient of labour, $\lambda$=factor of technological progress, and $\mu$=system error. If we use a regional variable, $D_1$ (where, $D_1=-1$ denotes the Western belt, $D_1=0$ denotes the Central belt, and $D_1=1$ denotes the Eastern belt) and a sectoral variable, $D_2$ (where $D_2=-1$ denotes the resource-exploiting enterprises, $D_2=0$ denotes the resource-processing enterprises, and $D_2=1$ denotes the high-tech enterprises), the modified Cobb–Douglas production function may be written as

$$Y=e^{\lambda_0}K^{(\alpha_0+\alpha_1 D_1+\alpha_2 D_2)}L^{(\beta_0+\beta_2 D_2+\beta_1 D_1)}e^\mu \qquad (8.2)$$

where, $\lambda_0$, $\alpha_0$, $\alpha_1$, $\alpha_2$, $\beta_0$, $\beta_1$, $\beta_2$ are constants to be estimated. Using the data of 500 top industrial enterprises compiled by CEEC (1990), we obtain a log-form regression equation:[17]

$$\ln Y=6.87+ (0.50-0.02D_1-0.17D_2)\ln K+(-0.10+0.03D_1+0.09D_2)\ln L \qquad (8.3)$$
$$(10.11)(-4.53)\ (-2.40) \qquad (-17.0)(4.94)\ (2.51)$$
$$(N=500,\ R^2=0.76,\ F=194.98)$$

*Table 8.6* The elasticities of $K$ and $L$ on the industrial production[a]

| Sector | Western belt $(D_1=-1)$ | | Central belt $(D_1=0)$ | | Eastern belt $(D_1=1)$ | |
|---|---|---|---|---|---|---|
| | $K$ | $L$ | $K$ | $L$ | $K$ | $L$ |
| Resource-exploiting $(D_2=-1)$ | 0.68 | −0.32 | 0.66 | −0.30 | 0.64 | −0.23 |
| Resource-processing $(D_2=0)$ | 0.51 | −0.13 | 0.50 | −0.10 | 0.48 | −0.07 |
| High-tech$(D_2=1)$ | 0.35 | −0.04 | 0.33 | −0.01 | 0.31 | 0.02 |

*Note*: [a] derived from Equation 8.3.

where, ln represents a natural logarithm, $R^2$ is a multiple correlation coefficient, F is the F-statistic and the figures in the parentheses under the parameters are the $t$ statistics. Using Equation 8.3, we may obtain the elasticities of capital $(K)$ and labour $(L)$ on production for each geographical belt and industrial sector (see Table 8.6).

From the perspective of the three belts, we may find that (1) the capital elasticity of the Western belt is larger than that of the Central belt, and the latter is larger than that of the Eastern belt, which suggests that the Western belt has the highest efficiency for capital input in large-sized enterprises; (2) the labour elasticity of the Eastern belt is larger than that of the Central belt, and the latter is larger than that of the Western belt, which suggests that the Eastern belt has the highest efficiency for labour input in the large-sized enterprises.

From the perspective of the three sectors, we may find that (1) the capital elasticity of the resource-exploiting enterprises is larger than that of the resource-processing enterprises, and the latter is larger than that of the high-tech enterprises, which suggests that the resource-exploiting enterprises have the highest efficiency for capital input in the large-sized enterprises; (2) the labour elasticity of the high-tech enterprises is larger than that of the resource-processing enterprises, and the latter is larger than that of the resource-exploiting enterprises, which suggests that the high-tech enterprises have the highest efficiency for labour input in the large-sized enterprises.

In addition, it is rather surprising that the labour elasticity is negative for all enterprises, except for high-tech enterprises in the Eastern belt of China, implying that there must have existed some problems in relation to labour productivity in China's large-sized enterprises.

# Rural industrialization

Labour force is equal to population in the productive age group multiplied by labour force participation rate. The labour force participation rate can be calculated as the ratio of the labour force to the population at a certain age or over. The international standard for the productive age is defined as 15 years or over. In a market economy, labour force demand is positively related to gross production output. When labour supply exceeds labour demand unemployment occurs.

In the early 1950s, almost eight-nineth of Chinese population lived in the countryside and earned their living from the land. Until the end of the 1990s, this proportion decreased gradually to two-thirds. But the total rural population increased during the same period. It is inevitable that the situation of a rapidly increasing rural population combined with limited cultivable land will generate a large rural labour surplus, particularly with the increased productivity resulting from the introduction of advanced technologies.

In 1978, more than 80 per cent of the population in China still lived in rural areas. In the following years, the rural population as a percentage of total population in China experienced a substantial reduction as a result of industrial expansion. However, it has still been higher than that in many countries, such as USA (3.9 per cent), Japan (10.7 per cent), UK (2.6 per cent), West Germany (4.9 per cent), South Korea (33.5 per cent), and India (66.2 per cent).[18] This resulted to a large extent from the long-standing government policy that strictly controlled rural–urban migration. With little prospect for expanding cultivated land and a large and still growing population, the Chinese government began to recognize the urgency of shifting the rural labour force from farming to more productive non-agricultural sectors. However, the government also remained convinced that this occupational shift must be achieved without significantly enlarging the urban population through rural-urban migration. Accordingly, the policy entitled *'litu bu lixiang, jinchang bu jincheng'* (leave the soil but not the countryside, enter the factory but not the city) has been implemented since the late 1970s.

The growth of the rural industrial sector has been extremely rapid and is largely responsible for the dramatic increases in income level in rural China. Almost overnight, a huge number of new industrial activities emerged and millions of private, share-holding or other enterprises (PSEs) and COEs were established in the countryside. Of particular importance is the rapid growth of enterprises that are collectively owned and operated by the townships and villages. The proliferation of township and village enterprises (TVEs) has had far-reaching consequences, because millions of rural workers have shifted from farming to industrial activities and in the process helped to transform the economic structure of rural China. For example, in 1978, the rural non-agricultural workers accounted for only 7.12 per cent of the total rural worker. In 2000, however, the share of rural non-agricultural workers in the total rural labours had quadrupled to more than 30 per cent.[19]

The growth of the TVEs is extraordinary. In 1978, there were only 1524 thousand TVEs in rural areas, while the number of TVEs increased dramatically to 22,027 thousand in 1995. Output has grown by over 30 per cent per annum since 1978. The share of value-added output in GDP rose from about 10 per cent in the early 1980s to over 30 per cent in 1995.[20] So far, the TVEs have created more than 120 million jobs for the surplus rural workers during the past years and is becoming a more and more important component of the Chinese economy. Total factor productivity in the TVEs is much higher than in the state sector and is growing by 5 per cent a year, more than twice the rate in the SOEs.

The World Bank (1996, p. 51) lists five factors contributing to the remarkable growth and superior record of efficiency of the TVEs:

- *Kinship and implicit property rights.* Strong kinship links among rural Chinese villagers encourage responsibility in entrepreneurs. The sharing of implicit, if fuzzy, property rights leads to a productive combination of risk and reward sharing between entrepreneurs and local government. None the less, incentives facing TVEs are more like those of private firms in that the residual profits accrue to a limited group: a traditionally stable local community and, in particular, its government and TVE managers.
- *Decentralization plus financial discipline.* The 1984 decentralization of fiscal power in China allowed sub-national governments to retain locally generated revenues, creating powerful incentives for the development of local industry. Under this system a non-performing TVE becomes an unaffordable drain on a limited local budget. In the end persistent money-losers are closed and the work force is shifted to more profitable lines.
- *Competition.* Studies also show intense competition for investment (including foreign investment) among communities with TVEs. Success in attracting investment is affected by reputation and local economic performance.
- *Market opportunities and rural saving.* A past bias against light industry and services has created vast market opportunities, buttressed by

high rural saving and demand following the agricultural reforms of 1978 and by the limited scoop for emigration from rural areas.

- *Links with the state enterprise sector.* The large state-owned industrial sector provides a natural source of demand, technology and raw materials for many TVEs. Foreign investment from Hong Kong and Taiwan (China) plays the same role for many others.

The proliferation of industrial activities in rural China stemming from rural reform have created more economic opportunities for China's rural population. The rural residents have seized these opportunities aggressively and shifted vast amounts of resources from agricultural to more profitable non-agricultural activities. It appears that large amounts of 'surplus labour' existing in China has facilitated the rapid rural industrial development. The problems that have emerged in the process of rural industrialization are, *inter alia*, the occupation of farm land by TVEs, possible adverse effects of rural industrial production on agriculture, waste of energy by TVEs, and environmental pollution.[21]

## Technological progress

Technological innovation has been the most fundamental element in promoting, either directly or indirectly, economic development and social change. Although it is very difficult to precisely measure its short-term impact, nobody would reject that technological progress is changing the world at an incredibly high rate. The most obvious contribution is transport and communication that have changed from the crude means (such as horses, carriages and hand-written letters) to such means as superjets, telephones, faxes as well as the increasingly efficient computer networks, of which the Internet has been increasingly becoming the most important means for transmitting information.[22] Mobile telephones, computer networks, and other technological inventions, which were considered to be either impossible or useless, are now becoming the necessities of our daily life.

Before the early 20th century, technological innovations had been contributed mainly by individual inventors or small-scale entrepreneurs. But now the great bulk of it – such as the invention of space shuttle and Internet, to list but two – has been conducted by prominent firms with substantial budgets, as well as by governments. As a result the process of technological innovation becomes more complicated than ever before. Specifically, the technological and related products are positively related to capital stock of and personnel engagement in technological innovation. In addition, technological innovation is also related to the educational level, as the content of education changes over time to accommodate to the growing stock of knowledge. There has been a proliferation of specialized intellectual disciplines to facilitate the absorption of knowledge and to promote its development through research.

The four great Chinese inventions (paper-making, gunpowder, movable-type printing and the compass) have greatly contributed to the world's civilization. In recent centuries, however, China lagged far behind Western nations.[23] After the PRC was founded in 1949, China began to import advanced technology from the Soviet Union. Unfortunately, this process was halted abruptly when Sino-Soviet relations worsed diplomatically in the late 1950s. Following its *râpprochement* with the United States and Japan, China gradually began to import advanced technology from the capitalist nations. But economic relations between China and the technologically advanced nations did not improved significantly until the late 1970s when the new CCP and the state leaders tried to abandon the 'leftist' ideology (self-reliance and independence). By the early 1980s, China's production technology in the iron and steel industry was still that of the advanced nations in the 1950s; the scientific and technological level of the electronic industry was approximately 15 to 20 years behind advanced international standards.[24] According to the national industrial census conducted in 1985, 23 per cent of the machines and equipment used by 8285 large- and medium-sized companies were produced during the period from 1949 to 1970.[25]

It must be mentioned that some important progresses in science and technology had been achieved during the pre-reform period. Particularly praiseworthy is the development of atomic bomb in 1964 and artificial satellite in 1970, which granted China a political seat in the superpowers. However, as this kind of technology has been controlled by the Science and Technology Commission for National Defense (STCND) and guided by the State Council and the Military Commission of the CCPCC, the transfer of military technology to social and economic uses is to some extent limited. In other aspects, China's metallurgical, coal, machine-building, oil, chemical, power, electric and precision instrument industries had acquired a stock of relatively advanced equipment. This provided the foundation for industrial modernization. Taken as a whole, however, the level of productivity still remained very low, as did the level of labour productivity.

In fact, the Chinese policy-makers has clearly realized the increasing role of technology in the Chinese economy and paid much attention to the acceleration of technological progress. Since the mid-1980s, China has implemented a package of plans for the development of new technology, high-technology and traditional technology. These plans include, *inter alia*,

- *'863' Plan*, which aims to track the frontiers of the high-tech, research and development;
- *Torchlight Plan*, which aims to promote the commercialization, industrialization, and internationalization of the high-tech products;
- *The Climbing Plan*, which aims to organize the research and application of new and high technologies;
- *Spark Plan*, which aims to spread applicable technologies to small- and medium-sized enterprises, TVEs, and other rural areas, and
- *Harvest Plan*, which aims to popularize various kinds of technology contributing to agriculture, herd and fishery.

However, many problems still exist in the Chinese science and technology sector. The expenditure on research and development (R&D) refers to all actual expenditure made for R&D (fundamental research, applied research, and experimental development). In 1995, China spent 28.6 billion yuan on R&D activities, which was only 0.50 per cent of GNP, compared with the R&D/GNP ratios of 0.93 per cent in 1979 and 1.12 per cent in 1986.[26] Obviously, China's proportion of R&D expenses to GNP has been reduced substantially since the mid-1980s. According to UNESCO (1995, table 5), the R&D/GNP ratio of China was much lower than that of many advanced countries, such as USA (2.9 per cent, 1988), Japan (3.0 per cent, 1991), France (2.4 per cent, 1991), UK (2.1 per cent, 1991), and so on. Even though Minami (1994, p. 116) finds that the R&D/GNP ratio rises sharply with respect to per capita GNP in developing countries when the per capita GNP is less than US$11,000 and in the NIEs, it is impossible for us to estimate any significant correlation between the R&D/GNP ratio and the per capita GNP for China. The main causes may derive from two aspects: (1) from the late 1970s to the mid-1980s, China spent large sum of money on R&D activities; (2) China's R&D/GNP ratio has declined rapidly since the mid-1980s alongside its GNP growth.[27]

# 9

# Population, Resource and Sustainable Development

Xishi, known for her peerless beauty, was beset by some sort of heart trouble, and so she was often seen knitting her brows and walking with a hand on her chest. Now there was an ugly woman, named Dongshi, in the neighbourhood who one day saw Xishi in the village street. In admiration she returned home determined to imitate Xishi' way of walking and mannerisms. But this only increased her ugliness. So much so that every time she walked abroad the rich would shut their doors tight and disdain to come out, while the poor with their wives and children would avoid her and quickly turn their steps away. Alas, that woman mistook frowning for something invariably beautiful, and was unaware that it only adds beauty to a real beauty.

Zhuangzi (c. 368–286 BC)

## General background

It was not until the late 1960s and early 1970s that the 'environment' became a firmly part of the political agenda in the developed nations. This was largely a response not only to the spectacular growth of the Western economies, but also to the continued extensive industrialization of the rest of the world. The phrase 'sustainable development' was firstly popularized by the World Commission for Environment and Development (1987). Since then, much attention for defining 'sustainable development' has been given by the worldwide environmentalists and economists. For example, Pearce *et al.* (1988, p. 6) state 'We can summarize the necessary conditions for sustainable development as constancy of the natural capital stock; more strictly, the requirement

174

for non-negative changes in the stock of natural resources, such as soil and soil quality, ground and surface water and their quality, land biomass, water biomass, and the waste-assimilation capacity of the receiving environments'. Another example cited by Solow (1991) from an UNESCO document is as '... every generation should leave water, air and soil resources as pure and unpolluted as when it came on earth'. The above two passages involve a category mistake being to identify the determinants of well-being with the constituents of well-being (for example, welfare, freedom, and so on), as sustainable development is defined as an impossible goal by these authors.

To be sure, a number of authors writing on sustainable development have consentaneously recognized that the starting point ought to be the realization of well-being over time. Based on this point, Dasgupta and Mäler (1995, p. 2394) give a more general interpretation of the idea of sustainable development that well-being (and, therefore, consumption) must never be allowed to decline over time. However, this definition seems also that the sustainable development is very difficult or, sometimes, impossible to be achieved by the existing economies.[1]

There are at least two characteristics for China: its population is huge and its economy has been growing very fast for at least one-quarter century. China has become the world's major player in both output and input markets. The data on the total consumption of various primary products presented in Table 9.1 reinforce the importance of China in world consumption markets. In metals and coal, China always is ranked first, with shares of 15 per cent to one-third of world consumption, and the United States is ranked second or third; in other energies, the United States is first and China is second or third. China also is important consumer of agricultural commodities, leading the world in consumption of wheat, rice, cotton, palm oil and rubber. India is ranked first in consumption of sugar and tea.[2]

During the past decades, China's rapid economic development has resulted in a substantial improvement in the ordinary people's standard of living. However, it also has generated environmental problems at an impressively high rate. $CO_2$, $SO_2$, $NO_X$, $CH_4$, CFCs and other hazardous waste and toxic materials have been increasingly produced in parallel with the industrial growth in China. Air pollution stemming from burning coal – China's major primary energy – has approximately reached the level of the developed countries in the 1950s and 1960s. Today, air, water, noise pollution, and land erosion together with the unprocessed garbage have prominently affected the Chinese society (see Figure 9.1). One striking example is that air pollution is estimated

*Table 9.1*    Shares in consumption of primary commodities for China, India and USA (%)

| | Commodity | China | India | USA |
|---|---|---|---|---|
| Metals 2005 | Aluminum | 22.5 (1) | 3.0 (8) | 19.4 (2) |
| | Copper | 21.6 (1) | 2.3 (11) | 13.8 (2) |
| | Lead | 25.7 (1) | 1.3 (15) | 19.4 (2) |
| | Nickel | 15.2 (1) | 0.9 (17) | 9.5 (3) |
| | Tin | 33.3 (1) | 2.2 (7) | 12.1 (2) |
| | Zinc | 28.6 (1) | 3.1 (8) | 9.0 (2) |
| | Iron ore | 29.0 (1) | 4.8 (5) | 4.7 (6) |
| | Steel production | 31.5 (1) | 3.5 (7) | 8.5 (3) |
| Energy 2003 | Coal | 32.9 (1) | 7.1 (3) | 20.6 (2) |
| | Oil | 7.4 (2) | 3.4 (7) | 25.3 (1) |
| | Total primary energy | 12.6 (2) | 3.6 (5) | 23.4 (1) |
| | Electricity generation | 11.4 (2) | 3.8 (5) | 24.3 (1) |
| Agriculture 2003 | Wheat | 15.2 (1) | 13.5 (2) | 5.4 (4) |
| | Rice | 29.7 (1) | 21.4 (2) | 1.0 (12) |
| | Maize | 17.0 (2) | 2.2 (6) | 32.5 (1) |
| | Soybeans | 19.2 (2) | 3.7 (5) | 24.0 (1) |
| | Soy oil | 24.4 (2) | 6.4 (4) | 25.7 (1) |
| | Palm oil | 15.8 (1) | 15.3 (2) | 0.6 (37) |
| | Sugar | 6.6 (3) | 15.2 (1) | 12.5 (2) |
| | Tea | 14.4 (2) | 17.5 (1) | 3.8 (7) |
| | Coffee | 0.4 (45) | 0.8 (27) | 16.8 (1) |
| | Cotton | 31.2 (1) | 12.8 (2) | 6.9 (5) |
| | Rubber | 23.5 (1) | 8.4 (4) | 12.9 (2) |

*Note*: Figures within parentheses are world rankings.
*Source*: Streifel (2006).

to have caused more than 400,000 excess deaths in 2003, and this figure will increase if action is not taken (Winters and Yusuf, 2007, p. 26)

Three elements have heavily lain upon the environmental damages in China: population growth, economic growth led by high-pollution making industry and coal-dominative energy structure. In 1949, the new government adopted the Soviet-type development model in which heavy industry was given priority while seeking the maximum self-sufficiency in the national economy. The Chinese leadership strongly believed that the economic independence and the national defense could only be guaranteed by the heavy industry. But the latter is also the main pollution-making source. Without good reason, the quickly expanded population, followed by the increasing demand for energy

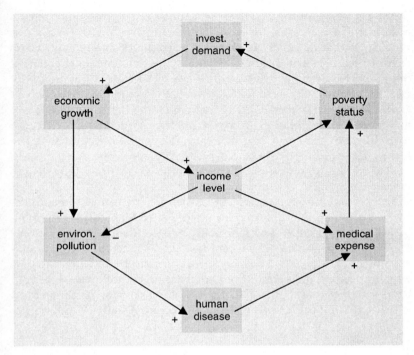

*Notes*: '+' denote positive relations; '–' denote negative relation; '→' denotes causal direction.

*Figure 9.1* A simplified model of economic, environmental and human relations

and food, will accelerate the deforestation and transference of forest-land and wetland into cropland. But the fragile ecosystem can only but accelerate the vicious circle of poverty. If these problems are not addressed properly, all efforts on the socialist market economic development with Chinese characteristics would be jeopardized inevitably.

## China's population problems

> People at present think that five sons are not too many and each son has also five sons, and there are already 25 descendants before the death of the grandfather. Therefore, people are more but wealth is less; they work hard but receive little.
>
> Hanfei (280–233 BC)

At the beginning of the 21st century, China's population surpassed 1.3 billion which accounted for more than one-fifth of the world's; it was nine times that of Japan, five times that of the USA, and three times that of the European Union as a whole. The dynamic mechanism of population growth has greatly influenced by China's population policies. When the PRC was founded in 1949, the population of mainland China was about 450 million. Since then China has experienced two major peaks of population growth. From the new Republic's year zero to 1958 when the Great Leap Forward movement was launched, the birth rate was as high as 3 to 4 per cent while, in contrast, the death rate decreased significantly. This dramatic population growth was largely encouraged by the government in line with Mao Zedong's thought 'the more population, the easier are the things to be done'. China's population began to grow rapidly once again after the famine period (1959–61) during which many people died from starvation.[3] The birthrate peaked at 4.3 per cent in 1963 and then decreased gradually but still ran at over 2 per cent until the early 1970s when the government realized the importance of population control (see Figure 9.2). Unfortunately, it was too late for China to control its population which has still been growing at the rate of more than 10 million per

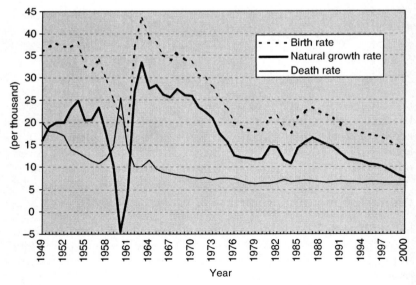

*Figure 9.2*   Birth, death and natural growth rates (1949–2000)

*Table 9.2*   Population forecasts for selective countries (million persons)

| Country | 1985 | 2000 | 2025 |
|---|---|---|---|
| China | 1050 | 1286 | 1493 |
| India | 769 | 1043 | 1446 |
| USSR | 277 | 308 | 351 |
| USA | 239 | 266 | 301 |
| Indonesia | 166 | 208 | 263 |
| Brazil | 136 | 179 | 246 |
| Japan | 121 | 129 | 129 |
| Pakistan | 103 | 162 | 267 |
| Bangladesh | 101 | 151 | 235 |
| Nigeria | 95 | 159 | 301 |

*Source*: United Nations (1988).

annum. In the coming decades, China will continue to be the most populous nation before it will have been overtaken by India in the 2030s, as reflected by the United Nations population projections in Table 9.2.

When the Chinese government was proud of its achievements which mainly relied upon the 'sea-of-manpower' approach, the population problem raised simultaneously. During the past decades when the population densities of some developed countries decreased gradually or kept constant, China's population density has sharply increased from 40 persons per sq. km of land area in 1949 up to 130 persons per sq. km of land area at the end of 1990s, which is more than three times that of the world as a whole. In fact, China's population density is not very high when compared with South Korea (443 persons/km$^2$), Japan (329 persons/km$^2$), India (290 persons/km$^2$), UK (237 persons/km$^2$), Germany (226 persons/km$^2$). However, as much of China's territory consists of mountains, desert and other uninhabitable lands, the number of persons per square kilometers of the *inhabitable* land area is much larger than the nominal population density in China. For instance, as will be discussed later, the population densities of many provinces in East China are more than 400 persons per square kilometers of land area, much higher than that of most of the most populous nations in the world.

Today, when looking at the poor living conditions in the countryside and the unemployment problem in urban China, one cannot help remembering the ridiculous debate on whether or not the population growth should be controlled effectively. Stimulated by the leftist idea of population equals production, some people believed blindly the link summed up by 'more people → more labour force → more production → faster economic development', which eventually resulted in China's over-population problem.[4]

In fact, confronted with the grim reality of population growth, even Mao Zedong acknowledged the increasing pressure of over-population on the Chinese economy in his late years and began to puzzle about his earlier prediction that 'Of all things in the world, people are the most precious. ... Even if China's population multiplies many times, she is fully capable of finding a solution.'[5] In the early 1970s, the Chinese government had to implement a birth control policy aiming to encourage late marriages, prolong the time period between births and reduce the number of children in each family. In 1978, the encouragement of birth control first appeared in Article 53 of the PRC's Constitution. Following the implementation of population control policy, the First National Conference on Birth Control (NCBC) was held in Beijing in 1979. The Conference requested 'that one couple has only one child and at most two children but with a three year interval. Those couples who do not plan to have a second child will be rewarded and those who have a third child will receive economic punishment.'[6]

Since the early 1980s, China has effectively controlled its population growth tendency by establishing a series of strict measures. The population growth rate declined drastically from 3 per cent in the 1960s to less than 1 per cent at the end of the 1990s. Obviously, without this reduction, China's population would have increased by more than 20 million (i.e. $(0.03–0.01) \times 1$ billion) per annum. In other words, as a result of China's population control effort, the population increase has been reduced by an amount equal to any medium-sized nation for every 2 to 3 years. Furthermore, the reduction of population growth also increased China's per capita GNP by more than 2.0 per cent (i.e. $1/(1–(0.03–0.01))–1$).[7] Despite these successes, some problems still remain.

First, China's population control policy has generated an imbalance between males and females. In poor and remote rural areas, the traditional discrimination against women has still remained very strong. Because there is very little social security in those rural areas, sons are the only hope for parents who are still earning living their by physical labour. This provides a strong incentive for people to have more than one child till they possess son(s). Partly as a result of the birth control policy and partly because of the increasing burden of having an additional child (girl), the inhumane practices of foeticide and infanticide are very common in rural areas where men have a higher social position than women, even though their practices have been prohibited by the Chinese government. China's national birth gender proportion (i.e., male to female) is much higher than the developed nations'.[8] If taking only the rural area into account, the birth gender difference would be much larger.

Second, a lower birth-rate will eventually result in a higher proportion of aged people. Already this has been a social problem in the advanced nations and will, sooner or later, affect the Chinese society. Thanks to the government's efforts in raising women's social position[9] and the strict domicile system for urban citizens, China's only-one-child policy has been successfully implemented in the urban area since the early 1980s. At present, it is very common in urban China for a couple to have only one child. However, the policy is to rigidly transform China's urban family pattern into a reverse pyramid in the coming decades. In 1953, the ratio of the population aged 65 or over was only 4.4 per cent in China. This ratio was further reduced to 3.6 per cent in 1964, but rose again to 4.9 per cent in 1982 and 5.6 per cent in 1990.[10] According to Du (1994, p. 88), the percentage of the aged population in China will increase steadily to 8.1 per cent in 2010, 10.9 per cent in 2020, 14.7 per cent in 2030, 19.8 per cent in 2040, and 20.9 per cent in 2050.

Third, population production has been largely imbalanced between the rural and urban areas of China. In rural and other poor areas, parents who would not receive any subsidies for living from the government after they retire have particularly strong incentives to have more children for whom, however, neither the government nor the parents are able to cover the educational costs. In urban and other relatively rich areas, parents who receive higher education and have lifetime social welfare usually have the trade-off between having more children and improving the living standards and quality of life. Faced with the cramped living space, high cost of education, as well as severe competition for university entrance, urban parents have no incentives to have a second child, not to mention that those who illegally raise more than one child would not receive the subsidies from the government and could be fired from their current posts. As an only child is more protected by its family than one with siblings, the children born in urban areas usually receive better care and education than those born in rural areas. In brief, the fact that the rural and poor people have more children than the urban and well-educated people will reduce the educational level of the Chinese population as a whole.

To illustrate the long-term effect of rural-urban imbalance of population growth, let's assume that $r_A$ ($P_A$) and $r_B$ ($P_B$) are the population growth rates (number of population) of urban (A) and rural (B) areas, respectively ($r_A<r_B$). Let $r_A=1\%$ and $r_B=2\%$. Assume $P_A=P_B=1$ when t=0; then when t=1, $P_A$: $P_B$= 1:1.01; t=10, $P_A$: $P_B$= 1:1.10; t=20, $P_A$: $P_B$= 1:1.22; t=30, $P_A$: $P_B$= 1:1.34; t=40, $P_A$: $P_B$= 1:1.48; t=50, $P_A$: $P_B$= 1:1.63. The above figures simply suggest that, given that the population growth rates in urban and rural areas are 1 per cent and 2 per cent, respectively, the number of population of the rural area which is equal to that of the urban area at the year zero will be 1 per cent, 10 per cent, 22 per cent, 34 per cent, 48 per cent, and 63 per cent larger than that of the urban area after 1, 10, 20, 30, 40, and 50 years, respectively.

## Natural and environmental resources

> You may fish by drying up lakes, then there would be no fisheries next year; you may hunt by firing woods, then there would be no animals next year.
>
> Lüshi Chunqiu

The environmental concerns stem from two kinds of human activities: resource depletion which covers the activities of the losses reflecting the deterioration of land and depleting reserves of coal, petroleum, timber, ground water, and so on; resource degradation which covers the consequences associated with air and water pollution, land erosion, solid wastes, and so on. Resource depletion is a concern because it would mean the quantitative exhaustion of natural resources that are an important source of revenues, obtained through exploitation and the discovery of new reserves. In the case of resource degradation, the issue is not the quantitative exhaustion of natural resources, but rather the qualitative degradation of the ecosystem, for example, through, amongst other things, the contamination of air and water as a result of the generation and deposit of residuals, and as a result of the environmental impact of producing garbage and solid wastes. In order to have a good picture of China's environmental situation, let us consider land, air, water, and deforestation and desertification in China first.

### Land

China has provided sustenance and other basic necessities for 22 per cent of the world's population with only 7 per cent of the world's cultivated land. But this kind of development pattern has also created many serious environmental problems resulting from inappropriate policies and approaches in agricultural production. During the 1960s and 1970s, the Chinese government was keenly 'taking grain production as the key link' (*yi liang weigang*) so as to maintain the maximum self-sufficiency in foodstuff supply. This policy has been generally known to ignore the comparative advantages between the regions differing in natural conditions, and accelerated the conversion of forestland, wetland, and marginal land into cropland.

Since the economic reform was introduced in the late 1970s, the transference of farmland to residential and industrial uses has been promoted. Consequently, the cultivated land decreased substantially. In order to increase the agricultural production, the only way was to rely upon the increase of land productivity, resulting in the intensive use of chemical fertilizers, continuous cropping, expansion of irrigation, excessive use of water, use of plastic sheeting and improved plant varieties. As reported by the SSB (1996, p. 361), the total consumption of chemical fertilizers had been almost quadrupled between 1983 and 1995. Nitrogenous fertilizers were the main fertilizers, while phosphate and potash fertilizers were still not very much utilized, particularly during the 1980s.

In practice, it is almost impossible for farmers to accurately count the proportion of nutrients that the soil needs. In most cases, the marginal cost and benefit do not determine the use of fertilizers. The government's subsidies on fertilizer consumption could distort the pricing mechanism and induce farmers to even more excessive and inefficient use of chemical fertilizers, which has, through the leaching of nitrates, caused the contamination of groundwater and the deterioration of soil structure. For instance, 59.1 per cent of farmland was in shortage of phosphorous, 22.9 per cent in shortage of potassium and over 60 per cent in lack of zinc, manganese and other trace metals in 1990 (NEPA, 1991, p. 5).

Organic manure and the leavened crop residues, stalks and straws have many advantages when used as fertilizers even if their value of nutrient per unit volume is lower than that of chemical fertilizers. Many farmers, however, have ignored the advantages of these *clean* fertilizers. In addition, the shortage of fuelwood for both cooking and heating results in the burning of straws, stalks and crop residues in rural China. Continuous cropping, instead of crop rotations, may cause the soil deficiency of some nutrients. For example, the cropping of soybeans causes deficiency of phosphorus and potassium in soil. The use of high-yielding and improved plant varieties makes crops more vulnerable to pest damages, which in turn results in the use of pesticides. Since the 1970s the use of pesticides has increased in both tonnage and concentration of active ingredients and, as a result, affected water, soil and food seriously.

The increasing use of plastic sheeting is a further threat. Farmers have been increasingly interested in the application of plastic sheets to conserve soil moisture and speed up the maturation of crops, particularly in northern China. But many farmers have ignored the fact that plastic sheets, if not treated properly after cropping, may be mixed with the soil and hence hinder the flow of water and root growth. According to NEPA (1991, p. 6), about 280,000 ton of plastic sheets had been used annually till the early 1990s.

In 1993, 100,000 square kilometers of farmland suffered from the damages of industrial wastes and urban rubbish and 9,000 square kilometers were occupied by piles of solid wastes and seriously damaged as a result of improper use of garbage and sludge (NEPA, 1994, p. 5). The sum of these circumstances has led to soil loss, especially in the area where ground cover was removed. The ecosystems of forests, wetlands, sloping and marginal lands are particularly fragile. Another form of soil contamination is the use of wastewater for irrigation, which ignores the fact that acids and toxic heavy metals in much of this water impair the soil chemistry and render it useless for agriculture.

Apart from the soil loss deriving from the erosion process, another consequence of soil over-exploitation and removal of ground cover is the increase of silt materials flowing into rivers. This leads to the rising of riverbeds undermining flood control, navigation and powergenerating capacity. The loess plateau area between Gansu, Shaanxi and Shanxi provinces has been cultivated since the Neolithic period and is now perhaps one of the most erodible areas in the world. Through this area, Yellow River carries 1.6 billion ton of sediment into Bohai sea by degrading a land from 260 to 330 square kilometers annually (Vaclav, 1992, p. 433). The average riverbed has been rising approximately one meter per decade with a consequent growing risk of catastrophic flooding. Yangtze river's load raises lake levels, particularly in Hubei and Hunan provinces. As a result, most lakes in East Hubei disappeared during the past decades, owing to the combination of silting and conversion to farmland.

In Northeast China plain (including Heilongjiang, Jilin, and Liaoning provinces and the eastern part of Inner Mongolia Autonomous Region), the soil has been seriously eroded, due mainly to the intense conversion of forested land and grassland to cropland and the abandon of traditional agricultural techniques. The Sanjiang plain at the confluence of Heilongjiang (Amur) River and Ussuri River in Northeast China is an alluvial marshland. In 1949 the farmland comprised only 3 per cent of the total land area. But in 1979 it had been expanded to 36 per cent of the total area (18 thousand square kilometers). The original 8 per cent of forest cover was reduced to 5 per cent in 1974 and almost disappeared entirely by the early 1980s (Vermeer, 1984, p. 9).

## Air

Clean air is the precondition for the living of the 1.3 billion population in China. During the past decades, however, China's air quality has been significantly decreased, particularly in urban areas. For example, China already shared 9.9 per cent of the world's greenhouse gas (GHG) emissions in the late 1980s, which is only behind the United States (22.3 per cent) and the former Soviet Union (17.4 per cent). The shares of European Union and Japan are 11.7 per cent and 6 per cent, respectively, and that of Brazil and India are each 4 per cent. China's GHG emissions are composed of about 68 per cent carbon dioxide ($CO_2$), 24 per cent methane ($CH_4$), and 8 per cent chlorofluorocarbans (CFCs) (WRI, 1992, tables 13.4 and 24.1; Perlack *et al.*, 1993, p.78). With respect to $CO_2$, about 80 per cent emissions come from coal and other solid fuels, 14 per cent from liquid petroleum fuels and the remainder from natural gas use and from chemical processes in the manufacturing of cement (CDIAC, 1990).[11]

When discussing the situation of China's GHG emissions, one is facing two different opinions: firstly, the country's per capita emissions are very low in comparison with the industrially developed countries and that the *onus* of global warming must rest elsewhere; secondly, compared with other countries, the GHG emissions per unit of GDP of China have been already very high – approximately 7.5, 17.7 and 6.9 times higher than that of the USA, Japan and the world as a whole, respectively (see Table 9.3). Moreover, some evidence suggests that China will have become the world's largest pollution maker before it may achieve the number one economy in the early 21st century. For example, using the GREEN model built by the OECD, Burnaux *et al.* (1992, fig. 2) present a detailed scenario for the world's GHG emissions of which China will constitute 29 per cent, far leading the shares of USA (12 per cent), the former USSR (13 per cent), and the European Union as a whole (7 per cent) by the year 2050.

In China, atmospheric pollution mainly comes from the burning of coal products which, under an optimistic scenario, will be unlikely

*Table 9.3*   China's GHG emissions in an international comparison

| Item | World | China | USA | Japan |
|---|---|---|---|---|
| GDP (billion US$) | 23555 | 372.4 | 5672.6 | 3618.0 |
| GHG (million ton) | 23152 | 2524 | 5163 | 1389 |
| GHG/POP (ton/person) | 4.30 | 2.18 | 21.0 | 11.21 |
| GHG/LA (ton/km$^2$) | 170.4 | 262.9 | 551.6 | 3674.6 |
| GHGs/GDP (kg/US$) | 0.98 | 6.78 | 0.91 | 0.38 |

*Notes*: GDP=gross national product; GHG=greenhouse gas; POP=population; LA=land area
*Sources*: UN (1993), IMF (1992), and WRI (1992, tables 13.4 and 24.1).

composed of less than the current three quarters of total primary energy consumption even by the year 2025 (Huang, 1990).[12] China's CFC and halon compound use is relatively minor given the size of the country. However, the potential for much greater use of CFCs is enormous. Moreover, the CFC emissions are projected to increase as a result of the economic growth and population increase. Country-specific estimates of $CH_4$ emissions put China's emissions at more than 10 per cent of the global flux. The specific sources of these emissions are, in order of amount, livestock, wet rice, natural gas pipeline leakage, solid waste disposal, and coal mining. In addition, China's large and still expanding population also suggests a concomitant increase of $CH_4$ for which there have not been any specific controlling targets (Perlack *et. al.*, 1993, p. 84).

In China, most of the proven coal reserves are bituminous, while only a small portion is lignite and anthracite. Therefore, coal is mainly responsible not only for the high $CO_2$ emissions but also for the high emissions of sulphur ($SO_2$), nitrogen oxide ($NO_x$), and total suspended particulate (TSP). In addition, as the northern (especially urban) areas usually use coal for heating in winter season, it is not surprising that the air pollution there is much more serious than that in the southern parts. All these pollutants have threaten public health seriously. The share of chronic obstructive pulmonary disease and cancers is rising. Acid rain is becoming more and more critical to the mankind. The high sulphur content of burning coal widely contributes to the high acidity levels of rainfall. Nationwide acid rain measurement which has been conducted since 1982 shows that the situation is particularly serious in southern China, where the pH values are often below 5.6.[13] Another noticeable factor is that the wind coming from Northwest region increase the neutralizing capability of atmosphere and transfers air pollutants to Southeast China and the neighbouring countries. In addition, lead (Pb) emissions from vehicles will increase substantially along with the rapid increase of vehicles in urban China.

## Water

Water scarcity, a matter of worldwide concern, is also plaguing China today. With 22 per cent of the world's population, China has only 8 per cent of the fresh water. In 2002, China's annual renewable water reserves were about 2.8 trillion cubic meters, which ranked fifth in the world, behind Brazil, Russia, Canada and Indonesia, but ahead of the U.S. However, in terms of per capita availability of water reserves, China is one of the lowest in the world – barely about one-fourth the world average (WRI, 2003). It is estimated that in 2030, along with its population reaching 1.6 billion, China will be water stressed as defined by the international standard of 1700 cubic meters per capita (Qian and Zhang, 2001).

Large-scale underground water extraction started in the 1950s and has been significantly increased in the past 20 years. Accordingly, underground water use as a percentage of the total water supply also increased from 14 per cent in 1980 to 20 per cent in 2001 (Chen and Cai, 2000). Ground water overexploitation has caused a marked and continuous drawdown of underground water levels in China. Deeper wells have to be installed from time to time. A recent survey indicates that the cones of depression in the deep aquifers have joined together to form a huge interprovincial cone of depression in the North China Plain. Competition for water between communities, sectors of the economy, and individual provinces is growing (Jiao and Wen, 2004).

With the formation of cones of depression, many cities, especially the coastal cities with thick unconsolidated soft soil layers, are suffering from land subsidence caused by the withdrawal of underground water in deep aquifers. The cities of Shanghai and Tianjin, with maximum subsidence of about 3 meters, are the most severe cases. Ground subsidence has caused a series of problems, such as sinking and splitting of railway bases, buildings, and underground pipelines, and an emerging flood crisis in areas near major rivers or the sea.[14]

The landmass of China is characterized by dramatic geographical, geological, and hydrogeological diversities. Its land surface ascends from north to south in four distinct zones: arid zone, semi-arid zone, semi-humid zone, and humid zone (see Table 9.4). The distribution of water is extremely irregular in China. In general, the northern part is poor in surface water, but modestly rich in groundwater in a few

*Table 9.4*  China's climatic zones

| Climatic Zone | % |
| --- | --- |
| Humid Zone (aridity<1.0) | 32 |
| Semi-Humid Zone (aridity 1.0–1.5) | 15 |
| Semi-Arid Zone (aridity 1.5–2.0) | 22 |
| Arid Zone (aridity>2.0) | 31 |

*Source*: NBS (2002).

provinces, such as Qinghai, Xinjiang, Inner Mongolia, and Heilongjiang. In particular, the Tarimu, Turpan and Qaidamu basins in Northwest region have less than 25 mm of precipitation per annum.

Figure 9.3 shows that the monthly precipitation has been rather uneven in both southern (such as Guangzhou and Shanghai) and northern (such as Beijing, Lanzhou, Shenyang, and Yinchuan) cities. Throughout China, rainfall usually occurs heavily in summer but not in winter. This is particularly so for Northwest cities (such as Lanzhou and Yinchuan), where there is almost no rainfall during October–May.

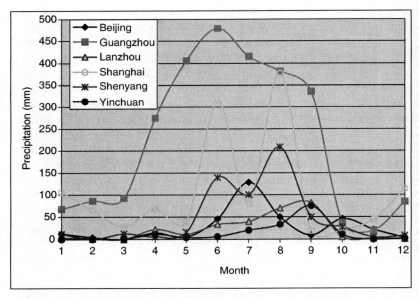

*Figure 9.3*  Monthly precipitation of selected cities in China (2001)

In China, water scarcity has been viewed as a major threat to its long-term security. In addition to water scarcity for China as a whole, water resources are unevenly distributed in China. The northern parts of the country are deficient in water, while the south is water-rich. The areas south of the Yangtze River, which account for only 37 per cent of the country's total territory, have 81 per cent of its total water resources. However, the areas north of the Yangtze, which make up 63 per cent of China's territory, possess only 19 per cent of the country's total water resources (Chen and Cai, 2000). Due to uneven distribution in some areas in north China, the per capita water rate is as low as one fifth the national average (Liaohe River Valley in the northeast) or one sixth (Haihe River Valley around Tianjin). Water shortage has become a major economic bottleneck to these areas (see Box 9.1).

---

*Box 9.1*  The South–North Water Diversion Project

China is plagued with unevenly distributed water and land resources: more water *vis-à-vis* less land in southern China and less water *vis-à-vis* more land in northern China. North China accounts for over one-third of the country's total population, near one half of cultivated land, but only one-eighth of the total water resources. Over 80 per cent direct water runoff in China takes place in the south. Since the 1980s the Haihe and Yellow river valleys have been stricken by chronic drought. Yet, further south, large amount of water from the Yangtze empties into the sea each year.

Given the existence of surface water surplus in southern China and freshwater shortage in northern China, is it feasible to transfer water from the water-rich south to the north? Transfer project had been discussed for more than two decades before it was started on 27 December 2002. The gigantic South-North Water Diversion project involves the construction of three canals running 1,300 kilometers across the eastern, middle and western parts of China, linking the country's four major rivers – the Yangtze, Yellow, Huaihe and Haihe rivers. The South-North Water Diversion project is expected to cost US$59 billion and to take 50 years to complete. If all goes well, the South-North Water Diversion project will carry annually more than 40 billion tones of water from the Yangtze River basin to Beijing and the other north provinces. However, this project cannot completely solve the water shortage problems in northern China.

There have already more than ten seawater desalination plants in China, with a total capacity of 5000 cubic meters per day in China. Besides, China has also planned to invest in a seawater desalination project so as to carry the desalinated seawater to Beijing before the year 2008 when the Olympic Games will be held. The production cost per tone of seawater ranges from US$1.1–2.5 in some countries. In China, it can be reduced to ¥5.0 (or about US$0.6), or even lower (¥3.7, or about US$0.46) for larger seawater desalination plants.[15] However, the problem with respect to the wide utilization of the desalinated seawater in the vast rural area is the cost. Many farmers in China are still neither able to nor willing to offer such a high price, since, in the traditional culture, waters in rivers and lakes are free of charge.

The constant and excessive extraction of groundwater has led to the continuous dropping of the watertable and the subsidence of land. The area of subsidence around large municipalities such as Beijing, Tianjin and Shanghai has been reported most serious. In the coastal areas of Hebei and Shandong provinces, the excessive drop of groundwater level has led to intrusion of saline water into the freshwater aquifers. In the loess plateau area of Northwest China, the drawing of underground water for irrigation is becoming extremely difficult, with increasing energy costs.

The excessive use of water without adequate drainage leads to water-logging, salinization and soil erosion. Salinization and alkalization are increasingly affecting the irrigated farmland. In Northeast region, cropping activities have increased the soil alkalinity to such a high level that it is very difficult to put them back into pasture. In the sandy soils of Northwest region, where the irrigation water seeps away quickly, strong winds and high evaporation contribute to easy alkalization of the soil. The rapid development of individually- and collectively-owned industrial enterprises are generally known to be responsible for the increasing water pollution in rural areas.

More than two-thirds of China's industrial wastewater has flown directly into rivers, lakes, seas, and reservoirs. The chemical industry is the largest wastewater producer. Other main sectors discharging wastewater are ferrous metals, papermaking and paper products, production and supply of power, steam and hot water, and so on.

Another top issue is the drinking water pollution in both urban and rural areas. Many groundwater sources have been affected as a result of infiltration of polluted surface water in urban areas. Rural water resources are even more contaminated due to fertilizers and pesticide run off, human and animal wastes, and pollutants from the township and villageowned enterprises. As a result, only one in seven people residing in the rural areas has safe drinking water (UNDP, 1994, p. 3). Seven-six per cent of the population drinks water with fecal coliform counts above the Chinese drinking water quality standard, and 59 per cent drinks water exceeding the WHO standard that is less stringent. About 60 per cent of the country's inhabitants do not have access to potable water (WRI, 1992, p. 410).

The river water pollution in the sections where rivers run through or near cities is the most serious in terms of ammonia nitrogen, fecal bacteria, volatile phenols, and biological oxygen demands (BOD).[16] Yangtze river which connects closely China's large industrial bases such as Chongqing, Wuhan, Nanjing and Shanghai is estimated by many observers to become the second 'Yellow river' sooner or later if no countermeasure is carried out. Huaihe river, the *black river* as people now refer to it, is believed the most polluted river in China.[17] In all of the 96 monitoring stations established by the National Environmental Protection Agency, only 35 monitoring stations obtained dissolved oxygen of more than 5 mg/l – a level that supports fishes; for BOD, only 24 of the 91 monitoring stations met the standard (i.e. 5 mg/l), while 21 stations violated it (NEPA, 1994, p. 4). In addition, pollution from heavy metals, such as mercury (Hg) and lead (Pb) and other toxic chemicals, are also affecting the river water seriously.

Pollution of nitrogen and phosphorus is common in lakes. Water pollution has not only endangered the local fishery and the collection of limnological plants, but it has also affected the daily lives and health of the nearby residents. According to a survey conducted in the Lake Weishan area, the frequency of cancer causing illnesses and tumors has been much higher in the lake region than in the inland areas nearby. Reported health events related to liver diseases, diarrhoea and birth defects have also been much more frequent in the polluted area than in the non-polluted area. For example the following case was reported:

> Located at the mouth of Chengguo River, Shadi village, Liuzhuang township in Weishan county, has a population of 1000 persons and an area of over 20,000 mu of shoaly land. Due to the lack of arable land (with a per capita area of only 0.013 mu), most of the residents were used to taking reeds, lotus-roots and other lake-related resources. Fishing and fishery cultivation has been their major sources of living. During recent years, as industrial and living waste water discharged from Tengzhou city into Lake Weishan via Chengguo River

has increased, water sources on which the residents have depended for their living have been seriously polluted. Consequently, fish stocks have been extinguished, and limnological plants have died. Even worse, the health conditions of the residents living in the region have been seriously affected. Since 1988, 26 young residents have died from diseases caused by, as diagnosed by hospitals at county or higher levels, the drinking of the polluted well water.[18]

In addition, petropollutants, inorganic nitrogen and inorganic phosphorus is common in the coastal water sources. Marine environments near large coastal cities are degraded due to the discharge of raw sewage and coastal construction. As a result, incidences of red tides have become frequent in many coastal areas, contaminated fish and mollusks have been common place and many fragile marine environments have been destroyed consequently. Marine pollution in northeastern and southern China is of particular concern since the industrial development is outpacing the environmental protection efforts in these areas.

### Deforestation and desertification

In spite of different estimates on the actual extent of forestland area,[19] the rapid decreasing in forestland has made China face the shortage of timber source. The causes of deforestation mainly come from the rapid growing population in rural area and the economic interests of the state. As the size of population expands, the needs of food, housing and energy will increase accordingly. The conversion of forestland, grassland and wetland to cropland and the illegal felling of trees for lumber and fuel increases. In the rural areas, the lack of fuels led to use of wood for both heating and cooking. But the traditional rural stoves have low combustion efficiency. In addition, much of the fuelwood consumed is low-quality brush and weeds collected from already deforested hills.

From the 1950s to 1970s, when a series of political and social movements (such as the Great Leap Forward and the Cultural Revolution) were under way, many natural and tropical forests were being destroyed seriously in China. For example, the natural tropical forest in Hainan island decreased by 72 per cent, from the previous 8630 square kilometers to 2450 sq. km in 1980 (Vermeer, 1984, p. 10). In Sichuan province, the forestland cover decreased from 19 per cent of the province's land area in the early 1950s to 12.6 per cent in 1988. During the 1980s the total forestland area decreased by 128 thousand sq. km (nearly 10 per cent of the total area) in Tibet Autonomous Region. From 1950 to 1985 some $54 billion worth of Tibetan timber was felled and processed, and 90 per cent of the timber, meat and minerals culled from the plateau are exported to other parts of China (Denniston, 1993, p. 9). In Tibet and many other provinces and autonomous regions, the process of forest degradation has started with a large-scale cutting of forests by the state or its contractors for commercial logging. This large-scale cutting combined with fuel necessities has denuded hillsides, resulting in the soil erosion and water loss. Vaclav (1992, p. 435) estimates that this had led to a 25 per cent increase in timber logging between 1979 and 1986 in China. The remaining natural forests in Northeast, Southwest regions and Hainan island are still being excessively logged so as to meet the increasing industrial and commercial demands.

To preserve the forestry richness and stabilize the soil structure, the government has started a massive reforestation program. The first afforestation project was initiated in 1978 to plant 667 thousand sq. km of trees covering 551 counties, cities and townships of 13 provinces and autonomous regions in the northern, western, central and eastern China areas. The other afforestation projects[20] plan to plant around 124 thousand square kilometers of trees (Qu, 1990, p. 14). It should noted that only a small portion of the plantings claimed by the government in the mass reforestation programs have managed to survive.

Covering about one-third of its total land area, China's grassland is concentrated on Inner Mongolia, Xinjiang and Tibet autonomous regions and a few of other provinces and autonomous regions, mostly in North and Northwest regions. As grassland is usually known as 'wasteland', the conversion of it into productive uses has been promoted for the past decades as a result of population growth. The conversion of grassland into crop cultivation has caused a constant decrease of grassland. The Eighth FYP (1991–95) proposed a plan to transfer, while among other provinces and autonomous regions, 1250 square kilometers of grassland in Inner Mongolia, 200 square kilometers in Xinjiang. At the same time, overgrazing is widely visible. Since the early 1980s, peasants have been allowed to raise their own animals. When the number of heads grows, the grassland decreases accordingly.[21]

During the last decades, desertification has become more and more serious and 176,000 sq. km of land have been desertified in northwestern China. Still expanding at a rate of 1560 sq. km per annum, the area of deserts and desertified lands is now 1,490,000 sq. km (i.e., 15.5 per cent of China's total land area), with, specifically, 41.8 per cent of rock and gravel (*gobi*) and 58.2 per cent of sandy (*shamo*).[22]

## Artificial weather modification

China's first man-made precipitation enhancement was conducted in 1958. It has now been the world's largest cloud seeder, using an array of methods to disperse chemicals into cloud layers to make rains: specialized airplanes, rocket shells and anti-aircraft guns are used to shoot canisters of chemicals like silver iodine, liquid nitrogen and calcium chloride into the sky so as to build up moisture in the clouds and increase rainfall. From 1995 to 2003, China spent a sum of US$266 million on rainmaking technology in 23 provinces, autonomous regions and municipalities, with some 35,000 people working in the field. In 2003 alone, China spent about US$50 million to disperse chemicals into clouds by using 30 airplanes, 3,800 rockets and 6,900 high artillery shells (China Meteorological Bureau, 2004). Besides, numerous aircrafts, old anti-aircraft guns, balloons and even mountaintop dispersing devices have been employed by provincial and local metrological bureaux and rainmaking authorities (note that private companies have not be entitled to conduct rainmaking activities in China) to fire chemicals into the clouds.

The man-made precipitation has also been part of local meteorological authorities' efforts to set up a long-term mechanism aimed to minimize losses caused by bad weather like prolonged heat waves or heavy fogs. Shanghai – the largest city of China – has resorted to artificial rain to cool down the city and slow down a power demand that is outstripping the supply. Shanghai suffered several power shortages in the summer of 2003, when an unprecedented heat wave hit the city. According to the report of *China Daily* (2004a), the maximum temperatures stayed above 35°C for a record 40 days in a row. Due to the soaring power demand at that time, power was even temporarily cut to some industrial sectors in a few cases. Local meteorological authorities have forecast that for year 2004, the city will have up to 21 days when temperatures will exceed 35°C. To precipitate the rain, an airplane travels over the city to create seed clouds with a catalyst like salt, silver iodide or dry ice. Any of the three can induces rainfall and thus lower the temperature. If the test goes smoothly, the approach will then be used during the city's hottest summer days, which are expected to match the peak periods for power demand.

China has virtually all the problems related to water resources faced by the rest of the world as a whole. China's rapid economic growth, industrialization and urbanization have outpaced infrastructure investment and management capacity, and have created widespread problems of water scarcity. Degradation of underground water resources and deterioration of underground water quality have become a striking environmental problem in many cities of China. In the areas of North China Plain, where about half of China's wheat and corn grows and peach orchards blossom, drought is an ever-looming threat.

Scientific rainmaking or precipitation enhancement began in 1946 when American scientists Vincent Schaefer and Bernard Vonnegu at General Electric (GE), following up on some laboratory observations, had 'seeded' a cloud with dry ice and then watched snowfall from its base. Until recent times it was thought that rain might be induced by explosions, updrafts from fires, or by giving the atmosphere a negative charge. Research showed that rain forms in warm clouds when larger drops of condensed water grow at the expense of smaller ones until they are big enough to fall; also that in cold clouds super-cooled water below –15°C freezes into ice crystals that act as nuclei for snow (Battan, 1962). On this basis, three methods resulted, which include (1) spraying water into warm clouds; (ii) dropping dry ice into cold clouds (where the dry ice freezes some water into ice crystals that act as natural nuclei for snow); and (iii) wafting silver iodide crystals or other similar crystals into a cold cloud from the ground or from an airplane over the cloud.[23]

It was also important to determine what kinds of clouds were suitable for seeding. It was found that, for reasons not at all well understood, there were important differences between clouds formed over land and over sea, with many more but much smaller droplets in continental clouds. Since larger droplets are needed if rain is to form, this meant that continental clouds were much less apt to release rain than were maritime ones, a discovery of considerable significance to would-be Australian rainmakers. Another crucial factor was found to be the temperature of the upper levels of the cloud. With both cumulus and stratiform clouds, provided this temperature was less than –7°C, seeding would inevitably be followed by precipitation within 20–25 minutes (Ryan and King, 1997, p. 21).[24]

Factors controlling the distribution of rainfall over the earth's surface are the belts of converging-ascending airflow, air temperature, moisture-bearing winds, ocean currents, distance inland from the coast, and mountain ranges. Ascending air is cooled by expansion, which results in the formation of clouds and the production of rain. Conversely, in the broad belts of descending air are found the great desert regions of the earth, descending air being warmed by compression and consequently absorbing instead of releasing moisture. If the temperature is low, the air has a small moisture capacity and is able to produce little precipitation. When winds blow over the ocean, especially over areas of warm water (where evaporation of moisture into the air is active) toward a given coastal area, that area receives more rainfall than a similar area where the winds blow from the interior toward the oceans. Areas near the sea receive more rain than inland regions, since the winds constantly lose moisture and may be quite dry by the time they reach the interior of a continent.

Production of rain by artificial means is now generally disregarded by many Western countries, though it is probable that rainmaking hastens or increases rainfall from clouds suitable for natural rainfall. The existing rainmaking techniques have been only moderately successful. Without clouds, there would be no rainfall, no matter how to fire the skies. So rainmaking activities cannot be relied upon in case of drought. On the other hand, it should be noted that some clouds would almost certainly result in rainfall, regardless of the artificial seeding. To judge the viability of a rainmaking program, it is important to establish that seeding made a difference – that is, it results in rain from clouds that would not otherwise have yielded it naturally. It was difficult to determine whether fluctuations in rainfall that occur at the time of cloud-seeding were produced by seeding or would have occurred naturally. Besides, the over-seeding can dissipate a cloud sometimes. Research conducted in China showed that even the best efforts of China's rainmakers produce only a 10 per cent or 15 per cent increase in rainfall. In addition, the vagaries of nature, such as wind direction and velocity, mean the effect of cloud-seeding on any given locality is difficult to predict.[25]

## Environmental protection in China

Since the late 1970s, several changes have taken place in the legislation of environmental protection in China along with the economic reform and opening up to the outside world. In 1978, a clause for environmental protection was firstly incorporated into the Constitution of the People's Republic of China. China's first Law on Environmental Protection (*huanjing baohu fa*) was formally promulgated in 1989 and was further revised in 1995 by the NPC. Since the early 1980s, a series of laws, regulations and national standards (*guobiao*, or GB) concerning the environmental protection (including four environmental laws, eight natural resource protection laws, more than 20 administrative decrees and more than 30 ministerial regulations for pollution prevention and 300-plus environmental standards) have been promulgated in China.[26] A relatively comprehensive legal system concerning environmental protection has initially taken shape, ending the past situation of no laws in this regard. Since 1980, China has joined or approved 18 international protocols on environmental protection, such as the UN Convention on Marine Law, Antarctic Treaty, Convention on International Trade in Endangered Species, Vienna Conference for the Protection of the Ozone Layer, Basel Convention on Transboundary Hazardous Waste Disposal, and the Montreal Protocol for Limiting use of CFCs, and so on.

However, problems still remain. For example, 'in the field of the environment and resources, there is no appropriate legislation on solid wastes and toxic chemicals, radioactive pollution prevention, and sustainable management of natural resources. Chinese legislation also faces the problems of coordination and consistency with international treaties and conventions'.[27] Moreover, as the Chinese legislation relating to sustainable development was to a large extent promulgated on the basis of a centralized planning system, many problems arose from China's economic transition. For example, there have been no environmentally related laws and regulations directly applicable to diversified economic sectors, i.e. for the environmental administration of township and village-based enterprises, foreign-funded enterprises and the tertiary sector.

It should be also noted that some articles of the environmentally-related laws have been only defined in principle but were not actionable. For example, in Article 44 of the Law on Mineral Resources (*kuangcan ziyuan fa*) (1986) '... those who use destructive methods to extract mineral resources should refund the loss of damages and be additionally charged if the resources have been seriously damaged, till the withdrawal of their certificates for mining permission at the most serious situation', there should be further clarified at least in the following points: (a) which kinds of extraction methods should be defined as 'destructive' to mineral resources; (b) how to set up the standard of the ' serious damages' to resources; (c) how to calculate the 'loss of damages' (d) how to determine the amount of 'additional charges'; and (e) what should be defined as the 'most serious situation', and so on.

Since the 1980s, a number of pieces of legislation relating to the exploitation and protection of water resources have been introduced. But the legislative foundation for the application of the man-made precipitation enhancement has been still weak. For example, China has not had any weather modification laws. It only had the 'Regulations of the People's Republic of China on Meteorological Services' promulgated by the State Council on 18 August 1994. The Meteorological Law was adopted at the 12th Meeting of the Standing Committee of the Ninth National People's Congress of the People's Republic of China on 31 October 1999 and went into effect as of 1 January 2000 (NPC, 2000). However, there are many contradictory issues in the Law. For example, in Article 5, the Law states:

> The competent meteorological department under the State Council is responsible for meteorological work nationwide. Local competent meteorological departments at different levels are responsible for meteorological work in their own administrative regions under the leadership of the competent meteorological departments at a higher level and the people's governments at the corresponding level.

This Article defines a dual-track system of leadership for the provincial and local meteorological departments. The problem of this system is its administrative efficiency, given that provincial and local meteorological departments are simultaneously subordinate to two different administrative organs. Regarding the prevention of meteorological disasters, Article 28 of the Law states:

> Competent meteorological departments at all levels shall make arrangements for joint monitoring and forecast of significant weather events among regions or departments, propose timely measures for preventing meteorological disasters and make assessment of severe weather disasters, which shall serve as the decision making basis for the people's governments at the corresponding levels to arrange prevention of meteorological disasters.

Obviously, this Article does not define the geographic scopes of and manners for interregional coordination in case that a meteorological disaster occurs. Our most serious concern now comes to that there has been no article relating to cross-border activities of weather modification in the Chinese laws. In 2002, it appears in the 'Regulations on Administration of Weather Modification' (rengong yingxiang tianqi guanli tiaoli) adopted at the 56th Executive Meeting of the State Council on 13 March (State Council, 2002). As defined in Article 14 of this Regulations,

Where weather modification operations are to be implemented crossing the boundaries of different provinces, autonomous regions or municipalities directly under the Central Government, the relevant people's governments of the provinces, autonomous regions or municipalities directly under the Central Government shall make a decision thereon through consultation; if no agreement is reached through consultation, the decision shall be made by the competent meteorological department of the State Council in consultation with the relevant people's governments of the provinces, autonomous regions or municipalities directly under the Central Government.

Clearly, this is nothing but an invalid article. And, therefore, its enforcement is weak. In most circumstances, weather modification activities of a province may not be carried out across land borders, but they could have serious impacts on the neighbouring provinces. Because of the geographic proximity in cross-border areas, the weather modification activities carried out within each side of a border may affect the territory of the other side.

In contrast to the Chinese regulations on weather modification, the 'Weather Modification Agreement signed by the Government of the United States of America and the Government of Canada' is much clearer in definition. For example, in Article I(b) of the Agreement, the term 'weather modification activities of mutual interest' is defined as

'... carried out in or over the territory of a Party within 200 miles of the international boundary; or such activities wherever conducted, which, in the judgment of a Party, may significantly affect the composition, behavior, or dynamics of the atmosphere over the territory of the other Party.'

In Article IV, 'each Party agrees to notify and to fully inform the other concerning any weather modification activities of mutual interest conducted by it prior to the commence of such activities. Every effort shall be made to provide such notice as far in advance of such activities as may be possible...'. Furthermore, the Agreement states:

The Parties agree to consult, at the request of either Party, regarding particular weather modification activities of mutual interest. Such consultations shall be initiated promptly on the request of a Party, and in cases of urgency may be undertaken through telephonic or other rapid means of communication.

For a long period, China followed an extensive development pattern and paid more attention to the construction of new industrial projects rather than the reconstruction of the old ones. It is often reported that outdated machinery and equipment is still used by many Chinese factories. Technologically outdated machinery and equipment implies low labour productivity and high energy consumption. In Table 9.5 the labour productivity in the Chinese steel, electricity and petrochemical industries is only 3 to 25 per cent that of the advanced nations; while the energy consumption level of China is 16 to 100 per cent higher than that of the advanced nations. The technologically outdated machinery and equipment also lead to poor quality products. According to the sample survey conducted by the State Technological Supervision Bureau (STSB) in 1995, only 86.8 per cent, 75.1 per cent and 24.2 per cent of the commodities produced by the SOEs, TVEs and PSEs, respectively, met the national standards (Wang, 1996, p. 11).

The large number of small-scale plants, particularly those in energy and heavy industries, widely contribute to this high-energy consumption. Besides, the use of inefficient facilities and equipment have induced by low energy prices. In market economies the energy price provides an incentive under which the efficient production and use of energy resources are guided properly. However, for a long period especially during the pre-reform era, China's energy price was officially fixed very low compared with the international level. Lower energy prices encour-

*Table 9.5*　A comparison of industrial production between China and the advanced nations

| Item | Advanced nations (1) | China (2) | (2)/(1) (3) |
|------|------------------------|-----------|--------------|
| A. *Labor productivity* | | | |
| Steel (ton/person) | 600–900 | 30 | 0.03–0.05 |
| Electricity (kW/person) | 2132[b] | 244 | 0.114 |
| Synthetic rubber (ton/person) | 200–300 | 20–50 | 0.067–0.25 |
| Ethylene (ton/person) | 150 | 30 | 0.2 |
| B. *Energy consumption*[a] | | | |
| Steel (kg/ton) | 629 | 1034 | 1.64 |
| Oil refinery (kg/ton) | 19 | 22 | 1.16 |
| Ethylene (1000 kal) | 420–550 | 840 | 1.53–2.0 |
| Electricity (g/kWh) | 150 | 30 | 1.28 |

*Notes*: [a] standard coal equivalent; [b] USA.

*Source*: IIE (1996, p. 40, and tables A and B).

aged people to operate those facilities in ways that used more energy than they would have done if managers had taken account of energy's true value. These results have been wasteful production of excess energy, idle factories and other facilities when sufficient energy is not available, and emission of more $CO_2$, $SO_2$ and other pollutants than necessary.

China's environmental situation is largely related to its energy policy. Coal has dominated more than 70 per cent of China's primary energy production (shown in Figure 9.4), with a production of 1.4 billion ton in 2000. This figure already makes China the world's leading coal producer. Moreover, Chinese coal industry is planning to increase its annual coal production and it has not been certain that the Chinese government is willing to significantly decrease the current proportion of coal in total energy consumption in the foreseen future. Environmental problems (such as acid rain, GHG TSP, land deconstruction, and so on) associated with the entire process of coal extraction, transportation, processing and consumption will, therefore, continue to seriously affect the sustainable development in China if no measures are adopted.

Coal resources concentrate on the North and Northwest, around 600–1000 km far away from the most industrialized provinces and

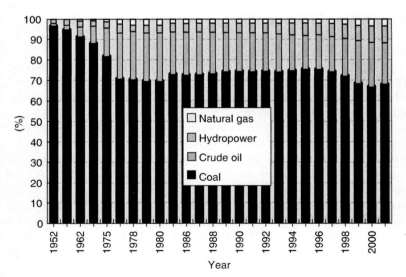

*Figure 9.4*   China's energy production structure (1950–2000)

municipalities in the Southeast. Coal is transported mainly by train and it accounts for more than 40 per cent of the country's railway freights. On the other hand, the building of thermal power stations near the coal mines (*kengkou dianzhan*) seems to be an efficient way, but faces substantial obstacles owing to the shortage of water needed for turbine cooling. Petroleum is currently supplied mainly by Northeast region, while Northwest region is rich in oil reserves and is looking forward to becoming the major oil supplier in the future. The locational disadvantages of the Northwest oil fields, however, will pose difficulties for the oil exploitation and transportation in China.

The government hopes to reduce the share of thermalpower in power generation by constructing large hydroelectric dams. The main hydroelectric dams are Gezhouba Dam in Hubei province, followed by Liujiaxia Dam in Gansu province, Longyang Dam in Qinghai province, Manwan Dam in Yunnan province, Baishan Dam in Jilin province, and so on. If all goes according to plan, China will have completed the world's largest dam in the Three Gorges of Yangtze river by the year 2009. The dam will increase the supply of affordable electricity throughout the Yangtze valley, control floods, boost the growing economy and reduce air pollution. The economic advantages coming from such a big dam, however, could be also reduced by the losses coming from the ecological and environmental costs and risks. The Chinese leadership realizes that developing nuclear power is an appropriate solution to improve local energy shortage in the eastern and southern coastal areas lacking of coal and petroleum resources.

In addition, the nuclear power stations are Qinshan in Zhejiang province and Daya Bay in Guangdong province. But the development of nuclear power stations also faces a series of uncertainties and risks, apart from the domestic technological constraints.

Theoretically, the structure of energy consumption may be largely readjusted through foreign trade. As a matter of fact, the Chinese government has treated energy as one of its 4 'strategic materials' since the PRC was founded. Under this condition, the energy production and consumption have been to a large extent guided in accordance to the principle of 'self-reliance and independence'. Besides the export of some coal and oil which was used as a source of foreign currency earning for many years. Recently, China has become a net-oil import nation, as a result of its increasing domestic demand. But it has not been clear that she is willing to further increase its energy (especially oil and natural gas) dependency to the outside world.

China's petroleum industry is currently under the administration of three state-owned corporations: China National Petroleum and Natural Gas Corporation (CNPC), China National Ocean Petroleum Corporation (CNOPC), and China National Petro-Chemical Corporation (CNPCC). The CNPC is responsible for the exploration and exploitation of the petroleum and natural gas resources within the territory of mainland China, while CNOPC specializes in the exploration and exploitation of ocean petroleum and natural gas resources. Using petroleum and natural gas as raw materials, CNPCC produces and sells finished oil products. In May 1994, the Chinese government began to reform the circulation system of crude oil and finished oil products which had been chaotically managed due to the large gap between the market price and planned price under the 'double-track system'. The reformed oil prices are officially fixed at two levels according to the quality and sources. In 1995, the crude oil prices were averaged at 860 yuan/ton, which is, after the value-added tax (125 yuan/ton) is excluded, only 70 per cent of the international level (SETC, 1996, p. 33).

Before the early 1980s, China did not have any formal administrative organs in charge of environmental protection. In 1984, the National Environmental Protection Agency (NEPA) was established. Thereafter, environmental protection bureaux, divisions, or offices have been established at all governmental levels, such as 'environmental protection offices' of the Commissions, ministries, and other government branches and the state-owned corporations at ministry or semi-ministry level, environmental protection bureaux' of the provinces and autonomous regions, and so on.

China's environmental protection network is virtually a complete one. Directly under the State Council, the NEPA – which has eight specific departments of planning, policy regulation, development supervision, pollution control, science and technology, nature conservation, personnel and foreign affairs – supervises China's environmentally-related activities through two parallel channels: (1) provinces and autonomous regions → prefectures or municipalities → counties and urban districts → non-state and private enterprises and (2) state commissions → ministries and other government branches and state corporations at ministry and semi-ministry levels → state-owned enterprises.

However, China's current administrative organs in charge of environmental protection and its environmentally-related law enforcement are still weak in strength, particularly at grass-roots level, compared to its increasing economic growth and social demands for environmental quality. NEPA is only a semi-ministry level government branch and, therefore, has sometimes less authority than those state-owned enterprises at ministry and semi-ministry levels. For example, NEPA can only exert its policy and professional directions to the provincial environmental protection bureaux, while the latter are appointed by and, naturally, mainly responsible to *their* respective provincial governments. The State Environmental Protection Committee (SEPC) with the participation of different ministries is not a permanent administrative body but a coordinating organization focusing on the interministerial actions. Furthermore, the importance of coordinating the economic development and environmental protection has not been brought home to some local governments and enterprises, due to the unawareness of their responsibility of implementation of the environmental protection laws. Motivated by partial economic interest, the government officials and enterprise managers often ignore environmental costs and benefits, as the yardstick of their achievements has been largely confined to the economic growth index. They are reluctant to carefully study whether such growth could be sustained, and even taken the developing economy as an excuse to evade the restraints of laws and regulations. The irrational aspects of the administrative system and unclear defined responsibility in various departments have impaired the efficiency of environmental management.

Along with the administrative decentralization and regional autonomy, it has been very common in China that laws, regulations and administrative decrees were either resisted or slowly implemented by local governments. For example, the small factories of 15 seriously polluting industries (like chemical paper pulp-making, leather processing and dye production) were ordered by State Council (1996) to close down by the end of September 1996, because of their primitive manufacturing techniques and equipment, excessive use of resources, discharge of untreated waste and damages to the environment. However, only 42,000 (about 80 per cent) of the total polluting factories had been closed before the deadline.[28] Among the 30 provinces, municipalities and autonomous regions, only Beijing, Jilin, Fujian, Hainan and Gansu had shut down all their listed enterprises. Central China's Henan province, which was ordered to close down 17117 small factories – the largest number in the current campaign – had fulfilled nearly 98 per cent of its target. Most of the others had shut down over 50 per cent of the polluting factories, except for Hunan, Yunnan and Zhejiang with the proportions of only 3.7 per cent, 32.9 per cent and 33.7 per cent of their tasks, respectively.[29]

# Summary

Environmental concerns stem from two kinds of human activities: resource depletion which covers the activities of the losses reflecting the deterioration of land and depleting reserves of coal, petroleum, timber, grounder water, and so on; resource degradation which covers the activities associated with air and water pollution, land erosion, solid wastes, and so on. Resource depletion is a concern because it would mean the quantitative exhaustion of natural resources that are an important source of revenues, obtained through exploitation and the discovery of new reserves. In the case of resource degradation, the issue is not the quantitative exhaustion of natural resources, but rather the qualitative degradation of the ecosystem, for example, through the contamination of air and water as a result of the generation and deposit of residuals, and as a result of the environmental impact of producing garbage and solid wastes.

There are further constraints for Chinese sustainable development. For example, China has expressed a willing to participate in an international global warming treaty. However, it is not likely that the Chinese are going to push GHG reductions up to the 'no-regrets' level, because they have more pressing problems. In addition, China has also promised to protect the endangered species in order to maintain a diversified ecosystem. Nevertheless, the relevant treaties and laws in this regard have only little constraint to those people with the habit of 'having wild animals in the tables'. Gains of today might be eventually the costs of tomorrow. The environmental costs resulting from industrialization often build up slowly and do not become critical for the initial years. The benefit of industrialization, however, is usually immediate. However, if the government, industrialists, and consumers are prepared to continue with various practices and leave future generations to worry about their environmental consequences, the problem is therefore a re-election of the importance that people attach to the present relative to the future.

China's economic development has basically followed a traditional development model that is characterized by high resource and energy (mainly coal) consumption and extensive management. This has not only led to a series of damages to the environment of today, but also affected its economic sustainability. Therefore, shifting the development strategy and embarking on the path to sustainable development is the only correct choice for the Chinese economy. We have in this chapter opened up more questions about the Chinese environmental issues rather than drawn up conclusions. It should be noted that China, like many other developing countries, is facing many pressing problems related to the economic development which might, at least in the short-run, be contradicted with environmental protection. However, environmental policies and measures should never be treated independently from economic policies. Moreover, they can serve as a dynamic mechanism for the maximization of the real well-being of the entire people.

# 10
## Economic Internationalization and China

A frog that lived in a shallow well said to a turtle coming from the East Sea: 'I am so happy! When I go out, I jump about on the railing beside the mouth of the well, and I rest in the holes on the broken wall of the well when I come home. If I jump into the water, it comes up to my armpits and holds up my cheeks. If I walk in the mud, it covers up my feet. I look around at the wriggly worms, crabs and tadpoles and non of them can compare with me. Moreover, I am lord of this trough of water and I stand up tall in this shallow well. My happiness is full. Why wouldn't you come here often and look around my place?'

Zhuangzi (c. 369–286 BC)

### Historical review

China had been a typical autarkic society for a long time before it was forced to open up to the outside world at the end of the First Opium War (1840–42).[1] Since then, the Chinese economy has been transformed as a result of the destruction of feudalism. Foreign capital inflowed gradually into the mainland, followed by the penetration of Western culture, representing the first signal for Chinese industrialization. Unfortunately, because of long civil wars as well as Japanese invasion, Chinese economic construction had not been given priority in the first half of the 20th century. During the First FYP period (1953–57), some economic progress was achieved. Thereafter, however, difficulties took place due to China's frequent domestic political struggles and fluctuating diplomatic relations with the capitalist bloc and then the socialist bloc.

As soon as the PRC was found on 1 October 1949, the Chinese government severed almost all economic ties with the capitalist world. Affected by the Korean War (1950–53) and the Taiwan strait crisis, the Eastern belt stagnated, compared with most parts of the Western belt which benefited geographically to a large extent from China's close relations with the former USSR. However, it should be noted that China's foreign trade with the CPEs usually remained at a minimum level, aiming at just supplementing any gap between domestic supply and demand. Such trade reflected natural resource endowments more than anything else. Therefore, China's close ties with the socialist economies did not result in significant economic effects on the Western belt. During the period from the early 1960s to the late 1970s, China practised autarkic socialism as a result of the Sino-USSR dispute as well as the 'self-reliance and independence' strategy.

China's economic internationalization strategy began to experience dramatic changes in the late 1970s when the top Chinese policymakers suddenly found that the Chinese economy, after having been socialistically constructed for almost 30 years, had lagged far behind not only the Western but also those once-ever backward economies along the western coast of the Pacific ocean. It is now generally believed that the Chinese outward-oriented development policy has been borrowed, in part, from East Asia's NIEs such as South Korea, Taiwan, Singaprore and Hong Kong. In order to attract foreign investment, China enacted the 'Law of the People's Republic of China Concerning the Joint Ventures with Chinese and Foreign Investment' in 1979. Also in this year, the CCPCC and State Council decided to grant Guangdong and Fujian provinces 'special policies and flexible measures' in foreign economic affairs. On 26 December 1979, the People's Congress of Guangdong province approved the Guangdong provincial government's proposal that a part of Shenzhen next to Hong Kong, Zhuhai next to Macau, and Santou be designed to experiment with a market-oriented economy with Chinese characteristics, namely, SEZ. This proposal was finally accepted by the NPC on 26 August 1980. At the same time, Xiamen in Southeast Fujian province *vis-à-vis* Taiwan also became a SEZ with the approval of NPC.

Thereafter, a series of open-door measures were implemented in the coastal area: in October 1983, Hainan island, Guangdong province, was allowed to conduct some of the special foreign economic policies granted to the SEZs; in April 1984, 14 coastal cities (including Tianjin, Shanghai, Dalian, Qinhuangdao, Yantai, Qingdao, Lianyungang, Nantong, Ningbo, Wenzhou, Fuzhou, Guangzhou, Ganjiang and Beihai) were designated by the CCPCC and the State Council as 'open cities'; in February 1985, three deltas of Yangtze River, Pearl River and South Fujian were approved as coastal economic development zones (EDZs); in March 1988, the EDZs of the three deltas were again approved to extensively cover larger areas while at the same time some cities and counties in Liaodong and Shandong peninsulas and Bohai Basin area were allowed to open up economically to the outside world; in April 1988, the NPC approved the establishment of Hainan province which was organized as an SEZ with even more flexible policies than other SEZs; in April 1990, Shanghai's suggestion of speeding up the development of Pudong area using some of the SEZ's mechanisms was approved by the CCPCC and the State Council.

Besides a 14,500 km coastline, China has over 22,000 km of international land boundaries through which nine frontier provinces are directly exposed to the outside world (see Table 10.1). Generally, cross-border economic cooperation and trade are naturally facilitated by the geographical factor as well as that people on both sides of the border often belong to the same minority group and share the same language and customs across the border. China's rapid border development has mainly benefited from its open-door policy and *râpprochement* with the neighbouring countries since the mid-1980s. In 1984 the Chinese government promulgated the 'Provisional Regulations for the Management of 'Small-volume' Border Trade' and opened hundreds of frontier cities and towns. In contrast to the eastern coastal development which was mainly fueled by FDI, China's inland frontier development has been characterized by border trade with foreign neighbours. Inspired by Deng Xiaoping's Southern Speech in early 1992, China has embarked on a deeper outward-looking policy in an attempt to promote the development in the frontier regions of the four provinces of Heilongjiang, Yunnan, Jilin and Liaoning and the four autonomous regions of Inner Mongolia, Xinjiang, Tibet and Guangxi. Since the early 1990s, a series of favourable and flexible measures to manage cross-border trade and economic cooperation have been granted to those frontier provinces. They include:

- 'Measures Concerning the Supervision and Favourable Taxation for the People-to-People Trade in Sino-Myanmer Border' (25 January 1992, Office of Custom, PRC);
- 'Notification Concerning the Further Opening up of the Four Frontier Cities of Heihe, Shuifenhe, Hunchun and Manzhouli' (1992, State Council);

- 'Notification Concerning the Further Opening up of the Five Frontier Cities and Towns of Nanning, Kunming, Pingxiang, Ruili and Hekou' (June 1992, State Council);
- 'Some Favourable Policies and Economic Autonomy Authorized to the Frontier Cities of Heihe and Shuifenhe' (June 1992, Heilongjiang);
- 'Resolution of Some Issues Concerning the Extension of Open-door and Promotion of Economic Development' (20 April 1991, Inner Mongolia);
- 'Notification of Promoting Trade and Economic Cooperation with Neighbouring and Eastern European Countries' (9 February 1992, Xinjiang);
- 'Resolutions Concerning the Further Reform and Opening up to the Outside World' (14 July 1992, Tibet);
- 'Provisional Regulations Concerning the Border Trade' (1991, Yunnan province).[2]

Since the reform and open-door policies were introduced in 1978, China has basically formed a pattern featuring gradual advance from east to west, from SEZs, then to other coastal areas, and finally to the inland area. Further progress has been made in opening border, riparian and inland areas to the outside world since 1992. This has also spread from processing industries to basic industries, infrastructure facilities and service

*Table 10.1*  Boundary conditions of the Chinese economy

| Frontier province | Neighboring countries (km of the borderline) | Open towns |
|---|---|---|
| Gansu | Mongolia (65) | none |
| Guangxi | Vietnam (1020) | 4 |
| Heilongjiang | Russia (3045) | 8 |
| Inner Mongolia | Mongolia (3640), Russia (560) | 10 |
| Jilin | North Korea (870), Russia (560) | 1 |
| Liaoning | North Korea (546) | 1 |
| Tibet | India (1906), Nepal (1236), Bhutan (470), Myanmer (188) | 4 |
| Xinjiang | Russia (40), Mongolia (968), Pakistan (523), Kazakhstan (1533), Kyrgyzstan (858), Tajikistan (540), Afghanistan (76), India (1474) | 10 |
| Yunnan | Myanmer (1997), Laos (710), Vietnam (1353) | 4 |

*Sources*: Liu and Liao (eds, 1993, pp. 3–152; (2) *China Atlas*.

trades, and is to intended to develop toward a multi level and all directional opening pattern. A glance at the PRC's history reveals that China's economic stagnation and prosperity have been closely related to its policy of economic internationalization. More specifically, when the autarkic policy was implemented, economic stagnation occurred; when the outward-looking policy was introduced, economic prosperity would be achieved accordingly. China's regional economic performances have also been decided in this way.

At the WTO's Fourth Ministerial Conference held in Doha, Qatar, China became the 143rd member of the WTO on 11 December 2001. In order to accede to the WTO, China agreed to take concrete steps to remove trade barriers and open its markets to foreign companies and their exports in virtually every product sector and for a wide range of services as represented in the Protocol of Accession of the People's Republic of China (Document No. WT/L/432, 2001). With China's consent, the WTO created a special multilateral mechanism for reviewing China's compliance on an annual basis. Known as the Transitional Review Mechanism, this mechanism operates annually for eight years after China's accession, with a final review by the tenth year.

The WTO membership will give China an improved external environment under which input of new technology and capital inflow can give China's industry a boost. Exports are expected to continue to grow, as China will be less strictly bound by trade quotas. China no longer needs to be concerned about the annual renewal of most-favoured nation status by the US Congress, as it did in the past two decades, telecommunications and other service industries of the rest of the world will be allowed to operate in China according to the negotiated timetable. The impact may eventually break up the status of monopoly and state control that have existed in China for about a half-century. Impact on social and political reforms can be highly significant in the long run.

## Foreign investment[3]

### General trends

Chinese FDI trends can be distinguished according to changes in policy directions. During the late 1970s and the early 1980s, the Chinese government established four SEZs in Guangdong and Fujian provinces, and offered special incentive policies for FDI in these SEZs. China has made continuous efforts to attract foreign capital in the forms of both foreign loans and FDI. Foreign loans include foreign government loans,

loans from international financial institutions, and buyers' credits and other private loans. In order to attract foreign investment, the NPC enacted the 'Law of the People's Republic of China Concerning the Joint Ventures with Chinese and Foreign Investment' in 1979. In the SEZs and other economic and technological development zones, foreign investors were afforded preferential treatment. Moreover, the government assumes responsibility for improving the landscape and constructing infrastructure such as water-supply and drainage systems, electricity, roads, post and telecommunications, warehouses, and so on. While FDI inflows into China were highly concentrated in these SEZs, the amount was rather limited at that period.

Since 1984, when Hainan Island and fourteen coastal cities across ten provinces were opened, the previously recorded modest FDI levels started to take off. Total FDI inflows amounted to US$10.3 billion in the 1984–88 period; with an annual average of US$2.1 billion. This remarkable upward trend, however, dropped steeply in 1989, mainly due to the impact of the Tiananmen incidents. The growth rates of FDI inflows into China slowed down at a meager 6.2 per cent level in 1989 and only 2.8 per cent in 1990. Even though FDI started to resume its growth path in 1991, by recording 25.2 per cent increase *vis-à-vis* the previous year, the annual growth rate for this overall period was lowered to 11.0 per cent, which paled in comparison to 38.1 per cent during 1984 to 1988 (OECD, 2000).

The third phase started in the Spring of 1992, when Deng Xiaoping circuited China's southern coastal areas and SEZs. His visit, which intended mainly to push China's overall economic reform process forward and to emphasize China's commitment to the open door policy and market-oriented economic reform, proved to be a success in garnering the confidence of foreign investors in China. China adopted a new approach, which turned away from special regimes toward more nation-wide implementation of open policies for FDI. The government issued a series of new policies and regulations to encourage FDI inflows. The results were remarkable: Since 1992 the inflows of FDI into China have accelerated and reached the peak level in the early 2000s.

Since it called for foreign capital participation in its economy in 1979, China has received a large part of international direct investment flows. China has become the second largest FDI recipient in the world, after the United States, and the largest host country among developing countries. China's position as a host to FDI is in fact too far removed from any other developing country – and most developed countries –

to be equaled. Beginning in 1993, China emerged as the largest recipient of FDI among developing countries. China's joining the WTO in 2001 provided a strong push for a new wave of foreign investment into China. In 2003, China overtook the United States as the world's biggest recipient of FDI, attracting US$53 billion. By the end of 2004, the accumulation of the established foreign-invested enterprises reached the number of more than ½ million with contracted foreign investment of more than US$1000 billion and actual use of foreign investment of more than US$500 billion (NBS, 2005), which is equivalent to 10 per cent of direct investment worldwide and about 30 per cent of the investment amount for all the developing countries put together.

Joint venture, cooperative and foreign enterprises have been three major forms of foreign investment in China. The scope of foreign investment has now extended from investments in tourism, textile, and building industries to cooperative ventures in oil exploration, transportation, telecommunications, machine building, electronics, and other industries. Regarding the origins of FDI, Hong Kong and Macau were the largest investor and contributed to 43.30 per cent of the total foreign investment, followed by Japan (10.62 per cent), Taiwan (6.58 per cent), USA (6.51 per cent), Singapore (3.87 per cent), South Korea (2.47 per cent), and UK (2.10 per cent) in 1995. In 2005, the top ten countries and regions with investments in China were as follows (in order of shares): Hong Kong, Virgin Islands, South Korea, Japan, the United States, Taiwan, Singapore, Cayman Islands, West Samoa and Germany, the total of which accounted for more than 80 per cent the total actual use of foreign investments in the country.[4]

During the 1980s, FDI was concentrated in traditional labour-intensive manufacturing industries (light industry), especially textiles, garments and real estate companies. Since 1992, it has gradually shifted to capital- and technology-intensive sectors, such as chemicals, machinery, transport equipment, electronics and telecommunications. In the second half of the 1990s, while foreign investments in traditional labour-intensive manufacturing industries stagnated, the IT industry became a new focus of investment. Investments in technology-intensive industries have become a new focus of investment. The goal to attract FDI inflows has been to introduce advanced technology, improve management and expand markets. The modes of foreign investment have undergone some systematic changes. The basic option in the early period of reform was to set up a contractual joint venture. Since 1986, equity joint ventures and wholly foreign-owned enterprise investments have become the main forms of foreign investment. Since the 1990s, the share of wholly foreign-invested enterprises gradually increased, along with foreign control in joint ventures also increasing. By 2000, the actual investment share of wholly foreign-owned enterprises exceeded that of joint ventures; the former became the main force in impelling growth in foreign trade. A related fact is that, apart from a few sectors, the Chinese government repealed restrictions on foreign control in joint ventures.

### Geographical distribution

Foreign investment has been unevenly distributed in China. FDI inflows have been heavily concentrated in China's coastal provinces, while Central and Western Regions have attracted only marginal shares. By 2000, foreign investments were felt in all parts of China, except in Tibet. The southeast coastal area has dominated as a recipient of inward foreign investments throughout. Not surprisingly, the most important determinant for the irregular absorption of foreign capital is geographical location. For example, the Eastern belt received most of the foreign capital, while only less than 10 per cent of the total foreign capital flowed into the central and Western belts which cover more than 85 per cent of China's territory. Nevertheless, this uneven pattern has gradually improved as a result of the government efforts to internationalize the inland economy.

This inequality stems from the FDI policies taken by the Chinese authority. The open door has started with the creation of SEZs and preferential regimes for fourteen coastal cities. This has resulted in an overwhelming concentration of FDI in the east. With the adoption of more broadly-based economic reforms and open door policies for FDI in the 1990s, FDI inflows into China have started to spread to other provinces. Among the eastern region provinces, Guangdong's performance in attracting FDI has been very impressive. Its share of accumulated FDI stock from 1983 to 1998 was 29.4 per cent of the national total, far exceeding all other provinces including Jiangsu and Fujian, each of which possessed around 10 per cent of the national total, and ranked second and third among China's thirty provinces. However, if we analyze this province group one step further, we find that the shares of each province have gradually changed. The share of Guangdong has declined from 46.13 per cent in the 1980s to 27.98 per cent in the 1990s. In contrast, the shares of other coastal provinces, such as Jiangsu, Fujian, Zhejiang, Shandong, Tianjin and Hubei, have increased steadily.

The share of the central provinces in the national total accumulated FDI stocks has increased gradually from 5.3 per cent during the 1980s to 9.2 per cent during the 1990s. The main contributors are Henan, Hubei, and Hunan provinces, and their shares of accumulated FDI in the national total doubled from the 1980s to the 1990s. These figures suggest that the provincial distribution of FDI inflows has spread somewhat from the opened coastal provinces into the inland provinces. The western less developed provinces received a very small amount of FDI inflows. Their share in the national accumulated FDI stocks has been declining from 4.7 per cent in the 1980s to 3.2 per cent in the 1990s. However, Sichuan and Shaanxi attracted relatively more FDI inflows than the other provinces in this group. In the final analysis, FDI inflows in the 1990s have diffused from the initially concentrated southern coastal areas towards the southeastern and eastern coastal areas as well as towards inland areas. The three provincial groups of the eastern, central and western regions experienced different patterns in FDI inflows. For the eastern region provinces FDI inflows have been increasing steadily with a remarkably high growth rate, particularly from 1992 to 1998. For the other two provincial groups, the inflows of FDI have been much less, especially for the western region provinces. As a result, the gap between the eastern region and the central and western regions in terms of the absolute magnitude of annual FDI inflows has actually broadened since 1992.

## Impacts on China's economy

The foreign investment has played an increasing role in the Chinese economy. The shares of foreign trade, GVIO and employees of the foreign-funded enterprises to China were only 17.4 per cent, 2.1 per cent and 1.4 per cent in 1990. In 1995, they increased dramatically to 39.1 per cent, 16.6 per cent and 10.8 per cent, up by 1.25, 6.67, and 6.71 times that in 1990, respectively.[5] What is more, the foreign enterprises have promoted the importation of the advanced technology, equipment, and management and, above all, the competition mechanisms from the advanced economies. Moreover, FIEs have generated nearly one-fifth of the total tax revenues and millions of job opportunities, employing about one-tenth of all urban workers.

Most of the foreign investments came from small and medium sized enterprises based in Hong Kong. The dominant position of Hong Kong is apparent through several factors. First, Hong Kong is geographically adjacent to Guangdong province, where Shenzhen – the most important SEZ of China – is located. Second, it was in the 1980s that Hong Kong made the transfer of its export-oriented labour-intensive manufacturing industry to Mainland China. This is the typical 'Flying Geese

*Table 10.2* FDI's Impacts on the Chinese economy

| A. *External effects* | B. *Domestic effects* |
|---|---|
| 1. China's comparative advantages | 1. An increasingly important source of capital |
| 2. Increased participation in the international segmentation of production | 2. Create jobs |
| 3. Impact on China's trade growth | 3. Upgrade skills |
| 4. Role of FIEs in processing trade | 4. Paid higher wages to employees |
| 5. Comparative trading performance of FIE firms | 5. Raise factor productivity and increased technology transfer |
| 6. Building dynamic specialization | 6. Modify China's industrial structure |
| 7. Domestic penetration of FIEs | 7. Foreign and domestic firms are different |
| 8. Rising local content | 8. FDI has increased domestic competition |
| 9. FIE export competitiveness and exchange rate policy | 9. FDI has increased industrial performance |
| 10. Domestic firms have lagged behind | |
| 11. Regional disparities have increased | |
| 12. Impact on China's balance of payments | |

*Source*: based on OECD (2000).

Paradigm' of international division of labour. Thirdly, especially since 1992, investments from Hong Kong took the advantage of preferential treatment given to foreign investors.

Table 10.2 summarizes the main findings of the research conducted under the cooperation program by the OECD and the Chinese Ministry of Foreign Trade.

There is large literature regarding FDI and exports as the driving force for China's success (see, for example, Berthelemy and Demurger 2000, Lemione 2000, and Demurger 2000). In this connection the roles of overseas Chinese and of Hong Kong and Taiwan are often emphasized. In contrast to the above view, Qian (2001) presents a quite different conclusion after simply considering a parallel experience in Germany. If Hong Kong or Taiwan could play such a powerful role on mainland China, West Germany should have been even more effective on East Germany, given that West Germany is much larger and stronger than Taiwan and Hong Kong combined and East Germany is much smaller than mainland China.[6] We argue that Qian's (2001) judgment would have been correct if only taking into account the direct influences of the FDI and foreign trade. However, the indirect effects of the FDI, though following a decreasing geographic order from coastal to middle and to western China, are also enomous. Besides, social and cultural influences of open-door policy should never be negelected, since they also determine economic development siginificantly. Anyone who has ever traveled to western and inland cities cannot fail to notice that their vibrant local economies were due largely to their interactions with the outside world. More important is the great potential of comparative advantages as well as close cultural lineages between Hong Kong, Macau, Taiwan and mainland China.

## Foreign trade

### General review

A country may benefit from exporting those commodities it can produce more cheaply and importing those which can be produced more efficiently abroad. This is particularly useful for China –a country with abundant natural and agricultural resources but lack of capital, technology – to import advanced scientific innovations, production techniques and management experience from advanced nations. To bring about socialist modernization in its own way, China did not adopt the strategy of 'founding a nation on trade' used by many industrially developed nations, rather, it was based on the principle of 'independence and self-reliance' during the first decades of the PRC. As a result, China lagged far behind the advanced nations. In order to achieve quickly the economic modernization, China must actively seek new technologies through foreign trade and cooperation.

China's foreign trade and economic relations during the early stage of the PRC reflected, to a large extent, the basic characteristics of a socialist economy. In the 1950s, because of a trade embargo imposed by the USA and other Western nations, most foreign trade was restricted to the Soviet bloc countries. Following the Sino-Soviet split in the early 1960s, foreign trade decreased dramatically. Guided by the principle of 'self-reliance and independence', China's foreign trade and economic relations had not been improved significantly before the early 1970s. Since then, its trade with the capitalist market increased gradually, as a result of the *râpprochement* with Japan, the USA, and some EU. However, because the autarkic economic policy had still been in operation before the late 1970s, both the volume of foreign trade

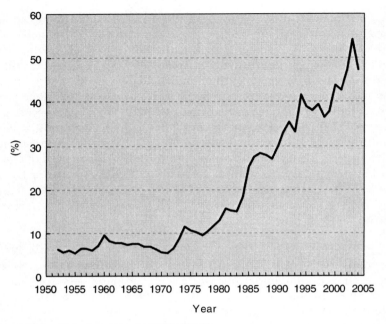

*Figure 10.1*   China's openness (1950–2005)

and the ratio of it to GNP were still very small at that time in China (see Figure 10.1).

Since the late 1970s, China has made many efforts to import advanced production equipment from abroad and use it to kick-start its economic take-off. Except for a few years such as 1982–83 and 1989–90, China's foreign trade during the reform period has grown with exceptional rapidity. When exports exceed imports, a trade surplus occurs. During the early period of the PRC, the Chinese economy sustained a large trade deficit. This seems to be reasonable because China, after many years of wars, needed more consumer goods as well as production materials than it could supply. From 1955 to 1977, China obtained a high level of trade surplus, with the exceptions of 1960, 1970, and 1974–75. Obviously, this beneficial foreign trade pattern had to large extent been shaped by China's 'self-reliance' policy for much of that period. China's attempt at speeding up economic development based on the 'imported' method was mainly responsible to the trade deficit in the late 1970s. A long-lasting trade deficit occurred between 1984–89. Trade surplus has accompanied the strong and growing exports since 1990, with the exception of 1993 (see Figure 10.2). This

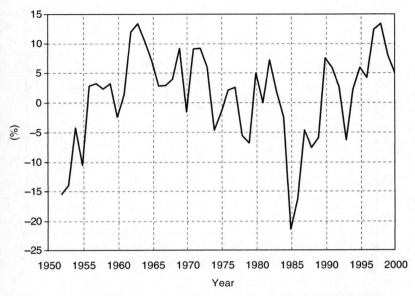

*Figure 10.2*   Foreign trade surplus (deficit) as % of total trade (1952–2000)

has also increased China's foreign deposits. However, this trade surplus has also led to large trade deficits for its trade partners, sometimes resulting in retaliations.[7]

Generally, foreign trade can be classified into four types according to the composition of imported and exported commodities in kind: (1) both imports and exports are dominated by primary goods; (2) imports are dominated by primary goods while exports by manufactured goods; (3) exports are dominated by primary goods while imports by manufactured goods; and (4) both imports and exports are dominated by manufactured goods. China's foreign trade has effectively transformed from pattern (1) to pattern (4) over the past decades. In the early 1950s, the shares of primary and manufactured goods were about 80 per cent and 20 per cent of total exports, respectively. Since then, the share of manufactured products to total exports has grown steadily and it eventually overtook that of primary products in the early 1980s. Since 1995, the share of manufactured goods to total exports has increased to more than 80 per cent (see Figure 10.3). This structural change of exports has been largely ascribed to China's strong push towards industrialization since 1949 (as discussed in Chapter 8). The composition of imported commodities includes a very

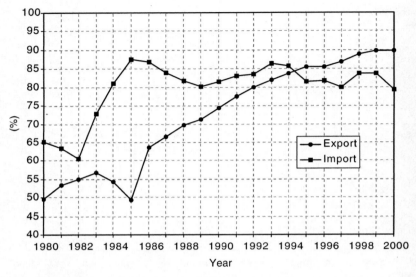

*Figure 10.3*   Share of manufactured commodity imports (exports) to total imports (exports), 1980–2000

small share of primary products compared with that of manufactured products, due to China's abundance in natural resources as well as its large agricultural sector.

### Determinants of foreign trade

It has been broadly assumed that a country's economic dependence on the outside world is negatively related to its land area.[8] This may be illustrated unambiguously by the relationship between the supply and demand of some basic resources for countries differing in size (land area).[9] Generally speaking, compared to large economies, small economies have a relatively limited variety of natural resources. Therefore, they have to import resources that they lack and that are essential to meeting diversified production and consumption needs. Eventually, the increased imports will stimulate the exportation in order to attain a balance.

Besides geographical area, a country's economic size (output) and population also influence its external economic activities. Generally, the larger the GDPs (or GNPs)[10] of trade partners, *ceteris paribus*, the larger the volume of trade between them; by contrast, population is a negative factor in the determination of international trade. This captures the well-known phenomenon that larger countries tend to be relatively less open to trade as a percentage of GDP (or GNP). Therefore, it is easy to understand that Hong Kong, Singapore and Luxembourg are more highly dependent on international trade than the United States, China or India. The former lack not only natural endowments but also room to exploit economies of scale in the domestic market, while the latter, engaging in far more trade in absolute terms (*versus* less trade as a percentage of GDP or GNP), can find more business opportunities inside their own territories.

Without considering geographical factor, it could be very difficult to understand the current patterns of both global and regional trade. For instance, bilateral trade flows across the US-Canadian border, between France, Italy, UK, Germany and the Netherlands, and along the western coast of the Pacific Ocean (including, *inter alia*, South Korea, Taiwan, Hong Kong and the mainland of China) have risen a great deal more quickly than between more remote and isolated economies. Besides distance, another proxy of geographical factor that influences international trade is adjacency. For example, bilateral trade between France and the United Kingdom will be due to their proximity but trade between France and Germany will be further boosted by their common border. One of many ways to include 'adjacency' in the international trade model is to treat it as a dummy variable.[11]

During the postwar period technological advances in transportation and communications have been of the greatest importance. The increasing proportion of economic value is weightless – that is, it can be transmitted over fiber-optic cable rather than transported in a container ship. At the same time, improvements in transportation networks and technology are reducing the costs of shipping goods by water, ground and air. More important are the improvements in information technology (IT) that have made it easier to manage the new interconnections world-wide. Among them is Internet, the fast-growing tool of communication. The Internet has provided a new means of commerce, with clear speed and cost advantages. Declining transportation and other distance-related costs should have increasingly contributed to the growth of global trade.

Past studies on the geographical influence on trade have raised more questions than they answered. For example, among the existing estimated results on the determinants of international trade (in logarithmic form), the statistically significant coefficients on the log of distance have ranged between $-0.51$ and $-1.50$, which demonstrates the respective decreases (in percentage) in international trade as a result of a

1.0 per cent increase in distance.[12] No observable tendency, however, has been found for the effect of geographical proximity to fall over time. Rather, the trend seems to be upward during the courses of, among others, 1950-88 in Boisso and Ferrantino (1997) and 1965–92 in Frankel *et al.* (1997). In their analyses on the negative correlation between distance and the interdependence for sovereign countries, Frankel *et al.* (1994) use the data of the 1980s and obtain slightly larger coefficients (around 0.5 to 0.6) on distance compared with Eichengreen and Irwin's (1995) interwar estimates (around 0.3 to 0.6) based on the data of the 1930s. Similarly, based on the panel data of 1970, 1980 and 1990, Rauch's (1999) results show little evidence that supports the decreasing tendency for trade with respect to distance from 1970 to 1990. Clearly this provides no evidence that, as a result of the declining transportation cost, there should have a decreasingly negative relation between trade and distance. Intuitively, we suspect that some powerful explanatory variables that may either resist or aid international trade must have been missing or simplified, which could in turn reduce to a greater or lesser extent the reliability of the estimated results.[13]

The determinants of international trade seem controversial in existing studies. For example, according to the Heckscher-Ohlin theorem, countries with dissimilar levels of per capita income will trade more than countries with similar levels (see Heckscher, 1919; and Ohlin, 1933). However, a number of empirical results indicate that if the distribution of national incomes across countries becomes more equal over time, the volume of trade should increase.[14] Moreover, Helpman (1987) and Krugman (1995) predict that the sum of the logs of per capita GDPs of two countries will have a positive effect on the log form of trade between the two countries. With regard to the East Asian case, the positive effect is found for both 1985 and 1995. But this does not apply to the case of China (see Table 10.3).

Among past literature relating to the determinants of international trade, the coefficients on the log of distance have ranged between –0.51 and –1.50, which demonstrate the decreases (in percentage) in international trade as a result of a 1.0 per cent increase in distance (see, for example, Linnemann, 1966; Brada and Mendez, 1983; Bikker, 1987; Oguledo and MacPhee, 1994; and Mansfield and Bronson, 1997).[15] No observable tendency, however, has been found for the effect of geographical proximity to fall over time. Rather, the trend seems to be upward during the courses of, among others, 1950–1988 in Boisso and Ferrantino (1997) and 1965–92 in Frankel *et al.* (1997). Frankel *et al.*

*Table 10.3* Gravity model regressions on foreign trade, China and East Asia

| Coefficient | East Asia | | China | |
|---|---|---|---|---|
| | 1985 | 1995 | 1985 | 1995 |
| Constant | −17.282 | 29.303 | −2.122 | −15.220 |
| | (1.666[a]) | −(1.225[a]) | (7.664) | (2.823[a]) |
| ln(GDP$_i$GDP$_j$) | 1.162 | 1.236 | 1.418 | 1.081 |
| | (0.032[a]) | (0.027[a]) | (0.166[a]) | (0.065[a]) |
| ln(GDPPC$_i$GDPPC$_j$) | 0.722 | 0.868 | −0.689 | 0.145 |
| | (0.059[a]) | (0.047[a]) | (0.330[b]) | (0.117) |
| ln(DISTANCE$_{ij}$) | −1.440 | −0.648 | −1.364 | −0.423 |
| | (0.147[a]) | (0.103[a]) | (0.631[b]) | (0.218[b]) |
| LANGUAGE$_{ij}$ | −9.048 | 2.860 | 14.375 | 2.600 |
| | (2.096[a]) | (0.862[a]) | (4.432[a]) | (1.017[a]) |
| RELIGION$_{ij}$ | 0.192 | 1.242 | −26.770 | 5.919 |
| | (0.410) | (0.330[a]) | (11.358[b]) | (4.069) |
| R square | 0.570 | 0.633 | 0.489 | 0.770 |
| F-statistic | 425.917 | 841.41 | 22.737 | 98.54 |
| No. of observations | 1612 | 2446 | 124 | 152 |

*Notes*: All regressions are based on ordinary least squares (OLS). Dependent variable is the natural log of bilateral trade (sum of exports and imports) in 1984 (since many East Asian economies suffered from bad recessions in 1985). Figures within parentheses are standard errors. [a] and [b] denote statistically significant at the 1% and 10% levels, respectively.

*Source*: Estimated by the author based on Appendix V.

(1994) use the data from the 1980s and obtain slightly larger co-efficients (around 0.5 to 0.6) on distance compared with Eichengreen and Irwin's (1995) interwar estimates (around 0.3 to 0.6) based on the data from the 1930s. Similarly, Rauch's (1999) results show little evidence that supports the decreasing tendency for trade with respect to distance-related barriers from 1970 to 1990 as a result of the declining transportation cost. I suspect that some factors that either resist or aid international trade might be missing in these empirical studies, especially for the post-Cold War era.

Obviously, a comparison of the estimated coefficients on the log of DISTANCE in 1985 and 1995 (see Table 10.3) provides evidence that supports the view that geographical influence on trade tends to be reduced in China and East Asia as well during the last decades of the 20th century. One of the major driving forces contributing to this tendency might be technological advance in transportation and communications. Intuitively, wide application of E-commerce and the declining of distance-related transactions costs have increasingly contributed to the growth of international trade in East Asia.

The estimated results reveal that, from 1985 to 1995, five individual languages (Bahasa, Chinese, English, Khmer and Thai) play different roles in foreign trade in East Asia (see Table 10.4). For inter-regional

*Table 10.4*   The growing role of 'Chinese' in foreign trade from 1985 to 1995

| Explanatory variable | Intra-regional trade | | Inter-regional trade | |
|---|---|---|---|---|
| | *1985* | *1995* | *1985* | *1995* |
| Constant | −46.816 | −39.547 | −12.519 | −33.077 |
| | (4.716[a]) | (3.079[a]) | (2.232[a]) | (1.833[a]) |
| $\ln(GDP_iGDP_j)$ | 1.147 | 1.107 | 1.148 | 1.260 |
| | (0.126[a]) | (0.079[a]) | (0.034[a]) | (0.029[a]) |
| $\ln(GDPPC_iGDPPC_j)$ | 1.313 | 1.093 | 0.642 | 0.742 |
| | (0.219[a]) | (0.169[a]) | (0.063[a]) | (0.053[a]) |
| $\ln(DISTANCE_{ij})$ | 1.069 | 0.601 | −1.795 | −0.112 |
| | (0.288[a]) | (0.210[a]) | (0.217[a]) | (0.178) |
| $RELIGION_{ij}$ | 2.697 | 2.332 | −0.206 | 0.454 |
| | (1.659) | (0.901[b]) | (0.419) | (0.360) |
| BAHASA | 1.893 | 1.478 | Excl. | Excl. |
| | (1.036[c]) | (0.753[b]) | | |
| CHINESE | 0.056 | 1.755 | 0.529 | 1.012 |
| | (0.694) | (0.483[a]) | (0.641) | (0.383[a]) |
| ENGLISH | 1.734 | −0.419 | 0.258 | 0.679 |
| | (0.710[b]) | (0.527) | (0.218) | (0.159[a]) |
| KHMER | 6.806 | 5.922 | Excl. | Excl. |
| | (2.277[a]) | (1.191[a]) | | |
| THAI | −3.406 | −1.211 | Excl. | Excl. |
| | (4.114) | (1.137) | | |
| R square | 0.565 | 0.641 | 0.569 | 0.625 |
| F-statistic | 19.341 | 48.71 | 322.188 | 605.96 |
| Number of observations | 143 | 255 | 1468 | 2190 |

*Notes*: All regressions are based on ordinary least squares (OLS). Dependent variable is the natural log of bilateral trade (sum of exports and imports) in 1984 (for 1985's regressions) and 1995 (for 1995's regressions). Hong Kong is excluded from regressions in 1985. Figures within parentheses are standard errors. 'Excl.' denotes the left-hand variable is deleted from the analysis since it has missing correlation. '[a]', '[b]' and '[c]' denote statistically significant at 1%, 5% and 10% levels, respectively.

*Source*: Guo (2007).

trade, Chinese and English, the only two languages with no missing correlation in the regressions, are statistically insignificant in 1985; but they become statistically significant in 1995. For inter-regional trade, Bahasa has a decreasing role from 1985 to 1995; English and Khmer are statistically insignificant in 1995 and statistically significant in 1985. For both years, Thai is not statistically significant. By way of contrast, Chinese language plays a dramatically increasing role from 1985 (with a statistically insignificant coefficient of only 0.056) to 1995 (with a statistically significant coefficient of 1.755).

Why does Chinese play a more important role in international trade than the other languages? I suspect that the stronger effect of linguistic influence on foreign trade might be attributable to Chinese Diaspora. Rauch and Trindade (2002), for example, find that ethnic Chinese networks have a quantitatively important impact on bilateral trade through the mechanisms of market information and matching and referral services, in addition to their effect through community enforcement of sanctions that deter opportunistic behavior. Their estimated results show that for trade between countries with ethnic Chinese population shares at the levels prevailing in Southeast Asia, the smallest estimated average increase in bilateral trade in differentiated products attributable to ethnic Chinese networks is nearly 60 per cent.

## Summary

It must be pointed out that China's foreign economic affairs have not been guided by a *laissez-faire* approach even since the outward-oriented development strategy was implemented in the 1980s. Intervention in the form of trade restrictions such as tariffs and licensing, subsidies, tax incentives and active contact with the world economy exists in both import and export sides. China used to manage its foreign trade through high tariff rates. This policy effectively promoted the development of its domestic industries which were still in the initial stage. However, it also negatively affected the Chinese economy. For example, under the high tariff rates, the products made in abroad have not an equal opportunity to enter the Chinese market as that made in China, which will inevitably prevent the importation of high-quality and cheap commodities from the advanced nations, harm the Chinese consumers, and finally provide less incentives for the Chinese producers to improve their competitiveness. China's import-regulating tax system was finally abolished in 1992. Since then, the Chinese government has reduced the tariffs three times. However, the average tariff rate had been still

*Box 10.1*   A guide to applying for visas

Since the late 1970s when the open-door policy was introduced, Chinese citizens have been freer to go abroad. However, problems still remain due to both the border control policy of China and the unavailability of visa-free access to most of the foreign nations. Chinese citizens going abroad for public affairs are able to apply for 'public affairs passports' (gongwu huzhao), while those who intend to go abroad for private affairs have to apply passports and visas through a complicated procedure. The diagram below shows a visa application process in the mid-1990s when I was invited by a European institution to write the first edition of this book:

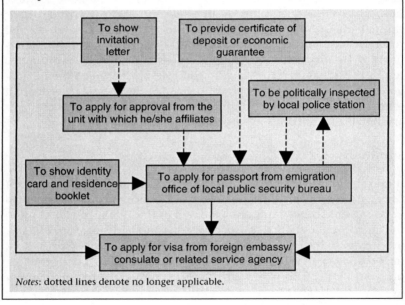

*Notes*: dotted lines denote no longer applicable.

higher than that of other developing countries before April 1996 when China began to reduce the tariff rates on more than 4000 items of imported commodities with an average reduction of over 30 per cent. Meanwhile, the preferentialities of tax exemption and reduction for the foreign-funded enterprises have been also abolished. After the reduction, China's average tariff rate was cut to 23 per cent from the previous level.

China's foreign exchange system used to be controlled severely by the government. Since China started its economic reform in the late 1970s, the foreign exchange system has been liberalized gradually. In the early 1980s, Chinese currency RMB was non-convertible and foreign exchanges were strictly supervised by the state. There existed two exchange rates at that period: an official rate published by the government and another special one for foreign trade. Such a system was aimed at enhancing the country's exports and restrict its imports, for then China seriously suffered from a lack of foreign exchange. In 1984, a new exchange retaining policy was adopted by the government as a result of the improvement in China's foreign trade and economy. It allowed domestic enterprises and institutions to retain a part of their foreign currency earnings, compared with the previous one in which these units turned in all their foreign currency earning to the state. Although a larger part of foreign exchanges was still in the control of the government, the new retaining policy stimulated domestic enterprises to increase their exports, and hence the foreign trade performance of China improved significantly. On 1 January 1994, China established a new unitary and floating exchange-rate system. Although it is based on market supply and demand, this system is still to a large extent determined by the government, as the People's Bank of China (PBC), China's central bank, takes the position of the largest demander of foreign exchange and the Bank of China (BOC) which is also owned by the state is the largest supplier of foreign exchange. What is more, the newly established foreign exchange rate system is still officially controlled and the central bank is one of the biggest participants in the market so as to keep RMB rate at a reasonable level.

Last but not least, China's economic liberalization has been hindered by both 'super-national remuneration' and 'sub-national remuneration' since the early 1980s. On the one hand, the foreign-funded enterprises have been greeted by a series of favourable policies such as tax exemption and low tax rates; on the other hand, they also have faced some unequal treatments and economic discriminations in such fields as communication, transportation, housing, advertising and so on.

Before ending this chapter, let us finishing reading the story by Zhuangzi (c. 369–286 BC) at the beginning of this chapter:

Before the turtle from the East Sea could get its left foot in the well, its right knee got struck. It hesitated and retreated. The turtle told the frog about the East Sea: 'Even a distance of a thousand *li* [500 km] cannot give you an idea of the sea's width; even a height of a thousand *ren* [approximately 666.67 m] cannot give you an idea of its depth. In the time of King Yu of the Xia dynasty, there were floods nine years out of ten, but the waters in the sea did not increase. In the time of King Tang of the Shang dunasty there were droughts seven years out of eight, but the waters in the sea did not decrease. The sea does not change along with the passage of time and its level does not rise or fall according to the amount of rain that falls. The greastest happiness is to live in the East Sea.'

# 11
## Comparative Economics for the Greater China

A man of the state of Lu was skilled in weaving hemp sandals and his wife was good at weaving fine white silk. The couple was thinking of moving out to the state of Yue in the south. 'You will be in dire straits,' he was told.' 'Why?' asked the man of the Lu. 'Hemp sandals are for walking but people of the Yue walk barefoot. White silk is for making hats but people of the Yue go about bareheaded. If you go to a place where your skills are utterly useless, how can you hope to do well?'

Hanfei (280–233 BC)

## Historical evolution

Greater China is defined in this chapter as one which includes Taiwan, Hong Kong, Macau and mainland China.[1] Against their common history, cultural and linguistic homogeneity during the past decades, the four independent Chinese areas have followed divergent political systems, from which different social and economic performances have resulted. As soon as the PRC was founded in 1949, mainland China had effectively adopted and practised a Marxist–Leninist command economy as imposed by the Soviet Union, before it decided to introduce structural reform in the late 1970s. As two colonial economies under the British and Portuguese administrations respectively, Hong Kong and Macau have been fundamentally incorporated into the Western-style society, whereas the Chinese culture and language are still accepted by most of the citizens living there. Taiwan had been colonially ruled by the Japanese for 50 years before it was liberated and returned to China in 1945. With the Civil War (1946–49) coming to an end, however, the newly reunified nation was separated by two

229

ideologically rival regimes – the Nationalists (KMT) in Taiwan and the Communists (CCP) in the mainland. Backed by the United States, the Taiwanese economy followed the capitalist road of economic development. While both sides of Taiwan strait have declared that there is only one *China* in the world and that their motherland should be reunified sooner or later, many political issues arising from the bloody war which was eventually detrimental to national cooperation remain unresolved.

The end of the Cold War and the implementation of economic reform and open-door policy in the mainland China in December 1978 heralded a new era. In January 1979 the USA established diplomatic relations with the mainland China and broke off its long-standing diplomatic relations with Taiwan. Ties between Hong Kong and the mainland developed very rapidly. The development of Mainland–Taiwan ties mainly took place after November 1987 when Taiwan lifted its ban on visits to the Mainland. Hong Kong and Macau reverted to Chinese sovereignty in 1997 and 1999, respectively, while preserving their capitalist system for 50 years under the formula of 'one country, two systems'. In economic terms, Hong Kong and Macu, each as an autonomous entity, are separate customs territories and founding members of the WTO. Each has an independent fiscal and monetary system, issuing its own currency that is linked to the US dollar. It issues its own passport and retains its legal system, maintaining its own court of appeal. It runs its internal affairs without interference from the central government, except in matters of defence and foreign affairs.

In order to help one to have an in-depth understanding of the economic mechanisms of the greater China area, let us briefly review the historical evolution of Hong Kong, Macau and Taiwan and the current situations of their economic relations with mainland China.

## Hong Kong

In ancient China, Hong Kong was initially included in Bao'an county, while the latter also included nowadays Donguan county and the Shenzhen municipality of Guangdong province. In 1573, Xin'an county was established and had administered Hong Kong for 268 years before Hong Kong island and Kowloon peninsula were ceded to the Great Britain according to two Sino-UK treaties which were unequally signed in 1842 and 1860, respectively. In 1898, the British government rented an area of the southern part of Bao'an county as its New Territories from the Qing dynasty (1644–1910). At present, Hong Kong is known to include Hong Kong island, Kowloon peninsula, and the New

Territories, with a 1068 square kilometers land area and 6.06 million population. For the past decades, there has existed a special geopolitical scenario between the two sides of Shenzhen river. Even though the Chinese character, Shenzhen, means a deep gutter, no one would have expected that the 'gutter' had served as a forbidden frontier between the socialist mainland China and the capitalist Hong Kong in the mid-20th century, and also has created an economic prosperity for Hong Kong and been still fueling up the industrialization of the South China area *vis-à-vis* the Britain's Hong Kong. On 19 December 1984, the Chinese and British governments jointly declared that the sovereignty of Hong Kong will be transferred from UK to PRC with effect from 1 July 1997.[2] Upholding national unity and territorial integrity, maintaining the prosperity and stability of Hong Kong, and taking account of its history and realities, China has decided that upon its resumption of the exercise of sovereignty over Hong Kong, a special administrative region (SAR) will be established in Hong Kong in accordance with the provisions of Article 31 of the Constitution of the PRC. Under the principle of 'one country, two systems', 'the socialist system and policies shall not be practised in the Hong Kong special administrative region, and the previous capitalist system and way of life shall remain unchanged for 50 years'.[3]

## Macau

Located in the west side the Pearl river (Zhujiang), Macau was included in Xiangshan county, Guangdong province before it was occupied by the Portuguese colonists in 1533. The Portuguese-rented land area in Macau increased after the Opium War (1840–42). Macau formally became a Portuguese colony in 1887. Bordering on Zhuhai municipality, Guangdong province, Macau has now 16.92 square kilometers of land area including Macau peninsula and Taipa and Toloane islands. Macau has a population of more than 400 thousand. According to the Sino-Portugal Joint Declaration signed in 15 January 1988, Macau will be handed over from the Portuguese administration to mainland China on 20 December 1999. After then, Macau will become the second SAR of the PRC under the principle of 'one country, two systems'.

## Taiwan

With 36,000 square kilometers of land and more than 20 million population, Taiwan is composed of Taiwan, Penghu, Mazu and other small islands adjacent to mainland China. The Sino-Japanese War was ended with the signing of the Shimonoseki Treaty on 17 April 1895. Under the Treaty, Japan seized Taiwan and the Penghu islands from Qing dynasty (1644–1911), subjecting Taiwan to colonial rule for half a century. At the end of World War II, together with the Allied forces, China defeated Japan. On 25 October 1945, Taiwan and Penghu islands returned unconditionally to the Chinese government, marking the end of Japan's colonization. However, with the civil war coming to an end, Taiwan and mainland China was again politically separated in 1949 when the Nationalist-led government fled to Taiwan and, consequently, the Communists took power in the mainland.

Since the late 1940s, China has been in practice ruled by two ideo-logically antagonistic regimes, each of which has laid claim to the sole sovereignty of the whole nation and treated the other side as its 'local' government.[4] The division of the Chinese nation extends through many phases of Chinese life–political, economic and social. The 50 year-long cross-Taiwan strait separation destroyed national unity, led to tragic conflicts and produced mutual distrust and many other human and national agonies. Since the 1980s, it has become the inviolable mission and long-term goal for the two regimes to achieve peaceful reunification and promote the all-around revitalization of the nation.

It can be seen that the greater China area has been undergoing a major transformation since the 1980s. Sino-Hong Kong and Sino-Macau rela-tions have been no longer treated internationally since 1997 and 1999, respectively. Regardless of the political separation, non-governmental relations between the two sides of the Taiwan strait have been devel-oped gradually since 1980 when the Standing Committee of the NPC (1979) firstly publicized 'Message to the Taiwan Compatriots', espe-cially since 1988 when private visits from Taiwan to the mainland were permitted by the Taiwnaese government. In the remainder of this Chapter, we will try to analyze economic performances and relations between Hong Kong, Macau, Taiwan and mainland China.

## A multiregional economic comparison

Against the common historical, cultural and linguistic homogeneity, the greater China economic area has followed different routes of economic developments. Hong Kong and Macau have been under the colonial administrations of the UK and Portugal, respectively. Taiwan served as the Japanese colony during 1895 and 1945 and, after a short period of reunification, has been operating independently from mainland China. As a result economic differences and mutual complementary conditions have existed significantly between the four parts of the area, especially since 1949. We will analyze them in detail.

Table 11.1 shows the basic social and economic indicators of the greater China in the early 2000s. In 2003, the GDP of Taiwan was 1.8 times that of Hong Kong. The GDP of the Mainland was 4.9 times that of Taiwan and 8.9 times that of Hong Kong. The Mainland's 2003 exports of US$438 billion surpassed Taiwan's exports of US$144 billion and also vastly surpassed Hong Kong's domestic exports (that is, exports made domestically in Hong Kong) of US$16 billion. The figure for Hong Kong's total exports (that is, including re-exports) of US$225 billion is large because Hong Kong is re-exporting Chinese products to third countries and third-country products to China. In other words, Hong Kong is China's gateway to the world in commodity trade.

From Table 11.1, one may also find that all parts of the greater China area have enjoyed higher annual GNP growth rates than most of the remaining economies in the world. Particularly noteworthy is the fact that mainland China's GNP growth rate is among the highest of the world's dynamic economies. If all goes according to plan, mainland China's economic size and per capita GNP will continue to increase at a higher rate than the other parts.

Hong Kong's economy was seriously affected by the Japanese invasion during World War II. The population decreased sharply from 1.6 million in 1940 to 0.60 million in August 1945 and 60 per cent of

*Table 11.1*  Basic indicators of the greater China

| Indicator | Taiwan | Hong Kong | Macau | Mainland |
|---|---|---|---|---|
| Area (sq. km) | 36188 | 1098 | 19 | 9600000 |
| Population (million) | 22.5 | 6.8 | 0.4 | 1284.5 |
| GDP (2003, US$bn) | 286.8 | 158.6 | 7.9 | 1416 |
| GDP per capita (2003, US$) | 12751 | 23311 | 17782 | 1090 |
| Average growth rate of GDP per capital (1978–2002, %) | 5.50 | 3.98 | 2.03[a] | 8.04 |
| Exports (2003, US$ bn) | 144.2 | 224.6(15.7[b]) | 2.6 | 438.4 |
| Life expectancy (1990s female/male, years) | 77/71.8 | 81.2/75.8 | | 71/68, |
| Adult literacy rate (1990s, female/male, %)[c] | 86/96 | 88/96 | 95.7[d] | 73/90 |

*Notes:* [a] Growth rate for 1982–2002; [b] Exports of Hong Kong goods (re-exports are excluded); [c] ADB (1996, pp. 11 and 28), SSB (1996, pp. 769, 781 and 803); [d] Xie (1992, p. 115) for the labor population.
*Source:* websites of the respective governments.

the buildings were destroyed (Wu and Liang, 1990, p. 235). Restricted by the shortage of land and other natural resources of its own and the closed-door policy in mainland China, Hong Kong's economy grew very slowly before the 1970s. Since then, however, it has grown rapidly, as a result of its favourable geographical location in the international trade and proximity to mainland China. Hong Kong has now been amongst the highest of the 'four Asian dragons' in terms of per capita GNP.

In mid-1997 the Asian Financial Crisis struck Hong Kong shortly after Hong Kong's reversion to China. Hong Kong's GDP contracted by more than 5 per cent in 1998, the first record of negative annual growth since official GDP figures were available since 1961. Though the Hong Kong economy recovered in 1999–2000, the slowdown of the US economy and the 11 September terrorist attack led to another recession, and GDP growth fell to 0.5 per cent in 2001. Recovery in the second half of 2002 was interrupted by the outbreak of SARS in March 2003. Since the Asian Financial Crisis, Hong Kong has tried to leverage on its connections with mainland China in order to boost its economy. Measures included relaxation of controls against tourists and skilled workers from the mainland, promotion of economic integration with the Pearl River Delta. Hong Kong also proposed forming an FTA (free trade area) with the mainland. The Mainland and Hong Kong CEPA was signed on 29 June 2003. This was the first free-trade agreement for either the mainland or Hong Kong.

For the past 400 years, the mixture of the western and Chinese societies has resulted in a unique cultural landscape for Macau. However, Macau's industrialization only began at the 1960s and had been restricted by many trade protectionism imposed on Hong Kong by the USA and the EU before the 1980s. Since the early 1980s, the economic development of Macau has greatly benefited from its proximity to both Hong Kong (one the freest markets in the world) and mainland China (one of the cheapest sources in labour and raw materials). Today, trade, tourism and casino and estate and construction are Macau's three major industries.

During the past decades, Taiwan has been successfully transformed from a colonized and agriculturally based economy to the newly industrialized economy and been internationally known as one of the 'Asian economic dragons'. In 1953, its per capita GNP was less than US$200, while this figure grew dramatically to more than US$12000 in the early 2000s. Economic development in Taiwan faced many obstacles such as lack of energy and industrial resources, high population density, large amount of defense expenditure so as to sustain a balance with mainland China (as shown in Table 11.3), a series of failures in foreign affairs as well as the increasing political pressure coming from the mainland, the affects of regional protectionism, and so on. The Taiwan miracle, however, has mainly ascribed to the indomitable spirit of the Taiwanese people themselves, as described by Kao and Shong (1994, p. 10) as 'the more difficulties they faced, the harder they would work'.

With the heterogeneous natural and social conditions, there exist great differences of real living standards in the greater China area. However, due to the differing personal consumption structures as well as the purchasing powers, it is very difficult for us to conduct a complete and reasonable comparison of the four parts. In brief, Hong Kong and Macau, as two municipal economies, have the highest level of living standards in the greater China area. Neverthless, the socioeconomic gap between Taiwan and mainland China should be narrowed substantially if the purchasing power differences are considered.

Other indicators, such as life expectancy, literacy and other physical quality-of-life indexes, not to mention political freedom of the individual (which is the most valuable criterion in Western nations), seem to indicate that there exist significant differences within the greater China area.

Mutually complementary conditions obviously exist in the greater China area in terms of natural resources, labor force, technology and industrial structure, as demonstrated in Table 11.2. For example, mainland China has adequate and various agricultural products and oil, coal, building materials, some high-tech products, excess and cheap labour, and a huge domestic market; while it lacks capital, advanced equipment, technology, and management experience. Taiwan, with high capital saving, advanced equipment ready to move out, and vanguard agricultural and industrial products and management experience, is scarce in energy and industrial resources, and facing increasing insufficiency and high costs of labour supply. Furthermore, its economic development seems to have been restricted by the limited domestic market. As the freest economies in the world, Hong Kong and Macau have capital surplus, favourable conditions for international trade, and advanced management experience in commercial and financial markets; while they are severely lacking agricultural and industrial resources, especially fresh water, foodstuff, energy and land. In addition, like Taiwan, Hong Kong and Macau are also facing a serious deficiency and high cost of labour.[5]

Both Hong Kong and Taiwan are strong in traditional labour-intensive, export-oriented industries: Hong Kong's niches are in clothing, toys, watches and electronics, while Taiwan's are in footwear, umbrellas, textiles and electronics. Such traditional industries have all but relocated to the mainland. The opening of the mainland came at the right time for Hong Kong and Taiwan as they had accumulated valuable human capital in the management and manufacturing of labour-intensive products for exports from the 1950s to the 1970s. However, successful export-oriented industrialization had raised their wages, and their labour-intensive industries were threatened in the 1980s. The majority of manufacturing firms in Hong Kong and Taiwan were small, and lacked the ability to operate internationally; for example, to relocate to Southeast Asia. Without the opening of the mainland, the vast majority of these small firms would have gone bankrupt. However, the opening of the mainland allowed small firms to relocate to a culturally familiar environment and thereby utilize their valuable know-how to build a 'global factory' (production base dominating the world market) there (Sung, 2004, p. 3).

Under the mutually complementary conditions, the multilateral economic cooperation may generate a series of positive effects on the economic development of the greater China area. Through trade and spatial relocation of production factors such as labour, raw materials, technology, capital and so on, the economic optimization will be undoubtedly increased in the greater China area.

## Cross-Taiwan Strait economic relations

Just as a clam came out to bask in the sun a snipe pecked at its flesh. The clam closed its shell and gripped the snipe's beak. The snipe said: 'If it does not rain today and tomorrow, you will become a dead clam.' 'If you cannot free yourself today and tomorrow, you will become a dead snipe,' replied the clam. Neither one would give way and eventually a fisherman caught both the clam and the snipe.

Zhanguoce (475–221 BC)

### Historical evolution

The Taiwan strait became a forbidden boundary in 1949 when the Nationalist-led government fled to Taiwan and, at the same time, the Communist-led government was founded on the mainland. Since then, Taiwan and mainland China have been two divergent regimes. Against the common cultural and linguistic homogeneity, mainland

*Table 11.2*  Mutually complementary conditions in the greater China area

| Economy | Advantages | Disadvantages |
| --- | --- | --- |
| Mainland China | Adequate and various agricultural products, energy, industrial materials, excess labor, some high-tech products, and huge domestic market. | Shortage of capital, equipment, technology, management experience, and less developed economic infrastructures. |
| Taiwan | High capital saving, advanced equipment ready to move out, vanguard agricultural and industrial products, and management experience. | Shortage of energy and industrial resources, limited domestic market, and insufficiency and high costs of labor supply. |
| Hong Kong and Macau | Capital surplus, favorable convenient conditions for international trade, the freest economic environment, and management experience in commercial and financial markets. | Severe shortage of agricultural and industrial resources, especially fresh water, foodstuff, energy, and land and deficiency of labor. |

China chose essentially socialism, while Taiwan followed the route of market-oriented capitalism. Furthermore, the two sides have also antagonistically treated each other, particularly they did so during the high tide of military confrontation, when the mainland claimed to liberate the Taiwan compatriots from the *black* society sooner or latter, while Taiwan maintained that they would use the 'three democratisms' to re-occupy the mainland eventually.[6]

The Taiwan-based Nationalists had been the internationally recognized government representing China as a whole before 15 October 1971 when the UN seat was changed from Taiwan to mainland China according to UN's Resolution No. 2758. Since then, the international positions of Taiwan and mainland China have been reversed. Following the United States' transference of its diplomatic relations with China from the KMT-led Taiwan to the CCP-led mainland in December 1978, more and more Western nations began to establish their formal ties with the mainland. As a result, Taiwan lost most of its friends.

Even though '[the cross-Taiwan strait] reunification does not mean that the mainland will swallow up Taiwan, nor does it mean that Taiwan

---

*Box 11.1*   Overseas Chinese economics

There have been more than 50 million overseas Chinese living in over one hundred countries (regions). Since World War II, especially the 1970s, the overseas Chinese wealth has been growing rapidly and played an increasing role in the world economy. According to an incomplete estimate from *The Economic Research Materials* (1996, p. 62), the overseas Chinese already had US$223.1 billion of foreign currency deposits by the end of 1993, which is mainly distributed in Taiwan (US$90.6 billion), Hong Kong (US$32.7 billion), Singapore (US$43.7 billion), Thailand (US$23.4 billion), Malaysia (US$15.4 billion), Indonesia (US$11.0 billion), the Philippines (US$4.3 billion), and other nations (US$2.0 billion). Furthermore, *The Economist* (1992, p. 17) offered an even more optimistic estimation that, excluding Taiwan and Hong Kong, the total capital owned by overseas Chinese could exceed US$150 to 200 billion. Briefly, several factors can explain this remarkable growth of the overseas Chinese economy:

1. thriftiness and hard working of the overseas Chinese,
2. an *élite* group of intellectuals,
3. a positive role of overseas Chinese organizations, and
4. closer socio-economic ties with mainland China

Since the early 1980s when the open-door policy was implemented in mainland China, the overseas Chinese have contributed greatly to the economic development of mainland China, especially the coastal area with which they have most close relations. Studies show that overseas Chinese investment has provided more than two-third of the total FDI in mainland China during the past years. Besides, China's growing exports have also been greatly promoted by the overseas Chinese networks (Rauch and Trindate, 2002).

---

will swallow up the mainland' (Jiang, 1995, p. 2), many critical issues concerning the cross-Taiwan strait relations still remain unresolved. For instance, even though both mainland China and Taiwan have declared to the outside world that they are pursuing the 'one China' policy, the contents of which are absolutely different from each other. Mainland China proudly stresses that the 'People's Republic of China' (PRC) has been one of the five permanent members of the UN's Security

*Table 11.3*   A comparison of military expenses between Taiwan and mainland China (1990s)

| Item | Taiwan | Mainland China |
|---|---|---|
| Defense expense (US$100m) | 104 | 562 |
| Forces (1000 persons) | 442 | 3,031 |
| Defense expense as % of GNP | 4.7 | 2.7 |
| Defense expense as % of budget | 20.0 | 16.2 |
| Per capita defense (US$) | 494 | 48 |
| Forces per 1000 population | 21.0 | 2.6 |

*Source*: Based on the US Academy of Defense Agency (1993) and SSB (1996, pp. 230, 580).

Council and of course should be and has already been the only legal government representing China of which, to be sure, Taiwan is only a province.[7] The Taiwanese government, however, strongly argues that the 'Republic of China' (ROC) founded by Dr. Sun Yatsen has existed since 1911 and is still in *râpport* with a certain number of independent nations. What is more important, along with Taiwan's remarkable economic growth and social progress, the Taiwanese government, after a long period of silence, has increasingly felt that it is time to expand internationally its political space and to let the outside world know the fact that there exists the 'Republic of China on Taiwan' at least in parallel with the 'People's Republic of China' in the mainland.

Nevertheless, progress towards the peaceful reunification has been registered in negotiations on specific issues. In order to find a practical way to keep touches, each of the two sides established a 'non-governmental' institution, namely, the Foundation of the Taiwan Strait Exchanges (FTSE) in Taiwan and the Association for the Taiwan Strait Relations (ATSR) in the mainland. Since the 1980s, the 'Wang Daohan–Koo Chenfu talks'[8] have represented forward steps in the relations between the two sides of the Taiwan strait. Particularly noteworthy is that the PRC has strongly opposed Taiwan's activities to 'internationally expand living space' which is aimed, as claimed by mainland China, at creating 'two Chinas' or 'one China, one Taiwan' and states that 'only after peaceful reunification is accomplished can Taiwan compatriots and other Chinese truly and fully share the international dignity and honour attained by our great motherland.'[9]

Taiwan's economy suffered from the Asian financial crisis, the 11 September terrorist attack and SARS. While economic difficulties have spurred Taiwan towards closer links with the mainland, Taiwan was less active than Hong Kong in capturing the mainland's market, owing to political animosity. Taiwan's GDP contracted by 1.9 per cent in 2001, the first record of negative annual growth since data were available in 1951. Taiwan's unemployment rate broke the 5 per cent barrier in 2002, the highest since 1964 when statistics on unemployment were regularly available (Sung, 2004, p. 7). While Taiwan's business community has been eager to improve relations with the mainland, the election of Chen Shui-bian (representing the pro-independence Democratic Progressive Party, or DPP) to Taiwan's presidency in 2000, exacerbated political tensions across the Taiwan strait. The long-awaited breakthrough on direct links has not been achieved.

However, where there is patience and willingness to compromise, there is still hope. The hope emerges when the two sides find that they are not fundamentally so different after all. Both sides will come to understand this 'sameness' and their basic heterogeneity if they can make further progress in the cross-Taiwan strait cooperation by establishing exchanges of, *inter alia*, sport, culture, education, science and technology, and high-level political groups.

### Bilateral trade and economic exchanges

Bilateral trade and economic exchanges between Taiwan and mainland China had been frozen before 1979, except for small amounts of indirect trade of, among others, Chinese medicine and other native products from mainland China to Taiwan (mainly conducted via Hong Kong). In 1979, mainland China's 'Taiwan policy' was transformed from 'liberating Taiwan' to 'peaceful reunification'. Since then, indirect trade between the two sides of the Taiwan strait and the Taiwanese investment in mainland China via Hong Kong and other regions have grown rapidly as a result of the cross-Taiwan strait *détente*. In addition, tourism, technological and labour cooperation between the two sides have also achieved much progress.

Since 1985 when the Taiwanese government carried out the 'non-interference' policy to Taiwan's exportation to mainland China, the restrictions of the cross-Taiwan strait trade have been gradually torn down under the principle of 'indirect trading', that is, the direct trade partners should be located outside mainland China and trade movements should be via third countries (regions). Till recently, the cross-Taiwan strait trade has still been managed through a 'concentrated' approach in mainland China, not allowing the mainland's foreign trade companies to deal directly with Taiwanese companies outside Hong Kong and Macau. This policy, nevertheless, has promoted the two sides' foreign trade companies to open up either sub-companies or branches of their own in Hong Kong and Macau.

During the early period, Taiwanese investment in mainland China was usually conducted under the names of investors from Hong Kong, Macau, overseas Chinese and others who would nominally be accepted by the two sides.[10] As a response to overcome the lack of foreign capital, mainland China introduces a flexible policy entitled 'attraction of the Taiwanese capital via Hong Kong and overseas Chinese' (*yi gang yin tai, yi qiao yin tai*) in order to promote the Taiwanese businessmen to invest in mainland China. Since October 1990 when the Taiwanese government formally allowed the Taiwanese businessmen to invest in mainland China, it has always required that the Taiwanese investors should be under the names of their sub-companies housed in the third areas. In order to promote the Taiwanese businessmen to invest in the mainland, mainland China promulgated the 'Regulations Concerning the Promotion of the Taiwanese Compatriots' Investment' in July 1988 and the 'Law of Protecting the Taiwanese compatriots investment' in March 1994, respectively.

Financial movement between Taiwan and mainland China had been strictly prohibited by the Taiwanese government before May 1990 when South China Bank (in Taiwan) was allowed to indirectly (via a British bank in Hong Kong) offer individual financial businesses from Taiwan to mainland China. Since then Taiwanese investment in the mainland China has increased dramatically. In July 1993, financial movements were able to extend from individual to business activities and in addition banks in the Taiwan area were able to receive funds sent indirectly from mainland China. As Taiwanese businessmen were only allowed to invest indirectly (i.e., via third regions or countries) in mainland China, this kind of investment is in theory one between the third region (country) and mainland China, which might result in many unresolved issues. We will discuss them later in detail in next section.

In Taiwan, the population is mainly identified by two groups – native Taiwanese and Han- and other ethnic Chinese who fled to Taiwan when the Nationalists (KMT) lost the mainland in 1949. Most of the latter have close ties with and relatives in mainland China. Besides the cross-Taiwan strait trade and Taiwanese investment in the mainland, other economic exchanges between the two sides of the Taiwan strait have also grown rapidly during the past years. Since November 1987 when Taiwanese citizens were first allowed to pay private visits to mainland China, visitors from Taiwan to the mainland have been increased year by year, resulting in a large amount of expenditure including the traveling expenses, donations, and others. In addition, exchanges in labour, science and technology between the two sides have also developed rapidly.

## Unresolved issues

Dividing the Chinese nation into two economically complementary but politically antagonistic counterparts, the Taiwan strait may have been perhaps one of the most special borders in the world. The nearest distance between Taiwan and mainland China is only within 1800 m. As direct links between the two sides have not been established officially, trade and economic relations have to be indirectly conducted via third countries (regions). For instance, the mainland's exports of raw coal to Taiwan has been nominally 'organized' by the Japanese and South Korean companies. According to China National Coal Industry Import and Export Corporation (CNCIE), US$0.5 has been charged by Japan and South Korea for each ton of the coal re-exported to Taiwan. In 1995, the total coal export was 400 million ton, which means a total loss of US$200 million for the mainland, not to mention the extra expenses resulting from the increased distance of transport.

Direct links for postal, air and shipping services and trade between the two sides are the objective requirements for their economic development and contacts in various fields, and since they are in the interests of the people on both sides, it is absolutely necessary to adopt practical measures to speed up the establishment of such direct links. Since the 1980s, efforts have been made to promote negotiations on the basis of reciprocity and mutual benefit and signing non-governmental agreements on the protection of industrialists and businessmen. However, substantial progress has not been achieved. According to CEC (1996), the direct cross-Taiwan strait links would have resulted in a net saving of US$731.5 million per annum for postal, remittance, air and shipping services between the two sides of Taiwan strait, including: (1) US$248.0 million for shipping service; (2) US$437.5 million (6.95 million hours) for air service; (3) US$24.0 million for postal service; and (4) US$22.0 million or more for remittance service.[11]

It should be noted that both the cross-Taiwan strait trade and Taiwanese investment in mainland China have still been to a large extent affected by the political uncertainties in the cross-Taiwan strait. In order to avoid 'putting all their eggs into one basket', the Taiwanese government has carried out a 'South-oriented' policy since 1993, encouraging Taiwanese investment to preferably move to ASEANs and other countries in Southeast Asia.[12] Obviously, this situation will be further accelerated by Taiwanese independence movement on the one hand and political pressure from the mainland on the other hand.[13]

## Future perspective

> When viewed with a belief that things are bound to change, there is not even a single element in the heaven and earth that does not change, while all materials in this world and the existence of myself who lives and dies are eternal when viewed from the standpoint that things do not change.
>
> Su Dongpo (AD 1037–1101)

In view of the development of the world economy in the 21st century, the cross-strait economic exchange and cooperation should be further accelerated. Only this can achieve prosperity for both sides and benefit the entire nation. The two sides have promised that political differences should not affect or interfere with economic cooperation between the sides. Under the principles of peace, equality and bilateralism, the Taiwanese government is willing to promote cross-Taiwan strait economic exchanges and treat the mainland as its hinterland. In order to seek the most efficient way of raising the level of the national economy, the PRC's government seems intent to continue to implement over a long period of time the policy of encouraging industrialists and businessmen from Taiwan to invest in the mainland. Along with the enforcement of the 'Law of the People's Republic of China for Protecting the Investment of the Compatriots of Taiwan' and safeguarding the legitimate rights and interests of industrialists and businessmen from Taiwan, the contacts and exchanges between the two sides will definitely increase and, surely, so too will the mutual understanding and trust.

It is close to a rule among practitioners and theorists that multilateral conflicts frequently arise from narrow individual interests and expectations of different communities on one hand, and a chaotic interdependent system on the other hand. Notwithstanding the political, economic and social differences within the greater China economic area, it looks more and more possible for all Chinese, under growing comparative advantages, mutual complementary conditions as well as the tendency towards the unanimity of political, social, especially economic points of view among different parts of the area, to find an appropriate approach that can maximize the benefits for all the parties concerned, while also taking into account their respective articulated objectives.

After the return of Hong Kong and Macau from the British and Portuguese governments to mainland China in 1997 and 1999, respectively, the economic development of the PRC will have gone ahead by approximately 2 to 3 years, given an average per capita GNP growth rate of 6 to 9 per cent for the minland.[14] However, nobody can predict when the greater China reunification will become a possibility.[15] With the Cold War coming to an end and private and semi-official cross-Taiwan strait contacts being guaranteed by the both sides, all Chinese see no reason why their country should be left out of the surging tide of *détente* and further divided by the man-made barriers. Regarding the possible direct links between the two sides of Taiwan strait, mainland China has intended to open as the first step six of its coastal ports (Qingdao, Dalian, Tianjin, Shanghai, Xiamen and Guangzhou) so as to deal with the cross-Taiwan strait shipping businesses; while Taiwan has also a plan in which a foreign shipping center is established in Kaohsiung. Both sides also try to reduce the political sensitiveness to the minimum level by, while among other actions, not hanging up the national flags.

While the Chinese economic areas are developing at an exceptional rate, all Chinese people have never forgoten that their motherland is still being artificially divided. Nevertheless, the creation of political harmony and reunification between Taiwan and mainland China may still require time and patience from both parties. It is a hopeful sign that the political regimes have promised to peacefully reunify as a single nation. Chinese people on both sides of the strait and the outside world as well will watch carefully.

Surely, the 'sleeping giant' is awaked!

# Appendices

## I Basic conditions of the ethnic minorities in China

| Ethnicity | Geographical distribution | Language(s) | Religion(s) |
|---|---|---|---|
| Achang | Yunnan | Achang | Buddhism |
| Bai | Yunnan, Guizhou | Bai, most also speak Chinese | animism |
| Baoan | Gansu | Baoan, Chinese (spoken and written) | Islam |
| Blang | Yunnan | Blang, Dai | Buddhism |
| Bouyei | Guizhou, Yunnan, Guangxi | Dai | Buddhism |
| Dai | Yunnan | Dai, most also speak Chinese | Buddhism |
| Daur | Inner Mongolia, Heilongjiang, Xinjiang | Daur (spoken), Chinese (written) | Lamaism |
| Deang | Yunnan | Deang | Buddhism |
| Dong | Guizhou, Hunan, Quangxi | Dong, Chinese | animism |
| Dongxiang | Gansu, Xinjiang | Dongxiang, most also speak Chinese | Islam |
| Drung | Yunnan | Drung | |
| Ewenki | Inner Mongolia, Heilongjiang | Ewenki (spoken), Mongolian (written), Chinese (written) | shamanism |
| Gaoshan | Taiwan, Fujian | Gaoshan (spoken), Chinese | |
| Gelao | Guizhou, Guangxi | Gelao, Chinese | Islam |
| Hani | Yunnan | Hani | animism |
| Hezhen | Heilongjiang | Hezhen (spoken), Chinese | |
| Hui | Ningxia, Gansu, Henan, Hebei, Qinghai, Shandong | Chinese | Islam |
| Jing | Guangxi | Jing, Chinese (spoken and written) | animism |
| Jingpo | Yunnan | Jingpo | |
| Jino | Yunnan | Jino | |
| Kazak | Xinjiang, Gansu, Qinghai | Kazaki | Islam |
| Kirgiz | Xinjiang, Heilongjiang | Kirgiz, Uygur (written), Kazaki (written) | Islam, Lamaism |
| Korean | Jilin, Liaoning, Heilongjiang | Korean, Chinese | individual choice |
| Lahu | Yunnan | Lahu | animism |

245

| Ethnicity | Geographical distribution | Language(s) | Religion(s) |
|---|---|---|---|
| Lhoba | Tibet | Lhoba (spoken) | Lamaism |
| Li | Hainan | Li, males and a small number of females also speak Chinese | animism |
| Lisu | Yunnan, Sichuan | Lisu | |
| Manchu | Liaoning, Jilin, Heilongjiang, Beijing, Inner Mongolia | most speak Chinese; only a small portion who speak Manchu can be found in Jilin and Heilongjiang | individual choice |
| Maonan | Quangxi | Maonan, Zhuang, Chinese (written) | Islam |
| Miao | Guizhou, Sichuan, Hunan, Hubei, Guangdong | Miao; the majority also assimilated into mainstream Chinese language | animism |
| Monba | Tibet | Monba, Tibetan | Lamaism |
| Mongol | Inner Mongolia, Xinjiang, Liaoning, Jilin, Heilongjiang, Gansu, Hebei, Henan, Qinghai | Mongolian, Mandarin | Lamaism |
| Mulam | Guangxi | Mulam and Zhuang (spoken), Chinese (written) | Lamaism |
| Naxi | Yunnan, Sichuan | Naxi, most also speak Chinese | Dongba |
| Nu | Yunnan | Nu | |
| Oroqen | Inner Mongolia, Heilongjiang | Oroqen (spoken), Chinese (written) | shamanism |
| Pumi | Yunnan | Pumi | |
| Qiang | Sichuan | Qiang (spoken) | Lamaism |
| Russian | Xinjiang, Heilongjiang | Russian | Eastern Orthodox |
| Salar | Qinghai, Gansu | Salar (spoken), Chinese (spoken and written) | Islam |
| She | Fujian, Zhejiang, Jiangxi, Guangdong | Chinese | animism |
| Shui | Guizhou, Guangxi | Shui, most also speak Chinese | animism |
| Tajik | Xinjiang | Tajik (spoken), Uygur | Islam |
| Tatar | Xinjiang | Tatar, Uygur, Kazaki | Islam |
| Tibetan | Tibet, Qinghai, Sichuan, Gansu, Yunnan, Xinjiang | Tibetan | Lamaism |

| Ethnicity | Geographical distribution | Language(s) | Religion(s) |
|-----------|--------------------------|-------------|-------------|
| Tu | Qinghai, Gansu | Tu, Chinese | Lamaism |
| Tujia | Hunan, Hubei | Tujia, most also speak Chinese | animism |
| Uygur | Xinjiang | Uygur | Islam |
| Uzbek | Xinjiang | Uzbek, Uygur, Kazaki | Islam |
| Va | Yunnan | Va | animism |
| Xibe | Xingiang, Liaoning, Jilin | Xibe | Islam |
| Yao | Guangxi, Hunan, Yunnan, Guangdong | Yao, most also speak Chinese | animism |
| Yi | Sichuan, Hunan, Guizhou, Guangxi | Yi (spoken), males also also speak and write Chinese | animism |
| Yugur | Gansu | Yugur, Chinese (spoken and written) | Lamaism |
| Zhuang | Guangxi, Guangdong, Yunnan and Guizhou | Zhuang (spoken), most males also speak Chinese; Chinese (written) | animism |

## II A list of major reforms and their outcomes (1978–2005)

| Year/M/D | Organizer(s) | Program | Outcome(s) |
| --- | --- | --- | --- |
| 18/12/1978 | Third Plenum of the 11th CCPCC | 'Decision of the CCPCC Concerning the Reform of Economic System' | Starting of China's economic reforms |
| 1979 | NPC | 'Law of the People's Republic of China Concerning the Joint Ventures with Chinese and Foreign Investment' | Promotion of the FDI and international trade |
| 1979 | CCPCC and State Council | Guangdong and Fujian provinces were granted with 'special policies and flexible measures' in foreign economic affairs. | Ibid, especially in Guangdong and Fujian provinces |
| 26/12/1979 | People's Congress of Guangdong province | Shenzhen next to Hong Kong, Zhuhai next to Macau, and Santou were designed as the SEZs, to experiment a market-oriented economy. | For example, they have the authority to approve foreign investment projects up to US$30 million, while other regions' authority remained much lower. |
| 1980 | State Council | Starting of the fiscal contract system | Transformation from 'having meals in one pot' to 'having meals in different pots'. |
| 26/8/1980 | NPC | Xiamen in Southeast Fujian province *vis-à-vis* Taiwan became a SEZ | Promotion of the economic tie with Taiwan |
| 9/1980 | CCP and State Council | Household Responsibility System (HRS) | Agricultural growth in rural area |

| Year/M/D | Organizer(s) | Program | Outcome(s) |
|---|---|---|---|
| 1984 | State Council | 'Provisional Regulations for the Management of 'Small-volume' Border Trade' | Promotion of inland border trade of China. |
| 4/1984 | CCPCC and the State Council | 'Design of 14 coastal open cities | Promotion of the FDI inflows into Tianjin, Shanghai, Dalian, Qinhuangdao, Yantai, Qingdao, Lianyungang, Nantong, Ningbo, Wenzhou, Fuzhou, Guangzhou, Ganjiang, and Beihai. |
| 10/5/1984 | State Council | 'Provisional Regulations on the Enlargement of Autonomy of State-owned Industrial Enterprises' | |
| 21/10/1984 | CCPCC | 'Decision of the CCPCC Concerning the Reform of Economic Structure' | Formal start of economic reform in urban areas and in industrial sector. |
| 2/1985 | State Council | The Yangtze River, Pearl River and South Fujian were approved as coastal economic development zones | Increase of FDI and foreign trade in the related areas. |
| 1986 | State Council | Regulations of Issues Concerning the Extensive Regional Economic Cooperation | Promotion of interprovincial cooperation. |
| 12/1986 | NPC | 'Bankruptcy Law Concerning the SOEs' | Not applied until 1994 due to fears of unemployment and social instability |
| 12/1986 | State Council | Encouraging the SOEs to adopt the contract system. | By the end of 1988, most SOEs had adopted various forms of the contract system. |
| 3/1988 | State Council | Liaodong and Shandong peninsulas and Bohai Basin area were allowed to open up to the outside world | Increase of FDI in the related areas. |

| Year/M/D | Organizer(s) | Program | Outcome(s) |
|---|---|---|---|
| 4/1988 | NPC | Hainan province was approved as a SEZ with even more flexible policies than other SEZs | |
| 8/1988 | State Council | Attempt of radical price reform | Ended with bankruptcy |
| 4/1990 | CCPCC and the State Council | Shanghai's Pudong area was granted to enjoy some of the SEZ's mechanisms | |
| 1991 | Yunnan province | 'Provisional Regulations Concerning the Border Trade' | Promotion of cross-border trade in related areas. |
| 14/7/1992 | Tibet autonomous region | 'Resolutions Concerning the Further Reform and Opening up to the Outside World' | Promotion of cross-border trade in related areas. |
| 20/4/1991 | Inner Mongolia autonomous region | 'Resolution of Some Issues Concerning the Extension of Open-door and Promotion of Economic Development' | Promotion of cross-border trade in related areas. |
| 1992 | State Council | 'Notification Concerning the Further Opening up of the Four Frontier Cities of Heihe, Shuifenhe, Hunchun and Manzhouli' | Promotion of cross-border trade in related areas. |
| 25/1/1992 | Office of Custom, PRC | 'Measures Concerning the Supervision and Favourable Taxation for the People-to-People Trade in Sino–Myanmar Border' | Promotion of cross-border trade in related areas. |

| Year/M/D | Organizer(s) | Program | Outcome(s) |
|---|---|---|---|
| 9/2/1992 | Xinjiang autonomous region | 'Notification of Promoting the Trade and Economic Cooperation with the Neighbouring and Eastern European Countries' | Promotion of cross-border trade in related areas. |
| 6/1992 | State Commission for Restructuring the Economic Systems | 'Provisional Regulations on Joint-Stock Companies' | |
| 6/1992 | State Council | 'Notification Concerning the Further Opening up of the Five Frontier Cities and Towns of Nanning, Kunming, Pingxiang, Ruili, and Hekou' | Promotion of cross-border trade in related areas. |
| 6/1992 | Heilongjiang province | 'Some Favourable Policies and Economic Autonomy Authorized to the Frontier Cities of Heihe and Shuifenhe' | Promotion of cross-border trade in related areas. |
| 22/7/1992 | State Council | 'Regulations on the Transformation of the Operating Mechanisms of State-owned Industrial Enterprises' | |
| 11/1993 | Third Plenum of the 14th CCPCC | Establishment of the Modern Enterprise System | |
| 14/11/1993 | Third Plenum of the 14th CCPCC | 'Decision of the CCPCC on Several Issues Concerning the Establishment of a Socialist Market Economic Structure' | Ideological victory of reformers over conservatives |
| 1994 | People's Bank of China | Separation of banking of commercial from policy lending; reducing of the number of the central bank's regional braches from 30 or more to only six. | The elimination of some of the structural inefficiencies of the financial system. |

| Year/M/D | Organizer(s) | Program | Outcome(s) |
|---|---|---|---|
| 1994 | State Council | Introduction of 'tax-sharing system' into all provinces | The central government collects all shared as central taxes, and local government collects only those designated as local taxes. |
| 1/1/1994 | People's Bank of China | Establishment of a new unitary and floating exchange-rate system | Devaluation of the RMB and promotion of export. |
| 9/1995 | Fifth Plenum of the Fourteenth CCPCC | Policy of 'grasping the large and releasing the small' | To turn a select group of 300 out of a list of 1000 already successful large enterprises and enterprise groups into world-class businesses; and to privatize or to contract out small SOEs or to let them go bankrupt. |
| 3/1998 | The Ninth NPC | Amendment was to Article 6 of the Chinese Constitution: 'public, instead of state, ownership as the main form of ownership of the means of production' | Individual, private and other forms of non-public ownership are 'important components of a socialist economy' and they 'supplement the system of socialist public ownership'. |
| 1999 | State Council | Debt-equity swap scheme (zhai zhuan gu) in four large state-owned banks | The bad loans to SOEs are converted into equity and then sold at a discount to investors. |
| 1/4/2000 | People's Bank of China | Adoption of 'real name' banking system | All the household bank deposits require a depositor's ID. |
| 11/2001 | WTO | China's access to TWO | Increase the possibility for China to integrate into the world economic system |
| 12/2003 | State Council | Transformation of Bank of China and China Construction Bank into joint stock ownership | |

Sources: (1) *Bulletins of the State Council, People's Republic of China*, various issues; (2) *Bulletins of the National People's Congress*, various issues.

# III    Specification to the model on system dynamics

## Quantifying the model

In order to quantify the model built in Chapter 5, we use system dynamics (SD) – a modeling method that first appeared in Forrester (1959). This SD, which was developed based on conceptions in control theory, organization theory, and on the available techniques of computer simulation, can be used to simulate the dynamic behaviors of the CPE under different initial and exogenous conditions. It is a unique tool for dealing with questions about the way complex systems behave through time.[1] Before building a system dynamics model, one must identify the correlations between the important factors that could influence the dynamic behaviors of the system of our interest endogenously. According to the principles of system dynamics, social systems, no matter how complicated they are, are composed of different feedback loops. A positive feedback loop means that the target grows without any limit, while a negative feedback loop will not grow after the target is achieved.[2] In order to enable the quantitative model suitable for computer simulation, we use DYNAMO (an abbreviation of 'dynamic model') software developed by Richardson and Pugh III (1981).

There are two categories for quantification of the causal relations described in our feedback model mentioned in Figure 5.1. The first category of causal relations includes those that can be precisely formulated. For example, the 'current market institution' (CGI) and 'speed of reform' (SOR) are formulated as the following:

$$CGI_k = CGI_j + DT \times SOR_{jk}, \text{ with } CGI_0 = I_0 \tag{A1}$$

$$SOR_{k\,l} = \frac{EGI - CGI_k}{T} \times Q_k \tag{A2}$$

Where, j, k and l are time marks, and j<k<l. DT is represented by the time interval from j to k (or from k to l). $I_0$ and EGI denote the initial market institution and the expected market institution respectively. In our analysis, EGI=1 (indicating that the policymakers expect a 100 per cent of market institutions after the reform is completed), and $I_0$ ranges from 0 to 0.5. The length of time of reform (T) represents how long the reform will last.[3] As defined in Assumption I, Q is used here to denote whether the reform goes ahead, stops, or is reversed. Specifically, it has three values: Q=1 denotes that the reform goes ahead (which needs that the value of political stability (PS) is larger than 1); Q=0 denotes that the reform stops (which needs that the value of PS is equal to 1); and Q=-1 denotes that the reform is reversed (which needs that the value of PS is less than 1).

The other category of causal relations includes those that can only be roughly determined. The rationale for this simplification relies on the fact that our analysis is not to precisely predict a set of time-series outputs of the macroeconomic indicators, but to show the general tendency of how the performances of the CPE will depend on exogenous variables. To this end, we use the following formula to determine the political stability (PS):

$$PS_k = PS_j + DT \times DPS_{jk} \tag{A3}$$
$$DPS = 2.0 \times GR - 5.0 \times SOR - 0.03O \tag{A4}$$

In Equation A3, DPS denotes the change of PS; and in Equation A4, GR is growth rate, and O=1 (for open-door policy) or 0 (for closed-door policy). GR=EG/Y (EG, which will be defined in Equation A6, is economic growth, and Y is the size of national income[4]). In our analysis, we stipulate that, in order for the reform to go ahead (that is Q=1), the value of PS is set as 1.001 at the starting time of reform.

Besides, there are some dependent variables that can be more precisely formulated based on the existing literature. However, this will increase the complexity of calculations by involving more explanatory variables. We will therefore simplify their mathematical formulations. For example, with regard to the determination of the foreign trade and FDI, we create a comprehensive term – foreign economic contribution (FEC), though the latter is not exactly the sum of foreign trade and FDI. The FEC is simply determined by the following formula:

$$FEC=0.05\times Y\times O\times IE \qquad (A5)$$

where Y=income level; IE=investment environment (which is positively related to political stability and income level).

As defined in Assumption VI, economic growth (EG) is contributed by three sources – the current market institution, the domestic political stability, and the foreign trade and FDI (that is, FEC). We use the following equations to roughly formulate the CPE's economic growth (EG) and the income level (Y) respectively:

$$EG=\{0.1\times CGI+0.03\times Min(Q,0)\}\times Y+0.5\times FEC \qquad (A6)$$
$$Y_k=Y_j+DT\times EG_{jk} \qquad (A7)$$

where CGI denotes the level of current market institution, and, as mentioned earlier, Q has three values, 1, 0 and –1. Since CGI is 0.3 and Q is 1 at the time zero, the economic growth expressed in Equation A6 will be: EG=(0.03+0.03) $\times Y+0.5\times FEC$ at the beginning of reform. With regard to the determination of FEC in Equation A5, given that O=1 and IE=1, we have FEC=0.05$\times$Y. We assume that the initial income level of the CPE is \$100, that is, $Y_0$=\$100 in Equation A7.

The level of investment environment (IE) and the change of investment environment (DIE) are determined by the following equations:

$$IE_k=IE_j+DT\times DIE_{jk} \qquad (A8)$$
$$DIE=1.0\times GR+0.5\times DPS \qquad (A9)$$

where GR=growth rate, DPS is defined in Equation A4. At time zero, the status quo of investment environment is assumed to be positively related to $PS_0$ and $Y_0$: that is, $IE_0=1.0+PS_0\times Y_0/1000$.

## Sensitivity analysis

Compared with other methods (such as econometrics), system dynamics (SD) does not pay much attention to specific parameters. Besides, due to the lack of any universal methods available, the test of the effectiveness of the SD model is much more difficult than that of the data based statistical and econometric models.

With regard to the sensitivity analysis of our SD model, we intend to clarify how the simulated results are sensitive to the parameter changes. In doing so,

*Table IIIA.1*  Sensitivity analysis of the simulated results

| | Income level under gradual reform ($Y_{T=10}$) | | | | |
|---|---|---|---|---|---|
| $I_0$ | $SR_B$ | $SR_1$ | $SSR_1$ | $SR_2$ | $SSR_2$ |
| 0.0 | 148 | 150 | 0.068 | 146 | 0.135 |
| 0.1 | 194 | 242 | 1.227 | 186 | 0.427 |
| 0.2 | 314 | 410 | 1.533 | 291 | 0.727 |
| 0.3 | 499 | 718 | 2.192 | 453 | 0.924 |
| 0.4 | 762 | 1194 | 2.837 | 680 | 1.073 |
| 0.5 | 1082 | 1766 | 3.158 | 1025 | 0.530 |

| | Income level under big bang reform ($Y_{T=2}$) | | | | |
|---|---|---|---|---|---|
| $I_0$ | $SR_B$ | $SR_1$ | $SSR_1$ | $SR_2$ | $SSR_2$ |
| 0.0 | 182 | 200 | 0.507 | 179 | 0.143 |
| 0.1 | 216 | 256 | 0.918 | 209 | 0.337 |
| 0.2 | 297 | 378 | 1.372 | 274 | 0.762 |
| 0.3 | 401 | 563 | 2.020 | 380 | 0.524 |
| 0.4 | 579 | 986 | 3.516 | 538 | 0.707 |
| 0.5 | 865 | 1527 | 3.828 | 817 | 0.554 |

| | Ratio of income levels under gradual and big bang reforms ($Y_{T=10}/Y_{T=2}$) | | | | |
|---|---|---|---|---|---|
| $I_0$ | $SR_B$ | $SR_1$ | $SSR_1$ | $SR_2$ | $SSR_2$ |
| 0.0 | 0.815 | 0.750 | 0.399 | 0.816 | 0.008 |
| 0.1 | 0.898 | 0.945 | 0.262 | 0.890 | 0.093 |
| 0.2 | 1.058 | 1.085 | 0.126 | 1.062 | 0.038 |
| 0.3 | 1.245 | 1.275 | 0.123 | 1.192 | 0.423 |
| 0.4 | 1.316 | 1.211 | 0.399 | 1.264 | 0.394 |
| 0.5 | 1.255 | 1.157 | 0.391 | 1.253 | 0.012 |

*Notes*
1. All simulations are based on $Y_0=100$ and $O=1$ and the simulated results are only reported for the last output (i.e. Time=20).
2. $SR_B$ denotes the basic simulated result (as reported in Figure 5.3); $SR_1$ denotes the simulated result in which the parameter of CGI (that is, 0.1) in Equation A6 is replaced with 0.12; and $SR_2$ denotes the simulated result in which the parameter of GR (that is, 2.0) in Equation A4 is replaced with 1.8.
3. $SSR_1$ and $SSR_2$ are the degrees to which the simulated results of $SR_1$ and $SR_2$ are respectively sensitive to parameter changes. We use the following formula:

$$SSR_N = \frac{\left| \dfrac{SR_B - SR_N}{SR_B} \right|}{\left| \dfrac{P_B - P_N}{P_B} \right|}$$

where $N=1$ or 2; $P_B$ and $P_N$ are the parameters assigned for the basic and new simulations respectively; $SR_B$ and $SR_N$ are the simulated results for the parameters $P_B$ and $P_N$ respectively; and $SSR_N$ is the degree to which the simulated result of $SR_N$ is sensitive to a change of the parameter from $P_B$ to $P_N$.

we try to calculate the degree to which the result of a simulation is sensitive to the changes of the parameters of the simulation. Numerically, the value of $SSR_N$ ($N$=1 and 2) in Table III-A.1 is the percentage change of the simulated result ($SR_N$) with respect to a one-percentage change of the parameter monitored. Obviously, the smaller is the value of $SSR_N$, the higher the effectiveness of the simulation ($SR_N$) is. From Table A1, we can find that, except for some simulated results for $SR_1$, the degrees of sensitivity are around or less than 1.0, indicating that the simulated results are not sensitive to parameter changes. More important is that the simulated results on $Y_{T=10}/Y_{T=2}$ are not sensitive with respect to the parameter changes, which is vital for the effectiveness of our proposed corollaries derived from Figure 5.3 and Table III-A.1. In addition, since the simulated results reported in Table III-A.1 are those of the last stage of the period monitored, the average level of estimation errors would be reduced if the whole period is considered.

# IV    Games between the Chinese radicals and conservatives

The following two games illustrate both the threat to radical economic reform and the value of the balance rule for precluding this threat. The first game is between three players: the radicals (R), the conservatives (S) and the incumbent bureaucrats (IB). The second game adds a fourth player who may veto the entire set of policies: backstage ruler (BSR). We assume that BSR holds the balance of political power between the R and S.

In addition, uncertainty affects how the players view the reform strategy. To make this circumstance concrete, we assume that uncertainty concerns the political stability: the country may experience normal (political stable) times or in a political crisis. Finally, we further assume: (i) R chooses a radical (big-bang) reform (labeled as BB) during the normal times; it chooses a gradual reform (labeled as GR) during a political crisis.[5] (ii) When R chooses BB, IB supports S; when R chooses GR, IB supports R during normal times and supports S during a political crisis. (iii) As defined by their very natures, R and S cannot reach an agreement concerning a reform in any circumstances, but they can compromise in the following ways: S does accept no reform policies (labeled as NR) when R advocates GR; and it accepts GR when R advocates BB. (iv) BSR can veto over both R's BB and S's NR; it instead tolerates all other reforms, no matter who will lead the reforms.

To simplify the decision tree, we assume in both games that the winner implements the policy it advocated. As to the information assumptions: We assume that R must choose in ignorance of the state of the political stability while IB knows the state of the political stability when it must choose.

The purpose of this exercise is to show the behavioral implications of the BSR's veto, particularly its effects on economic reform initiatives. The game is a highly stylized representation of post-Mao politics.

## Game 1: Rational choice of reform in the absence of a BSR veto

Understanding the game's implications require calculation of the equilibrium outcomes. To begin this step, consider the sequence of choices made by the players. The game represents uncertainty over the society by a non-strategic player, called political stator (PS), who has the first move (see Figure IVA.1). With probabilities of $\pi$ and $1-\pi$, PS chooses normal times and a political crisis respectively. The move by PS represents a convenient way to express the uncertainty facing the second player, who must choose prior to knowing the state of the political stability.

After PS moves, R moves and may advocate either BB or GR. The shadowed area around R's two decision nodes in Figure IVA.1 indicates that R does not know the state of the political stability at the time of its decision. After taking into account the characteristics of China's political evolutions, we suppose that R must choose in ignorance of the state of the political stability, while IB knows the state of the political stability when it must choose.[6] The outcomes are summarized as follows. If R wins BB, the outcome is A; if it wins GR, the outcome is B if IB and S do not form a coalition and is C if IB and S form a coalition. If S wins, the outcome is 'no reform' (D). The preferences of R, IB, S and BSR are given in Table IVA.1.

257

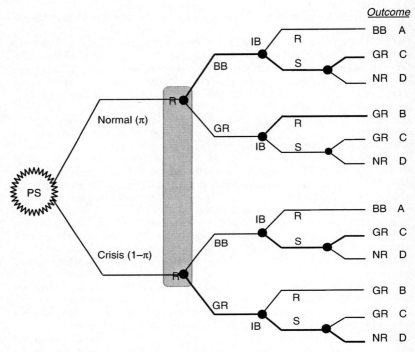

*Figure IVA.1*  Choice of reform without a BSR Veto (game 1)

The radicals' preferences depend on the state of political stability. During the normal times, IB ($IB_N$) prefers R's gradual reform (B) to S's no reform (D). The four outcomes are ranked as follows: R's gradual reform (B) is preferred to no actions on reforms (D), which are preferred to S's gradual reform (C) and lastly,

*Table IVA.1*  Players' preference ranking

| $R_N$ | $R_C$ | $IB_N$ | $IB_C$ | S | BSR |
|-------|-------|--------|--------|---|-----|
| A | B | B | D | D | B, C |
| B | A | D | C | C | |
| C | C | C | B | B | A, D |
| D | D | A | A | A | |

*Notes:* (1) the reason for $R_C$ to rank C after A is that in a political crisis R losses supporters in both cases it would be more likely to stake a big-bang reform (A) than to exercise a gradual reform (B); (2) the reason for $IB_N$ to rank D and C after B is that in normal times, a gradual reform means more benefits rather than costs; and (3) since it is difficult to differentiate C from B and D from A, we equally treat B and C and A and D.

to R's big-bang reform (A). During a political crisis, however, IB (IB$_C$) prefers S's policies to R's policies, ranking the four outcomes as follows: no reform (D) is preferred to S's gradual reform (C), which are preferred to R's gradual reform (B) and lastly, to R's big-bang reform (A). Regardless of the state of the political stability, S ranks the outcomes as D, C, B, A, and BSR ranks the outcomes as B(C), A(D).

To determine the outcome of the game, we solve a subgame-perfect equilibrium, requiring that an action be specified for each decision-maker at each node of the game. Consider IB's choices in Figure IVA.1. During normal times, if R chooses BB, IB will cooperate with S for a gradual reform (C); if R chooses GR, IB will cooperate with R for a gradual reform (B). Although the final outcomes of B and C are the same, the cost of implementing B is lower than that of implementing C, since in C there is an extra risk for reversing BB to GR. As a result, IB prefers the R-advocated gradual reform (B) to the S-advocated gradual reform (C). This leads to the following behavior by IB: during normal times, IB will cooperate with R for a gradual reform (B) if R advocates GR, otherwise IB will cooperate with S for a gradual reform (C); during a political crisis, IB will cooperate with S for a gradual reform (C) if R advocates BB, otherwise IB will cooperate with S for no reform (NR). In both cases, R will lose its power in the country during a political crisis.

IB's behavior sets the stage for R's decisions. R does not know whether there will be a political crisis. Because it does not win regardless of its decision if there is a political crisis, and because it wins during normal times only if it chooses GR, it will choose GR.

In this game, S is able to attract IB in normal times if R advocates BB and in a political crisis regardless of R's choices. By contrast, R is often isolated and, without careful treatment, R is in trouble.

## Game 2: Rational choice of reform under a BSR veto

The sequence of action in the second game adds an additional (fifth) move by BSR to the four moves in the first game. BSR may veto the entire set of policies (Figure IV4.2), resulting in a payoff of 0 to IB and BSR. If R leads reforms, BSR prefers B to A; if S leads reforms BSR prefers C to D (see Table IVA.2).

We again solve for the equilibrium by backward induction. Although this game has 24 end nodes, there are only four possible outcomes, making it relatively easier for us to solve. In the game's last move, BSR must choose between the outcome arrived at by the previous move or, by exercising its veto. Because BSR prefers 0 only to outcomes A and D, it will exercise its veto only when the previous moves yield A and D. In all other circumstances, a veto would make BSR worse off. The following contingent rule for exercising its veto summarizes BSR's behavior at its 12 decision nodes: BSR's exercises its veto if and only if R chooses BB and S chooses NR. This implies that BSR exercises its veto only at its first and last decision nodes (numbering the nodes from top to bottom).

Working background the next set of decision nodes requires a choice by S and IB, who take BSR's behavior as given. Consider normal times. If R advocates BB, it will not receive any support from IB; even worse, it will lead IB and S to form a coalition, in addition that it will face a veto by BSR. As a result, R will choose GR instead of BB. If instead R advocates GR, choosing R yields outcome B, whereas choosing S yields outcome C. In both cases, IB prefers R's GR to S's.

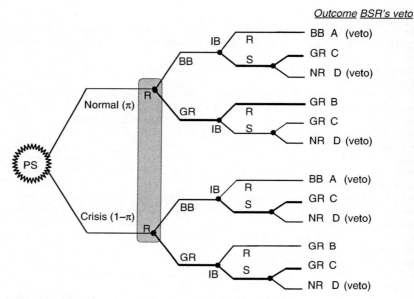

*Figure IVA.2*    Choice of reform under a BSR veto (game 2)

In a political crisis, IB never supports R even though the latter chooses a moderate reform strategy (GR). Choosing S yields outcome C if R advocates BB and outcome D if R advocates GR. But since S knows in advance that BSR will veto over outcome D (no reform), choosing S will yield outcome C in both cases.

Next consider R's decision at the first node. Taking IB and BSR's behavior as given, we observe that IB never chooses R during a political crisis, whereas during normal times IB choose R if R advocates GR. R can never win by advocating BB, but it can win during normal times and if it advocates GR. So R will choose GR as long as the possibility of political stability p, exceeds zero.

In the equilibrium of this game, S will win when the relative frequency of political crisis is high ($\pi$<0.5). In the face of a BSR veto, both R and S will temper their radical initiatives.

Game 2 demonstrates that the outcome changes when the BSR holds a veto over both R and S. Because the BSR will veto R when R attempts to implement the big-bang economic reform policies, IB prefers S to R when R advocates BB, This leads to a change in R's behavior and it instead advocates only GR policy. R's behavior under balance implies that IB prefers S to R during bad times and R to S during good times.

Both the radicals and the conservatives could have decided the extent of their cooperation in negotiating a mutually accepted strategy of reforms. At the same time, they could have also initiated a costly confrontation with each other so as to gain supremacy over the Chinese society. This situation may be depicted as a repetitive, complete information game (Bates *et al.*, 1998, p. 30).

The analytical framework presented in this section sets out to deal with the characteristics of the set of mutual deterrence (sub-game perfect) equilibria (MDEs).[7] In such equilibria, the confrontation between the radicals and the conservatives does not occur. Concentration on these equilibria is motivated by two considerations. First, the stable and mutually accepted reforms during most, if not all years of the 1980s and 1990s indicates that each side of the radicals and the conservatives was indeed deterred from challenging the other. Second, since confrontation is costly, refraining from it was economically efficient. Furthermore, since implementing reforms was efficient, studying whether the need for the Chinese political system to be self-enforcing affected its economy is to examine whether this need constrained cooperation in reaching an MDE with the efficient reform strategy (i.e., the length of time for the reforms to be completed).

Examining whether China's self-enforcing political system reached an MDE with the efficient reform strategy requires analyzing the incentives for the radicals and the conservatives to cooperate with each other. For simplicity, our analysis first examines the MED for a given set of reform strategies; only then is it extended to allow the reforms to be determined endogenously. This approach reveals the distinct political and economic characteristics of efficient and inefficient MDEs, enabling us to compare the insights gained from the theoretical finding with the historical evidence.

To understand the implications of the incentives for the policymakers to implement reforms, the relations between the radicals and conservatives should be made explicit. For ease of analysis, we assume that (i) the radicals prefer a big-bang to gradual reform, and (ii) the conservatives do not prefer any reforms or at least prefer a gradual to big-bang reform. Since both the radicals and the conservatives can recruit supporters through their contributions to the growth of incomes, the tradeoff between them was inherent in the nature of the political exchange through which reforms were implemented.

Assume that there is a fixed length of time for the reforms to be completed, $T^*$, that maximizes the (gross) income for the radicals and the conservatives.[8] Hence, if the actual length of time for the reforms is shorter than that length, the income for the radicals is larger than for the conservatives; by contrast, if it is longer than that length, the income for the conservatives is larger than for the radicals.

The analysis can now be extended to examine the reform strategy in acquisition of which both the radicals and the conservatives would find it optimal to cooperate, in other words, to examine the length of time by which to implement the reforms. The analysis addresses the following question: Does the efficient MDE maximize the conservatives' incomes? If the answer to this question is affirmative, it can be concluded (at least from the static point of view) that the need to sustain China's self-enforcing political system did not theoretically entail economic cost. If the answer to this question is negative, however, it can be concluded that, theoretically, the need to sustain China's self-enforcing political system hindered economic efficiency, since the conservatives would not cooperate in achieving the efficient MDE. If this is the case, we can also use the model to identify the exact sources of this inefficiency.

Addressing these questions requires examining an MDE implies an increasing numbers of supporters. In Condition 1, if there are no reforms, it implies no gains from cooperation. Hence, in the absence of reforms, the conservatives would neither increase the incomes of their own, nor recruit supporters from the society. At the same time, since the reform could increase incomes for all sides concerned, the radicals would be able to provoke challenges if they were facing resistance from the conservatives. By contrast, incentives for the conservatives to cooperate with the radicals decrease in Condition 2, since each side only obtained a decreasingly marginal gain.

Let us now come to Condition 3 and to examine how external policy influences the choice of reform strategies.[9] Why open-door policy yielded incentives for policymakers to choose the gradual *vis-à-vis* big-bang reforms in China? To understand this case, one must bear in mind the characteristics of the political evolutions in China. During the 1980s and 1990s, most political elites (especially those conservatives) still treated open-door policy as both good (economically) and bad (politically) things (we have addressed them in Figure IV-A.1).

In considering the profitability of faster reforms, the conservatives take into account not only the benefit from the reforms but also the political cost stemming from the possibility losing supremacy over the society. Since deterrence implies cost, the reform strategy that both players (radicals and conservatives) would find optimal to cooperate does not equate the marginal economic benefit with the marginal economic cost. Instead, a player's optimal strategy of reforms equates the marginal economic cost with the marginal economic and political costs. In other words, it is political cost that creates a wedge between the efficient and optimal strategies of reforms. Although the MDE with the efficient strategy of reforms maximizes the radicals' gross payoff, it does not maximize it net payoff. The radicals would find it optimal to have an MDE with slower reforms in which the marginal economic gains from cooperation equal the marginal political and economic costs.[10]

This analysis has been motivated by the quest to identify the possible sources for political order in China and, specifically, by the inability of narrative to resolve two conflicting interpretations of the prevalence of economic reforms during most of the 1980s and 1990s. Our theory indicates that both interpretations can be correct: On the one hand, a slow (gradual) reform can be correct; on the other hand, a fast (big-bang) reform can also be optimal. The analysis enables us to determine the conditions under which the reforms are optimal.

Specifically, a faster reform is more likely to occur when the initial institutional conditions are less favourable; and a slower reform is more likely accepted by the policymakers (including both radicals and conservatives) when the latter are facing political threats from the outside world.

# V  Literature on the determinants of foreign trade

## Analytical Framework

There is a widely held view that easily observable impediments, such as transportation and other distance-related costs, do not adequately capture transactions costs in international trade. One response has been to directly investigate the possible role of transborder business networks or ethnic diasporas in reducing transactions costs (Rauch, 1999; Rauch and Trindade, 2002; and Combes et al., 2005). Besides, Guiso et al. (2004) and Guo (2006) suggest that more diffuse cultural affinity or similarity may be another channel. They argue that cultural distance – as proxied by, among other things, the genetic differences across national populations – is a robust explanator of the volume of international trade in the context of a conventional gravity model.

Among the quantitative studies of international trade, the gravity model is the tool most commonly used by economists.[11] The classic extensive early application of the model was by Linnemann (1966), who continued work first reported in Tinbergen (1962) and then in Pöyhönen (1963). The most recent work on the application of the model was Frankel et al. (1997), Rauch (1999) and Rose (2004), among others. Generally, a gravity model assumes that the volume of trade between any two economies will be directly proportional to the product of their economic masses (measured by GDP or GNP) and inversely proportional to the distance between them. Per capita incomes (measured by product of per capita GDPs or GNPs) have become a standard covariate in the gravity models of, for example, Eaton and Tamura (1994), Frankel et al. (1997) and Rauch (1999).

In order to apply the gravity model to test the effects of the linguistic and religious influences on trade, I control other political and social variables. My consideration here springs from that 'language' is an effective tool of communication and that 'religion' can provide the insights into the characteristics of culture. Studies such as that of Frankel et al. (1995, 1997) also employ dummies for 'membership' in the geographical areas of East Asia, Western Hemisphere, and so on. Including these dummy variables could, as stated by Rauch (1999, n. 6), shrink the estimated coefficients on 'distance'. In this research, dummies for membership are excluded from analysis because they could compound the problem of interpretation that will be presented by the cultural variables employed. 'Adjacency' – another dummy that has been used in the above studies – is also excluded here since most East Asian economies do not share a common land border with the outside world (such as Japan, Philippines, Singapore, and Taiwan) or their land boundaries cannot be used as efficient trade ports (such as the 38th Parallel of North and South Korea, Mts. Upper Kapuas and Iran in Kalimantan between Indonesia and Malaysia, the boundary between Myanmar and Thailand, as well as the Himalayas and the Pamirs separating China and its western neighbors).

The basic form of the gravity model to be used in my empirical analysis is as the following:

$$\ln(TRADE_{ij}+1)=\alpha_0+\alpha_1\ln(GDP_iGDP_j)+\alpha_2\ln(GDPPC_iGDPPC_j) \quad (A10)$$
$$+\alpha_3\ln DISTANCE_{ij}+\alpha_4 LANGUAGE_{ij}+\alpha_5 RELIGION_{ij}$$

In Equation (A10), 'ln' represents natural logarithm; $TRADE_{ij}$, measured in thousand US dollars, is the sum of exports and imports between economies $i$ and $j$. In order to make the natural logarithm of TRADE become mathematically meaningful when TRADE=0, I use ln(TRADE+1) to approximately equal ln(TRADE).[12] This seems to be reasonable since the size of TRADE is, if not zero, always far larger than one thousand US dollars. $GDP_iGDP_j$ is the product of purchasing power parity (PPP)-adjusted GDPs of the $i$th and $j$th economies. $GDPPC_iGDPPC_j$ is the product of PPP-adjusted per capita GDPs of the $i$th and $j$th economies. $DISTANCE_{ij}$ represents the distance between the geographical centers of gravity of the $i$th and $j$th economies (in kilometers). $LANGUAGE_{ij}$ and $RELIGION_{ij}$, the measurement of which will be discussed below, denote the extents to which the $i$th and $j$th economies are linguistically and religiously linked each other, respectively.

The major task here is to quantitatively investigate the sources for changes in East Asia's foreign trade over time. Thus, the use of the cross-sectional data from the East Asian economies in different years enables that the estimated results are not artifact of any particular time period and to allow for changes in coefficients on the linguistic and religious variables. Generally a time period with ten years or so is fairly appropriate for such kind of research: a shorter period could not reflect social and economic changes and a longer one would bear significant changes in transportation and communication technologies. Besides, since international trade performance might differ during the Cold War era and the post-Cold War era, it is useful if the gravity model is tested using the data from both eras. Technically the cross-sectional data of more years should be considered in order that each period can be better represented. But this would result in difficulties in the collection and calculation of the linguistic and religious data. I choose 1985 and 1995 as the years representing the Cold War era and the post-Cold War era, respectively. Since many East Asian economies suffered from bad recessions in 1985, data on trade from 1985 are replaced with those from 1984.

Data sources for the abovementioned economic variables are as follows. The data on TRADE are available from the NBER-UN Trade Data for 1962–2000 (available at http://cid.econ.undavis.edu/data/undata/undata.htm). As emphasized in Feenstra *et al.* (2005), it is generally better to use data from the importing country because it is usually much easier to measure imports than exports. Country A's exports to country B is based on country B's import data, not country A's export data. The reasons that I do not use the IMF-reported data on trade are shown below. First, the large amount of the 'entrepot trade' in Hong Kong and Singapore is not included in the IMF's statistics. Second, data discrepancies between exporting and importing economies exist, particularly in China, Hong Kong, Indonesia and Singapore. For example, discrepancies in bilateral trade statistics as reported by China and its trading partners exist, particularly with industrial countries. Trade with these countries is classified by China as trade with Hong Kong Special Administrative Region (HKSAR) if it passes through HKSAR ports. However, the NBER-UN data have not solved all the problems included in the IMF's data. Although the problematic data of many East Asian economies (including Indonesia and Singapore) have been modified, those on Hong Kong's trade are revised only for years from 1988 onwards. The only practical way to provide an adequate explanation in this regard is to conduct a sensitivity analysis for the gravity model estimates in 1985.[13] Specifically, the sensitivity analysis may compare estimates excluding trade flows involving

Hong Kong (a very strange economy with a large amount of entrepot trade with China) and alternative estimates excluding these trade flows.

The PPP-adjusted GDP and GDPPC data are based on the Penn World Table (PWT) v6.1 (available at http://pwt.econ.upenn.edu/php_site/pwt_index.php).[14] The PWT includes 168 economies, from which Brunei (1985 and 1995), North Korea (1985 and 1995), Lao PDR (1985 and 1995), Myanmar (1985 and 1995) and Vietnam (1985) are not available. My estimates of the unreported PPP-adjusted data of the East Asian countries are based on each country's nominal GDP per capita (which are available from World Bank (1986 and 1996) for the years 1985 and 1995, respectively) and the PPP conversion factors of an economically similar or geographically neighbouring country. For example, China's PPP conversion factor is applied to North Korea, Singapore's to Brunei, and Cambodia's to both Lao PDR and Myanmar. Vietnam's PPP-adjusted GDP per capita in 1985, which is not reported in the above source, is estimated based on its PPP conversion factor in 1995. Besides, since the 1985's GDP per capita data (in exchange rates) are not available in Cambodia, Laos and Vietnam, the figures estimated by Zhao (2002) are used.

The data on the DISTANCE variable are measured by the author based on the *World Atlas* (1994).

I am now most interested in the process in which the linguistic and religious variables may resist or aid international trade. The emphasis on the role of cultural linkage in international economic activities may trace back to a biological basis in which cooperation among animals is importantly influenced by genetic similarity (Wilson, 1980). Trade and economic cooperation are based on cultural commonality, as it is easier and more efficient for people with the same cultural identity (language, religion, or any other cultural element) to trust and communicate each other than for those with different cultural identities. The differences between intra- and inter-cultural behaviors can be summarized as four aspects: (1) feelings of superiority (and occasionally inferiority) toward people who are perceived as being very different; (2) fear of and lack of trust in such people; (3) difficulty of communication with them as a result of differences in language and what is considered civil behavior; (4) lack of familiarity with the assumptions, motivations, such as relationships, and social practices of other people (Huntington, 1996, p. 129).

To a certain extent, linguistic differences have decisively influenced international trade and marketing. Although it is not the only tool in building trusting relationships, doors usually open more quickly when knocked on by someone who speaks a familiar language. Sharing a common language, however, does not necessarily mean effective communication in technical terms. For example, when a Japanese manager say in a business negotiation 'It is very difficult' (which is a polite manner of refusal in Japanese society), the American partner would probably ask the Japanese side to find a solution, finding the expression to be more ambiguous. In contemporary Chinese society, by contrast, 'We have some difficulties' implies 'It would be OK under certain conditions.' Compared to language, religion can provide more insights into the characteristics of interpersonal behaviors. What is more important, religion can have a deep impact not only on attitudes towards economic matters but also on values that influence them. Specifically, religious attitudes and values can help to determine what we think is right or appropriate, what is important, what is desirable and so on.

As will be mentioned in the next section, the data on some, if not all, linguistic groups remain problematic, at least compared with the other variables in Equation (A10). Given the difficulty of improving the reliability of LANGUAGE as a continuous variable, and as alternative measures for linguistic linkage, five internationally employed languages are selected as dummy variables: Bahasa (Indonesian or Malay), Chinese, English, Khmer, and Thai. Consequently the gravity model on trade is written as:

$$\ln(\text{TRADE}_{ij}+1)=\beta_0+\beta_1\ln(\text{GDP}_i\text{GDP}_j)+\beta_2\ln(\text{GDPPC}_i\text{GDPPC}_j) \quad (A11)$$
$$+\beta_3\ln\text{DISTANCE}_{ij}+\beta_4\text{RELIGION}_{ij}+\beta_5\text{BAHASA}$$
$$+\beta_6\text{CHINESE}+\beta_7\text{ENGLISH}+\beta_8\text{KHMER}+\beta_9\text{THAI}$$

In Equation (A11) different formula are used to the construct of dummy variables. Specifically, I assume that BAHASA=1, CHINESE=1, KHMER=1, and THAI=1 if economies $i$ and $j$ speak Bahasa, Chinese, Khmer, and Thai, respectively; and that BAHASA=0, CHINESE=0, KHMER=0, and THAI=0 otherwise. It has been recognized that most international trade contracts and documents are processed in English, especially in East Asia where different phylums exist.[15] As a result English reading/writing ability has been an important linguistic trait that reduces trade-related transactions costs. In order to warrant some special treatment of English ability, I define English to include not only mother tongue but also lingua franca and bilingual English. Besides, the following formula is used for the construct of the English dummy: ENGLISH=0 if economies $i$ and $j$ do not speak in English; and ENGLISH=1 otherwise.

Equations (A10) and (A11) can be estimated by using standard statistical techniques. In order to further account for the potential impacts of multicollinearity between geographical and linguistic and religious variables, we perform additional regressions by excluding the linguistic and religious variables. Specifically, if correlation coefficients of each pair of explanatory variables are fairly large, they could suggest potential multicollinearity that can cause imprecise regression results (Greene, 2002, pp. 255–8). Besides, since the cross-sectional data are employed, it is also necessary to conduct tests for heteroscedasticity. More specifically, while ordinary least squares (OLS)-estimated coefficients are unbiased, weighed least squares (WLS) estimation can provide more efficient results in terms of smaller coefficient standard errors (Greene, 2002, p. 499).

## Constructing similarity indexes

Linguistic and religious similarity indexes can be measured by different methods. The simplest method is to use a dummy index: that is, using '1' for economies to be linguistically or religiously linked with each other; and using '0' otherwise. Although it has been applied in a number of studies (see, for example, Havrylyshyn and Pritchett, 1991; Foroutan and Pritchett, 1993; Frankel and Wei, 1995; and Frankel *et al.*, 1997), this method cannot be used to precisely measure the extent to which economies are linguistically or religiously linked each other, particularly when the economies are linguistically or religiously diversified.

I will use a comprehensive method for the measurement of linguistic and religious similarity indexes. Suppose that the population shares of $N$ linguistic (religious) groups are expressed by ($x_1$, $x_2$, ..., and $x_N$) and ($y_1$, $y_2$, ..., and $y_N$) for economies $X$ and $Y$, respectively. $x_i$ and $y_i$ (where, $x_i \geq 0$ and $y_i \geq 0$) belong to the same linguistic (religious) group. Mathematically, the linguistic and religious similarity indexes (denoted by LANGUAGE and RELIGION, respectively) between the economies $X$ and $Y$ can be measured according to the following formula:[16]

$$\sum_{i=1}^{N} \min(x_i, y_i) \tag{A12}$$

In Equation (A12), 'min (...)' denotes the minimization of the variables within parentheses. In fact, several other methods can also be used to comprehensively measure linguistic and religious similarity indexes.[17] The values of LANGUAGE and RELIGION range between 0 and 1. In the extreme cases, when LANGUAGE (RELIGION) =1, the two economies have a common linguistic (religious) structure (that is, for all $i$, $x_i = y_i$); when LANGUAGE (RELIGION) =0, the two economies do not have any linguistic (religious) links with each other (that is, for all $i$, $x_i$ (or $y_i$)=0 and $x_i \neq y_i$). In the other cases, the greater the value of LANGUAGE (RELIGION), the more linguistically (religiously) similar the economies concerned.

Languages considered here are Bahasa (Malay or Indonesia), Cham, Chinese, English, Japanese, Kazak, Khmer, Korean, Kyrgyz, Miao, Mongol, Thai, Yao, Uighur, and Vietnamese. Population shares of the major linguistic groups are shown in Table VA.1. Restricted by data unavailability, the population shares of most linguistic groups are based on first, native language speakers. To overcome the above shortcoming, I include both mother tongue and lingua franca and bilingual Englishes in the English-speaking group. For some countries, the shares of national (official) language speakers, if their data seem to be unreliable, are roughly represented by literacy rates. It may be worthwhile to consider the similarity of two languages that are either within a language phylum or characterized by some form of connection. For example, many Taglog speakers in the Philippines find it relatively easy to communicate with Bahasa speakers in Indonesia or Malaysia. Besides, many Japanese and Korean business managers can read (or guess the meaning of) Chinese characters that are used in both mainland China (under the simplified form) and Taiwan and Hong Kong (under the complex form). But I would rather separate these languages from each other. The reason relates to the fact that, since many neighbouring countries' languages have a certain degree of similarity or connection in East Asia, including this kind of inter-linguistic connection could result in the multicollinearity problem (with the 'distance' variable) in Equation (A10).

Religious groups considered here are roughly classified by Christianity (including all western Christians, such as Anglican, Roman Catholic, Protestant, Methodist, and so on), Islam (including Sunni and Shia), Buddhism (including Mahayana and Hinayana (Theravada) Buddhism), Chinese folk-religion (a mixture of Confucianism and Taoism, which still finds followers in, besides China, some Southeast Asian economies), and Hinduism. Subdivisions of Christianity and Islam are not further done since they do not seem to be necessary in East Asia compared to those in Western nations and Middle East, respectively. Hinayana Buddhism, which has followers in Southeast Asia (especially in Cambodia, Myanmar, and Thailand) and in East Asia, is not separated from Mahayana Buddhism, which is concentrated in Southwest and Northwest China. Population shares of the major religious groups are shown in Table VA.2. In selecting the religions used for the measurement of RELIGION indexes, such religions as 'folk religion' (but 'Chinese folk-religion' is an exception), 'traditional religion', 'atheism' and

*Table VA.1*  Shares of major linguistic groups in East Asia (%, 1985 and 1995)

| Economy | Bahasa[a] | | Chinese | | English[b] | | Khmer | | Thai | |
|---|---|---|---|---|---|---|---|---|---|---|
| | 1995 | 1985 | 1995 | 1985 | 1995 | 1985 | 1995 | 1985 | 1995 | 1985 |
| Brunei | 82.03 | 64.73 | 9.48 | 20.54 | 3.27 | NA | | | | |
| Cambodia | | | 3.08 | NA | | | 88.63 | NA | | |
| China | | | 92.06 | 88.65 | | | | | | |
| Hong Kong | | | 76.56 | 98.58 | 20.29 | 20.29[c] | | | | |
| Indonesia | 85.00[d] | 77.00[d] | NA | NA | | | | | | |
| Japan | | | 0.17 | | 0.06 | | | | | |
| Korea, North | | | 0.16 | | | | | | | |
| Korea, South | | | 0.11 | | | | | | | |
| Laos | | | | 1.09 | | | 16.41[e] | 7.00[e] | | |
| Malaysia | 84.30[f] | 76.30[f] | 33.60[g] | 33.60[g] | 24.61 | 24.61[c] | | | | |
| Myanmar | | | | | | | | | | |
| Philippines | | | 0.05 | 0.25 | 29.54 | 29.54[c] | | | | |
| Singapore | 10.30 | 14.70 | 56.26 | 76.66 | 27.23 | 27.23[c] | | | | |
| Taiwan | | | 97.85 | 97.85 | | | | | | |
| Thailand | 3.65 | 3.80 | 12.13 | 11.31 | | | 1.27 | 1.40 | 80.15 | 81.36 |
| Vietnam | | | 1.40 | | | | 1.38 | 1.35 | 1.62 | 1.32 |

*Notes:* (1) Cham, Japanese, Kazak, Korean, Kyrgyz, Miao, Mongol, Taglog, Yao, Uighur, and Vietnamese, which are also taken in to account in the measurement of linguistic similarity index, are not shown in this table. (2) 'NA' denotes data are not available. (3) Blanks denote that figures are less than 0.005% or data are not available. (4) Totals in the table may not be added up to 100 due to the existence of bilinguists. [a] Include 'Bahasa Indonesia' and 'Bahasa Malay'. In some countries populations also include second language speakers as well as other relevant linguistic groups (such as 'Malay–Chinese', 'Malay–English', 'Malay–Chinese–English', and 'Malay–others'). [b] Include mother tongue, lingua franca, and bilingual Englishes. [c] As of 1995 due to the data unavailability or unreliability in 1985. [d] Represented by literacy rates, based on Jalal and Sardjunanu (2006). [e] As for 'Mon-Khmer' or 'Lao-Theung'. [f] Represented by literacy rates, based on "Literacy Facts and Figures at National level" (available from www.accu.or.jp/litdbase/stats/mys/dl/02_mys.xls). [g] As of 1979. Based on *Languages of the World*, 14th Edn (available from www.ethnologue.com/14/show_country.asp?name=Malaysia).

*Source:* Calculated by the author based on *Britannica Book of the Year* (1986 and 1996), except those that are noted otherwise.

*Table VA.2* Shares of selected religious groups in East Asia (%, 1985 and 1995)

| Economy | Christian | | Muslim | | Buddhist | | Hindu | | Chinese folk-religion | |
|---|---|---|---|---|---|---|---|---|---|---|
| | 1995 | 1985 | 1995 | 1985 | 1995 | 1985 | 1995 | 1985 | 1995 | 1985 |
| Brunei | | | 67.21 | 63.39 | | 13.84 | | | | |
| Cambodia | 5.95 | | 2.12 | | 95.00 | | | | | |
| China | 8.47 | 9.51 | 1.47 | 2.40 | 8.48 | 6.00 | | | 20.13 | 20.10 |
| Hong Kong | | 7.50 | | | 21.88[a] | 20.80[a] | | | 51.93[a] | 69.69[a] |
| Indonesia | | | 87.21 | 83.60 | 1.03 | | 1.83 | | | |
| Japan[b] | 0.69 | 0.74 | | | 40.86[b] | 41.82[b] | | | | |
| Korea, North[c] | | | | | | | | | | |
| Korea, South[c] | 24.06[d] | 25.69 | | | 24.35 | 37.40 | | | 17.51[e] | 17.51 |
| Laos | | | | | 57.81 | 58.00 | | | | |
| Malaysia | 6.39 | 5.60 | 52.92 | 52.90 | 17.33 | 17.30 | 6.99 | | 11.59 | 11.60 |
| Myanmar | 4.91 | | 3.82 | 3.60 | 89.45 | 87.20 | 0.51 | | | |
| Philippines | 90.68 | 84.10[f] | 4.57 | | | | | | | |
| Singapore | 12.89 | 10.35 | 14.92 | 16.21 | 15.97[a] | 26.76 | 3.29 | | 37.90[a] | 29.30 |
| Taiwan | 3.45 | 7.40 | 0.23 | | 22.95 | 43.00 | | | 18.85[g] | 48.50 |
| Thailand | 0.54 | | 4.04 | 3.80 | 94.80 | 95.00 | | | | |
| Vietnam | 8.68 | 7.40 | | | 66.67 | 55.30 | | | | |

*Notes:* (1) Atheism, traditional religion and non-religion are not listed in this table since they cannot be taken into account in the calculation of religious similarity index. (2) 'Christian' includes all western Christians, such as Anglican, Roman Catholic, Protestant, Methodist, etc. (3) Blanks denote that figures are less than 0.005 or data are not available. [a] Include Taoist and Chinese folk-religion). [b] These figures are much smaller than the corresponding numbers reported by the religious organizations in Japan, but they are closer to the surveyed data (Ash, 1997, p. 160). [c] Both North and South Korea are also religiously linked by Chondogyo – a Korean folk-religion that is not listed in this table. [d] Only include Protestant. [e] As of 1985. [f] Only include Roman Catholic. [g] Only include Taoist and Confucian.

*Source:* Calculated by the author based on *Britannica Book of the Year* (1986, 1996).

'non-religion' were removed from Equation (A12).[18] This is due to the fact that these religions should not be measured as a common religion in the religious similarity index. For example, 'traditional or folk religionists' from one nation (say, Togo) and 'traditional or folk religionists' form the other (say, China) do not have a common religious ground for people to trust each other. In addition, Chondogyo, which only exists in North and South Korea (two economies that have not set up formal economic and trade relations), and Shintoist, which only exists in Japan, are excluded from the calculation.

Estimates of the percentage of Japanese who are Buddhism vary widely. Perhaps 85 per cent of the population will cite Buddhism if asked what their preferred religion is, but about 75 per cent of them claim to nonreligious – to practice and believe in no religion. Frequently seen high figures of 85 per cent or 90 per cent of Japanese being Buddhism come primarily from birth records, following a longstanding practice of family lines being officially associated with a local Buddhist temple. In Japan there has been a large and thriving Buddhist community, but surveys indicate that the numbers of veritable Buddhism are far fewer than those of nominal Buddhism (Ash, 1997, pp. 160–1).

16 economies (Brunei, Cambodia, China, Hong Kong, Indonesia, Japan, Laos, North Korea, South Korea, Malaysia, Myanmar, Philippines, Singapore, Taiwan, Thailand and Vietnam are chosen in this research. Restricted by the data unavailability, I exclude Cambodia and Taiwan from 1985, as well as Macau from both 1985 and 1995. For each East Asian economy in the sample, 162 and 196 trade partners (economies) are selected for the estimates of 1985 and 1995, respectively. As a result the maximum number of observations is 2268 (14×162) for 1985 and 3136 (16×196) for 1995. The data on LANGUAGE and RELIGION are calculated by the author based on Equation (A12) and *Britannica Book of the Year* (1986 and 1996).[19]

The above sample includes economies at vastly different political and cultural conditions. The attractive feature of this broad sample is that it encompasses great variation in the explanatory variables that are to be evaluated. It is impossible to use the experience of one or a few countries to get an accurate empirical assessment of the long-term growth implications from a set of social, economic and cultural variables. However, one drawback of this kind of diverse sample is that it creates difficulties in measuring variables in a consistent and accurate way across countries and over time. For example, one reason that China, Japan and Korea may have relatively low transaction costs is because they share a common Buddhist/Confucian/Taoist past which left them with similar cultural legacies. The other empirical issue is the sorting out of directions of causation. From a longer perspective of the human history, there is an argument that the change of culture (especially of language and religion, which appear in our model as explanatory variables) is to a more or less extent determined or influenced by international exchanges and trade (which appears in our model as dependent variable). But this kind of causation is very weak for a shorter period of time (since there are always far fewer linguistic and religious changes than economic variables!)

# VI  Indexes of China's cultural linkages with the rest of the world

| Country | Language | Religion |
|---|---|---|
| Afghanistan | 0.0000 | 0.0147 |
| Albania | 0.0000 | 0.0663 |
| Algeria | 0.0000 | 0.0147 |
| American Samoa | 0.0000 | 0.0595 |
| Andorra | 0.0000 | 0.0595 |
| Angola | 0.0000 | 0.0595 |
| Antigua and Barbuda | 0.0000 | 0.0595 |
| Argentina | 0.0000 | 0.0742 |
| Armenia | 0.0000 | 0.0000 |
| Aruba | 0.0000 | 0.0595 |
| Australia | 0.0167 | 0.0595 |
| Austria | 0.0000 | 0.0595 |
| Azerbaijan | 0.0000 | 0.0147 |
| Bahamas,The | 0.0000 | 0.0595 |
| Bahrain | 0.0000 | 0.0147 |
| Bangladesh | 0.0000 | 0.0147 |
| Barbados | 0.0000 | 0.0595 |
| Belarus | 0.0000 | 0.0595 |
| Belgium | 0.0000 | 0.0595 |
| Belize | 0.0000 | 0.0595 |
| Benin | 0.0000 | 0.0742 |
| Bermuda | 0.0000 | 0.0595 |
| Bhutan | 0.0000 | 0.0848 |
| Bolivia | 0.0000 | 0.0595 |
| Bosnia and Herzegovina | 0.0000 | 0.0742 |
| Botswana | 0.0000 | 0.0595 |
| Brazil | 0.0000 | 0.0595 |
| Brunei | 0.0948 | 0.0147 |
| Bulgaria | 0.0000 | 0.0147 |
| Burkina Faso | 0.0000 | 0.0742 |
| Burundi | 0.0000 | 0.0595 |
| Cambodia | 0.0308 | 0.0994 |
| Cameroon | 0.0000 | 0.0742 |
| Canada | 0.0105 | 0.0747 |
| Cape Verde | 0.0000 | 0.0595 |
| Central African Republic | 0.0000 | 0.0742 |
| Chad | 0.0000 | 0.0742 |
| Chile | 0.0000 | 0.0595 |
| Colombia | 0.0000 | 0.0595 |
| Comoros | 0.0000 | 0.0214 |
| Congo, Dem. Rep. of the | 0.0000 | 0.0734 |
| Congo, Rep. of the | 0.0000 | 0.0742 |
| Costa Rica | 0.0020 | 0.0595 |

| Country | Language | Religion |
|---|---|---|
| Cote D'lvoire | 0.0000 | 0.0742 |
| Croatia | 0.0000 | 0.0721 |
| Cuba | 0.0000 | 0.0147 |
| Cyprus | 0.0000 | 0.0496 |
| Czech Republic | 0.0000 | 0.0595 |
| Denmark | 0.0000 | 0.0595 |
| Djibouti | 0.0000 | 0.0420 |
| Dominica | 0.0000 | 0.0595 |
| Dominican Republic | 0.0000 | 0.0595 |
| Ecuador | 0.0000 | 0.0595 |
| Egypt | 0.0000 | 0.0247 |
| El Salvador | 0.0000 | 0.0595 |
| Equatorial Guinea | 0.0000 | 0.0595 |
| Eritrea | 0.0000 | 0.0147 |
| Estonia | 0.0000 | 0.0595 |
| Ethiopia | 0.0000 | 0.0742 |
| Faroe Islands | 0.0000 | 0.0595 |
| Fiji | 0.0000 | 0.0742 |
| Finland | 0.0000 | 0.0595 |
| France | 0.0000 | 0.0742 |
| French Guiana | 0.0000 | 0.0595 |
| French Polynesia | 0.0291 | 0.0595 |
| Gabon | 0.0000 | 0.0595 |
| Gambia, The | 0.0000 | 0.0147 |
| Gaza Strip | 0.0000 | 0.0147 |
| Georgia | 0.0000 | 0.0147 |
| Germany | 0.0000 | 0.0742 |
| Ghana | 0.0000 | 0.0742 |
| Gibraltar | 0.0000 | 0.0595 |
| Greece | 0.0000 | 0.0133 |
| Greenland | 0.0000 | 0.0595 |
| Grenada | 0.0000 | 0.0595 |
| Guadeloupe | 0.0000 | 0.0595 |
| Guam | 0.0145 | 0.0595 |
| Guatemala | 0.0000 | 0.0595 |
| Guernsey | 0.0000 | 0.0000 |
| Guinea | 0.0000 | 0.0579 |
| Guinea-Bissau | 0.0000 | 0.0655 |
| Guyana | 0.0000 | 0.0742 |
| Haiti | 0.0000 | 0.0595 |
| Honduras | 0.0000 | 0.0595 |
| Hong Kong | 0.7656 | 0.1443 |
| Hungary | 0.0000 | 0.0595 |
| Iceland | 0.0000 | 0.0595 |
| India | 0.0000 | 0.0570 |
| Indonesia | 0.0000 | 0.0250 |
| Iran | 0.0000 | 0.0147 |

| Country | Language | Religion |
|---|---|---|
| Iraq | 0.0000 | 0.0448 |
| Ireland | 0.0000 | 0.0595 |
| Isle of Man | 0.0000 | 0.0595 |
| Israel | 0.0000 | 0.0147 |
| Italy | 0.0000 | 0.0717 |
| Jamaica | 0.0000 | 0.0595 |
| Japan | 0.0034 | 0.0917 |
| Jersey | 0.0000 | 0.0595 |
| Jordan | 0.0000 | 0.0501 |
| Kazakstan | 0.0090 | 0.0358 |
| Kenya | 0.0000 | 0.0742 |
| Kiribati | 0.0000 | 0.0595 |
| Korea, North | 0.0033 | 0.0000 |
| Korea, South | 0.0028 | 0.1443 |
| Kuwait | 0.0000 | 0.0147 |
| Kyrgyzstan | 0.0011 | 0.0147 |
| Laos | 0.0000 | 0.0848 |
| Latvia | 0.0000 | 0.0595 |
| Lebanon | 0.0000 | 0.0742 |
| Lesotho | 0.0000 | 0.0595 |
| Liberia | 0.0000 | 0.0742 |
| Libya | 0.0000 | 0.0147 |
| Liechtenstein | 0.0000 | 0.0595 |
| Lithuania | 0.0000 | 0.0595 |
| Luxembourg | 0.0000 | 0.0595 |
| Macau | 0.9206 | 0.0848 |
| Macedonia | 0.0000 | 0.0147 |
| Madagascar | 0.0000 | 0.0742 |
| Malawi | 0.0064 | 0.0742 |
| Malaysia | 0.0695 | 0.1589 |
| Maldives | 0.0000 | 0.0147 |
| Mali | 0.0000 | 0.0247 |
| Malta | 0.0000 | 0.0595 |
| Marshall Islands | 0.0000 | 0.0595 |
| Martinique | 0.0000 | 0.0595 |
| Mauritania | 0.0000 | 0.0147 |
| Mauritius | 0.0035 | 0.0742 |
| Mayotte | 0.0000 | 0.0459 |
| Mexico | 0.0000 | 0.0595 |
| Micronesia | 0.0000 | 0.0595 |
| Moldova | 0.0000 | 0.0000 |
| Monaco | 0.0000 | 0.0595 |
| Mongolia | 0.0052 | 0.0994 |
| Morocco | 0.0000 | 0.0147 |
| Mozambique | 0.0064 | 0.0742 |
| Myanmar (Burma) | 0.0000 | 0.1486 |
| Namibia | 0.0000 | 0.0595 |

| Country | Language | Religion |
|---|---|---|
| Nauru | 0.0435 | 0.0595 |
| Nepal | 0.0000 | 0.0926 |
| Netherlands, The | 0.0000 | 0.0742 |
| Netherlands Antilles | 0.0000 | 0.0595 |
| New Caledonia | 0.0000 | 0.0595 |
| New Zealand | 0.0000 | 0.0595 |
| Nicaragua | 0.0000 | 0.0595 |
| Niger | 0.0000 | 0.0147 |
| Nigeria | 0.0000 | 0.0742 |
| Northern Mariana | 0.0389 | 0.0595 |
| Norway | 0.0000 | 0.0595 |
| Oman | 0.0000 | 0.0545 |
| Pakistan | 0.0000 | 0.0346 |
| Palau | 0.0088 | 0.0595 |
| Panama | 0.0030 | 0.0595 |
| Papua New Guinea | 0.0000 | 0.0595 |
| Paraguay | 0.0000 | 0.0595 |
| Peru | 0.0000 | 0.0595 |
| Philippines | 0.0005 | 0.0742 |
| Poland | 0.0000 | 0.0595 |
| Portugal | 0.0000 | 0.0595 |
| Puerto Rico | 0.0000 | 0.0595 |
| Qatar | 0.0000 | 0.0147 |
| Reunion | 0.0198 | 0.0742 |
| Romania | 0.0000 | 0.0501 |
| Russia | 0.0010 | 0.0238 |
| Rwanda | 0.0000 | 0.0698 |
| St. Kitts and Nevis | 0.0000 | 0.0595 |
| St. Lucia | 0.0000 | 0.0595 |
| St. Vincent and the Grenadines | 0.0000 | 0.0595 |
| Samoa | 0.0000 | 0.0595 |
| San Marino | 0.0000 | 0.0595 |
| Sao Tome and Principe | 0.0000 | 0.0595 |
| Saudi Arabia | 0.0000 | 0.0147 |
| Senegal | 0.0000 | 0.0349 |
| Seychelles | 0.0000 | 0.0595 |
| Sierra Leone | 0.0000 | 0.0742 |
| Singapore | 0.5626 | 0.1589 |
| Slovakia | 0.0000 | 0.0595 |
| Slovenia | 0.0000 | 0.0595 |
| Solomon Islands | 0.0000 | 0.0595 |
| Somalia | 0.0000 | 0.0147 |
| South Africa | 0.0000 | 0.0742 |
| Spain | 0.0000 | 0.0709 |
| Sri Lanka | 0.0000 | 0.1589 |
| Sudan, The | 0.0000 | 0.0742 |
| Suriname | 0.0000 | 0.0742 |

| Country | Language | Religion |
|---|---|---|
| Swaziland | 0.0000 | 0.0595 |
| Sweden | 0.0000 | 0.0595 |
| Switzerland | 0.0000 | 0.0595 |
| Syria | 0.0000 | 0.0699 |
| Taiwan | 0.9206 | 0.1213 |
| Tajikistan | 0.0000 | 0.0147 |
| Tanzania | 0.0019 | 0.0742 |
| Thailand | 0.1213 | 0.1049 |
| Togo | 0.0000 | 0.0742 |
| Tonga | 0.0000 | 0.0595 |
| Trinidad and Tobago | 0.0000 | 0.0742 |
| Tunisia | 0.0000 | 0.0147 |
| Turkey | 0.0000 | 0.0147 |
| Turkmenistan | 0.0010 | 0.0147 |
| Tuvalu | 0.0000 | 0.0595 |
| Uganda | 0.0000 | 0.0742 |
| Ukraine | 0.0000 | 0.0595 |
| United Arab Emirates | 0.0000 | 0.0147 |
| United Kingdom | 0.0000 | 0.0738 |
| United States | 0.0077 | 0.0820 |
| Uruguay | 0.0000 | 0.0595 |
| Uzbekistan | 0.0028 | 0.0147 |
| Vanuatu | 0.0000 | 0.0595 |
| Venezuela | 0.0000 | 0.0595 |
| Vietnam | 0.0233 | 0.1443 |
| Virgin Islands (US) | 0.0000 | 0.0595 |
| West Bank | 0.0000 | 0.0742 |
| Western Sahara | 0.0000 | 0.0147 |
| Yemen | 0.0000 | 0.0147 |
| Yugoslavia | 0.0000 | 0.0730 |
| Zambia | 0.0000 | 0.0595 |
| Zimbabwe | 0.0000 | 0.0595 |

Source: Calculated based on Britannica Book for the Year 1996 and Equation (A12).

# Notes

## 1 A Brief History of China

1. With a paucity of verifiable facts, records of the rise of the Chinese nation of this time, however, were primarily written down almost a thousand years later, based on the oral transcriptions, for which, therefore, some doubts may remain.
2. The archaeologists discovered in ruins of Shang city in Anyang, central China's Henan province, some 10000 pieces of oracle bones and other relics of the dynasty, suggesting that China experienced relative stability and prosperity in that period (Li, 1957).
3. According to the Zhongfa system, the eldest son born of the highest ranking wife of a member of the royal household or nobility was called the 'major branch' and inherited the right of succession to his father's throne or noble title. Other son(s) was (were) known as 'minor branch(s)'.
4. Historically, the Han dynasty is divided into two periods: the Western Han had its capital in Chang'an in the west; while the Eastern Han had its capital in Loyang in the east.
5. Historians refer to the period from AD 265 to 581 as the Sixteen Kingdoms.
6. The period from AD 907 to 960 is known as the Five Dynasties and Ten Kingdoms (wudai shiguo).
7. The major events that occurred in the Chinese society during the 20th century are listed below in a chronological order: 1912, China's last dynasty, the Qing, was replaced by the Republic of China (ROC); 1937, Japan invaded China and the War of Resistance Against Japan (WRAJ) began; 1945, Japan surrendered unconditionally and, thereafter, the Civil War between the Nationalists and the Communists broke out; 1949, the People's Republic of China (PRC) was founded, followed by the large-scale land reform and socialist transformation of capitalist industry and commerce in mainland China.
8. This first of the World Bank reports was given prominence in *The Economist* (28 November, 1992). Subsequent reports appeared in *The Financial Times* (26 April 1993) and *The Economist* (15 May 1993).
9. Under the best guess projection, the US share of the world output falls down to 19.2 per cent in 2003, Japan experiences a declining share to something on the range of 7.6–8.1 per cent. In contrast, China's share jumps unambiguously up to 13.0 per cent in the best guess scenario and 15.5 per cent in the high growth scenario (Noland, 1995, p. 95, table 1).

## 2 The Spatial Division of the Chinese Economy

1. More often than not, the Chinese nation, as it is now called *zhongguo* (central state) in pinyin form, had another name, *jiuzhou* (nine states). The

reason for the latter may be plausibly explained by the fact that the remaining three states (Binzhou, Youzhou, and Yingzhou) had been independent from China before the central and peripheral states were unified as a single nation.

2. *Zhongshu-xingsheng* and *xingsheng* (the latter evolved to *sheng*) referred to the central government ministerial representative agencies to the provinces.

3. Notice that the Chinese character *dao* is being used as 'province' in Korea and that *sheng* used as 'ministry' in Japan.

4. It has been virtually the most important power body in making decisions on the Chinese state affairs.

5. See Yang (1993), p. 248.

6. Examples of literature on the application of the six great regions would include Hu *et al.* (1988, pp. 171–381), Yang (1989, p. 92), and Wei (1992, pp. 62–3).

7. The NPC is the supreme legislative organ of China. It includes several thousand representatives from different regions and sectors, meeting regularly in the Great Hall of the People in Beijing to discuss state affairs, appoint key government officials of the State Council and issue laws and regulations.

8. See *Guangming Daily*, 6 April 1986, p. 1.

9. For example, Wu and Hou (1990, p. 116), Hu *et al.* (1988, pp. 182–4), Yang (1990, pp. 38–43), Liu (1994, pp. 1–13), and Hsueh (1994a, pp. 22–56) give the same definition.

## 3   China's Economic Foundations

1. Other sources suggest different estimates on China's cultivated land. For instance, after summing up the official data from the provincial statistics, the total cultivated land area is no more than 100,000,000 ha, while other estimates (such as 120,000,000 ha, 133,333,000 ha, and 146,667,000 ha) have been also conducted by different institutions based on satellite photographs and sample surveys respectively (Cheng, 1990, pp. 1–18). In 1979, the Chinese official statistics defined the forestland area at 1,220,000 sq. km while the World Bank (1992) puts the figure to 1,150,000 sq. km for the year 1980. According to Vaclav (1992, p. 434), China's forestland area was estimated as 124,650,000 ha in the third national survey (1984–8) and was reported by SSB and Ministry of Forestry of China as 1,246,000 sq. km and 1,092,000 sq. km respectively for the year 1989. NEPA (1993, p. 4; 1994, p. 5) evaluates it at 1,309,000 sq. km in 1992 and 1,337,000 sq. km in 1993, respectively.

2. Source: Zhu (1990a, pp. 727–36).

3. Notice that the monetary values of the mineral resources might have been underestimated due to the use of low and officially fixed prices for the mineral products before the 1990s. But it does not matter here. Our aim is only to multiregionally estimate the relative shares, nothing more.

4. Data source: SSB (1996), p. 71.

5. Notice that only in 1995 did the Chinese government decide to implement a nine-year compulsory education system (that is, six years of primary school and three years of junior middle school), aiming at universal access

to junior middle school within six years in urban and coastal areas and within ten years in the remaining areas.

6. According to the PRC's Constitution, workers are the leading class in China.
7. According to Chenery and Syrquin (1975, p. 20), when the per capita GNP grows from US$100 to US$400 in developing countries, the ratio of educational expenditure to GNP increases from 3.3 per cent to 3.5 per cent accordingly.
8. Data source: UNESCO (1995), table 4.1.
9. See North and Thomas (1973), North (1981 and 1990) and Abramovitz (1986) for the varieties of European experience on the importance of institutions or differential social capability.
10. Chinese today treat themselves as the Hua-Xia descendants. The Hua people, who first settled around Mt. Hua of China's western mountain range, together with the Xia people, who established themselves near the Xia river (the upper course of the Han river, a tributary of the Yangtze river), were referred to as the Hua-Xia people. Both areas were located in the central southern region of Shaanxi province.
11. Cited in *China Ethnic Statistical Yearbook*, 1997, pp. 299–300.
12. For details about the historical evolution of Chinese characters, see Box 3.1.
13. See Chao (1970) and Ramsey (1989) for more detailed analyses.
14. Developing his ideas further, Confucius said: 'Regulated by the edicts and punishments, the people will know only how to stay away out of trouble, but will not have a sense of shame. Guided by virtues and the rites, they will not only have a sense of shame, but also know how to correct their mistakes of their own accord.'
15. For more details, see Weber (1964).

# 4   China's Economic Systems in Transition

1. The centralized planning model is based upon the supposition that 'society' (in practice the planning agencies, under the authority of the political leadership) knows or can discover what is needed, and can issue orders incorporating these needs, while allocating the required means of production so that the needs are economically met (Nove, 1987, p. 881).
2. Even though the term 'commodity' in the Chinese understanding is closely related to the concept of market economy, we may assume that it was used here to literally distinguish the Chinese economy from the Western style market system.
3. The term was firstly publicized in bold headlines in the CCP's official newspapers, such as *People's Daily*, *Workers' Daily*, etc. in early 1988.
4. For details of the Speech, see Deng (1992, pp. 370–83).
5. See Appendix II for a list of major reforms and their outcomes.
6. Data source: SSB (1990b). The concepts GVIO, GVAO, and national income are based on the MPS used during the pre-reform period. For more details about the MPS, see Chapter 5.
7. Data source: Liu (1982, p. 31).
8. For more detailed analysis of the Great Leap Forward and its impacts on the Chinese economy, see Chapter 8.

9. See, for example, Liu (1982, pp. 28–51) for more details.
10. This boring bargaining between the state planners and the managers usually reached a high tide during the national planning meetings arranged by the State Planning Commission (SPC) annually.
11. Data source: State Council (1988a, p. 198).
12. Data source: Liu (1995, p. 53).
13. 'Price release' in fact implies alteration of the price mechanism, from planned pricing to market pricing.
14. As noted by Lin (1995), China's SOEs enjoyed far less autonomy than their Soviet antecedents, as the Soviet enterprises operated under the Economic Accounting System (*khozraschet*) which endowed state enterprises with a limited degree of financial autonomy with them being allowed to retain a proportion of profits, depreciation reserves, and major repairs funds. But national shortages of productive resources and severe weakness in enterprise management in China during the 1950s compelled a much more centralized system which left SOEs without any substantive decision-making or financial autonomy.
15. According to SICA (1995), the number of *getihu* grew by over 11 times, from 1828 thousand in 1981 to 22,390 thousand in 1995, while that of *shiyingqiye* grew by over five times, from 91 thousand in 1989 to 563 thousand in 1995. Notice that the actual number could be larger as some PSEs could have reported under the name of 'COEs' in order to evade the 'individual income' tax.
16. Notice that as soon as the Tian'anmen Square incident (May–June 1989) was clam down, the Chinese leadership began to re-emphasize the role of the working class in the Chinese economy.
17. Note the state ownership only includes the SOEs, while the public ownership include the SOEs and COEs (see Figure 4.2).
18. The following is cited from Liew (2000), which also gives other references.
19. The literature of the evolution in central–local fiscal arrangement over the pre-reform era would include Lardy (1975, pp. 25–60), Donnithorne (1976, pp. 328–54) and Oksenberg and Tong (1991, pp. 1–32).
20. That is, the marginal and average propensity to tax each province from its collected revenue ranged between 12 per cent and 90 per cent (Oksenberg and Tong, 1991, p. 24).
21. In what follows in this paragraph, the fiscal parameters in parentheses are defined in Table 4.3.
22. Data source: Wei (1994, pp. 297–9).
23. Cited from Knight and Li (1995, p. 5).
24. Knight and Li (1995, p. 16) explain three main reasons for why the provinces have retained an increasing proportion of the revenue they collect: (1) the growing importance of extra-budgetary revenue in total revenue; (2) under the lump-sum contract system the marginal rate of tax was unity if the target was not achieved and zero for revenue in excess of the target; and (3) the increasing cross-section responsiveness of budgetary expenditure to budgetary revenue.
25. They are Shanghai, Tianjin, Shenyang, Nanjing, Ji'nan, Wuhan, Guangzhou, Chengdu, and Xi'an, with additional two administrative departments housed in Beijing and Chongqing municipalities.

26. Before the crisis, there had been a crying call for the SOEs to be reconstructed according to the Korean model. But obviously this idea has been abandoned as soon as the Korean cheobals met strategical difficulties.
27. For example, they have the authority to approve foreign investment projects up to US$30 million, while other regions' authority remained much lower (Montinola *et al.*, 1995).
28. As defined by McKinnon (1991a) and Weingast (1995), the Chinese system provides a partial basis for a special kind of federalism called *market-preserving federalism*. Central to the success of market-preserving federalism is the element of political durability built into the arrangements, meaning that the decentralization of power is not merely at the discretion of the central political authorities.

## 5  How Well the Chinese-style Reform Performs

1. It should be noted that the judgment of a reform as being 'successful' or 'unsuccessful' is based on some available data and literature. Frankly speaking, there is no mandatory standard for this definition since each reform – no matter whether not it has been 'successful' ('unsuccessful') – has both positive and negative effects on the Chinese economy. Besides, the terms 'radical' and 'gradual/partial' reforms used in this section are also elastically defined, since according to international standard, China's reforms as a whole were implemented via only but a gradual/partial approach during the past two decades.
2. Note that as a result of three decades of effective CCP control on the one hand and of the closed-door policy on the other, most, if not all peasants in rural China had been accustomed to obeying political and economic orders coming from Beijing.
3. The resulting near-zero incentives in post-reform Russia look similar to the pre-reform China but stands in sharp contrast to the post-reform China (Qian, 2002).
4. I still clearly remember that when the news of discussions about radical price reform was released to the media in August 1988, there was a nationwide run on the banks and panic buying by consumers. The incident ended ideas of further speeding up the pace of price reform, and lent support to a gradual reform.
5. Source: Liew (2000), which also gives other references.
6. See, for example, Jiang's (1998, p. 2) speech at the meeting commemorating the twentieth anniversary of the Third Plenum of the Eleventh CCP National Congress.
7. Young (2000), based on the pre-1990s data, find that China's economic reform have resulted in a fragmented internal market with fiefdoms controlled by local officials whose economic and political ties to protected industry resemble those of the Latin American economies of past decades. It seems plausible that the endogenous response of actors to the rent-seeking opportunities created by gradualist reform could give rise to new distortions, whose lifespan far exceeds that of the rents which motivated their arrive (Young, 2000). Based on the data from 1988 to 2000, Cai *et al.*

(2002), however, argue that the decentralization of authority has already generated comparative advantages for interregional cooperation in manufacturing sector during the reform period. If both results are correct, the Chinese reform might suggest that Big bang tends to be optimal in the early stage of reform and that gradualism tends to be optimal in the late stage of reform.

8. More detailed analysis can be found in Shen and Dai (1990); Li (1993); and Wedeman (1993).

9. Discussions in this regard would include, for example, Garnaut and Huang (1995), Corbet (1996), Keidel (1995), Wu (1996), Mastel (1996, 1998), and Morici (1997).

10. Here we use a much simpler definition of a closed economy than the others. Sachs and Warner (1995), for example, define a closed economy as one that has one of the following characteristics: non-tariff barriers cover 40 per cent or more of trade; average tariff rates of 40 per cent or more; a black-market exchange rate that is depreciated by 20 per cent or more relative to the official rate, among others.

11. As for the FSU's relatively weakness of market economy, Mikhail Gorbachev's speech on 11 September 1990 might be revealing: 'Our brains just could not handle this idea of a market' – Cited from Hwang (1993, p. 147).

12. Examples that support big bang reforms would include Lipton and Sachs (1990), A[o]slund (1991), Berg and Sachs (1992), Boycko (1992), Murphy *et al.* (1992), Sachs (1993), Frydman and Rapaczynski (1994), and Woo (1994).

13. Examples that support gradual reforms would include Svejnar (1989), Portes (1990), McKinnon (1991b), Roland (1991), Dewatripont and Roland (1992a, b, 1995), McMillan and Naughton (1992), Murrell (1992), Aghion and Blanchard (1994), Litwack and Qian (1998), and Wei (1993).

14. For simplification, we only use the income levels at the final stage of reform (that is, at time 20 in this simulation) in calculation.

15. In fact, it is difficult to consistently identify the radicals and conservatives throughout the whole period of reform. Those who had been treated as radicals during a period might become conservatives later on; and that a CCP senior who can be a radical reformer in one reform agenda (such as agricultural or other domestic sector reform) might be considered as a conservative in the other (such as external economic sector or political reform in general).

16. The most typical example would be the smooth implementation of the agricultural reform during the early 1980s (as discussed in Section 1.1).

17. Note that this result does not depend on the process through which the re-distribution of incomes from the radicals and conservatives has been determined.

18. Source: http://edition.cnn.com/SPECIALS/1999/china.50/inside.china/profiles/li.peng/. For a theoretical demonstration of Chinese political games, see Appendix IV.

19. Since the institutional decentralization and concentralization might occur simultaneously in different sectors, authors with different analytical purposes may identify the *fang-shou* circle differently. For example, Baum (1994, pp. 5–9, 369–76) offers a plausible explanation of the *fang-shou* cycle

during 1978–93: the decentralization (*fang*) policy was concentrated on 1978, 1980, 1982, 1984, 1986, 1988, and 1992; while the concentralization (*shou*) policy was concentrated on 1979, 1981, 1983, 1985, 1987, 1989, and 1993. Shirk (1993), Dittmer and Wu (1993, pp. 10–12) reach a similar conclusion, sketching out four relatively complete, synchronous cycles of *fang* and *shou* during 1980 to 1989: *fang* is predominated in 1979–80, 1984, and 1988, while *shou* is predominated in 1981, 1985–86, 1987, and 1988–89.

20. In a survey conducted in 1992, 30 per cent of surveyed officials were thinking about *xiahai* (Chen, 1993). In another survey of local government officials in 1995, close to 20 per cent were planning on *xiahai* (SCSR, 1996). Of those, 35 per cent were looking for joint-venture enterprises, 21 per cent for private enterprises, and 1.5 per cent for SOEs. Tang and Parish (1998) find in their large survey that 99 per cent of those officials who planned to quit the bureaucracy wanted to join businesses – Cited from Li (1998).

21. This can be witnessed by, for example, Yu's (2004) article in which some influential Chinese economists are criticized for their favouritism to the rich *vis-à-vis* the poor.

22. One example is the 'real name' banking system which was introduced on April, 2000. Frankly speaking, this change was not so much about increasing tax revenue, but to reduce political corruption by making the flow of money transparent. What is interesting is that it followed a dual-track approach: the real name policy only applies to the new deposits made after 1 April 2000. Withdrawing from the existing deposits, which amount to about 6 trillion yuan (or more than 60 per cent of China's GDP), continued to be anonymous (Qian, 2002).

23. Cited from www.wsws.org/articles/2002/nov2002/chin-n13.shtml.

# 6   A Multiregional Economic Comparison

1. It is worth noting that the SNA has some shortcomings and is not a complete measure of economic welfare from which humankind may benefit. In fact, as illustrated in UN (1990a, b), the SNA-based GNP (or GDP) indicator ignores the costs of both the depletion and degradation of natural and environmental resources.

2. More evidence may be found in Tsui (1993, pp. 30–1).

3. See, for example, Guo and Han (1991, pp. 10–21) for a more detailed explanation and the critical evaluation on the quality of Chinese GDP data.

4. Therefore, national income equals GVSP minus all material costs including depreciation of capital.

5. According to a survey conducted by JPSB (1990, pp. 27–8), the rural GVIO data reported to the SSB might have been 21.8 per cent higher than the real data in Jilin province in 1989.

6. All data are estimated according to World Bank Atlas method of converting national currency to current US dollars.

7. The World Bank (1996, pp. 394–5) defined low-income economies, lower-middle-income economies, upper-middle-income economies and high-income economies with per capita GNPs of US$725 or less, US$726–2,895, US$2,896–8,955 and US$8,956 or more, respectively.

8. As a matter of fact, the reason why the Chinese government rejected the PPP-enlarged GDP may arise from, among others, the fears that it could affect China as a less-developed country obtaining the favourable loans and economic assistance from the international organizations (Zheng, 1996, p. 1).

9. Cited from *Asia-Pacific Economic Times*, 22 October 1996. See Box 6.1 for more details about 'underground economic activities'.

10. Data sources: SSB (1989, p. 29; 1994, p. 33; 1996, p. 42; and 1996b, pp. 13 and 15). As the SNA-based data for the period from 1978 to 1984 had been only crudely estimated by the SSB, we exclude them from estimation.

11. For more evidence of the overstatement on China's GNP for the post-1992 period, one may also refer to *China Youths* (1995, p. 2), Ling *et al.* (1995, pp. 18–19), *People's Daily* (1995, p. 2), *The Economist* (1995, p. 19), *Huang* (1996, pp. 157–62), and so on.

12. Of course, this approximation is only a crude one, but it would be at least better than taking no action at all, when one intends to obtan an inequality index including all the provinces (see Chapter 6, pp. 124–8).

13. Data source: SSB (1986, p. 563 and 1996, p. 282).

14. Notice that according to Khan *et al.* (1993, p. 34), the difference between the incomes of an average urban household and an average rural household is much higher than the official estimate. The true ratio of urban to rural incomes, for instance, would be 2.42 in 1988 as compared to a ratio of 2.05 estimated by the SSB (1989, p. 719). Li (2004) further argues that, if taking into account the subsidies and other non-wage earnings, the actual ratio would be as high as 5–6 times, which was the largest in the world.

15. Data source: SPC (1996, pp. 37–40).

16. See, for example, Yang (1989, pp. 95–6) and Liu *et al.* (1994, pp. 142–3) for the application in the Chinese economic analyses.

17. Examples of literature for the application in the Chinese economic analyses would include Lardy (1980, pp. 153–90), Denny (1991, pp. 186–208), Tsui (1991, pp. 1–21), Lyons (1992, pp. 471–506), and Yang (1992, pp. 70–4).

18. Literature of the multidimensional measurement of regional inequalities would include Atkinson (1970, pp. 244–63), Kolm (1976a, pp. 416–42; 1976b, pp. 82–111; 1977, pp. 1–13), Maasoumi (1986, pp. 771–9), and Atkinson and Bourguigon (1992, pp. 140–53). In addition, as a demonstration in which two indices (per capita GDP and per capita hospital beds) are considered, Tsui (1994, pp. 181–92) applies the multidimensional GE method to calculate China's regional disparities between 1978 and 1989. Due to the complexity of the multidimensional measurement, we will not conduct it here.

19. See, for example, Guo and Wang (1988), Yang (1990, 230–57), Denny (1991, pp. 186–208), Tsui (1991, pp. 1–21), Dong (1992, pp. 63–4), Lyons (1992, pp. 471–506), Wei (1992, pp. 61–5), Yang (1992a, pp. 70–4; 1992b, pp. 65–6), Wei and Liu (1994, pp. 28–36), Zhang (1994, pp. 296–312), and Song (1996, pp. 38–44).

20. See, for example, Yang (1991, pp. 504–9; 1993, pp. 129–45), Liu *et al.* (1994, pp. 141–66), and Tsui (1993).

21. Data source: SSB (1990b). All data are based on comparable prices.

22. The per capita GDPs are estimated according to the method in Section 4.2 for the provinces whose GDP data are not officially reported.

23. See Khan *et al.* (1993, p. 69).

24. Data sources: Higgins (1981, pp. 69–70), Nair (1985, p. 9), Smith (1987, p. 41), Kim and Mills (1990, p. 415), Savice (1992, p. 191), Ottolenghiand and Steinherr (1993, p. 29), Hill and Weidemann (1989, pp. 6–7), and Hu *et al.* (1995, p. 92).

## 7  Can the Chinese Economy Be Spatially Optimized?

1. Cited from www.answers.com/topic/authoritarianism
2. Similar arguments are made by Alesina and Spolarore (1997, p. 1029).
3. See Guo (2006, pp. 186–92) for a mathematical proof of the following propositions. After reviewing the Chinese history, one may find an interesting phenomenon: during the prosperous period, China's political (economic) cores would move to its geographical peripheries (centers); while during the stagnant period, China's political (economic) cores would move to its geographical centers (peripheries). This issue will be included in another research and therefore is not analyzed in the chapter.
4. Examples of literature would include *Economic News* (1987, p. 1; 1988, p. 1), Zhu (1990b, pp. 20–4), Hu (1992, p. 1), and Guo (1993, pp. 118–23; 1996, pp. 70–1).
5. See *Baokan Wenzhai* (1989, p. 4).
6. For more discussions about the interregional separation and its affects on the Chinese economy, see Chapter 9 (pp. 194–9).
7. This phenomenon has been described as *Zhuhou Jingji* (feudal prince economy) or *Duli Wangguo* (independent kingdom). See, for example, Shen and Dai (1990, p. 12), Li (1993, pp. 23–36), and Wedeman (1993, pp. 1–2) for more detailed analyses.
8. More detailed evidence may be found in Sun (1993, pp. 95–104), Feng (1993, pp. 87–94), Guo (1993, pp. 201–5), and Goodman (1994, pp. 1–20).
9. See Young and Ho (1993, pp. 9–13).
10. Cited from Standler (2002).
11. Cited from www.dragontv.cn/detail.php?InfoID=21232
12. Cited form *Washington Post* (2004, p. A12). There is also encouraging news reported by the *People's Daily* (2004, p. 16). In 2004 more than 50 counties and cities in the interprovincial border area of Hubei, Henan, Sichuan, Shaanxi, and Chongqing decided to establish a Regional Meteorological Community so as to share with each other the meteorological data and information and to jointly utilize the atmospheric resources. Moreover, China Meteorological Bureau also submitted a proposal concerning the construction of man-made precipitation enhancement bases in such areas as the upper reaches of Heihe River, the Qilianshan Mountain area, the upper reaches of Songhuajiang River and so on, in order to build up a mechanism unifying command and coordination for interprovincial rain-making activities.
13. See, for example, Oi (1992, pp. 99–129), Wong (1992), Shirk (1993), and Jin *et al.* (2001).
14. See, for example, Shen and Dai (1990, pp. 1–13), and Li (1993, pp. 23–36).
15. More detailed evidence may be found in Feng (1993, pp. 87–94), Sun (1993, pp. 95–104), and Goodman (1994, p. 1–20).

16. See *Beijing Youth*, 2 December 2002 (available at www.sina.com.cn).
17. See CCPCC (1984).
18. Examples of the literature would include CASS (1992) and Guo (1993, pp. 189–95; 1996, pp. 146–50).
19. http://www.westchina.gov.cn/english/asp/showinfo.asp?name=2. 11.11.2003
20. http://www.chinadaily.com.cn/highlights/nbc/news/319wen.htm. 21.3.2003.
21. *Beijing Review*, 29 May 2000.
22. Cited from Goodman (2002).

# 8 Industrialization and Technological Progress

1. Data source: Liao (1982, p. 130).
2. Cited from Mao (1956, p. 285).
3. See Mao (1957, p. 491).
4. Data source: Liu (1982, p. 32).
5. Data source: SSB (1990b).
6. During the Great Leap Forward period, large amounts of material and labor were invested in heavy industry at the expense of agriculture and light industry. Millions of peasants abandoned farming to dig for ore and fell trees in order to make steel using indigenous methods. The harvest was poor despite the high yields, which eventually resulted in a three-year famine.
7. Data source: Liang (1982, p. 60).
8. The read might be interested in reading a pessimist model on world dynamics (Box 8.1).
9. Data source: Jao and Leung (1986, pp. 3 and 6).
10. Examples of literature on the third-front area would include Lardy (1978), Leung (1980), Maruyama (1982, pp. 437–71), Liu (1983), Riskin (1987), Naughton (1988, pp. 227–304), Bo (1991, pp. 1202–3, 1209), and Chen (1994, pp. 329–42).
11. Data source: Hu *et al.* (1995, p. 5).
12. Data source: Liu (1984, p. 270).
13. Data source: Liang (1982, pp. 61–2). This clearly went too far beyond the real capacities of this country.
14. Data source: Liang (1982, p. 56, table 3).
15. See SSB (1996, pp. 405–1).
16. Data source: Yang (1993, p. 179).
17. The units used are yuan for $Y$ and $K$ and person for $L$.
18. Data source: UNFAO (1992).
19. Rural workers are classified by main activity: for example, those engaged primarily in agriculture and secondly in commerce are classified under agriculture.
20. Data source: SSB (1996, pp. 387–90).
21. More details may be found in He *et al.* (1991, pp. 124–41). In the 1990s, increasing institutional checks and balances increase of the security of foreign investors, and FDI replaced the TVEs as a major driver of manufac-

turing growth (Winters and Yusuf, 2007, p. 29). There will be a detailed analysis of the FDI as well as its contributions to the development of the Chinese economy in Chapter 10.

22. For example, people in almost everywhere of the world now can immediately get access to the latest information about technological progress and download electronic products from the Internet. However, the intercontinental spread of technological inventions was both costly and time-consuming in the ancient times, which usually took decades or even centuries.

23. Lu Xun, a well-known writer, ironically noted that while Western nations used powder to make firearms and compass for navigation, China used powder to make firecrackers and compass to align the spiritual location within the landscape (*fengshui*).

24. Data source: Liao (1982, p. 138).

25. Data Source: SSB (1987b, p. 100).

26. Data sources: (1) SSB (1996, p. 661) for the data of 1995; (2) SSTC (1988, p. 267) for the data of 1986; (3) As Ma and Sun (1981, p. 614) estimate that China's R&D expenses were 0.54 per cent of GVIAO in 1979, using the estimated GVIAO/GNP ratio in Equation 4.3, we can obtain an approximation of R&D/GNP ratio (0.54/0.58≈0.93).

27. According to UNESCO (1986), the R&D/GNP ratio of China was, although lower than that of USA, Japan, West Germany, UK, and Switzerland whose R&D/GNP ratios exceeded 2.0, higher than that of Pakistan, Indonesia, Thailand, and the Philippines whose R&D/GNP ratios ranged from 1.0 to 0.4, and much similar to that of Austria, Australia, Denmark, Italy, and South Korea whose R&D ratios ranged from 1.0 to 1.2 during 1980–85.

## 9  Population, Resource and Sustainable Development

1. In this chapter, we will less strictly (but more practically) define sustainable development as 'the maximization of the total well-being over a long period of time'.

2. Increasing commodity demand from the giants obviously supports prices, other things being equal, but prices also depend on supply. Most analysts hold that, in recent years, Chinese demand has increased most metals prices because supply growth has not kept up with demand (Winters and Yusuf, 2007, pp. 16–17). The exception that proves the rule is aluminum, for which China is a net exporter and produces about 25 per cent of the world total. Compared with price increases of 379 per cent for copper from January 2002 to Jun 2006, aluminum prices have increased modestly – up only 80 per cent (Streifel, 2006).

3. Wakabayashi (1989, p. 14) estimates that 14 million people died from starvation between 1959 and 1961. In addition, Minami (1994, p. 197, fn. 8) puts the number of deaths higher.

4. The literature of this arguments would include Wang and Dai (1958, pp. 10–14), He *et al.* (1960, pp. 20–5), and Zhang (1982, pp. 12–14).

5. Cited from Mao (1949, pp. 453–4).

6. Cited from Minami (1994, p. 197).
7. If considering the contribution of capital saved as a result of the reduced birth rate, this figure would be higher.
8. According to a sampling survey conducted on 1 October 1995, the birth gender proportions for population at the ages of 0, 1, 2, 3, 4 years were 116.57:100, 121.08:100, 121.26:100, 119.17:100, and 115.01:100 respectively (SSB, 1996, p. 72).
9. According to the PRC's Constitution, women and men shall have the same right to be employed and paid the same wage if they do the same job. However, this does not always apply in rural areas where labour productivity is to a large extent physically determined.
10. Data source: SSB (1993b, p. 153). The population age composition also differs among regions. In 1982, Shanghai became the first province whose population aged 65 years or over exceeded 7 per cent of the total population – a criterion that is generally known to be an aged society. At the end of the 1990s, the old-aged provinces further covered Beijing, Tianjin, Jiangsu, Zhejiang, Shandong, Guangdong, Liaoning, Sichuan and so on.
11. The CDIAC estimates for 1988 were extrapolated based on the 1990 figures for primary energy output as reported in *Beijing Review*, 7–11 March 1991.
12. Notice that Wang (1995), and Wang and Li (1995) even extend the year to 2050.
13. pH values below 5.6 are indicative of acid rain.
14. For example, embankments have had to be constructed to prevent flooding of seawater into some areas of Tianjin after significant ground subsidence.
15. Source, *Beijing Evening News* (25 May 2004).
16. As oxygen is required to aerobically decompose biologically degradable compounds, the higher the level of BOD, the poorer the water quality
17. Source: the CCTV special program on 16 August 1996.
18. Cited from Guo (2005, pp. 204–5).
19. In 1979, for example, the Chinese official statistics defined the forestland area at 1.22 million square kilometers, while the World Bank (1992) puts the figure to 1.15 million square kilometers for the year 1980. According to Vaclav (1992, p. 434), China's forestland area was estimated as 124,650,000 ha in the third national survey (1984–88) and was reported by the SSB and Ministry of Forestry of China as 1,246,000 sq. km and 1,092,000 sq. km in 1989, respectively. NEPA (1993, p. 4; 1994, p. 5) estimated it at 1,309,000 sq. km in 1992 and 1,337,000 sq. km in 1993, respectively.
20. According to NEPA (1992), these projects include: (1) 'Forest System of the Upper and Middle Reaches of the Changjiang River', with a planned afforestation space of around 66 thousand square kilometers; (2) 'Coastal Shelter-Forest System' with 25 thousand sq. km; and (3) 'Afforestation Project of the Taihang Mountains between Shanxi, Hebei and Henan provinces, and Beijing and Tianjin Municipalities', with 33,000 sq. km.
21. Sheehy (1992, p. 303) estimates that the desertified grazingland has increased at a rate of over 10,000 sq. km per annum.
22. Data source: Fullen and Mitchell (1994, p. 131).
23. For more detail about these methods, see UWRL (1971).
24. Cited form Home (2004).

25. Source: China Meteorological Bureau (2002). The enthusiasms in rainmaking in China, however, have been increasingly spurred by factors including drought and the need for irrigation water. See Box 7.2 for details.
26. These laws, regulations, and other relevant official documents have covered a broader range from air, inland water pollution control, protection of endangered wildlife, to the control of domestic marine pollution from offshore oil drilling and waste release into territorial seas.
27. Cited from ACCA21 (1994, p. 1-1A-1).
28. Cited from *Legal Daily* (1996, p.1).
29. Cited from *China Daily* (1996, p. 1). Notice that the above percentages could be to some extent miscalculated, as some of the factories which had been closed during the official inspection period might re-open their business after the inspection.

# 10   Economic Internationalization and China

1. According to *Guangxu Da Qing Huidian Shili* (vol. 775, p. 4 and vol. 776, p. 13), *haijin* (close-door policy) included: (1) the export of cereals and five metals (gold, silver, copper, iron and tin) were strictly prohibited; (2) private trade and contacts between Chinese and foreign businessmen were illegal; (3) foreigners' activities in China were only allowed on the conditions that 'At most ten foreigners may take a walk together near their hotel three days a month on the 8th, 18th and 28th', 'Overseas businessmen should not stay in Guangdong in winter', and 'Women from foreign countries are prohibited to enter this country', and so on; (4) Chinese businessmen going abroad were subject to the conditions that 'At most one liter of rice may be carried by a seaman a day' and 'At most two guns may be installed in a ship'; and (5) manufacture of seagoing vessels of more than 500 *dans* in weight and 8 meters in height was prohibited – Translated from Zheng (1992, pp. 30–1).
2. Source: *Bulletins of the State Council, People's Republic of China*, various issues.
3. In this section only FDI inflows are discussed. China's FDI outflows, though small amounts at present, are growing larger at an annual rate of US$5.5 billion (Winters and Yusuf, 2007, p. 23), mostly in Asia (especially Hong Kong), Latin America and Africa. In face the net wealth of Chinese affiliates abroad can be measured in hundreds of billion dollars. Officially, the Chinese SOEs had as many as 5666 affiliates abroad at the end of 1998 with a combined FDI of US$6.33 billion (Chandra, 1999).
4. Data source: NBS (1996, 2006).
5. See IIE (1996, pp. 274–5).
6. According to Qian (2001), the role of the FDI in China is vastly overstated in the press. For the entire 1980s, FDI in China was tiny. FDI only started to increase substantially in 1993, and at its peak it accounted for about 10 per cent of total investment. On per capita basis, China's FDI was not high by the international standard. The direct contribution of foreign trade and investment to large countries cannot be quantitatively as important as to those small countries. Like FDI, China's exports were very concentrated in coastal provinces. However, contrary to a popular perception, China's

growth was not just a phenomenon of coastal provinces – it is across-board, both coastal and inland. Inland provinces grow fast while coastal provinces just faster.

7. There have been some remarkable differences in estimating China's imports and exports due to differing statistical systems. For instance, statistics from the US Department of Commerce indicated that Sino-US trade had been in favour of the US side during the 1979–82 period, but the US started registering deficit in 1983, and the figure amounted to US$39.5 billion in 1996. Chinese statistics from the Customs of the PRC, however, suggested that China had recorded deficit in the bilateral trade between 1979 and 1992. Surplus first appeared in 1993, and rose to US$10.5 billion in 1996 – cited from SCIO (1996, p. 21).

8. In an estimation of international trade, Frankel and Romer (1996, table 1) find that, for every 1 per cent increase in land area, trade falls by about 0.2 per cent accordingly.

9. Based on the data of 93 countries, Guo (1996, pp. 85–6) finds that, for every increment of about 132.56 million ha of land area, a new metal will appear in a country.

10. Linnemann (1966) and Frankel *et al*. (1997) have estimated the effects of both GDP and GNP on trade, but no significant difference is found.

11. Frankel *et al*'s (1997, p. 66) estimated coefficients on 'adjacency' range between 0.5 and 0.7. Because trade is specified in natural logarithmic form in their estimates, the way to interpret the coefficients on adjacency is to take the exponent: that is to say, two countries that share a common border will, *ceteris paribus*, increase their trade by about 65–101 per cent compared with two otherwise countries.

12. For example, Linnemann (1966) puts the estimated coefficient as –0.77, Brada and Mendez (1983) and Oguledo and MacPhee (1994) as 0.76, Bikker (1987) as –0.90 to –1.1, Mansfield and Bronson (1997) as –0.51 to –0.69 (for 1950–90), and Rauch (1999) as –0.62 to –0.70 (1970–90).

13. In fact, as witnessed in Guo (2004; 2006), the exclusion of one or more cultural variables that have played a much more important role in international economic activities in the post-Cold War era than the Cold War era could have artificially magnified the effects of distance on trade, especially for the post-Cold War era.

14. For example, Linder (1961) predicts that countries with similar levels of per capita income will tend to have similar preferences with somewhat differentiated marketable goods, and thus will trade more with each other.

15. Specifically, Linnemann (1966) estimates the coefficient as –0.77, Brada and Mendez (1983) and Oguledo and MacPhee (1994) as 0.76, Bikker (1987) as –0.90 to –1.1, and Mansfield and Bronson (1997) as –0.51 to –0.69 (for 1950–1990).

# 11 Comparative Economics for the Greater China

1. There have been different names for the greater China economic area, such as 'the Chinese circle' (Wen, 1987), 'the Chinese community' (Hwang, 1988; and Zhou, 1989, p. 924), 'the greater China community' (Zheng,

1988), 'China economic circle' (Feng, 1992, pp. 6–9; Fei, 1993, p. 54), 'Chinese economic area' (Segal, 1994, p. 44), 'China economic zone' (Zhou, 1992, pp. 18–21; Yang, 1995), and so on. In addition, Dong and Xu (1992, pp. 10–3) and Wei and Frankel (1994, pp. 179–90), while among others, add Singapore, Malaysia, Indonesia, Thailand and the Philippines to this area.

2. See 'Joint Declaration of the Government of the United Kingdom of Great Britain and Northern Ireland and the Government of the People's Republic of China on the Question of Hong Kong', Beijing, 19 December 1984.

3. See 'Basic Law of the Hong Kong Special Administrative Region of the People's Republic of China', Article 5, the Third Session of the Seventh NPC, 4 April 1990.

4. For example, the Mainland Commission has still been established by the Taiwanese government so as to officially manage its 'mainland affairs', while in mainland China, the Office for Taiwan Affairs is also authorized by the State Council to deal with the 'Taiwan affairs'.

5. During the early 1990s, average labour cost in Hong Kong, Macau, and Taiwan is 10–20 times that in mainland China (Yang, 1992, p. 3).

6. A comparison of military expenditures between Taiwan and mainland China is illustrated in Table 11.3.

7. The PRC's attitude towards the Taiwan's position in the international community may be briefly summarized by Jiang (1995, p. 2) as that under the principle of one China and in accordance with the charters of the relevant international organizations, Taiwan has become a member of the Asian Development Bank, the Asian-Pacific Economic Cooperation Forum and other international economic organizations in the name of 'Chinese Taipei.'

8. Wang Daohan was the President of the ATSR and Koo Chenfu was the Chairman of the FTSE.

9. Cited from Jiang (1995, p. 2).

10. In 1985, Chen Guoshun, a Taiwanese businessman was sentenced in Taipei to 12 years in prison for 'rebellious' activities. The prosecutor charged Chen with illegally entering mainland China in 1984, signing a contract, and engaging in direct investment in the mainland. Chen's sentence sent a shock wave to those who had engaged or intended to conduct direct business activities (*Pai Shing Semimonthly*, 1 March 1986, p. 52).

11. Cited from *Cankao Xiaoxi* (1996, p. 8).

12. Until 1995, the number of the Taiwanese funded projects in the ASEANs are 4249, the total investment of which reaches US$28.02 billion, accounting for more than 11 per cent of Taiwan's total foreign investment (Li, 1996, p. 2).

13. A survey conducted in Taiwan in Feburary 2000 reveals that, when the responders were asked if they were Chinese or Taiwanese, 45.0 per cent replied 'Taiwanese', 39.4 per cent answered 'both Taiwanese and Chinese', 13.9 per cent considered themselves as 'Chinese'. But in the survey conducted in September 1992, these ratios are 16.7 per cent, 36.5 per cent and 44.0 per cent respectively (Chen and Chen, 2001, p. 91).

14. Let $GNP$=gross national product, $POP$=population, $mc$=mainland China, $x$=Hong Kong, Macau, or Taiwan, $r_{mc}$=the average annual growth rate of per capita GNP for mainland China within a certain period in the future, and $T(x)$=time period (in years) by which the per capita GNP of mainland

China will reach that of mainland China and $x$ as a whole, the average economic level for a territorially-enlarged China is determined mathematically by an equation as

$$\frac{GNP_{mc} + GNP_x}{POP_{mc} + POP_x} = \frac{GNP_{mc}}{POP_{mc}}(1 + r_{mc})^{T(x)}, \text{ with } \frac{GNP_x}{POP_x} \gg \frac{GNP_x}{POP_x} \text{ and } r_{mc} > 0.$$

Using the above equation and the data in Table 11.1, we can calculate $T(x)$ for a constant rate $r_{mc}=7\%$: $T$(Hong Kong)=2.51 years, $T$(Macau)=0.03 year and $T$(Taiwan)=4.58 years. In sum, the reunification of Hong Kong, Macau, and Taiwan with mainland China will accelerated the development of the unified China by 7.12 years.

15. Kan (1994, pp. 172–3) maps out seven assumptions for the triangle relationships between Taiwan, Hong Kong and mainland China and argues that the successful transition of Hong Kong is believed to be the critical factor on which the future reunification of the greater China area will depend.

# Appendices

1. One of the most influential research using the SD methodology would include Meadows (1972).
2. For more knowledge about the SD approach, see Forrester (1969) and Day (1985, pp. 55–64).
3. Obviously, $1/T$ represents the average speed of the reform.
4. Since we have defined the size of the population as constant in Assumption III, the size of national income and income level are used interchangeably here.
5. This assumption is simply based on the very fact that all radicals have a CCP background and do not want any reforms that could lead to the collapse of the CCP-dominated nation.
6. As a matter of fact, due to its deep influence on the Chinese society, the behaviour of the IB per se can represent the state of political stability, or at least there is a positive correlation of the two.
7. We borrow this term from Bates *et al.* (1998, p. 31).
8. Note that if the expected length of time for the reforms is $T_{BB}$ for the radicals and $T_{GR}$ for the conservatives, we have $T_{BB} \leq T^* \leq T_{GR}$.
9. Note that in Conditions 1 and 2 the optimal reform strategies have nothing to do with open-door policies.
10. Note that this result does not depend on the process through which the re-distribution of incomes from the redicals and conservatives has been determined.
11. The earliest application of the gravity model can be traced back to the 1940s (see, for example, Zipf, 1946; Stewart, 1948; and Isard, 1949).
12. Note that if there are a significant number of zero values in the pair-wise trade, then Tobit regressions techniques should be used. In this research, the number of observations identified by 'TRADE=0' (that is, there is no trade) is quite small.
13. This idea is largely based on the suggestion by an anonymous referee.

14. A country's GDP indicator in 1985 or 1995 can be easily obtained by multiplying its GDP per capita (GDPPC) by its population (the latter is available from United Nations 1986 and 1996).
15. For example, there are five phylums in in East Asia: Sino-Tibetan phylum, Ural-Altaic phylum (such as Mongolian, Manchu-Tungas, etc.), Dravidian phylum (such as Telugu, Malay, etc.), Austronesian phylum, Austro-Asiatic phylum (such as Khmer, Mon, Vietnamese, etc.), and other phylums (such as Japanese, Korean, Papuan).
16. This formula has been used in Guo (2004, 2006) and Noland (2005).
17. Boisso and Ferrantino (1997), for example, use $\Sigma x_i y_i$ as the construct of similarity index. However, using Equation (A12) can prevent the index from further reduction when the values of $x_i$ and $y_i$ are small.
18. Atheism and non-religion were each treated as a 'religious affiliation' in China, but they were grouped as a single religious group in North Korea (*Britannica Book* of the year 1996, pp. 775, 776).
19. As an example, the data on China's bilateral linguistic and religious similarity indexes are shown in Appendix VI.

# Bibliography

(*Note*: the titles of Chinese references are listed in English translations followed by *pinyin* forms in parentheses.)

Abramoritz, M. (1986), 'Catching Up, Forging Ahead and Falling Behind', *Journal of Economic History*, vol. 56 (June), 23–34.

Administrative Committee of China Agenda 21 (1994), *Priority Programs for China's Agenda 21*, First Tranche, State Planning Commission and State Science and Technology Commission, Beijing.

"Agreement between the United States of America and Canada Relating to the Exchange of Information on Weather Modification Activities," Washington, D.C.: Government of the United States of America; and Ottawa: Government of Canada, available at: www.americansovereign.com/articles/weather.htm

Agarwala, R. (1992), 'China: Reforming Intergovernmental Fiscal Relations', *World Bank Discussion Papers*, no. 178, Washington, DC: World Bank.

Aghion, P. and O. Blanchard (1994), 'On the Speed of Transition in Central Europe', *National Bureau for Economic Research Macroeconomics Annual*, pp. 283–319.

Alesina, A. and E. Spolaore (1997), 'On the Number and Size of Nations', *The Quarterly Journal of Economics*, vol. 112 (Nov), 1027–56.

Anderson, D. (1987), *The Economics of Afforestation*, Baltimore: Johns Hopkins University Press.

Argawala, R. (1992), 'China: Reforming Intergovernmental Fiscal Relations', *World Bank Discussion Papers*, no. 178, Washington DC: World Bank.

Ash, R. (1997), *The Top 10 of Everything*, New York: DK Publishing.

Asian Development Bank (1996), *Key Indicators of Developing and Asian Countries 1996*, vol. XXVII, Economics and Development Resource Center, Asian Development Bank (ABD), Manila, published by Oxford University Press.

*Asia-Pacific Economic Times*, 22 October 1996.

Åslund, A. (1991), 'Principles of Privatization', in L. Csaba (ed.), *Systemic Change and Stabilization in Eastern Europe*, Aldershot: Dartmouth, pp. 17–31.

Atkinson, A.B. (1970), 'On the Measurement of Inequality', *Journal of Economic Theory*, vol. 2, pp. 244–63.

Atkinson, A.B. and F. Bourguignon (1992), 'The Comparison of Multidimensional Distributions of Economic Status', *Review of Economic Studies*, pp. 140–53.

*Baokan Wenzhai* (1989), 'The Armed Disputes in China's Internal Borders' (zhongguo bianjie da xiedou), *The Digest of Newspapers and Magazines*, 13 June, p. 4.

Bates, R., A. Greif, M. Levi, J.-L. Rosenthal, and B. Weingast (1998), *Analytic Narratives*, Princeton, NJ: Princeton University Press.

Battan, L.J. (1962), *Cloud Physics and Cloud Seeding*, San Francisco: Double Day.

Baum, R. (1994), *Burying Mao: Chinese Politics in the Age of Deng Xiaoping*, Princeton: Princeton University Press.

Berg, A. and J. Sachs (1992), 'Structural Adjustment and International Trade in Eastern Europe: The Case of Poland', *Economic Policy*, vol. 14, pp. 117–74.

Berthelemy, J.-C. and S. Demurger (2000), 'Foreign Direct Investment and Economic Growth: Theoretical Issues and Empirical Application to China', Paris: OECD Development Center.

Bikker, J. (1987), 'An International Trade Flow Model with Substitution: An Extension of the Gravity Model', *Kyklos*, vol. 40, 315–37.

Bo, Y. (1991), *A Retrospect of Some Key Decisions and Incidents of China* (ruogan zongda juece yu shijian de huigu), vol. I, Beijing: The CCPCC Literature Press.

Boisso, D., and M. Ferrantino (1997), 'Economic Distance, Cultural Distance and Openness in International Trade: Empirical Puzzles', *Journal of Economic Integration*, vol. 12, 456–84.

Boycko, M. (1992), 'When Higher Incomes Reduce Welfare: Queues, Labour Supply, and Macroeconomic Equilibrium in Socialist Economies', *Quarterly Journal of Economics*, vol. 107, pp. 907–20.

Brada, J., and J. Mendez (1983), 'Regional Economic Integration and the Volume of Intra-Regional Trade: A Comparison of Developed and Developing Country Experience', *Kyklos*, vol. 36, 589–603.

*Britannica Book of the Year* (various years), Chicago: Encyclopedia Britannica.

Brooks, S. (1949), 'The Legal Aspects of Rainmaking', *California Law Review*, vol. 37, pp. 114–21.

Brown, G. and C.B. McGuire (1967), 'A Socially Optimal Pricing Policy for a Public Water Agency', *Water Resources Research*, vol. 3, pp.13–43.

Brown, L. (1993), *The New Shorter Oxford English Dictionary*, Oxford: Clarendon Press.

Burnaux, J.M., J.P. Martin, G. Nicoletti and J.O. Martins (1992), 'The Costs of Reducing $CO_2$ Emissions: Evidence from GREEN', OECD Economics Department Working Paper no. 115, Paris.

Byrd, W.A. (1987), 'The Impact of the Two-Tier Plan/Market System in Chinese Industry', *Journal of Comparative Economics*, September.

Cai, F., D. Wang and M. Wang (2002), 'China's Regional Specialization in the Course of Gradual Reform', *The Economic Research* (in Chinese), No. 9, pp. 24–30.

Campos, N.F., and F. Coricelli (2002), 'Growth in Transition: What We Know, What We Don't and What Should', *Journal of Economic Literature*, vol. XL (September), pp. 793–836.

*Cankao Xiaoxi* (1996), 'Reference News – Taiwan', 16 October, p. 8, Beijing.

Carbon Dioxide Information Analysis Center (1990), *Trends '90*, Oak Ridge, TN: Oak Ridge National Laboratory.

CCPCC (1984), 'Decision of the CCPCC Concerning the Reform of Economic Structure', Beijing: the Third Plenum of the 12th CCPCC, Beijing, 21 October.

CCPCC Party School (ed.) (1988), *The Basic Plans for China's Economic Reform, 1979–87* (zhongguo jingji tizhi gaige guihuaji, 1979–87), Beijing: CCPCC Party School Press.

Chan, J. (2002), 'Chinese Communist Party to Declare Itself Open to the Capitalist Elite', available at: http://www.wsws.org/articles/2002/nov2002/chin-n13.shtml.

Chandra, N.K. (1999), 'FDI and Domestic Economy: Neoliberalism in China', EPW Special Articles (www.epw.org.in/34–45/sa3.htm).

Chao, Y.R. (1970): *A Grammar of Spoken Chinese*, Berkeley, CA: University of California Press.

Chen G. (1994), *China's Regional Economic Development: A Comparative Study of the East, Central, and West Belts* (zhongguo quyu jingji fazhan: dongbu zhongbu he xibu de bijiao yanjiu), Beijing: Beijing University of Technology Press.

Chen Z. (1994), 'An Analysis of the Industrial Development in the Third-front Area', in Liu, S., Q. Li and T. Hsueh (eds), *Studies on China's Regional Economic Development* (zhongguo diqu jingji yanjiu), Beijing: China Statistics Publishing House, 1994, pp. 329–42.

Chen, C. (1992), 'Modernization in Mainland China', *American Journal of Economics and Sociology*, vol. 51 (1), pp. 57–68.

Chen, L., Y. Yee and R. Shu (1993), 'A Study of the Feasibility of Opening the Indirect Commercial Funds Sent to the Mainland Area' (kaifang dui dalu diqu shangye xing jianjie huikuan kexing xing zhi yanjiu), Research Project prepared to the Mainland Commission, Taipei.

Chen, M. and Z. Cai (2000), *Groundwater Resources and the Related Environmental–Hydrogeologic Problems in China* (in Chinese), Beijing: Seismological Press.

Chen, R. (1993), *The Craze of Xiahai* (xiahai kuangchao), Beijing: Tuangjie.

Chen, Z. and F. Chen (2001), 'Probing into Taiwan's Development in Democratic Elections from its Political Characteristics', *Asian Studies* (Hong Kong), No. 41.

Chenery, H. and M. Syrquin (1975), *Patterns of Development, 1950–1970*, published for the World Bank, New York: Oxford University Press.

Cheng, H. (1990), 'A Brief Introduction to China's Natural Resources' (zhongguo zhiran zhiyuan gaishu), in Commission of Integrated Survey on Natural Resources (ed.), *Handbook of Natural Resources in China* (zhongguo zhiran zhiyuan shouce), Chinese Academy of Sciences, Beijing: Science Press, 1990, pp. 1–20.

Chi, F. (2000), 'The WTO Accession and the Second Reform in China', *Business Management*, No. 11.

China Daily (1996), 'State Closes 42,000 Polluting Factories' (CD News), Beijing, 12 October, p. 1.

*China Daily* (2004a), 'Man-Made Rain to Cool Shanghai's Power Demand' (by Liang Yu), 15 June, Beijing: China Daily.

*China Daily* (2004b), 'Hey, You! Get Off of My Cloud', 14 July, Beijing: China Daily.

*China Daily*, 17 November 1993.

China Enterprise Evaluation Center (1990), *China's Top 500 Enterprises*, published by *Management World* magazine for the Development Research Center of the State Council, Beijing.

*China Ethnic Statistical Yearbook*, Beijing: National Ethnic Commission of China, 1997

China Meteorological Bureau (2004), *China Meteorological Report* (in Chinese), Beijing: China Meteorological Bureau.

*China Youths*, 3 January 1995.

Chinese Academy of Sciences (CASS) (1989), *Ecological Deficit: The Biggest Crisis of the Nation's Survival in the Future*, Chinese Academy of Sciences, and State Science and Technology Commission, Beijing.

Chinese Academy of Social Sciences (CASS) (1992), *China's Yearbook for Horizontal Economy* (zhongguo hengxiang jingji nianjian), Beijing: China Social Sciences Press.

Chung, Y-W (2004), *Greater China: An Emerging Economic Reality*, London: Palgrave Macmillan.

*Cihai* (1988), 'State' (*zhou*), *Cihai*, Shanghai: Shanghai Cishu Press.

CISNR (Commission of Integrated Survey on Natural Resources) (ed.) (1990), *Handbook of Natural Resources in China* (zhougguo zhiran zhiyuan shouche), Chinese Academy of Sciences, Beijing: Science Press.

Clark, C. W. (1976), *Mathematical Bioeconomics: The Optimal Management of Renewable Resources*, New York: John Wiley.

Coase, R. (1992), 'The Institutional Structure of Production', *American Economic Review*, vol. 82, (Sept.), 713–19.

Combes, P.-P., M. Lafourcade, T. Mayer (2005), 'The Trade-Creating Effects of Business and Social Networks: Evidence from France', *Journal of International Economics*, vol. 66, no. 1, 1–29.

Commission of Economic Construction (CEC) (1996), 'The Opening of the Three Direct Links of the Special Economic and Trade Zones May Save US$700 million' (kaitong jingmao tequ santong, niansheng qiyi meiyuan), Taipei, *Central Daily*, 14 October.

Cooper, R. (1975), 'An Economist's View of the Oceans', *Journal of World Trade Law*, vol. 9, pp. 357–77.

Corbet, H. (1996), 'Issues in the Accession of China to the WTO System', *Journal of Northeast Asian Studies*, vol. 15, No. 3.

Cremer, R.D. (1989), 'The Industrialization of Macau', in Jao, Y.C., V. Mok and L.S. Ho (eds.), *Economic Development in Chinese Societies: Models and Experiences*, Hong Kong: Hong Kong University Press, 1989, pp. 18–32.

Crook, F.W. and X. Diao (2000), 'Water Pressure in China: Growth Strains Resources', *Agricultural Outlook*, January–February, pp. 25–9.

Dasgupta, P. (1982), *The Control of Resources*, Oxford: Basil Blackwell.

Dasgupta, P, and Mäler, K.-G. (1995), 'Poverty, Institutions, and the Environmental Resource-Base', in Behrman, J. and Srinivasan, T.N. (eds), pp. 2331–463), *Handbook of Development Economics*, vol. III, Amsterdam: Elsevier Science B. V.

Davis, R.J. (1968), 'Special Problems of Liability and Water Resources Law', in Taubenfeld, H.J. (ed.), *Weather Modification and The Law*, Mumbai: Oceana Publications, pp. 103–62.

Day, R.H. (1985), 'Dynamics Systems Theory and Complicated Economic Behaviors', *Environment and Planning*, vol. 12, pp. 55–64.

De Melo, M., C. Denizer, A. Gleb and S. Tenev (1997), 'Circumstances and Choice: the Role of Initial Condition and Politics in Transition Economies', *Policy Research Working Paper* No. 1866, Washington, DC: The World Bank.

Deardorff, A. (1997), 'Determinants of Bilateral Trade: Does Gravity Work in a Classical World?' in Frankel, J. (1997, ed.), *The Regionalization of the World Economy*, Chicago: University of Chicago Press, pp. 110–30.

Demurger, S. (2000), 'Economic Opening and Growth in China', *Review of Development Economics*, vol. 4(2), 140–55.

Deng X. (1992), 'The Key Points of the Speeches in Wuchang, Shenzhen, Zhuhai, Shanghai, etc.' (zai in wuchang, shenzhen, zhuhai, shanghai deng di de jianghua yiaodian), in Literature Editing Committee of CCPCC (ed.), *Selected Works of Deng Xiaoping* (Deng Xiaoping wenxue), Beijing: The People's Press, 1993, pp. 370–83.

Denniston, D. (1993), 'Plunder Behind the Bamboo Curtain', *World Watch*, May–June, pp. 9–36.

Denny, D.L. (1991), 'Provincial Economic Differences Diminished in the Decade of Reform', in US Congress Joint Economic Committee (ed.), *China's Economic Dilemmas in the 1990s: the Problems of Reforms, Modernization, and Interdependence*, vol. 1, pp. 186–208, Washington DC: the US Government Printing Office, vol. 1, pp. 186–208.

Dewatripont, M. and G. Roland (1992a), 'Economic Reform and Dynamic Political Constraints', *Review of Economic Studies*, vol. 59, pp. 703–30.

Dewatripont, M. and G. Roland (1992b), 'The Virtues of Gradualism and Legitimacy in the Transition to a Market Economy', *Economic Journal*, vol. 102, pp. 291–300.

Dewatripont, M. and G. Roland (1995), 'The Design of Reform Packages under Uncertainty', *American Economic Review*, vol. 85, pp. 1207–23.

Dittmer, L., and Y. Wu (1993), 'The Political Economy of Reform Leadership in China: Macro and Micro Informal Politics Linkages', paper presented to the Annual Meeting of the Association of Asian Studies, Los Angles.

Dodsworth, J. and D. Mihaljek (1997), 'Hong Kontg, China: Growth, Structural Change, and Economic Stability During the Transition', International Monetary Fund Occasional Paper No. 152, Washington, DC: IMF.

Dong F. (1982), 'Relationship Between Accumulation and Consumption', in Xu, D. and others (eds), *China's Search for Economic Growth: The Chinese Economy Since 1949*, Beijing: New World Press, 1982, pp. 79–101.

Dong F. (1992), 'Some Comments on Analyses of Interregional income Gaps' (guanyu diqu jian shouru chaju biandong fenxi de jidian shangque yijian', *The Economic Research* (jingji yanjiu), no. 7, pp. 63–4.

Dong S. and C. Xu (1992), 'Some Issues Relating to the Greater China Economic Cooperation' (da zhonguo jingji xiezuo de jige wenti), in Youths Committee of China Society of Natural Resources (ed.), *The Cross-Taiwan Strait: Sustainable Development of the Issues of Resources and Environment*, Beijing: China Science and Technology Press, 1992, pp. 10–13.

Donnithrone, A. (1976), 'Centralization and Decentralization in China's Fiscal Management', *China Quarterly*, vol. 66, pp. 328–54.

Du, P. (1994), *A Study of the Process of Population Aging in China* (zhongguo renkou laohua yanjiu), Beijing: The People's University of China Press.

Eaton, J., and A. Tamura (1994), 'Bilateralism and Regionalism in Japanese and U.S. Trade and Direct Foreign Investment Patterns', *Journal of the Japanese and International Economics*, vol. 8, 478–510.

*Economic News*, 11 February 1987; 21 December 1988.

Eichengreen, B. and D. Irwin (1995). 'Trade Blocs, Currency Blocs and the Reorientation of Trading the 1930's, *Journal of International Economics*, vol. 38(2), 89–106.

Fairbank, J.K. (1980), *The United States and China: Policies in Chinese–American Relations*, Cambridge MA: Harvard University Press.

Fanelli, J. (2004), 'Understanding Reform: A Global GDN Research Project', paper presented at the Fifth Annual Global Development Conference

'Understanding Reform, organized the Global Development Network (GDN), New Delhi, India, 28–30 January.

Feenstra, R.C., R.E. Lipsey, H. Deng, A.C. Ma and H. Mo (2005), 'World Trade Flows: 1962–2000', NBER Working Paper No. 11040, National Bureau of Economic Research, Cambridge, MA (available from http://cid.econ.ucdavis.edu/data/undata/undata.html).

Fei W. (1993), 'Economic Analysis of China Economic Area' (dui zhongguo jingji quan de fenxi), *Asia-Pacific Economic Review*, no. 2, pp. 54–9.

Feng, L. (1993), 'On the 'Wars' over the Purchase of Farm and Subsidiary Products', *Chinese Economic Studies*, vol. 26, no. 5, pp. 87–94.

Feng, Y. (1992), 'The Trends of Asian–Pacific Regional Cooperation and the Formation and Development of the Chinese Economic Circle', in Youths Committee of China Society of Natural Resources (ed.), *The Cross-Taiwan Strait: Sustainable Development of the Issues of Resources and Environment*, Beijing: China Science and Technology Press, 1992, pp. 6–9.

Fewsmith, J. (1999), *China Since Tian'anmen: The Politics of Transition*, Cambridge: Cambridge University Press.

Fidrmuc, J. and A.G. Noury (2003), 'Interest Groups, Stakeholders, and the Distribution of Benefits and Costs of Reform', Thematic Paper, Washington DC: GDN.

*Financial Times, The*, 26 April, 1993

Fischer, S. and A. Gelb (1991), 'The Process of Socialist Economic Transformation', *Journal of Economic Perspectives*, vol. 5, pp. 91–105.

Food and Agricultural Organization (1987), *FAO Production Yearbook 1987*, Rome: FAO.

Foroutan, F., and L. Pritchett (1993), 'Intra-Sub-Saharan African Trade: Is It Too Little?' *Journal of African Economics*, vol. 2 (May), 74–105.

Forrester, J.W. (1959), 'Advertising: A Problem in Industrial Dynamics', *Harvard Business Review*, March–April.

Forrester, J.W. (1969), *Industrial Dynamics*, Cambridge, MA: The MIT Press.

Frankel, J.A. and D. Romer (1996), 'Trade and Growth', NBER Working Paper No. 5476, Cambridge MA: National Bureau of Economic Research.

Frankel, J. and S. Wei (1995), 'European Integration and the Regionalization of World Trade and Currencies: The Economics and the Politics', in B. Eichengreen, F. Frieden, and J. von Hagen (eds), *Monetary and Fiscal Policy in an Integrated Europe*, New York: Springer-Verlag.

Frankel, J., D. Romer and T. Cyrus (1995), 'Trade and Growth in East Asian Countries: Cause and Effect?' Pacific Basin Working Paper Series No. 95–03, San Francisco: Federal Reserve Bank of San Francisco.

Frankel, J., E. Stein and S. Wei (1994), 'Trading Blocs: The Natural, the Unnatural, and the Super-natural', Center for International and Development Economics Research (CIDER) Working Paper No. C94–034, University of California, Berkeley, April.

Frankel, J., E. Stein and S. Wei (1997), *Regional Trading Blocs in the World Economic System*, Washington, DC: Institute for International Economics.

Frydman, R. and A. Rapaczynski (1994), *Privatization in Eastern Europe: Is the State Withering Away?*, London: Central European University Press.

Fullen, M.A. and Mitchell, D.J. (1994), 'Desertification and Reclamation in North–Central China', *Ambio*, vol. 23, no. 2, March, pp. 131–5.

Garnaut, R. (1999), 'Introduction', in R. Garnaut and L. Song (eds), *China: Twenty Years of Reform*, Canberra: Asia Pacific Press, pp. 1–20.

Garnaut, R. and Y. Huang (1995), 'China and the Future International Trading Systems', in *China and East Asia Trade Policy*, Pacific Economic Papers, No. 250, Australia–Japan Research Center, Australian National University.

Gilley, B. (2004), 'The 'End of Politics' in Beijing', *The China Journal*, No. 51, pp. 115–35.

Goodman, D.S.G. (1994), 'The Politics of Regionalism: Economic Development Conflicts and Negotiation', in Goodman, D.S.G. and G. Segal (eds), *China Deconstructs: Politics, Trade, and Regionalism*, London and New York: Routledge, 1994, pp. 1–20.

Goodman, D.S.G. (1997), 'China in Reform: The View from the Provinces', in D.S.G. Goodman (ed.), *China's Provinces in Reform – Class, Community and Political Culture*, London: Routledge.

Goodman, D.S.G. (2002), 'The Politics of the West: Equality, Nation-building and Colonization', *Provincial China*, vol. 7 (2), December.

Gottmann, J. (1973), *The Significance of Territory*, Charlottesville: University of Virginia Press.

Goulet, D. (1980; 1995), *Development Ethics: A Guide to Theory and Practice*, New York: Apex Press.

Greene, W.H. (2002), *Econometric Analysis*, 5th edn, Upper Saddle River, NJ: Prentice-Hall.

Groves, T., Y. Hong, J. McMillan and B. Naughton (1994), 'Autonomy and Incentives in Chinese State Enterprises', *Quarterly Journal of Economics*, vol. 109(1), pp. 183–209.

Gu J. (1995), 'Analyses on the Causes of Income Variable among Regions in China', Proceedings of the Fifth Annual Meeting of the Congress of Political Economists (COPE), International, pp. 45–51, Seoul, South Korea, 5–10 January.

Gu, H. (1997), 'China's Economic Marketization: An Estimate and Forecast' (zhonguo jingji shichang hua chengdu de zuixin guji yu yuce), *Management World*, no. 2, pp. 52–5.

Gu, M. (1986), 'Advances in Pollution Control', Environmental and Policy Law, vol. 16, no. 6, pp. 211–14.

Guiso, L., P. Sapienza, and L. Zingales (2004), 'Cultural Biases in Economic Exchange', NBER Working Paper Series 11005, Cambridge, MA: National Bureau of Economic Research, December.

Guo, F. and W. Wang (1988), *Poverty and Development* (pinkun yu fazhan), Hangzhou: Zhejiang People's Press.

Guo, R. (1991), 'A Preliminary Study of Border–Regional Economics: Theory and Practice of China' (bianjie diqu jingji xue cutan: lilun yu zhongguo shijian), PhD thesis, CUMT.

Guo, R. (1993), *Economic Analysis of Border-Regions: Theory and Practice of China* (zhongguo shengji bianjie diqu jingji fazhan yanjiu), Beijing: China Ocean Press.

Guo, R. (1995), 'The Impacts of Provincial Borders on the Economic Development of China: The N-dimensional Model of Spatial Economies' (shengji bianjie dui zhongguo jingji de yingxiang), *Xitong Gongcheng Lilun Yu Shijian* (Journal of China System Engineering Society), vol. 15, no. 4, pp. 38–43.

Guo, R. (1996), *Border–Regional Economics*, Heidelberg: Physica-Verleg.

Guo, R. (2004), 'How Culture Influences Foreign Trade: Evidence from the U.S. and China', *The Journal of Socio-Economics*, vol. 33, 785–812.

Guo, R. (2005), *Cross-Border Resource Management – Theory and Practice*, Amsterdam and Boston: Elsevier.

Guo, R. (2006), *Cultural Influences on Economic Analysis: Theory and Empirical Evidence*, London and New York: Palgrave Macmillan.

Guo, R. (2007), 'Linguistic and Religious Influences on Foreign Trade: Evidence from East Asia', *Asian Economic Journal*, vol. 21(1), 101–21.

Guo, R., S. Li and Y. Xing (2003), 'Ownership Reform and Income Distribution in China's State-Owned Enterprises: The Case Study of Guangzheng and Chuangda' (zhongguo guoyou qiye gaizhi yu zhigong sgouru fenpei: guangzheng gongsi yu chuangda gongsi de anli yanjiu), *Management World*, No. 4, pp. 103–11.

Guo, S. and W. Han (1991), *The Distribution and Utilization of China's GNP* (zhongguo GNP de fenpei he shiyong), Beijing: The People's University of China Press.

Haggard, S. and S. Webb (1994), 'What Do We Know About the Political Economy of Economic Policy Reform?' *The World Bank Research Observer*, vol. 8(2), pp.143–68.

Havrylyshyn, O., and L. Pritchett (1991), 'European Trade Patterns after the Transition', Policy, Research and External Affairs Working Paper Series No. 74, Washington, DC: World Bank.

He, B., R. Gu, Y. Yan, and Z. Bao (1991), *Studies on the Non-agricultural Development in Jiangsu's Rural Area* (jiangsu nongcun feinonghua yanjiu), Shanghai: Shanghai People's Press.

He, J., Z. Zhu and J. Liao (1960), 'Criticizing Ma Yinchu's Reactionary 'New Population Theory'' (pipan Ma Yinchu fandong de 'xin renkou lun'), *The Economic Research* (jingji janjiu), no. 4, pp. 20–5.

Heckscher, E.F. (1919), 'The Effect of Foreign Trade on the Distribution of Income', *Ekonomisk Tidskirift*, 497–512.

Helpman, E. (1987), 'Imperfect Competition and International Trade: Evidence from Fourteen Industrial Countries', *Journal of the Japanese and International Economies*, vol. 1 (Mar.), 62–81.

Heston, A., R. Summers and B. Aten (2006), 'Penn World Table Version 6.2', Center for International Comparisons of Production, Income and Prices at the University of Pennsylvania, September.

Higgins, B. (1981), 'Economic Development and Regional Disparities: A Comparative Study of Four Federations', in Mathews, R.L. (ed.), *Regional Disparities and Economic Development*, Canberra: The Australian National University, 1981, pp. 69–70.

Hill, H. and A. Weidemann (1989), 'Regional Development in Indonesia: Patterns and Issues', in Hill, H. (ed.), *Unity and Diversity: Regional Economic Development in Indonesia Since 1970*, Singapore: Oxford University Press, 1989, pp. 1–7.

Home, R.W. (2004), 'Science for a Dry Continent: The Rise and Fall of CSIRO's Rainmaking Project', in Sherratt, T., T. Griffiths and L. Robin (eds), *A Change in the Weather: Climate and Culture in Australia*, Sydney: Halstead Press in association with the National Museum of Australia.

Hong F. (1945a), 'On the New Provincial Regions' (xin shengqu lun), *Dagong pao*, 2 October.

Hong F. (1945b), 'Reconstruring Provincial Regions: A Preliminary Discussion' (chonghua shengqu fang'an chuyi), *Oriental Journal*, vol. 43, no. 6.

Horwitz, J. (1998), 'All Life Is Connected: the Shaman's Journey', available at www.users.dircon.w.uk/~snail/scss/Articles/All%20Life.htm

Hsueh, T. (1994a), 'A Synthesized Development Index System for China's Regions' (zhongguo diqu zhonghe fazhai zhibiao tixi), in Liu, S., Q. Li, and T. Hsueh (eds.), *Studies on China's Regional Economic Development* (zhongguo diqu jingji yanjiu), Beijing: China Statistics Publishing House, 1994, pp. 22–56.

Hsueh, T. (1994b), 'The Regional Economic Development Pattern in China and Its International Comparison' (zhongguo diqu jingji fazhan de xingtai, jianyu guoji jian de biaojiao), in Liu, S., Q. Li, and T. Hsueh (eds), *Studies on China's Regional Economic Development* (zhongguo diqu jingji yanjiu), Beijing: China Statistics Publishing House, 1994, pp. 74–99.

Hsueh, T., Q. Li and S. Liu (1993), *China's Provincial Statistics*, Boulder: Westview Press.

Hu, A., S. Wang, and X. Kang (1995), *Regional Disparities in China* (zhonguo diqu chayi baogao), Shenyang: Liaoning People's Press.

Hu, B. (1994), 'Inspection of Enforcement of Environmental Protection Laws', *China Environmental Science*, vol. 5, no. 1, pp. 1–8.

Hu, H. (1991), 'The Past, Present, and Future Administrative Divisions in China' (zhongguo xingzheng qu de guoqu, xianzai he weilai), in Chinese Society for Administrative Divisions (ed.), *Studies of China's Administrative Divisions* (zhonguo xingzheng quhua yanjiu), Beijing: China Social Press, 1991, pp. 144–67.

Hu, H. and J. Ding (1990), 'The Past, Present, and Future of China's Administrative Divisions' (woguo xingzhengqu de guoqu, xianzhai he jianglai), *Journal of East China Normal University*, no. 2, pp. 10–17.

Hu, X. (1993), 'On the Typology and Organization of Economic Regions in China' (lun zhonguo jingjiqu de leixing yu zhuzhi), *ACTA Geographica Sinica*, no. 3, vol. 48, pp. 193–202.

Hu, X. and G. Yang (eds.), *China's Coastal Port Cities* (zhongguo yanhai gangkou chengshi), Beijing: Science Press, 1990.

Hu, X., X. Shao, and F. Li (1988), *Chinese Economic Geography* (zhonguo jingji dili), Lixin Financial Economics Series, Shanghai: Lixin Accounting Books Press.

Hu, Y. (1992), 'Guizhou Recovers its Broken Roads with the Neighbouring Provinces' (Guizhou yu linsheng xiutong duantou lu), *People's Daily*, 20 September, p. 1.

Huang, W. (1996), *The Hidden Economy in China* (zhongguo de yinxing jingji), Beijing: China Commercial Press, the second edition.

Huang, Y. (1990), 'Developing the Energy Industry and Protecting the Environment', International Conference on the Integration of the Economic Development and Environment in China, Hainan, China.

Huang, Y. (1999), 'State-Owned Enterprise Reform', in R. Garnaut and L. Song (eds), *China: Twenty Years of Reform*, Canberra: Asia Pacific Press, pp. 95–116.

Huntington, S.P. (1996), *The Clash of Civilization and the Remaking of World Order*, New York: Simon & Schuster.

Hwang, E-G (1993), *The Korean Economies: A Comparison of North and South*, Oxford: Clarendon Press.

Hwang, Q. and W. Cheng (1994), *The 400 years of Macau Economy* (aomen jingji sibai nian), The Macau Foundation, Macau.

Hwang, Z. (1988), *The United States' 203 years: An Analysis of the History and Future for the 'American System'* (meiguo 203 nian: dui 'meiguo tixi' de lishi yu weilai xue de fenxi), Hong Kong: Zhongliu Press.

Institute of Industrial Economics (IIE) (1996), *China's Industrial Development Report* (zhongguo gongye fazhan baogao), Beijing: The Economics and Management Press.

International Labour Office (1993), *Statistical Yearbook*, Washington, DC.

International Monetary Fund (various years), *Direction of Trade Statistics*, Washington, DC: the International Monetary Fund (IMF).

Isard, W. (1949; 1990), 'Gravity, Potential, and Spatial Interaction Models', in Christine Smith (ed.), *Practical Methods of Regional Science and Empirical Applications: Selected Papers of Walter Isard*, vol. 2, New Work: New York University Press.

Jalal, F., and N. Sardjunani (2006), 'Increasing Literacy in Indonesia', Paris: UNESCO, available from http://portal.unesco.org/education/en/file_download.php/5a47778d61b0875d540b0bd837b65ce8Jalal.doc

Jao, J.C. and C.K. Leung (eds), *China's Special Economic Zones: Policies, Problems and Prospects*, Oxford: Oxford University Press, 1986.

Jian, T. (1996), 'The Disequilibrated of Regional Economic Development and the Reform of Fiscal System in China' (zhongguo quyu jingji bu pingheng fazhan yu shuizhi gaige), *Economic Highlights* (jingjixue xiaoxi bao), 18 October, no. 198, p. 2.

Jian, T., J.D. Sachs and A.M. Warner (1996), 'Trends in Regional Inequality in China', *China Economic Review*, vol. 7, no. 1, pp. 1–22.

Jiang, Z. (1995), 'Continue to Promote the Reunification of the Motherland', *China Daily*, 2 February, pp. 1 and 2.

Jiang, Z. (1998), 'Speech Commemorating the 20th Anniversary of the Party's Third Plenum of the 11th Party Congress', 19 December, Beijing: the Great Hall of the People.

Jiang, Z. (2002), 'Report to the 16th National Congress if the CCP', 8 November, Beijing: the Great Hall of the People.

Jiao, J.J. and D. Wen (2004), 'Perspectives on Chinese Ground Water Resources', *Ground Water*, vol. 42, No. 4, pp. 488–90.

Jin, G. and Q. Liu (1984), *Prosperity and Crises – On the Ultrastable Structure of the Federal System in China* (xingsheng yu weiji–lun zhongguo fengjian shehui de chao wending jiegou), Changsha: Hunan People's Press.

Jin, H., Y. Qian, and B.R. Weingast (2001), 'Regional Decentralization and Fiscal Incentives: Federalism, Chinese Style', mimeo, Stanford University.

JPSB (1990), 'Please Read the Results of An Investigation to Evaluate the Quality of Data for the Three Indices' (sanxiang zhibiao shuju zhiliang ruhe, qingkan diaocha pinggu jieguo), by Jilin Provincial Statistical Bureau, *China Statistics* (zhongguo tongji), no. 2, pp. 27–8.

Kan, C-Y (1994), *The Emergency of the Golden Economic Triangle – Mainland China, Hong Kong and Taiwan*, Taipei: Lifework Press.

Kang, X. (2002), 'An Analysis of Mainland China's Political Stability in the Coming 3–5 Years', *Strategy and Management* (in Chinese), no. 3, pp. 1–15.

Kao, C. and E. Shong (1994), 'A Positive Analysis of the Indirect Trade between the Two Sides of the Taiwan Strait via the Third Areas', Chunghua Institution for Economic Research, Taipei, September.

Keidel, A. (1995), 'China's Regional Disparities', World Bank.

Khan, A.R., K. Griffin, C. Riskin and R. Zhao (1993), 'Household Income and Its Distribution in China', in Griffin, K. and R. Zhao (eds), *The Distribution of Income in China*, New York: St. Martin's Press, 1993, pp. 25–73.

Kim, K-H and E.S. Mills (1990), 'Urbanization and Regional Development in Korea', in Kwon, J.K. (ed.), *Korean Development*, New York: Green Press, 1990.

Knight, J. and S. Li (1993), 'The Determinants of Educational Attainment in China', in Griffin, K. and R. Zhao (eds), *The Distribution of Income in China*, New York: St Martin's Press, 1993, pp. 285–330.

Knight, J. and S. Li (1995), 'Fiscal Decentralization, Redistribution and Reform in China', Working paper, no. 168, Institute of Economics and Statistics, Oxford University.

Kolm, S.-C. (1976a), 'Unequal Inequalities I', *Journal of Economic Theory*, vol. 12, pp. 416–42.

Kolm, S.-C. (1976b), 'Unequal Inequalities II', *Journal of Economic Theory*, vol. 13, pp. 82–111.

Kolm, S.-C. (1977), 'Multidimensional Equaliterianisms', *Quarterly Journal of Economics*, vol. 91, pp. 1–13.

Kornai, J. (1992), *The Socialist System*, Princeton, NJ: Princeton University Press.

Krugman, P.R. (1995), 'Growing World Trade: Causes and Consequences', *Brookings Papers on Economic Activity*, no. 1, 327–62.

Lam, W.W. (1999), *The Era of Jiang Zemin*, Singapore: Prentice Hall.

Lardy, N.R. (1975), 'Centralization and Decentralization in China's Fiscal Management', *China Quarterly*, vol. 61, pp. 25–60.

Lardy, N.R. (1978), *Economic Growth and Income Distribution in the People's Republic of China*, New York: Cambridge University Press.

Lardy, N.R. (1980), 'Regional Growth and Income Distribution in China', in Denberger, R.F. (ed.), *China's Development Experience in Comparative Perspective*, Cambridge: Harvard University Press, 1980.

Lau, L., Y. Qian, and G. Roland (2000), 'Reform without Losers: An Interpretation of China's Dual-Track Approach to Reforms', *Journal of Political Economy*, vol. 108, pp. 120–63.

Lee, F. (1995), 'The Development of the Cross-Taiwan Strait Trade Relations: Present Situation, Issues, and Measures', *Taiwan Studies*, no. 2.

Legal Daily, 11 October, 1996, Beijing.

Lemione, F. (2000), *FDI and the Opening Up of China's Economy*, Paris: Centre d'etudes Prospectives et d'Informations Internationales (CEPII).

Lenssen, N. (1993), 'All the Coal in China', World Watch, March–April, pp. 22–30.

Leung, C.K. (1980), *China: Railway Patterns and National Goals*, Department of Geography, The University of Chicago, Research Paper no. 195.

Li, C. (1957), *The Beginnings of Chinese Civilization: Three Lectures Illustrated with Finds at Anyang*, Seattle: University of Washington Press.

Li, D. (1998), 'Changing Incentives of the Chinese Bureaucracy', *American Economic Review*, vol. 88(2), pp. 393–7.

Li, J. and M. Fan (1994), 'A Comparison of the Regional Structures for the Economic Development in China During Pre- and Post-reform Periods' (gaige kaifang qianhou zhongguo jingji fazhan quyu jiegou de bijiao), pp. 57–73, in Liu, S., Q. Li and T. Hsueh (eds), *Studies on China's Regional Economic Development* (zhongguo diqu jingji yanjiu), Beijing: China Statistics Publishing House, 1994.

Li, N. (1997), 'Pearl River Delta Heading Towards Modernization', *Beijing Review*, vol. 40, no. 4, pp. 12–13.

Li, S. (2004), 'China's Urban and Rural Income Surveys', *Journal of Financial Economics* (caijing zazhi), No. 3.

Li, S., Z. Wu, and C. Wu (1994), 'A Quantitative Analysis of the Inter-Regional Linkages in China' (zhongguo quji lianxi de shuliang fenxi), in Development Research Center of the State Council (ed.), *The Regional Coordinate Development Strategy in China* (zhonguo quyu xietiao fazhan zhanlue), Beijing: China Economy Press, 1994, pp. 139–75.

Li, W. (1997), 'The Impact of the Chinese Reform on the Performance of Chinese State-Owned Enterprises, 1980–89', *Journal of Political Economy*, vol. 105, pp. 1080–1106.

Li, X., W. Zhang, and J. Zhong (1989), 'Set-up the Wage System Oriented at Improving Efficiency' (jianli yi tigao xiaolu wei daoxiang de gongzhi zhidu), *The Economic Research*, no. 2, pp. 34–40.

Li, Y. (1996), 'Taiwan to Enhance the 'South-Oriented Policy' and Enlarge the Investment Area' (Taiwan kuoda 'nanxia zhengce' touzhi fanwei), *International Trade News*, 16 May, p. 2.

Li, Z. (1993), 'In-Depth Exploration of the Question of Regional Blockades', *Chinese Economic Studies*, vol. 26, no. 5, pp. 23–36.

Liang, W. (1982), 'Balanced Development of Industry and Agriculture', in Xu, D. and others (eds.), *China's Search for Economic Growth: The Chinese Economy Since 1949*, Beijing: New World Press, 1982, pp. 152–78.

Liang, Z. (1978), 'The Political Corruption and Social Uprisings in the Late Qing Dynasty: A Quantitative Analysis' (wanqing zhi zhengzhi yu shehui shaoluan), *Journal of the Research Institute for Chinese Culture*, vol. 9, Chinese University of Hong Kong.

Liao, J. (1982), 'Size of Industrial Enterprises Operation and Choice of Technology', in Xu, D. and others (eds), *China's Search for Economic Growth: The Chinese Economy Since 1949*, Beijing: New World Press, 1982, pp. 130–44.

Liew, L. (1999), 'The Impact of the Asian Financial Crisis on China: the Macroeconomy and State-Owned Enterprise Reform', *Management International Review*, vol. 39 (4), pp. 85–104.

Liew, L. (2000), 'China's Economic Reform Experience: the End of a Pareto-Improving Strategy', *China Information*, vol. 14 (2), pp. 129–68.

Liew, L. Bruszt, and L. He (2003), 'Causes, National Costs, and Timing of Reform', Thematic Paper, Washington, DC: GDN.

Lin, C. (1995), 'The Reform of State-owned Enterprises in China', unpublished draft, University of Oxford, Oxford.

Lin, F. and J. Liu (1996), 'Towards the 21st Century: the Regional Disparities of China's Population' (maixiang 21 shiji: zhongguo renkou de diqu chayi), *Population Studies* (renkou yanjiu), no. 2, pp. 10–14.

Lin, J. (1992), 'Rural Reforms and Agricultural Growth in China', *American Economic Review*, vol. 82, pp. 34–51.

Linder, S.B. (1961), *An Essay on Trade and Transformation*, New York: John Wiley.

Ling, Y., F. Xu and J. Chen (1995), 'Be Attention to the Overstatement Wind!' (jingti! fukua feng), *Economic Tribune* (jingji luntan), no. 7, pp. 18–19.

Linnemann, H. (1966), *An Econometric Study of International Trade Theory*, Amsterdam: North-Holland.

Lipton, D. and J. Sachs (1990), 'Creating a Market Economy in Eastern Europe: The Case of Poland', *Brookings Papers on Economic Activity*, vol. 75–133.

Litwack, J. and Y. Qian (1998), 'Balanced or Unbalanced Development: Special Economic Zones as Catalysts for Transition', *Journal of Comparative Economics*, vol. 26, pp. 117–41.

Liu, B. and J. Liao (1993, eds.), *China's Frontier Opening and the Neighbouring Countries* (zhongguo yanian kaifang yu zhoubian guojia shichang), Beijing: The Legal Press.

Liu, G. (1984), *A Study of China's Economic Development Strategy Issues* (zhonguo jingji fazhan zhanlue wenti yanjiu), Shanghai: Shanghai People's Press.

Liu, G. (1994), 'China's Regional Economic Development Strategy – An Evaluation and Prospect' (zhongguo diqu jingji fazhan zhanlue de pinggu yu zhaiwang), in Liu, S., Q. Li, and T. Hsueh (eds), *Studies on China's Regional Economic Development* (zhongguo diqu jingji yanjiu), Beijing: China Statistics Publishing House, 1994, pp. 1–13.

Liu, G. (2004), 'A Legal Blank Results from the Competition of Rainmaking by Five Cities and Prefectures in Henan province' (in Chinese), *Dahe Bao* (The Big River News), 12 July, Zhengzhou, Henan Province, also cited by *China Daily* (2004b).

Liu, J. (1996), *China's Administrative Divisions: Theory and Practice* (zhongguo xingzheng quhua de lilun yu shijian), Shanghai: East China Normal University Press.

Liu, K.L. (1991), *100 Ancient Chinese Fables*, Beijing: China Foreign Translations Publishing House and the Commercial Press (Hong Kong) Ltd.

Liu, S. (1982), 'Economic Planning', in Xu, D. and others (eds), *China's Search for Economic Growth: The Chinese Economy Since 1949*, Beijing: New World Press, 1982, pp. 28–51.

Liu, S., Y. Gong, Q. Li and Y. Wu (1994), 'The Regional Income Disparity in China: Measurement, Analysis, and Policy Suggestions' (zhongguo ge diqu shouru chayi de jishuan, fenxi yu zhengze jianyi), in Liu, S., Q. Li, and T. Hsueh (eds), *Studies on China's Regional Economic Development* (zhongguo diqu jingji yanjiu), Beijing: China Statistics Publishing House, 1994, pp. 142–3.

Liu, T. (1995), 'Changes to China's Economic System Structure' (zhongguo jingji tizhi jiegou de yanbain), *Management World*, no. 3, pp. 51–6.

Liu, Z. (1983), 'On the Construction of the Third-front Area' (lun shanxian jianshe), Department of Planning and Statistics, The People's University of China, Beijing.

Liu, Z. (1994), 'The Overall Production Allocation and the Regional Coordinate Development' (zhongti shengchanli peizhi he quyu xietiao fazhan), in Development Research Center of the State Council (ed.), *The Regional Coordinate Development Strategy in China* (zhonguo quyu xietiao fazhan zhanlue), Beijing: China Economy Press, 1994, pp. 15–63.

Lo, C. (2004), 'Bank Reform: How Much Time Does China Have?' *The China Business Review*, available at: http://www.chinabusinessreview.com/public/0403/chilo.html.

Lyons, T. (1992), 'Interprovincial Disparities in China: Output and Consumption, 1952–1957', *Economic Development and Cultural Change*, vol. 39, pp. 471–506.

Ma, H. and S. Sun (1981) (eds), *A Study of the Economic Structure of China – Part 2* (zhongguo jingji ji egou ynagiu, xia), Beijing: the People's Press.

Maddison, A. (1996), A Retrospect for the 200 Years of the World Economy, 1820–1992, Paris: OECD Development Centre.

Maasourmi, E. (1986), 'The Measurement and Decomposition of Multidimensional Inequality', *Econometrica*, vol. 54, pp. 771–9.

Maddison, A. (2001), *The World Economy: A Millennial Perspective*, Paris: OECD Development Centre.

Magrath, W. and P. Arens (1989), 'The Costs of Soil Erosion in Java: A Natural Resource Accounting approach', World Bank Environmental Department Working Paper no. 18.

Mäler, K.-G. (1974), *Environmental Economics: A Theoretical Enquiry*, Baltimore: Johns Hopkins University Press.

Mansfield, E., and R. Bronson (1997), 'The Political Economy of Major-Power Trade Flows', in Mansfield, Edward, and Helen Milner (eds), *The Political Economy of Regionalism*, New York: Columbia University Press.

Mao, Z. (1949), 'The Bankrupt of the Idealist Conception of History', pp. 451–9, in *Selected Works of Mao Tse-tung*, vol. IV, Beijing: Foreign Languages Press, 1975.

Mao, Z. (1956), 'On the Ten Major Relations', in *Selected Works of Mao Tse-tung*, vol. V, Beijing: Foreign Languages Press, 1975.

Mao, Z. (1957), 'Be Activists in Promoting the Revolution', pp. 483–97, in *Selected Works of Mao Tse-tung*, vol. V, Beijing: Foreign Languages Press, 1975.

Marea, P. (1985), *Dollar GNPs of the USSR and Eastern Europe*, Baltimore: Johns Hopkins University Press.

Markusen, J. (1986), 'Explaining the Volume of Trade: An Eclectic Approach', *American Economic Review*, vol. 76 (Dec.), 1002–1011.

Maruyama, N. (1982), 'The Mechanism of China's Industrial Development: Background to the Shift in Development Strategy', *The Developing Economies*, vol. 20, pp. 437–71.

Mastel, G. (1996), 'The WTO and the Nonmarket Economies', *The Washington Quarterly*, 1998 (Summer), vol. 21.

Mastel, G. (1998), 'Beijing at a Bay', *Foreign Policy*, autumn, No. 104.

McKinnon, R. (1991a), 'Financial Control in the Transition from Classical Socialism to a Market Economy', *Journal of Economic Perspectives* vol. 5, pp. 107–22.

McKinnon, R. (1991b), *The Order of Economic Liberalization*, Baltimore: John Hopkins University Press.

McMillan, J. and B. Naughton (1992), 'How to Reform a Planned Economy: Lessons from China', *Oxford Review of Economic Policy*, vol. 8, pp. 130–43.

Meadows, D. H. (1972), *Limits to Growth: A Report of the Club of Rome's Project on the Predicament of Mankind*, Rome: the Club of Rome.

Minami, R. (1994), *The Economic Development of China: A Comparison with the Japanese Experience*, English edition, London: Macmillan Press.

Ministry of Energy (MOE) (1991), *Energy in China*, Beijing: Ministry of Energy.

Mizoguchi, T., H. Wang and Y. Matsuda (1989) 'A Comparison of Real Consumption Level Between Japan and the People's Republic of China: The First Approach to the Application of the ICP Method to Chinese Data', *Hitotsubashi Journal of Economics*, June.

Montinola, G., Y. Qian and B. Weingast (1995), 'Federalism, Chinese Style: the Political Basis for Economic Success in China', *World Politics*, vol. 48, pp. 50–81.

Morici, P. (1997), 'Barring Entry? China and the WTO', *Current History*, September, vol. 96.

Murphy, K., A. Shielfer, and R. Vishny (1992), 'The Transition to a Market Economy: Pitfalls of Partial Reform', *Quarterly Journal of Economics*, vol. 107, pp. 889–906.

Murrell, P. (1992), 'Evolution in Economics and in the Economic Reform of the Centrally Planned Economies', in C. Clague and G. Raisser (eds.), *The Emergence of Market Economies in Eastern Europe*, Cambridge: Blackwell, pp. 35–53.

Nair, K.R.G. (1985), 'Inter-State Income Differentials in India, 1970–71 to 1979–80', in Mishra, G.P. (ed.), *Regional Structure of Development and Growth in India*, New Delhi: Ashish Publishing House, 1985.

Naughton, B. (1988), 'The Third Front: Defense Industrialization in the Chinese Interior', *China Quarterly*, vol. 115, pp. 227–304.

NBS (various years), *China Statistical Yearbook*, various issues, Beijing: China Statistics Publishing House.

NEPA (various years), *Report on the State of the Environment*, Beijing: National Environment Protection Agency.

Newcombe, K. (1984), 'An Economic Justification of Rural Afforestation: The Case of Ethiopia', Energy Department Paper no. 16, World Bank, Washington, DC.

Nolan, P. and J. Sender (1992), 'Death Rates, Life Expectancy and China's Economic Reforms: A Critique of A. A. Sen', *World Development*, vol. 20, pp. 1279–303.

Noland, M. (1994), 'Implications of Asian Growth', Washington: Institute for International Economics, mimeo.

Noland, M. (1995), 'The United States and APEC', in Kee, W.S, I-T Hyun and K. Kim (eds.), *APEC and A New Pacific Community: Issues and Prospects*, Seoul: The Sejong Institute, 1995, pp. 69–99.

Noland, M. (2005), 'Affinity and International Trade', Institute for International Economics, Washington, DC, Working Paper Series No. WP 05–3, June.

North, D.C. (1990), *Institutions, Institutional Change and Economic Performance*, Cambridge, Cambridge University Press.

North, D.C. (1997), 'The Contribution of the New Institutional Economics to an Understanding of the Transition Problem', WIDER Annual Lectures, March.

North, D.C. and R.P. Thomas (1973), *The Rise of the Western World*, Cambridge: Cambridge University Press.

North, D.C. (1981), *Structure and Change in Economic History*, New York: Norton.

Nove, A. (1987), 'Planning Economy', in Eatwell, J., M. Milgate and P. Newman (eds), *The New Palgrave: A Dictionary of Economics*, London: The Macmillan Press Limited, 1987, pp. 879–85.

NPC (1979), 'Law of the People's Republic of China on the Joint Ventures with Chinese and Foreign Investment' (zhonghua renmin gongheguo zhongwai hezi qiye fa), Beijing: National People's Congress of China.

NPC (1980), 'The Regulations Concerning the Special Economic Zones of Guangdong Province, the People's Republic of China' (zhonghua renmin gongheguo guangdong sheng jingji tequ de youguan tiaoli), Beijing: National People's Congress of China, 26 August.

NPC (1993), 'Anti-unfair Competition Law' (fan bu zhengdang jingzhen fa), Beijing: National People's Congress of China.

NPC (1994), 'Law of Protecting the Taiwanese Compatriots' Investment' (baohu Taiwan tongbao tuzhi fa), Beijing: National People's Congress of China, March.

NPC (2000), 'Meteorological Law of the People's Republic of China', Beijing: the 12th Meeting of the Standing Committee of the Ninth National People's Congress of the People's Republic of China, 31 October.

OECD (2000), 'Main Developments and Impacts of Foreign Direct Investment on China's Economy', Directorate for Financial, Fiscal and Enterprise Affairs Working Papers on International Investment, No. 2000/4, Paris: OECD, December

Oguledo, V., and C. MacPhee (1994), 'Gravity Models: A Reformulation and an Application to Discriminatory Trade Arrangement', *Applied Economics*, vol. 26, 107–20.

Ohlin, B. (1933), *Interregional and International Trade*, Cambridge, MA: Harvard University Press.

Oi, J. (1992), 'Fiscal Reform and the Economic Foundations of Local State Corporatism in China', *World Politics*, vol. 45 (Oct.). 99–129.

*Oxford Advanced Learner's Dictionary*, 1974, 3rd edn, Oxford: Oxford University Press.

Oksenberg, M. and J. Tong (1991), 'The Evolution of Central–Provincial Fiscal Relations in China, 1971–1984: the Formal System', *The China Quarterly*, March, pp. 1–32.

Ottolenghi, D. and A. Steinherr (1993), 'Yugoslavia: Was It A Winner's Curse?', *Economies of Transition*, vol. 1, no. 2.

*Pai Shing Semimonthly*, 1 March 1986.

Pearce, D., E. Barbier and A. Markandya (1988), 'Sustainable Development and Cost-Benefit Analysis', Paper Presented at the Canadian Assessment Workshop on Integrating Economic and Environment Chinese Economic Sustainability Assessment.

*People's Daily* (1992), 'On Regional Economy' (lun quyu jingji) (editorial), 5 November, Beijing.

*People's Daily* (2004), 'A Reflection on the Competition of Rainmaking by Five Cities and Prefectures' (in Chinese), Beijing: People's Daily, 22 July, p. 16.

*People's Daily*, 18 January 1995.

*People's Daily*, 26 November 1989, Beijing.

Perlack, R.D., M. Russell and Z. Shen (1993), 'Reducing Greenhouse Gas Emissions in China: International Legal and Cultural Constrains and Opportunities', *Global Environmental Change*, March.

Portes, R. (1990), 'Introduction to Economic Transformation of Hungary and Poland', *European Economy*, vol. 43, pp. 11–18.

Pöyhönen, P. (1963), 'A Tentative Model for the Volume of Trade Between Countries', *Weltwirtschaftliches Archiv*, vol. 90 (1), 93–9.

Price Yearbook of China (PYC), 1995, Beijing: China Price Press.

Qian, Y. (2001; 2002), 'How Reform Worked in China', draft, also in D. Rodirk (ed.), *In Search of Prosperity: Analytic Narratives on Economic Growth*, Princeton, NJ: Princeton University Press, 2004, pp. 297–333.

Qian, Z. and G. Zhang (2001), 'Comprehensive Report on the Sustainable Development of China's Water Resources', *Research Report on Sustainable Development on China's Water Resources*, vol. 1, pp. 3–32.

Qu, G. (1990), 'Thoughts about the Policies for the Coordinated Development of China's Economy and Environment', presented at the International Conference on the Integration of Economic Development and Environment in China, Beijing, September, pp. 1–15.

Ramsey, S.R. (1989), *The Languages of China*, Princeton, NJ: Princeton University Press.

Rauch, J.E. (1999), 'Networks versus Markets in International Trade', *Journal of International Economics*, vol. 48, 7–35.

Rauch, J.E. and V. Trindade (2002), 'Ethnic Chinese Networks in International Trade', *Review of Economics and Statistics*, vol. 84(1), 116–30.

Repetto, R. *et al.* (1989), Wasting Assets: Natural Resources and the National Income Accounts, Washington, DC: World Resources Institute.

Reti, P. (2001), 'China's Path toward a Market Economy: Interview with a Prominent Reformer', *Transition Newsletter*, Oct.–Nov.–Dec., pp. 17–19.

Ricardo, D. (1817), 'On the Principles of Political Economy and Taxation', in Sraffa, P. (ed.), *The Works and Correspondence of David Ricardo*, vol. 1, Cambridge: Cambridge University Press, 1951, ch. vii.

Richardson, G. P. and A. L. Pugh III (1981), *Introduction to SD Modeling with DYNAMO*, Cambridge, MA: The MIT Press.

Riskin, C. (1987), *China's Political Economy: The Quest for Development Since 1949*, Oxford: Oxford University Press.

Riskin, C. (1994), 'The Distribution of Income and Poverty in Rural China' (zhonguo nongchun de shouru fenpei yu pingkun), in Zhao, R., K. Griffin (eds), *The Household Income Distribution in China* (zhongguo de jumin shouru fenpei), Beijing: China Social Science Press, pp. 313–51.

Rodrik, D. (1996), 'Understanding Economic Policy Reform', *Journal of Economic Literature* vol. XXXIV (March), pp. 9–41.

Roland, G. (1991), 'Political Economy of Sequencing Tactics in the Transition Period', in L. Csaba (ed.), *Systemic Change and Stabilization in Eastern Europe*, Aldershot: Dartmouth, pp. 47–64.

Rose, A.K. (2004), 'Macroeconomic Determinants of International Trade', NBER working paper, Cambridge, MA: National Bureau of Economic Research.

Russell, M. (1990), 'Energy in China', presented at the International Conference on the Integration of 'China', *Ambio*, vol. 21, no. 4, pp. 303–7.

Ryan, B.F. and W.D. King (1997), 'A Critical Review of the Australian Experience in Cloud Seeding', *Bulletin of the American Meteorological Society*, vol. 78, pp. 239–54.

Sachs, J. (1993), *Poland's Jump to the Market Economy*, Linel Robbins Lectures, London: MIT Press.

Sachs, J. and A. Warner (1995), 'Economic Reform and the Process of Global Integration', *Brookings Papers on Economic Activity*, vol. 1995, No. 1, pp. 1–95.

Sachs, J. and W.T. Woo (1994), 'Structural Factors in the Economic Reforms of China, Eastern Europe, and the Former Soviet Union', *Economic Policy*, vol. 18, No. 1.

Savcie, D.J. (1992), *Regional Economic Development: Canada's Search for Solution*, 2nd edn, Toronto: University of Toronto Press

SCSR (1996), 'The Environment of Changes in the Role of the Government in China: Analysis of a Survey', in State Commission of System Reform (ed.), *Chinese Economic Almanac 1996*, Beijing: China Statistical Press.

Segal, G. (1994), 'China's Changing Shape', vol. 73, *Foreign Affairs*, pp. 40–65.

Sen, A. (1992), 'Life and Death in China', *World Development*, pp. 1305–1312

Sen, A. (2004), 'Remarks at the Inaugural Meeting of the GDN Conference on Understanding Reform', Global Development Conference, New Delhi, 27 January.

Shanker, R. (1996), 'Diversity and Development', Québec, Canada: International Development Information Center.

Shen, L. and Y. Dai (1990), 'Chinese Federal Economy: Mechanisms, Impacts, and Sources' (zhongguo de zhuhou jingji: jizhi, houguo he genyuan), *Jingji Yanjiu* (Economic Research Journal), no. 3, pp. 10–13.

Shirk, S. (1990), 'The Political Price of Reform Cycles: Elite Politics in Chinese-Style Economic Reforms', ms.

Shirk, S. (1993), *The Political Logic of Economic Reform in China*, Berkeley, CA: University of California Press.

Shirk, S. (1994), *How China Opened Its Door*, Washington, DC: Brookings Institution.

Shorrocks, A. (1980), 'The Class of Additionally Decomposable Inequality Measures', *Econometrica*, vol. 48, pp. 613–25.

Shorrocks, A. and J.E. Foster (1987), 'Transfer Sensitive Inequality Measure', *Review of Economic Studies*, vol. 54, pp. 485–97

Sloman, J. (1991), *Economics*, Hertfordshire: Harvester Wheatsheaf.

Smith, A.H. (1890) (1972), *Chinese Characteristics*, 5th edn, Shaunow, Ireland: Irish University Press.

Smith, D.M. (1987), *Geography, Inequality and Society*, Cambridge: Cambridge University Press.

Solorzano, R. *et al.* (1991), 'Accounts Overdue: Natural Resource Depreciation in Costa Rica', Washington, DC: World Resources Institute.

Solow, R.M. (1991), 'Sustainability – An Economist's Perspective', Department of Economics, Massachusetts Institute of Technology, Cambridge, MA.

Song, X. (1996), 'China's Regional Economic Development and Its Convergence', *The Economic Research*, no. 9, pp. 38–44.

*South China Morning Post* (2004), 'Soldiers Could Shoot at Clouds to End Drought', Hong Kong: *South China Morning Post*, July.

SPC (1996), *China Price* (zhonguo wujia), Institute of Market and Prices, State Planning Commission, Beijing, January.

SSB (1987b), *Materials of the 1985 Industry Census in the People's Republic of China* (zhonghua renmin gonghe guo 1985 nian gongye pucha zhiliao), Beijing: China Statistics Publishing House.

SSB (1988b), *China Population Statistical Yearbook* (zhongguo renkou nianjian), Beijing: China Statistics Publishing House.

SSB (1989b), *China Yearbook for Price Statistics* (zhongguo jiage tongji nianjian), Beijing: China Statistics Publishing House.

SSB (1990b), *A Compilation of Historical Statistical Materials of China's Provinces, Autonomous Regions and Municipalities (1949–89)* (quanguo ge sheng, zhiziqu, zhixiashi lishi tongji zhiliao huibian 1949–1989), Beijing: China Statistics Publishing House.

SSB (1991b), *China Energy Statistical Yearbook* (zhongguo nengyuan tongji nianjian), Beijing: China Statistics Publishing House.

SSB (1991c), *Some Statistical Materials of Social Development for the Major Countries and Regions 1990* (shijie zhuyao guojia he diqu shehui fazhan bijiao tongji zhiliao 1990), Beijing: China Statistics Publishing House.

SSB (1993b), *China Population Yearbook* (zhongguo renkou nianjian), Beijing: China Statistics Publishing House.

SSB (1994b), *The 1993 Abstracts of International Economic and Social Statistics* (guoji jingji he shehui tongji tiyao 1993), Beijing: China Statistics Publishing House.

SSB (1996b), *China Industrial Economic Statistical Yearbook 1995*, Beijing: China Statistics Publishing House.

SSB (various years), *China Statistical Yearbook*, various issues, Beijing: China Statistics Publishing House.

Standing Committee of NPC (1979), 'Messages to the Taiwanese Compatriots' (gao Taiwan tongbao shu), Beijing: National People's Congress of PRC, January.

Standler, R.B. (2002), 'Weather Modification Law in the USA', draft, available at: www.rbs2.com/index.htm

State Council (1980a), 'Provisional Regulations Relating to the Development and Protection of Socialist Competition' (guanyu fazhan yu baohu shehui zhuyi jingzheng de zhanxing tiaoli), Beijing: State Council.

State Council (1980b), 'Provisional Regulations Concerning the Promotion of Economic Unification', Beijing: State Council.

State Council (1981), 'Regulations of the P. R. China Concerning the Resolutions of the Disputes on Borders of the Administrative Divisions' (zhonghua renmin gongheguo xingzhengqu bianjie zhengyi culi tiaoli), Beijing: State Council.

State Council (1982), 'Notice Relating to the Prohibition of Blockades in the Sale of Industrial Products' (guanyu jinzhi gongye chanpin xiaoshou bilei de tongzhi), Beijing.

State Council (1984), 'Provisional Regulations on the Enlargement of Autonomy of State Industrial Enterprises', 10 May, Beijing: State Council.

State Council (1986), 'Regulations on Some Issues Concerning the Further Promotion of Horizontal Economic Unification', Beijing: State Council, 26 March.

State Council (1988a), 'Regulations of the P. R. China Concerning the Resolutions of the Disputes on Borders of the Administrative Divisions', Beijing: State Council, revised version.

State Council (1988b), 'A Retrospect on the Reforms of the Economic System and the Prospects on the Basic Thought of the Future Reforms' (jingji tizhi gaige de huigu yu jinhou gaige de jiben shilu), in CCPCC Party School (ed.), *The Basic Plans for China's Economic Reform, 1979–87*, Beijing: the CCPCC Party School Press.

State Council (1990), 'An Administrative Order to Remove all Regional Blockades to Trade', Beijing: State Council.

State Council (1992), 'Regulations on the Transformation of the Operating Mechanisms of State-owned Industrial Enterprises', Beijing: State Council, 22 July.

State Council (1993), 'Resolution Concerning the Promotion of the Development of the TVEs in the Central and Western Area', Beijing: State Council, December.

State Council (1996), 'Decision of the State Council on Several Issues Relating to Environmental Protection', 3 August, Beijing: State Council.

State Council (2002), 'Regulations Concerning the Artificial Weather Modification', Rule of the State Council of the People's Republic of China, No. 248, 19 March, Beijing: State Council.

State Council Information Office (SCIO) (1996), 'On Sino-US Trade Balance', *Beijing Review*, vol. 40, no. 14, pp. 20–7.

State Economic and Trade Commission (1994), 'China Energy Annual Review' (zhongguo nengyuan nianping), Department of Resources Conservation & Comprehensive Utilization, State Economic and Trade Commission, People's Republic of China.

State Economic and Trade Commission (1996), China Energy Annual Review (zhongguo nengyuan nianping), Department of Resources Conservation & Comprehensive Utilization, State Economic and Trade Commission and China Energy Society, Beijing.

State Industrial and Commercial Administration (SICA) (1995), *A Compilation of Industrial and Commercial Statistics* (gongshang xingzheng guanli tongji huibian), Beijing: State Industrial and Commercial Administration.

State Planning Commission and State Science and Technology Commission (1994), *China's Agenda 21 – White Paper on China's Population, Environment, and Development in the 21st Century*, Beijing: China Environmental Science Press.

State Science and Technology Commission (1988), *Guide to China's Science and Technology Policy* (zhongguo kexue jishu zhengce zhinan), Beijing: Science and Technology Compilation Press.

Statistical Division of Hong Kong Government: *Re-exports by All Countries of Origin by Importing Countries by Items*, various years.

Stewart, J.Q. (1948), 'Demographic Gravitation: Evidence and Applications', *Sociometry*, vol. 2, 31–58.

Stigliz, J. E. (1999), 'Whither Reform? – Ten Years of Transition', Keynote Address to the World Bank Annual Bank Conference on Development Economics, Washington, DC: World Bank.

Streifel, S. (2006), 'Impact of China and India on Global Commodity Markets: Focus on Metals and Minerals and Petroleum', draft, Development Prospects Group, World Bank, Washington, DC.

Study Group of CASS (1994), 'Theoretical Thinking and Policy Choice on Chinese Economy Towards the 21st Century' (zhongguo jingji jinru 21 shiji de lilun shikao yu zhengce xuanzhe), *Economic Research Journal* (jingji yanjiu), no. 8, pp. 1–14.

Summers, L. (1992), 'The Rise of China', *Transition Newsletter*, Vol. 3, no. 6, The World Bank, Washington, DC.

Summers, R. and A. Heston (1991), 'The Penn World Table (Mark 5), An Expended Set of International Comparisons, 1950–1988', *Quarterly Journal of Economics*, pp. 327–68.

Sun J. (1987), *Territory, Resources, and Regional Development* (guotu, zhiyuan kaifa he quyu fazhan), Beijing: People's Education Press.

Sun, G., S.G. MacNulty, J. Moore, C. Bunch, and J. Ni (2002), 'Potential Impacts of Climate Change on Rainfall Erosivity and Water Availability in China in the Next 100 Years', the 12th International Soil Conservation Conference, Beijing, China, May.

Sun, Z. (1993), 'Causes of Trade Wars over Farm Products, Their Effects, and Suggested Solutions', *Chinese Economic Studies*, vol. 26, no. 5, pp. 95–104.

Sung, Y.-W. (2004), *Greater China: An Emerging Economic Reality*, New York: Palgrave Macmillan.

Svejnar, J. (1989), 'A Framework for the Economic Transformation of Czechoslovakia', *Planning Economic Report*, vol. 5, pp. 1–18.

Tang, T. (1982), 'The Economic Responsibility System and Accounting in China's Enterprises', *Caiwu Yu Kuaiji* (property and accounting), January, pp. 7–11.

Tang, W. and W. Parish (1998), *The Changing Social Contract: Chinese Urban Life Under Reform*, New York: Cambridge University Press.

Teng, W. (1982), 'Socialist Modernization and the Pattern of Foreign Trade', in Xu, D. and others (eds), *China's Search for Economic Growth: The Chinese Economy Since 1949*, Beijing: New World Press, 1982, pp. 167–92.

*The Economic Research Materials*, no. 6, 1996, p. 62.

*The Economist*, various issues.

Tinbergen, J. (1962), 'An Analysis of World Trade Flows, the Linder Hypothesis, and Exchange Risk', in Jan Tinbergen (ed., 1962), *Shaping the World Economy*, New York: The Twentieth Century Fund.

Topping, A.R. (1995), 'Ecological Roulette: Damming the Yangtze', *Foreign Affairs*, September/October, pp. 132–46.

Toshiyuki, M., H. Wang and Y. Matsuda (1989), 'A Comparison of Real Consumption Level Between Japan and the People's Republic of China: The First Approach to the Application of the ICP Method to Chinese Data', *Hitotsubashi Journal of Economics*, June.

Tsui, K. (1991), 'China's Regional Inequality, 1952–1985', *Journal of Comparative Economics*, vol. 15, pp. 1–21.

Tsui, K. (1993), 'Economic Reform and Interprovincial Inequalities in China', Working paper no. 31, Economics Department, the Chinese University of Hong Kong, Hong Kong.

Tsui, K. (1994), 'A Multiregional Measurement of China's Inequalities', in Liu, S., Q. Li and T. Hsueh (eds), *Studies on China's Regional Economic Development* (zhongguo diqu jingji yanjiu), Beijing: China Statistics Publishing House, 1994, pp. 180–98.

UNDP (1994), *China Environment and Sustainable Development Resources Book: A Compendium of Donor Activities*, Beijing: UNDP, April.

UNESCO (various years): *Statistical Yearbook*, Paris: UNESCO.

UNFAO (1992), *Statistical Yearbook*, Rome: United Nations Food and Agricultural Organization.

United Nations (1986; 1996), *Annual Statistical Yearbook*, New York: United Nations.

United Nations (1988), *World Population Prospect*, New York: United Nations.

United Nations (1990a), *SNA Handbook on Integrated Environmental and Economic Accounting*, Preliminary draft of Part I, 'General Concept', New York: United Nations.

United Nations (1990b), *Revised System of National Accounts*, Preliminary draft, New York: United Nations.

United Nations (1994), *Human Development Report 1994*, New York: Oxford University Press.

US Academy of Defense Agency (1993), 'US Arm Control and Disarmament', Washington, DC: US Academy of Defense Agency.

Utah Water Research Laboratory (UWRL) (1971), 'Development of Cold Cloud Seeding Technology for Use in Precipitation Management', Logon: Utah State University, available at: www.encyclopedia.com/html/r1/rainmaki.asp.

Vaclav, S. (1992), 'China's Environment in the 1980s: Some Critical Changes', *Ambio*, vol. 21, no. 6, pp. 431–6.

Vermeer, E.B. (1984), 'Agriculture in China- A Deteriorating Situation', *The Ecologist*, vol. 14, no. 1, pp. 6–14.

von Gemert, H. (2001), 'China's Great Financial Challenge', *Transition Newsletter*, vol. 12 (2), pp. 10–11.

Wakabayashi, K. (1989), *China's Population Problem*, Tokyo: University of Tokyo Press (in Japanese).

Walker, T. (1995), 'Five Nations in Pact to Develop NE Asian Region', *Financial Times* (News: Asia-Pacific), 31 May.

Wang, J. and J. Li (1996), 'China's Energy Development Strategy for the First Half of the 21st Century' (21 shiji qian banye zhongguo de nengyuan fazhan zhanlue), The Research of the Chinese Economic Development Strategy for the First Half of the 21st Century, Report Series no. 8, Institute of Industrial and Tech-Economics, State Planning Commission (SPC), Beijing.

Wang, Q. (1995), 'A Study of the Energy Strategy in China' (zhongguo nengyuan zhanlue yanjiu), Beijing: Academy of Coal Science and Ministry of Coal Industry.

Wang, S. (2003), 'China's Public Health Care: Crisis and Transitions' (zhongguo gonggong weisheng de weiji yu zhuanji), *Comparative Analysis* (Bijiao), vol. 4, 52–88.

Wang, W. (ed., 1986), *China's Special Economic Zones and 14 Coastal Cities*, Beijing: China Zhanwang Press.

Wang, Z. and Y. Dai (1958), 'A Critique on the 'New Population theory'' ('xin renkou lun' pipan), *The Economic Research* (jingji yanjiu) no. 2, pp. 10–14.

Washington Post (2004), 'Chinese Rainmakers Competing for Clouds: Widespread Drought Leads to Regional Rivalries' (by Edward Cody), Foreign Service, 2August, p. A12.

WCCD (1995), *Our Cultural Diversity*, Paris: World Commission for Culture and Development.

Weber, M. (1964), *The Religion in China*, London: Collier Macmillan.

Wedeman, A.H. (1993), 'Editor's Introduction to Chinese Economic Studies', *Chinese Economic Studies*, vol. 26, no. 5 (special issue on regional protection), pp. 1–2.

Wei, H. (1992), 'On the Changing Pattern of The Interregional Income Gaps in China' (lun woguo quji shouru chaju de biandong geju), *The Economic Research* (jingji yanjiu), no. 4, pp. 61–5.

Wei, H. and K. Liu (1994), 'The Analysis of the Regional Differences in China and the forecast of their changing trends' (woguo diqu chayi biandong qushi fenxi ji yuce), *China Industrial Economic Research*, no. 3, pp. 29–36.

Wei, S. (1993), 'Gradualism vs. Big Bang: Speed and Sustainability of Reforms', Mimeo, Harvard University, Cambridge, MA.

Wei, S. (1994), 'Comrade Deng Xiaoping's Concept of 'One country, two systems' and Its Practice', *Foreign Affairs Journal*, no. 33, September, pp. 1–7.

Wei, S. and J. Frankel (1994), 'A 'Greater China' Trade Block?', *China Economic Review*, vol. 5, no. 2, pp. 179–90.

Wei, W. (1994), 'The Imbalance of Regional Economic Development and Disequilibrated Growth of China' (woguo diqu jingji fazhan shiheng yu feijunheng zhengzhang), in Hu, N. and R. Yang (eds.), *Studies of the Disequilibrated Development Issues in the Chinese Economy* (zhongguo jingji feijunheng fazhan wenti yanjiu), Taiyuan: The United Press of Shanxi Universities, 1994, pp. 279–309.

Weingast, B.R. (1995), 'The Economic Role of Political Institutions: Market-Preserving Federalism and Economic Growth', *Journal of Law, Economics, and Organization*, vol. 11.

Wen, Y. (1987), 'The Prospects of the Asia-Pacific Area and the Chinese Circle: An Interview with Chen Kunyao, Director of Asian Studies Center of Hong Kong University' (yatai diqu jingji qianjing he zhongguo: fang xianggang daxue yazhou yanjiu zhongxin zhuren Chen Kunyao), *Economic Review*, 30 November.

Williamson, J. (1965), 'Regional Inequality and the Process of National Development: A Description of the Patterns', *Economic Development and Cultural Change*, vol. 13, no. 4, pp. 165–204.

Williamson, J.C. (1994), 'In Search of a Manual for Technopols', in J. Williamson (ed.), *The Political Economy of Police Reform*, Washington, DC: Institute for International Economics.

Williamson, J. (1995), 'What Washington Means by Policy Reform', *The International Political Economy and the Developing Countries*, vol. 1, 514–28.

Wilson, E.A. (1980), *Sociobiology*, Cambridge, MA: Belknap.

Winters, L.A. and S. Yusuf (2007), 'Introduction: Dancing with Giants', in Winters, L.A. and S. Yusuf (eds), *Dancing with Giants: China and India, and the Global Economy*, pp. 1–34, Washington, DC: World Bank Publications.

Wolf, T. (1985), 'Exchange Rates, Foreign Trade Accounting and Purchasing Power Parity for Centrally Planned Economies', World Bank Staff Working Papers, no. 779.

Woo, W. (1994), 'The Art of Reforming Centrally Planned Economies: Comparing China, Poland and Russia', *Journal of Comparative Economics*, vol. 21, pp. 276–308.

Wong, C. (1992), 'Fiscal Reform and Local Industrialization', *Modern China*, vol. 18 (April), 23–42.

*World Atlas*, Rand McNally & Company, 1994.

World Bank (1981), *China: Development of a Socialist Economy* (zhonguo: shehui zhuyi jingji de fazhan), Beijing: the World Bank.

World Bank (1983), *China: The Development of a Socialist Economy*, Washington, DC: the World Bank.

World Bank (1986), *World Bank Atlas*, Washington, DC: the World Bank.

World Bank (1990), *China: Revenue Mobilization and Tax Policy*, Washington, DC: the World Bank.

World Bank (1991), 'Mexico in Transition: Towards a New Role for the Public Sector', Report 8770–ME, Washington, DC: the World Bank.

World Bank (1992), *STAR–World Development Indicators 1991, Socio-economic Time-series Access and Retrieval System*, Version 2.5, April 1992

World Bank (1993), *World Development Report*, Washington, DC: the World Bank.

World Bank (1996), *From Plan to Market: World Bank Development Report 1996*, New York: Oxford University Press.

World Bank (1997), *China 2020*, Washington, DC: the World Bank.

World Bank (1999), *World Development Indicators CD-ROM*, Washington DC: the World Bank.

*World Bank Atlas 1996*, Washington, DC: the World Bank.

World Commission for Environment and Development (1987), *Our Common Future*, New York: Oxford University Press.

World Resources Institute (WRI) (1985), Tropical Forests.- A Call for Action, International Task Force Report convened by the World Resources Institute, the World Bank, and the United Nations Development Program, Washington, DC.

World Resources Institute (WRI) (1992), *World Resources 1992–93*, Oxford: Oxford University Press.

World Resources Institute (WRI) (2003), *Water Resources and Freshwater Ecosystems*, Washington, DC: World Resources Institute, available at: http://earthtrend.wri.org

Wright, T. (1984), *Coal Mining in China's Economy and Society 1895–1937*, Cambridge: Cambridge University Press.

Wu, C. and F. Hou (1990), *Territorial Development and Planning* (guotu kaifa ahengzi yu guihua), Nanjing: Jiangsu Educational Press, 1990.

Wu, J. and R. Zhao (1987), 'The Dual Pricing System in China's Industry', *Journal of Comparative Economics*, vol. 14 (Nov.).

Wu, R. and Y. Liang (1990), 'Hong Kong – The First Financial and Trade Center in the Far East' (yuandong diyi jinrong maoyi zhongxin–xianggang), in Hu, N. and R. Yang (eds), *Studies of the Disequilibrated Development Issues in the Chinese Economy* (zhongguo jingji feijunheng fazhan wenti yanjiu), Taiyuan: The United Press of Shanxi Universities, 1994, pp. 234–44.

Wu, R.-I. (1996), 'Importance of Integrating China and Taiwan into the WTO System', *Journal of Northeast Asian Studies*, vol. 15, No. 3.

Xiao, L. (1993), 'China's Economic Internationalization: A Prospect', unpublished draft, Institute of American Studies, Chinese Academy of Social Sciences.

Xie, H. (1992), 'The Industrial Development in Macau', in Youths Committee of China Society of Natural Resources (ed.), *The Cross-Taiwan Strait: Sustainable Development of the Issues of Resources and Environment*, Beijing: China Science and Technology Press, 1992, pp. 110–16.

Xu, D. (1995), 'China: Contradictory Measures Frustrate Bank Reform', *Economic Reform Today* (Banking and Financial Reform), No. 1, Center for International Private Enterprise, Washington, http://www.cipe.org/publications/fs/ert/e15/china.htm

Yan, Z. (1995), 'The Cross-Taiwan Strait Financial relations: Situation, Issues, and Prospect', *The Central Bank Quarterly*, vol. 17, no. 4, pp. 54–74.

Yang, D. (1990), 'Patterns of China's Regional Development Strategy', *China Quarterly*, no. 122, pp. 230–57.

Yang, K. (1989), *A Study of Regional Development in China* (zhongguo quyu fazhan yanjiu), Beijing: China Ocean Press.

Yang, K. (1991), 'The Theory and Application of Regional Structure – An Application of the Regional Structure in China' (quyu jiegou lilun yu yingyong–zhongguo quyu jiegou yanjiu), in Sun, S. (ed.), *The Economic Structure: Theory, Application and Policy* (jingji jiegou de lilun, xingyong yu zhengce), Beijing: China Social Science Press, 1991.

Yang, K. (1993), *For a Spatial Integration: China's Market Economy and Regional Development Strategy* (maixiang kongjian yiti hua: zhongguo shichang jingji yu quyu fazhan zhanlue), 'Across the Century Series', Chengdu: Sichuan People's Press.

Yang, S. (1990), 'The Issues of China's Economic Regions' (zhongguo jingji quyu wenti), in Yang, S., Liu Zhenya and Gao Lianqing (eds), *Studies of Chinese Economic Regionalization* (zhongguo jingji quhua yanjiu), Beijing: China Zhanwang Press, pp. 38–43.

Yang, W. (1989), *The Locational Principles – An Economic Analysis of Industrial, Urban, and Regional Locations* (quweilun yuanli: chanye, chengshi he quwei de jingji fenxi), Lanzhou: Gansu People's Press.

Yang, W. (1992a), 'An Empirical Analysis of the Changes in Interregional Income Inequalities' (Diqu jian shouru chaju biandong de shizheng fenxi), *The Economic Research* (jingji yanjiu), no. 1, pp. 70–4.

Yang, W. (1992b), 'Answers to Comrade Dong Fan's Comments' (dui dong Fan tongzhi shangque de dafu), *The Economic Research* (jingji yanjiu), no. 7, pp. 65–6.

Yang, X. (1992), 'The Resource Exploitation and Economic Development in the Greater China Economic Circle' (da zhonuo jingji quan de ziyuan yu jingji fazhan), in Youths Committee of China Society of Natural Resources (ed.), *The Cross-Taiwan Strait: Sustainable Development of the Issues of Resources and Environment*, Beijing: China Science and Technology Press, 1992, pp. 1–5.

Young, A. (2000), 'The Razor's Edge: Distortions and Incremental Reform in the People's Republic of China', *Quarterly Journal of Economics*, vol. 115(4), pp. 1091–1136.

Young, J.C. and H.H. Ho (1993), 'China Moves Against Unfair Competition', *East Asian Executive Report*, September.

Yu, J. (2004), 'Why We Don't Believe Economists', *Sohu Online Paper* (in Chinese), 15 September, available at: http://culture.news.sohu.com/20040915/n222055879.shtml

Zhang, L. (1982), 'A Review of the Discussions on Two Production Theories' (liangzhong shengchan lilun de taolun zhongshu), *Population Studies* (renkou yanjiu), no. 5, pp. 12–14.

Zhang, P. (1994), 'The Peasant Income Distribution among Rural Areas' (nongchun jian de shouru fenpei), pp. 296–312, in Zhao, R. and K. Griffin (eds), *The Household Income Distribution in China* (zhongguo de jumin shouru fenpei), Beijing: China Social Science Press.

Zhang, W. (1990), 'Reform Well China's Administrative Division for the Continuous Peace and Stability of the Nation' (chong guojia changzhi jiu'an chufa, gaohao xingzheng qu hua de gaige), *Journal of East China Normal University*, no. 2, pp. 1–9.

Zhao, G. (2002), 'The Determinants of Transnational Water Pollution in the LMB', MSc thesis, CUMT, Beijing, China.

Zhao, R. (1993), 'Three Features of the Distribution of Income during the Transition to Reform', in Griffin, K. and R. Zhao (eds), *The Distribution of Income in China*, New York: St. Martin's Press, 1993, pp. 74–94.

Zhao, R. (2003), 'Strengthening the Reform of Income Distribution Systems' (shenhua shouru fengei zhidu gaige), in M. Wang (ed.), *China's Steps Towards a Market Economy Retrospect and Prospect*, Chuigu yu qianzhan: zhouxiang shichang jingji de zhongguo), pp. 255–94, Beijing: China Economics Press.

Zhao, R. (1999), 'Review of Economic Reform in China: Features, Experiences and Challenges', in R. Garnaut and L. Song (eds.), *China: Twenty Years of Reform*, Canberra: Asia Pacific Press, pp. 185–200.

Zhao, R. (2001), 'Increasing Income Inequality and Its Causes in China', in C. Riskin, R. Zhao and Li Shi (eds), *China's Retreat from Equality: Income Distribution and Economic Transition*, New York: M. E. Sharpe, pp. 25–43.

Zheng, J. (1996), 'How Large is China's Per Capita GDP in US Dollar?' (zhongguo de renjun GDP wei duoshao meiyuan), *Economic Highlights* (jingjixue xiaoxi bao), 13 September, no. 193, p. 1.

Zheng, P. (1992), *A Concise Modern History of China* (jiangming xiandai zhongguo shi), Beijing: Beijing Normal University Press.

Zheng, Z. (1988), 'A Framework of the Greater China Community' (da zhonghua gongtong ti shichang de gouxiang), *Economic Review*, 13 June.

Zhou, B (1989), 'The Chinese Community and Southeast China Free Trade Zone' (zhongguo ren gongtongti hua dongnan zhiyou maoyi qu), *Economic Review*, 6 November.

Zhou, F. (1994), 'Measuring the Interregional Inequalities in Terms of Single Index and Multiple Indices' (zhuhe zhibiao he danyi zhibiao de diqu jian bu pingdengxing chedu), in Liu, S., Q. Li, and T. Hsueh (eds), *Studies on China's Regional Economic Development* (zhongguo diqu jingji yanjiu), Beijing: China Statistics Publishing House, 1994, pp. 193–200.

Zhou, J. 1992), 'To Establish the Greater China Economic Area between Hong Kong, Macau, Taiwan and Mainland China: A Basic Framework' (zhongguo dalu yu gang ao tai goujian da zhonghua jingji quan de jiben gouxiang), in Youths Committee of China Society of Natural Resources (ed.), *The Cross-Taiwan Strait: Sustainable Development of the Issues of Resources and Environment*, Beijing: China Science and Technology Press, 1992, pp. 18–21.

Zhu, W. (1990a), 'A Brief Introduction to China's Mineral Resources' (zhongguo kuangchan zhiyuan gaishu), in Commission of Integrated Survey on Natural Resources (ed.), *Handbook of Natural Resources in China* (zhongguo zhiran zhiyuan shouche), Chinese Academy of Sciences, Beijing: Science Press, 1990, pp. 627–36.

Zhu, W. (1990b), 'A Preliminary Study of the Economic Development in the Border-Region of Zhejiang, Fujian, and Jiangxi Provinces' (zhe min gan shengji bianjie diqu jingji fazhan cutan), unpublished MBA thesis, School of Economics and Management, Qinghua University, Beijing.

Zhuravskaya, E. V. (2000), 'Incentives to Provide Local Public Goods: Fiscal Federalism, Russian Style', *Journal of Public Economics*, 76(3), pp. 337–68.

Zipf, G.K. (1946), 'The $P^1P^2/D$ Hypothesis: On the Intercity Movement of Persons', *American Sociological Review*, vol. 11(6), 677–86.

# Index

Abramovitz, M., 278
Achang, 37, 245
ADB, 233, 290
Administrative Committee of China
    Agenda 21 (ACCA21), 288
Afghanistan, 1, 210, 271
Aghion, P., 281
Albania, 271
Alesina, A., 284
Algeria, 271
American Samoa, 271
analytic narrative, 76, 105
Andorra, 271
Angola, 271
Anhui, 12, 14–18, 20, 23–6, 53–4, 67,
    69, 117–18, 138
Antigua and Barbuda, 271
APEC (Asia-Pacific Economic
    Cooperation), 147, 242, 290
Argarwala, R., 67
Argentina, 271
Armenia, 271
artificial weather modification, 141–3,
    194, 198–9
Aruba, 271
ASEAN (Association of Southeast
    Asian Nations), 147
Ash, R., 269, 270
Asian Development Bank, see ADB
Asian financial crisis, 71–2, 87, 234,
    239
*Asia-Pacific Economic Times*, 283
Asia-Pacific, 120–1
Åslund, A., 281
atheism, 43, 45, 267, 269
Atkinson, A.B., 283
Australia, 21, 120, 130, 195, 271,
    286
Austria, 271, 286
authoritarianism, 76, 131–4, 284
autonomous region, 11–13, 17, 66,
    86, 135, 140, 145–6, 153, 193–4,
    199, 203–4, 209, 250–1; *compare*

municipality, province, *see also*
    under individual names
Azerbaijan, 271

Bahamas, The, 271
Bahrain, 271
Bai, 12, 33, 34, 37, 245
Bangladesh, 128, 179, 271
Bao'an, 230
Baoan, 245
Barbados, 271
Bates, R., 260, 291
Battan, L.J., 195
Baum, R., 281
Beijing, 6, 12, 14–18, 20, 23–4, 29, 42,
    53–4, 66–7, 81, 99, 104, 109,
    116–18, 124, 135, 138, 144, 162,
    180, 188–90, 204, 246, 277,
    279–80, 285, 287, 290
Belarus, 271
Belgium, 6, 271
Belize, 271
Benin, 271
Berg, A., 281
Bermuda, 271
Berthelemy, J.-C., 216
Bhutan, 210, 271
big bang, 76, 91, 93–4, 100, 105, 255,
    257–62, 281
Bikker, J., 222, 289
Blang, 35, 37, 42, 245
Bo, Y., 285
Boisso, D., 222, 292
Bolivia, 271
Bosnia and Herzegovina, 271
Botswana, 271
Bourguignon, F., 283
Bouyei, 37, 245
Boycko, M., 281
Brada, J., 222, 289
Brazil, 22, 179, 185, 271
*Britannica Book*, 37, 43, 268–70, 275,
    292